A Practical Approach to Land Law

Fourth Edition

D1638282

Judith-Anne MacKenzie, LLM, AKC, Barrister

Mary Phillips, MA, LLM, Barrister

BLACKSTONE
PRESS LIMITED

This edition published in Great Britain 1993 by Blackstone Press Limited
9-15 Aldine Street, London W12 8AW. Telephone: 081-740 1173

First edition 1986
Second edition 1989
Third edition 1991
Reprinted 1992
Fourth edition 1993

ISBN: 1 85431 266 9

British Library Cataloguing in Publication Data.
A CIP catalogue record for this book is available from the British Library

Typeset by Kerrypress Ltd, Luton
Printed by Bell & Bain Limited, Glasgow

Contents

— Giving notice and obtaining consent — Tenant for life is trustee of his powers —Defective dispositions — Role of trustees of settlements — End of a settlement — Trusts for sale — Definition of a trust for sale — Creation of a trust for sale — Role of trustees — Position of a purchaser — Nature of the beneficiary's interest under a trust for sale —Comparison of the two forms of settlement — Statutory transformation of certain accidentally created settlements — The rule against perpetuities

Preface

I am pleased to be able, once again, to thank those who have written to me with comments on and criticisms of this book. I do read anything which is sent and take your views seriously, even if I am not able to respond to your letters. I am also grateful for the many words of support that I have received from readers.

This edition has again been prepared without the assistance of Mary Phillips, whose other obligations have kept her fully occupied, and accordingly any faults should be laid entirely at my door.

The first edition of this book was written for the Bar Diploma students Mary and I were teaching at the time. I am pleased to say that many of those students are now successful practitioners. However, this book is now widely used for other courses, covering a wide range of readers—from surveyors to degree students and including trainee legal executives and those studying for solicitors' examinations. To cater for such a wide audience I have tried to concentrate on the fundamentals of the subject, particularly since these often prove a stumbling block for those studying land law for the first time. I hope that once the basics have been understood it will prove easier for students to tackle the weightier tomes produced on this subject and particularly the learned works designed for professional lawyers, which will provide essential information to anyone who hopes to master this area of the law in all its complexity.

This book does not contain any reference to the leasehold enfranchisement provisions of the Housing and Urban Development Bill, which have received much press coverage recently. At the time of writing, amendments to the Bill have imposed such stringent requirements on tenants before the right to purchase the reversion can be exercised that it seems likely that this right will prove of less importance in practice than many had hoped. In particular, it will be very difficult for the tenants of large blocks of flats with a rapidly changing population to reach the necessary majorities. I have not dealt with these provisions as they remain unsettled and cannot be regarded as forming part of the fundamental structure of the law relating to leases.

As I was for part of the time covered by this book employed as Assistant Parliamentary Counsel, and as I continue to be employed in Government service, I must emphasise that the views expressed in this book are purely personal opinion and carry no official weight. Nor have they been arrived at on the basis of any 'insider' information.

My thanks go as always to the team at Blackstone Press, whose enthusiasm and hard work continue to be an inspiration to all their authors.

Finally, as always, my thanks and love go to Paul, who has given me a great deal of support and encouragement over the years during which this book has been produced, who has brewed endless cups of tea and who has never complained about being neglected in favour of a little black (and yellow) book.

Judith-Anne MacKenzie

Introduction

Both of us have been fascinated by land law ever since our first encounters with the subject as undergraduates. Accordingly we have always been disappointed to note that the majority of law students (and many practitioners) regard the subject with dislike. We feel that one source of confusion, and often boredom, in the student is produced by the traditional method of teaching land law, in which the historical background to the subject is heavily emphasised. Whilst we find the history of the subject both intriguing and informative, we are well aware that most modern students are interested primarily in the law as it is, rather than as it was. As a result, during the years in which we taught together we developed a new approach to the subject which concentrates on its modern and practical aspects. However, we found our efforts hampered by the lack of a text which suited our methods, and were therefore pleased to be offered the opportunity to present our style of teaching in book form. We hope that this text will encourage an interest in a lively and important subject and that it will, perhaps, prove to be a comfort to the confused and faint-hearted. Our method has led us to leave a discussion of the question, 'What is land?' to the end of the book. This is one of the more technical areas of the subject and it demonstrates to the student, who, we trust, will by this point have grasped the basic principles of land law, that its history can be of value when a more profound understanding of the subject is required.

We have not included a general introduction to equity in this book because it is now common for students to study land law and equity (trusts) at the same time, and in such a case your studies in your equity course will provide the background knowledge which is needed for land law. If, however, your studies in land law precede those in equity, or if you are not required to study equity in detail, you may find it helpful to read one or all of the following brief introductions before starting to read this book: *What Is Equity About?* by Anne Everton (London: Butterworths, 1970), *The Law of Trusts* by D.J. Hayton (Sweet and Maxwell) and lectures 1, 2 and 3 in F.W. Maitland's *Lectures on Equity*, revised ed. (Cambridge University Press, 1969).

A NOTE ON TRANT WAY

Trant Way, Mousehole, in the county of Stilton is a purely fictional street and so are its inhabitants, and the other characters and institutions in this book are all inventions and bear no relation to any real persons or bodies, living or dead. The purpose of the given examples is to assist the reader in applying the law to typical practical situations. Since Trant Way exists only in our joint imagination we must explain that we visualise it as a street on the outskirts of an old county town. The houses at the end of the street closest to the centre of the town (e.g., numbers 1–6) stand in a typical suburban environment, whereas the houses at the far end of the street (number 15 onwards) stretch out into the countryside surrounding Mousehole and in some cases are flanked by open farmland. We enjoyed inventing Trant Way, and its inhabitants have provided light relief for many of our students. We hope that they will assist you in understanding land law and demonstrate that the subject is not as 'stuffy' as some may have you believe.

THE PROPERTY LEGISLATION

Much of this book refers to the body of legislation passed in 1925 and which came into force on 1 January 1926. This legislation consolidated earlier amendments to land law, put into statutory form some common law rules and introduced further reforms. This turning-point in land law was contained in the following statutes:

Settled Land Act 1925.
Trustee Act 1925.
Law of Property Act 1925.
Land Registration Act 1925.
Administration of Estates Act 1925.
Land Charges Act 1925.

These statutes have been amended by later enactments and in some cases are largely superseded by later statutes. For convenience we have used the following abbreviations throughout the book, giving the year in each case, in order to avoid confusion where there are two or more statutes with similar names:

SLA — Settled Land Act
LPA — Law of Property Act
LRA — Land Registration Act
LCA — Land Charges Act

Judith-Anne MacKenzie   Mary Phillips

Table of Cases

Table of Statutes

Table of Statutory Instruments

1 Estates and Interests in Land

Anyone who has looked in the window of an estate agent will have seen advertisements similar in form to the two following examples:

Trant Way, Mousehole, Stilton.
Freehold House.
Victorian house on 3 floors.
Completely modernised throughout.
Central heating. Large garden.
3 recep. 2 bedrm. 2 bathrm.
sep WC. Large kitchen.
£65,000.

2 Trant Way, Mousehole, Stilton.
Leasehold maisonette. 99-yr lease.
Pleasant maisonette, being ground and
first floor of this elegant Victorian property.
2 recep. 2 bedrm. bathrm. sep WC.
Spacious kitchen/breakfast room.
£50,000.

Thus the terms 'freehold' and 'leasehold' are in common public use, though most members of the public will have no idea of what those terms mean to a lawyer. In land law, specialised terminology is of great importance and it is necessary to consider how these layman's terms translate into more legal language.

WHAT AM I BUYING?

The answer to this question, as far as the purchaser is concerned, is usually, 'I'm buying a house'. For the lawyer, however, the answer to the same question is rather different and may at first seem unnecessarily complicated. It is certainly true that the scheme underlying the lawyer's answer is unique to England and Wales. A Scottish lawyer will answer the same question in an entirely different manner because the system of land ownership in Scotland is completely different. Thus this book is concerned only with the law relating to England and Wales.

The first thing to note about land law is that no subject can own land!

Theoretically all land belongs to the Crown and the only person who is capable of owning land is the monarch. This is an idea which dates from the Norman conquest in 1066 and which persists even today. The subject cannot therefore own the land upon which he lives or runs his business, but he is allowed the use of the land by the Crown. What the subject owns is a series of rights and duties in relation to that piece of land. Understandably lawyers have given a name to the interest in land which the subject holds, and that name is an 'estate in land'. So the land belongs to the Crown and the subject owns an estate in the land, which gives him certain rights in relation to it. Thus a freehold owner is said to 'hold land of the Crown'. At one time it was usual for an estate owner to render services to the Crown in return for the right to use the land, but these services are now only paid in the rarest of cases and tend to be regarded as an honour rather than as an obligation (for example, the duty to supply a pair of gloves for the monarch to wear at his coronation).

The relationship between the freehold owner and the Crown is called 'tenure' (from the Latin word '*tenere*' which means 'to hold'). At one time there were many types of tenure, classified according to the nature of the services to be rendered by the estate owner. Today only one form of tenure remains and that is called 'free and common socage'. For all practical purposes the doctrine of tenure has little modern significance, and most freehold owners are completely unaware of their tenurial relationship with the monarch.

Today there are only two estates in land which are recognised at law and these are set out in LPA 1925, s. 1(1):

The only estates and interests in land which are capable of subsisting or of being conveyed or created at law are—
  (a)   an estate in fee simple absolute in possession;
  (b)   a term of years absolute.

The two terms in paragraphs (a) and (b) correspond to the common terms 'freehold' and 'leasehold' and require further detailed consideration.

ESTATE IN FEE SIMPLE ABSOLUTE IN POSSESSION

The fee simple is the larger of the two legal estates, in that it is of greater duration. The technical name describes the characteristics of the estate as it existed *before* 1 January 1926. At this date a number of statutes passed by Parliament in 1925 came into force and made considerable changes to the law relating to property. (These Acts are listed at p. x.) As a result some of the characteristics of the fee simple estate were changed but the old name continues to be used. We have therefore to explain what the words meant under the old law, but we will do this very briefly.

It is the phrase 'fee simple' which really causes the difficulty because of the changes made by the 1925 legislation. The word 'fee' denoted an inheritable interest in land and the word 'simple' tells us that the estate could be inherited by the 'general heirs'. This means that the estate would last as long as there were heirs to inherit. If a man died intestate (without making a will), any fee simple estate which he had owned would pass to his heir—a single individual who was identified according to complicated rules. If the deceased had children, the heir would be his eldest son. If the eldest son predeceased his father but had himself left a son, that grandson would be his grandfather's heir. If there were no sons to inherit, any daughters inherited the estate jointly. If the deceased had no descendants, his heir would be found amongst his brothers and sisters, or their issue, with preference being given once again to the oldest male. If still no heir could be found, the search would continue amongst the deceased's ancestors; his father, or uncles and aunts, or their descendants. It might be therefore that the estate would pass to a fairly remote relation, as long as he was the closest living relative.

All this is now a matter of history, because the 1925 legislation abolished the old concept of the heir. Instead new statutory rules of inheritance were imposed (and still apply, with modifications), so really after 1925 one cannot define a fee simple by calling it an estate 'inheritable by heirs general'. What remains true is that the fee simple is an estate which can endure indefinitely, as long as there are persons entitled to take the property under the provisions of the will of the previous owner, or under the statutory rules relating to an intestacy. Very occasionally no person entitled to the estate can be discovered after the rules have been applied. In such cases the estate will at this point come to an end and the land will revert to the Crown.

The explanation of the word 'absolute' gives rise to further complications. The word indicates that the fee simple should not be subject to any restriction whereby it may not endure as long as there are persons entitled to inherit. So, if I try to give Fred a fee simple estate 'until he qualifies as a solicitor', the gift cannot be of a fee simple estate. The estate will not necessarily last for ever (as long as there is someone to inherit) because it will end earlier should Fred ever become a solicitor. This sort of arrangement is called a 'determinable fee' and, together with its relative the 'conditional fee', it is considered in detail in chapter 3.

The final words in the legal term for a freehold estate are 'in possession'. This means that the estate must be current, rather than being one which is to give the owner the use of the land at some time in the future. Thus, if I give Paul an estate to start in five years' time, I have not given him a legal estate. Future interests in land are dealt with in more detail in chapters 3 and 5.

It should be noted that the estate owner does not have to be in physical possession of the land itself in order to have a legal estate. For example, the property may be let to a tenant, in which case the tenant will be in physical possession of the land, whilst the landlord has the right to receive the rent payable under the lease. In this case the landlord still has a legal estate because LPA 1925, s. 205(1)(xix), says:

'Possession' includes receipt of rents and profits or the right to receive the same, if any.

Some examples of interests which do not come within the definition of the fee simple

It will be obvious that there are many kinds of arrangement which one may wish to make concerning a piece of land, but which cannot amount to a legal estate in fee simple. Many of these other arrangements are dealt with by using a trust of the property (see chapter 5). Some examples of arrangements which fall into this category are:

(a)   an interest for life;
(b)   an interest to start at some time in the future—a future interest;
(c)   an entailed interest.

The 'entailed interest' requires some explanation. If you refer back to our remarks on the fee simple you will recall that that estate was inheritable by general heirs, the heir being drawn from a wide range of relatives of the deceased. In the case of an 'entail', however, the heir had to come from a more limited class. This class was the 'heirs of the body', meaning the lineal descendants of the original tenant in tail. Sometimes this class was limited even further, to the 'heirs of the body male' (or, rarely, 'female'). In such a case the estate could not pass to an heir of the wrong sex, nor could it pass to the ascendants or siblings of the original tenant. It would pass only to his direct descendants of the correct sex. If no such heir existed the estate would come to an end and the property reverted to the fee simple owner who had originally created this more limited estate (or to his general heir had he died). The person who had this right to recover the property should the entail come to an end was said to have a 'reversion'. Before 1926 the entail and the life interest were regarded as lesser types of legal estate but this was altered by the 1925 legislation, so that today they amount only to equitable interests in the property and are dealt with behind a trust of the fee simple.

TERM OF YEARS ABSOLUTE

The 'term of years absolute' is what is more commonly called a lease. It too is a legal estate but it is inferior to the fee simple estate because it is of limited duration. The essential requirement is that a lease must be for a fixed 'term of years', though this can include periods of less than a year (LPA 1925, s. 205(1)(xxvii)) and can include arrangements such as weekly or monthly tenancies. The word 'absolute' does not seem to add anything to the meaning because a lease does not cease to be a legal estate merely because it will terminate on the occurrence of some event (e.g., if the rent is unpaid).

To give one example of an arrangement which cannot qualify as a legal estate under LPA 1925, s. 1(1)(b), one may consider the case of *Lace* v *Chantler* [1944] KB 368, in which there was an attempt to create a lease 'for the duration of the war'. This was not a legal lease because it was not for a fixed period.

It should be noted that the owner of a term of years does not hold the land of the Crown. The leaseholder derives his title from that of his landlord, who will be either the owner of a fee simple estate or of a longer leasehold estate.

The lease is of considerable importance in land law and it is considered in far greater detail in chapter 3.

INTERESTS IN LAND

It will be obvious to the reader that the legal estates are not the only rights to land which one might own. Normal daily life often requires that one person should be given a right which is enforceable against the land of another. For example, it is frequently the case that owners of neighbouring land share a common driveway to their houses, the drive being constructed partly on one piece of land and partly on the other. Before either owner can use such a driveway he must be given a right to use the half of the drive which is on his neighbour's property. Unless each owner has a right which he can enforce against the other's estate, the drive will be useless to both of them. Another example of a third-party right to land arises when an estate owner borrows money from a building society in order to finance the purchase of the estate. In order to provide security for the loan, the building society will take a mortgage of the property, which will give it rights over the estate should the borrower fail to repay the debt. Thus the society will have a right which is enforceable against the estate of the borrower and that right is a third-party right in land. A third example might arise if the purchaser of an estate uses partly his own money and partly the money of his girlfriend. The legal estate in the property may be transferred to the purchaser alone, but it is obviously unfair that he should be allowed to treat the property as wholly his (unless the money was advanced as a loan). Often this arrangement will be regarded as giving an interest in the property to his girlfriend because she paid for part. In such a case it is possible for a trust of the estate to arise so that the purchaser becomes a trustee in relation to the property, the beneficiaries under the trust being himself and his girlfriend. Thus the girlfriend would have an interest arising from the land, even though the legal estate belonged solely to her boyfriend.

Such third-party rights are very common and come in a multitude of shapes and sizes. They may all, however, be divided into two important classes:

(a) rights recognised by *law*; and
(b) rights recognised by *equity*.

LEGAL INTERESTS

The two legal estates are the largest and the most important of the rights to land which are recognised by law, as opposed to operating in equity. However, there are lesser rights which are accepted at law and which are not relegated to an existence in equity only. These lesser interests are called 'legal interests or charges' and they are listed in LPA 1925, s. 1(2), (in which the words given here in brackets have been repealed):

The only interests or charges in or over land which are capable of subsisting or of being conveyed or created at law are—

    (a) An easement, right, or privilege in or over land for an interest equivalent to an estate in fee simple absolute in possession or a term of years absolute;

    (b) A rentcharge in possession issuing out of or charged on land being either perpetual or for a term of years absolute;

    (c) A charge by way of legal mortgage;

    (d) [Land tax, tithe rentcharge] and any other similar charge on land which is not created by an instrument;

    (e) Rights of entry exercisable over or in respect of a legal term of years absolute, or annexed, for any purpose, to a legal rentcharge.

What follows is a brief introduction to each of these rights, some of which are considered in greater detail later in the book.

Section 1(2)(a): Legal easements, rights or privileges

Easements are not easily defined but are easily recognisable once encountered. Essentially, they are rights attached to one piece of land, either entitling its occupants to do something on another's property, or preventing the owner of that other property from interfering with the passage of some benefit to the first piece of land. Thus one may have the right to walk over one's neighbour's land (a right of way), or perhaps the right to prevent the neighbour building so as to block the passage of light to one's windows (a right to light). In each case there is a piece of land which is benefited by the easement and a piece of land which is burdened with it. There are many types of easement, such as rights to storage or drainage, the right to water and a great number of others. A list of common examples is given in chapter 8.

Related to easements, and also capable of being recognised at law under s. 1(2)(a), are profits à prendre. These are rights to take something from land which belongs to another estate owner; for example, a right to cut wood on another's property. These rights are also considered in detail in chapter 8.

It should be noted that for either of these rights to be legal, as opposed to being enforceable in equity only, they must be granted for a term equivalent to a legal estate. This means that they must last for the same period as one of the two legal estates: that is, effectively in perpetuity (like a fee simple) or for a fixed period (like a term of years). Accordingly, a right of way given to Jane for her lifetime cannot be a legal easement because it is to last for an uncertain length of time (Jane's life). Such an easement may, however, be enforceable as an equitable interest.

Section 1(2)(b): Rentcharges

The first thing to note about the term 'rentcharge' is that it does not refer to rent which is payable under a lease, but to other arrangements whereby land is charged with the payment to someone of an annual or periodic sum. If the money is not paid, the person with the benefit of the rentcharge is entitled to enter upon the land in order to enforce payment (e.g., by taking from the income of the land the sum which he is owed). At one time, and in certain parts of the country, it was rare for an estate in fee simple to be sold for a single payment of money; instead the vendor took a lump sum plus a rentcharge securing an annual payment. However the Rentcharges Act 1977 prevents the creation of any new rentcharges of this type, provides that any existing ones are to end after 60 years, and gives the estate owner of the charged land the right to redeem the rentcharge earlier on the payment of compensation. The 1977 Act does not, however, abolish rentcharges altogether and it is still possible to create them for certain purposes. Thus it is still possible to leave a property to a person, subject to a rentcharge obliging him to make a periodical payment to your widow or widower, or to some other member of your family, in order to provide for the maintenance of such person. This sort of rentcharge gives rise to a trust of the land under SLA 1925, s. (1)(v), and is considered in chapter 5. It is also still possible to create 'estate rentcharges', which are used to ensure that the estate owner of the charged land makes a payment towards the upkeep of facilities on other land. An example of this type is the rentcharge obliging the estate owner to pay an annual sum towards the maintenance of a road on his neighbour's property. These rentcharges are a means of providing for the enforcement of positive covenants in freehold land and they are further considered in chapter 9.

For a rentcharge to be a legal interest in land it must last for the same period as one of the two legal estates; that is, either in perpetuity or for a fixed period.

Section 1(2)(c): Charge by way of legal mortgage
A mortgage is the means whereby an estate in land is charged with the repayment of a debt or the performance of some other obligation. For example, the borrower (who grants the mortgage over his estate and is called the 'mortgagor') provides security for a loan by granting a mortgage to the lender (who becomes the 'mortgagee'). The mortgagee obtains an estate or interest in the mortgaged property by virtue of this arrangement. If the borrower fails to repay the loan, the mortgagee may take the mortgagor's property and sell it to satisfy the debt.

The charge by way of legal mortgage is one of the three types of mortgage recognised by LPA 1925, ss. 85-7. The other two are not mentioned in LPA 1925, s. 1(2), because they are created in a manner which gives the mortgagee a legal estate in the mortgaged property (in fact a lease) and are therefore legal by virtue of s. 1(1). The three types of legal mortgage are described in more detail in chapter 7.

Section 1(2)(d): . . . and any other similar charge on land which is not created by an instrument
The rather peculiar wording of this section is due to the repeal of the first four words, which originally referred to 'land tax' and 'tithe rentcharge'. The charges in this category are all created by statute and are rarely encountered.

Section 1(2)(e): Rights of entry
This heading includes rights of entry included in leases or annexed to rentcharges. It is usual to include in a lease a clause which allows the landlord to recover, or 're-enter', the property, should the tenant be in breach of any of his obligations under the lease. This right is a legal right in itself under s. 1(2)(e) and is regarded as an interest in land. A similar right is usually included in a rentcharge, so that the owner of the rentcharge may enter the land should the owner of the charged estate fail to pay the sums due.

EQUITABLE INTERESTS

Any interest which does not qualify as a legal interest must necessarily be an equitable interest, if it is to be regarded as an interest in land at all (LPA 1925, s. 1(3)). This means that, if one is claiming an interest in land which does not appear on the list in s. 1(2), the interest will be enforced in equity only.

Creation of equitable interests

Equitable interests may be divided into two categories. The 'traditional' ones are equitable because historically equity provided a remedy when law would not help. Other interests, which are today equitable, were originally legal but were pushed back into equity as a result of the statutory reforms of land law. We have already seen that interests which do not fall within the definitions of legal estates and interests in LPA 1925, s. 1(1) and (2), now exist only in equity.

Traditional equitable interests

The interest of a beneficiary under a trust
Trusts are extremely important in land law and are considered further in chapter 5. However, it is not possible to proceed very far with a study of this subject without having a basic idea of what a trust is, and so a brief explanation will be included here.

A trust arises when property is held by a person or persons 'upon trust' for another person or persons. Thus Anne may hold a legal estate upon trust for Bob. Anne is called a 'trustee', whilst Bob is called a 'beneficiary'. It is the trustee's job to hold the legal estate for the benefit of the beneficiary. It is the beneficiary who is entitled to the benefits of the estate, whilst the trustee is a bare legal owner and he must not use the estate for his own benefit. It may be easier to understand this idea if one compares the estate with a banana: the trustee is regarded as the owner of the banana-skin, whereas the beneficiary is the owner of the banana inside! (See Everton, *What is Equity About?*, or D.J. Hayton, *The Law of Trusts*, for a further introduction to trusts.)

Historically, common law did not recognise such a separation of ownership and enjoyment and would not assist the beneficiary if the trustee used the estate for his own benefit. Equity did, however, protect the beneficiary, who accordingly does have an enforceable right to the property. The rights of the beneficiary are enforceable only in equity and not at law.

Where there is a trust of the legal estate there are therefore effectively two owners:

(a)   the trustee owns the legal estate; and
(b)   the beneficiary owns an equitable interest.

In addition to trusts which are created expressly by the owner of property, there are situations which the courts will interpret as giving rise to a trust, sometimes to give effect to the presumed intention of the owner, but on other occasions very much against his will. We have already seen an example of this in the trust which may arise where the purchaser's girlfriend has contributed to the purchase price (p. 5).

Trusts which are recognised by the courts in this way, without express creation, are said to be 'implied', 'resulting' or 'constructive' trusts. The definition of these terms is somewhat unclear, and in some cases they seem to be regarded as interchangeable and are not always used very accurately. For our purposes, not a great deal seems to turn on whether a particular trust is more properly described, for example, as resulting or constructive, and we will leave you to pursue the matter in your study of trusts. What is of considerable importance, though, is that you should recognise the situations in which a trust will arise—the label to be attached to that trust is of less significance.

Interests under contracts to create legal estates or interests
Equitable interests also arise because equity regards contracts to create legal estates or interests in a special way. If, for example, Victor, the fee simple owner of Blackacre, agrees to sell his estate to Peter, this agreement is protected in two ways if either party breaks the contract. The legal remedy available is that of damages for breach of contract. Equity, however, goes further and will give an order for specific performance of the contract. Specific performance is an order which will make the parties to a contract perform their promises— in our example Victor can be compelled to convey the estate and Peter can be made to pay the purchase price. Obviously, before enforcing the contract, equity will require sufficient evidence that it does exist. This need for satisfactory evidence is subject to the statutory rules provided by s. 2 of the Law of Property (Miscellaneous Provisions) Act 1989, which are considered in chapter 2. Specific performance is, of course, a remedy which lies in the discretion of the court, because it is equitable in origin and all equitable remedies are discretionary.

Interestingly, the application of an equitable maxim, that 'Equity regards as done that which ought to be done', produces the result that a contract which can be specifically enforced is regarded as creating an interest in equity. The operation of this rule can best be explained by reference to our example of the sale by Victor to Peter. 'That which ought to be done' is the conveyance of the estate to Peter. However, from the time that the contract is made, equity acts as though that conveyance had already been completed. As a result Peter is treated as being the owner in equity from the date that the contract is made, whilst Victor remains the legal owner until the deed conveying the legal estate is made, and until that time is regarded by equity as holding the legal estate upon trust for Peter.

This special way in which equity treats contracts to create or convey estates or interests in land leads us on to the third type of equitable interest.

Interests which are improperly created

Usually in order to convey, transfer or create a legal estate or interest in land it is necessary to use a deed. A deed is a document which has been executed in accordance with certain formalities in order to ensure that its validity can be proved. The nature of the formalities required depends on the date at which the deed was executed. Since 31 July 1990, the Law of Property (Miscellaneous Provisions) Act 1989, s. 1, has required that to be a deed a document must:

(a)   make it clear on the face of the document that it is intended to be a deed; and

(b)   be signed—

(i)   by the person executing in the presence of a witness who attests the signature (this means that the witness also signs as such), or

(ii)   by another person at the direction of the person who wishes to execute the deed in the presence of two witnesses who attest the signature (this is used where for some reason the person executing cannot sign something and he has to ask someone to sign on his behalf); and

(c)   be delivered by the person executing or by someone else on his behalf.

So basically the document must be signed, witnessed and delivered.

Deeds executed before 31 July 1990 are subject to the traditional rules which required a deed to be signed, SEALED, and delivered. At one time it was a person's seal that was essential in order to prove the authenticity of a document but for many years the habit of using sealing wax and a real seal had been abandoned and the seal was represented by a red sticker on the document. In *First National Securities Ltd* v *Jones* [1978] Ch 109, it was held that a printed circle containing the letters 'LS' would suffice if it were shown that it was intended that these should represent a seal. It should be noted that in relation to these older documents no witness was necessary though most deeds were in fact witnessed.

In the case of both the old and the new rules it is technically necessary for the deed to be delivered formally. Correctly this used to be done by the person concerned placing his hand on the seal on the document and saying, 'I deliver this as my act and deed'. Today formal delivery is usually dispensed with, a practice which was approved in *Stromdale & Ball Ltd* v *Burden* [1952] Ch 223.

The requirement that legal estates and interests must be granted by deed is an ancient rule, but it is now contained in LPA 1925, s. 52(1):

All conveyances of land or of any interest therein are void for the purpose of conveying or creating a legal estate unless made by deed.

So an attempt to create an estate or interest without a deed will be totally ineffective at law. Equity, however, may help here, by regarding the attempted grant as a contract to create such an estate or interest. Specific performance may be available to compel the creation of a legal estate or interest in the proper form, by requiring one party to make a grant by deed. Moreover, as we explained above, the maxim that, equity regards as done that which ought to be done, may enable equity to treat the person entitled to the grant as already having the interest in equity.

We may illustrate this principle with the following example:

If Len purports to grant a lease of a flat to Tom for 10 years without using a deed, Tom does not obtain a legal term of years. Tom may, however, seek an order for specific performance to compel Len to grant the lease by deed, and meanwhile, if specific performance could be granted, Tom is regarded by equity as having an equitable lease of the property for the specified period. (On this point see *Walsh* v *Lonsdale* (1882) 21 ChD 9.)

Interests arising under restrictive covenants

A final example of equity's willingness to provide a remedy when the law would not do so relates to restrictive covenants. These are promises under seal (made in a deed) by which the promisor, or 'covenantor', undertakes not to do certain things on his land. If, for example, Pip is buying a house he might covenant not to carry on a business on the premises. Law will enforce this promise against Pip, the original covenantor, as a matter of contract. If Pip later sells the property to Quentin, law will not enforce the covenant against Quentin, because he was not a party to the original contract. This is the ordinary contractual rule which requires 'privity of contract'. However, in certain circumstances, which are explained in chapter 9, equity will enforce the covenant against Quentin. The person who is seeking to enforce the covenant will therefore have a right which is enforceable in equity against the owner for the time being of the property. This is a rule which originally arose in situations in which equity, as a matter of conscience, ruled that a purchaser should be bound by the covenant. The issue of 'conscience' has over the years become formalised into a series of rules which govern the position.

Interests which became equitable as the result of statutory reform

Any interest in land which does not satisfy s. 1(1) or s. 1(2) of LPA 1925 can only be created in equity. Thus if I try to give Tim a 'fee simple for life', I have not given him a legal estate or interest in the property because it is neither a full fee simple nor a lease. Similarly, an easement granted for life cannot be a legal interest because it does not satisfy s. 1(2). Both of these rights can, however, exist as equitable interests in the land.

Some of these rights can only exist behind a trust of the legal estate, so that trustees hold the property upon trust for the person or persons having equitable interests. Any attempt to give someone a life interest in property, or to create an entailed interest, is dealt with in this way, as are certain other types of interest. These arrangements are discussed in chapter 5.

All the other equitable interests do not create trusts of the legal estate but are simply regarded as third-party rights to land which are enforceable if equity so allows.

LEGAL INTERESTS AND EQUITABLE INTERESTS COMPARED

The fact that a right is recognised only in equity and not at law is of great practical significance, since all equitable rights are enforceable only at the discretion of the court. Thus although, since the Supreme Court of Judicature Acts 1873 and 1875, the rules of law and equity may both be administered by the same courts, it is still important to know whether one is dealing with a legal interest or an equitable interest. One has no absolute right to the protection of an equitable interest—remedies are at the discretion of the court. In this context the old equitable maxim that, 'He who comes to equity must come with clean hands', is of great importance. It may be the case that Tim can show that he has an equitable interest in land, but this would be of little use to him if he has 'dirty hands' and accordingly would be refused any remedy by the courts. For example, if Tim claims to have an equitable easement entitling him to walk across another estate owner's land, he may find that he is refused a remedy to enforce his right of way if he has behaved improperly himself (perhaps by exceeding the limits of his right or by causing damage). Legal rights, however, are enforceable as of right, and once the existence of the right is established it is not really open to the court to consider the merits of the situation before giving a remedy.

Another important difference between legal and equitable rights is found in the rules governing the enforceability of those rights against a third party, for example, against the purchaser of the estate which is subject to the rights. Thus one might discover that whereas a legal easement over a piece of land could be enforced against a purchaser of any estate in that land, an equitable easement over the same piece of land might not be enforceable against certain categories of purchaser. This is a rule which has its origins in the separate evolution of law and equity. Legal rights are said to be rights *in rem*; that is, rights in the land itself ('in the thing', from the Latin word '*res*', meaning 'thing') and hence generally can be enforced against any person who acquires an estate or interest in the land. However equitable rights are only rights *in personam*; that is, rights which are enforceable against certain categories of person. These general rules have been amended in modern law by statutory provisions which require that certain interests should be protected in a formal manner, usually by registration, if they are to be enforceable against later acquirers of the land. However, the distinction is still important where there is no statutory regulation and also sometimes when deciding which statutory provisions should be applied. This whole area is considered in detail in chapter 2.

A MULTIPLICITY OF INTERESTS

It will be obvious from what we have said so far that one piece of land may be subject to a large number of interests all at the same time. Indeed the doctrine of estates may be responsible for encouraging the development of such multiple interests, because it encourages one to think in terms of owning rights in land rather than of owning the land itself. As we will see, in England and Wales land law is not really concerned with absolute rights but rather with balancing the relative claims to land which may be made by a number of people. Thus one piece of land could be subject to *all* the following interests at the same time:

(a)   a fee simple owned by Amy;

(b)   a 99-year lease granted by Amy to Bob;

(c)   a weekly tenancy granted by Bob to Carol;

(d)   a legal mortgage of the freehold granted by Amy to a building society;

(e)   an equitable mortgage of the 99-year lease granted by Bob to his bank;

(f)   a right of way over the property granted to David in perpetuity (a legal easement);

(g)   an estate rentcharge granted by Amy to Eric, a neighbouring owner, to ensure that Amy contributes to the cost of maintaining a shared drive;

(h)   a restrictive covenant which prevents the land from being used for business purposes.

CLASSIFICATION OF PROPERTY

Although we are leaving questions about the definition of land, and other technical matters, until the last chapter, we must make a brief mention here of the lawyers' classification of property and a few of the technical terms connected with it.

Property is divided into two main categories: 'real' property and 'personal' property (or 'realty' and 'personalty'). Real property consists of all the estates and interests in land which we will be considering in this book, with the exception of leases which, for historical reasons, are regarded as a form of personal property. The reason for this is described in chapter 10.

Personal property is divided into three categories:

(a)   Tangible objects other than land, which can be physically possessed (such as cars, books and clothes) and which are called 'choses in possession'. 'Chose' is another word meaning 'thing' but this time lawyers use a French word rather than the Latin one.

(b)   Intangible rights, other than those relating to land, of which one cannot take physical possession and which depend for their existence on enforcement by the courts. In this category are placed debts, copyrights and patents, amongst other rights. The technical name for such types of property is 'choses in action'.

(c)   Leases are in a category on their own and are known technically as 'chattels real' (because although they are chattels they are like real property— see p. 337).

2 Acquisition of Estates and Interests in Land

In this chapter we intend to concentrate on the acquisition of a fee simple estate in land and of any interests, legal or equitable, in that land. Acquisition of leases will be dealt with in detail in chapter 3, in which the term of years absolute is further discussed. Although estates and interests in land may be acquired by way of gift, either in the lifetime of the donor or on his death, we are primarily concerned here with acquisitions for value, and will, in the main, be describing the process by which a purchaser buys an estate in land from a vendor. We will also discuss another manner of acquiring an estate, which may occur in circumstances in which the owner of the estate has no intention of transferring the estate to another person. This may happen when the other person takes possession of the land and remains upon it for a prescribed period of time; the title so acquired is commonly known as 'squatter's rights' but is more technically called 'title by adverse possession' and is further explained below at p. 75. The acquisition of title by adverse possession is not a frequent occurrence but it does happen and its possibility should be noted from the outset and we will make references to it in the course of this chapter.

Although land law and conveyancing are normally taught separately they are in fact inextricably linked: the law relating to conveyancing is unintelligible without an understanding of the underlying structure of land law and land law seems pointless unless one has an appreciation of how the theory of the law is applied in practice. Here we are concentrating on the rules of land law rather than those of conveyancing but we will set the land law rules in their conveyancing context as this will make it easier to appreciate their purpose. To this end we will consider in this chapter the steps necessary to purchase two properties, Nos. 1 and 3 Trant Way.

1 Trant Way

This property has already been mentioned in chapter 1. It is a large Victorian house with a garden. The current owner of the fee simple is Victor Venn. Mr Venn bought the property in 1982 but is now obliged to move to another part of the country. Mr and Mrs Armstrong (Arnold and Arriety) are interested in buying the property for £65,000.

3 Trant Way

Number 3 is another large house but it has been divided up so that the top floor provides a separate 'granny flat', with its own internal front door but sharing the street door with the rest of the house and using the internal stairs for access. The current fee simple owner is Victoria Ventnor who bought the property in 1978. Barbara Bell is interested in buying the house for £70,000. Barbara has an elderly father, Bob Bell, and she hopes that he will agree to come and live in the top-floor flat so that she 'can keep an eye on him'.

Mousehole

Before we consider the legal steps required to purchase these properties it is necessary to give some background information about Mousehole.

Mousehole is the county town of Stilton. Many of the suburban streets (such as Trant Way) stretch into the surrounding countryside. The outskirts of the town have extended considerably over the past 50 years and many of the outlying houses have been built on land which was once farm land.

The whole of Stilton became an area of compulsory land registration on 1 January 1980. As is explained on p. 17, some of the properties in the area have to be dealt with according to the rules of the old, unregistered system of conveyancing, and some under the new registered system.

BACKGROUND TO CONVEYANCING

Problems for the buyer

Any person who reflects for a few moments will realise that a buyer of any property (or normally his solicitor) has two main concerns. First, he must be sure that the vendor of the property is really entitled to sell it. Thus the buyer must insist that the vendor proves that his title to the land is good and that he can pass to the purchaser the estate which he is offering to sell. Secondly, the purchaser will want to know whether any third parties have rights to the land which might interfere with his intended use of it. These third-party rights might include covenants restricting use, rights of way, tree preservation orders or even mortgages obliging the owner of the estate to make payments to a creditor. Concern about these matters will lead the purchaser, or his representatives, to make extensive enquiries before the purchase of the estate is finally concluded.

Unfortunately for the student of English land law, there are two totally separate systems of proving title to land and investigating third-party rights in it. The newer (and now more common) system is the registered land system; the older system is usually called the unregistered system of conveyancing. The inquiries to be made by a purchaser differ depending on whether the title to the property he wishes to buy is registered or unregistered. For the student this means learning two totally different sets of laws: one governed by statute, the Land Registration Act 1925; the other governed by the old rules of common law and equity as amended by statute (chiefly now the Law of Property Act 1925 and the Land Charges Act 1972).

Which system applies?

The first thing which you must ascertain when dealing with any piece of land is which system of conveyancing is to be applied to it. In other words you must ask yourself whether the estate in the land is (or should be) registered or not.

Areas of compulsory registration
The current system of land registration exists under the provisions of s. 1 of the LRA 1925:

> There shall continue to be kept at His Majesty's Land Registry a register of title to freehold land and leasehold land.

You will note from the wording of this provision that the register did exist before 1925. The change made by the 1925 Act was that in future registration of title to land was to become compulsory in areas designated as areas of compulsory registration by central government. As it was not possible to introduce the registration system to the whole country immediately (largely due to cost) the practice was adopted of making only certain places areas of compulsory registration, and gradually increasing those areas as time went on. Originally it was thought that the whole country would soon be covered, but economic depression, followed by a war and further recession, held up the extension of the system. In 1984 the government pledged that it would make the entire country an area of compulsory registration within ten years. That promise has been fulfilled and the last areas became compulsory registration areas on 1 December 1990. Accordingly, now all land stands in an area of compulsory registration and any person dealing with a property simply needs to ask the Land Registry whether the title has in fact been registered.

Although we will tend to make reference to 'the Land Registry' you should be aware of the fact that in reality there is not one registry but a number of District Land Registries spread around the country which deal with the registrations for their local areas. The records maintained by the Land Registry are now being computerised.

Under the provisions of LRA 1966, ss. 1 and 2, areas had to be designated compulsory areas of registration by statutory instrument. Our imaginary town of Mousehole became an area of compulsory registration on 1 January 1980.

Has the title to the estate been registered?
One has to ask this question because estates did not have to be registered as soon as the area in which the land stands became an area of compulsory registration. To require otherwise would involve estate owners in unexpected costs, for Land Registry fees are payable on all registrations. Instead, estates have to be registered at the time of the first dealing for value (usually a

sale) with the estate after the area became a compulsory area. Thus in Mousehole all estates which have been dealt with since 1980 should have been registered at the Land Registry. Accordingly the title to 1 Trant Way will be registered (dealing in 1982), whilst the title to 3 Trant Way will not be registered (last dealing in 1978). In fact there is nothing in the Act which says that you must register an estate but, as we will see later, if you fail to do so you may either lose the estate which you had bought or discover that you have not acquired a legal estate at all (LRA 1925, ss. 123(1) and 19).

The result of this rule is that the title to some pieces of land will be registered, whilst the title to others will not. If you are not sure whether a registration has been made you can find out by making an 'index map search' (Land Registration Rules 1925, r. 286) which will tell you whether the estate has been registered (but which will not reveal any other information, such as the name of the estate owner). Further details may be obtained by making a full search of the register. (Since 3 December 1990 it has no longer been necessary to obtain the consent of the estate owner to make a search.)

While most registered land has been entered on the register due to a need to comply with the rules making registration essential, there are also cases in which registration is appropriate on a voluntary basis. For example, a developer planning to build a large housing estate on land which is currently unregistered may choose to register the title to the whole estate voluntarily. He can then agree an estate plan for all the new properties with the Land Registry before he starts to sell the individual plots. This makes conveyancig of each plot of land easier once purchasers are found and is convenient for the developer, the purchasers and the Registry. Voluntary registration is also sometimes used to solve a problem which has arisen in relation to the property, for example, if the title deeds have been destroyed in a fire or due to an accident. In these cases voluntary registration can avoid many difficulties when the estate owner comes to sell because the registry entry will replace the missing deeds. You can even find properties which were registered voluntarily at a time at which the area in which they stand was not an area of compulsory registration. However, this possibility is no longer relevant because the whole of England and Wales is now covered by the compulsory registration system and voluntary registration has always been possible for any property within a compulsory area.

Unregistered land
Any land which is not shown as being registered on the Land Registry index map is necessarily unregistered land (even though it is in an area of compulsory registration). As such it is covered by the older system of conveyancing rules which are substantially different, particularly as regards the protection of third-party rights.

CONVEYANCING PROCEDURE

Most readers will be aware that in England and Wales conveyancing is normally conducted in two stages:

(a)   contract; and
(b)   conveyance (or transfer, in registered land).

The steps up to and including the formation of a legally binding contract are essentially the same for both registered and unregistered land. It is after the contract is concluded that the major differences appear and we will delay a discussion of the two conveyancing systems until that point. Let us first consider all that happens before a contract is made.

Steps before a contract is concluded

Enquiries before contract
Before they enter into contracts to buy 1 and 3 Trant Way, Mr and Mrs Armstrong and Miss Bell will want confirmation of certain information about the property: they will want to know how much the Council Tax is; whether the price includes any fittings, such as carpets; whether there have been any disputes in respect of the land (e.g., boundary disputes); and, no doubt, a great deal else. In addition their solicitors may wish to query portions of the draft contract each has received from the vendors' solicitors. These assorted enquiries are usually collected together into a set of 'enquiries before contract' to be answered by the vendors and their legal advisers. Unfortunately, due to fears about liability for misrepresentation, many lawyers give very evasive answers to such questions. A standard form of typical enquiries can be obtained from any legal stationers.

Local land charges
Before entering into a contract to buy an estate in land, it is usual also to make a search about the property in the local land charges register. These registers are maintained by the local authorities for the properties in their areas under the Local Land Charges Act 1975. They contain details of a variety of 'charges' (burdens) on the land. Thus you might discover from searching the register that the property is in a smoke control zone, or that a tree in the garden is the subject of a tree preservation order, or that the local authority has a claim against the land because the Council Tax has not been paid. You might also discover planning restrictions or that the building is listed as being of outstanding architectural or historical importance. As all these matters might have a considerable effect upon the use to which the land can be put, it is essential that a purchaser should make a search. Oddly, a purchaser of an estate will be bound by any charge which exists, even if it has not been registered. However, a search is still worthwhile because, if a purchaser obtains an official search certificate, compensation can be claimed under s. 10 of the Local Land Charges Act 1975 if later a charge is discovered which was not revealed by the certificate. This right to compensation arises whether the search was clean because the charge had not been registered or because the local authority made a mistake when issuing the certificate. The compensation is paid by the local authority, even if the loss is due to the mistake of some third party who has failed to register a charge (the authority may seek to recover from the third party any sums so paid).

In addition to providing an official search of the local land charges register, the local authority will also provide, if asked, a wide range of other information about the property (including, for example, details of any planned local road alterations). Standard forms are used for both searches and for raising extra enquiries with local authorities and a fee is payable for both.

The contract

Once a purchaser is satisfied with the answers to his preliminary enquiries and has received a satisfactory local search, has made any necessary arrangements to finance the transaction, and has had a surveyor's report on the property (if he so wishes), the point will have been reached at which the parties are ready to conclude a legally binding contract. Until a contract is concluded neither party is legally bound to continue with the transaction and either can back out of the negotiations without liability. However, once a contract has been concluded, each party is legally obliged to give effect to the transaction, unless the other party is in breach of the terms of the contract. It is therefore crucial to know at which point an enforceable contract has come into existence.

To some extent, a contract for the sale of an estate or an interest in land is just like any other contract. It must comply with the basic requirements for a contract not under seal: there must have been an offer and an acceptance, there must be consideration, and the parties must have intended to create a legal relationship. However, due to the considerable value of land, it is not surprising that for many years greater formality has been required in relation to contracts to convey, transfer or create estates or interests in land. Once again the nature of the formalities required will depend upon the date at which the contract was made because new rules for making of such contracts were introduced by the Law of Property (Miscellaneous Provisions) Act 1989. These new rules apply to contracts made on or after 27 September 1989. Older contracts are still subject to the old rules and, since it is quite possible to come across a dispute involving an old contract, we will set out both sets of rules.

Contracts made before 27 September 1989

The rules regarding contracts for the disposition of estates or interests in land, made before 27 September 1989, were contained in s. 40(1) of the LPA 1925:

> No action may be brought upon any contract for the sale or other disposition of land or any interest in land, unless the agreement upon which such action is brought, or some memorandum or note thereof, is in writing, and signed by the party to be charged or by some other person thereunto by him lawfully authorised.

The provisions of this section must now be considered in detail.

'No action may be brought'
The wording of s. 40 does not render an oral contract either void or voidable: it is merely unenforceable by action in the courts. This may seem like splitting hairs but the distinction can be important as is illustrated by the case of *Low* v *Fry* (1935) 51 TLR 322. In that case the parties made an oral agreement for the sale of an estate in land and the purchaser gave the vendor a cheque for a portion of the purchase price. Later the purchaser decided not to proceed with the transaction and told his bank to stop payment of the cheque. The vendor was unable to enforce the contract to sell because of s. 40, but was able to recover on the cheque: this was not a case in which a cheque had been issued for a consideration which had totally failed, because the contract, though unenforceable, was valid.

'Any contract'
It is necessary to show that a contract exists and therefore the document used to satisfy s. 40 must contain certain essential details:

(a)   the names of the parties or a description which allows them to be identified;
(b)   a clear description of the property;
(c)   the consideration;
(d)   any additional material terms of the contract other than any which are implied by operation of law.

If any essential detail is missing then the courts will not enforce the contract. The existence of a memorandum cannot make enforceable any agreement which is not a binding contract.

'Sale or other disposition'
The inclusion of these words means that s. 40 applied to a wide range of transactions. Thus, for example, an agreement to grant a legal charge (mortgage) had to comply with s. 40 (*Pattle* v *Anstruther* (1893) 69 LT 175), as did a contract to grant a lease (*Biss* v *Hygate* [1918] 2 KB 314).

'Land or any interest in land'
The section applied to dispositions of any estates or interests in land. So an agreement to grant an interest, such as an easement or profit à prendre, would also need to comply with the section (*Webber* v *Lee* (1882) 9 QBD 315).

'Unless the agreement . . . or some memorandum or note thereof, is in writing'
Section 40 was satisfied if there was either a written contract or a written record of a pre-existing oral contract. Thus an oral contract could be enforced if at some point a memorandum was made of the terms of the contract. Accordingly, if an intending purchaser of an estate made an oral contract and then later wrote a letter which stated that he had agreed to buy the property from the vendor for so much money, then the letter can constitute a s. 40 memorandum and be used to prove the contract (even if the purchaser

sent his letter to his own solicitor: *Smith-Bird* v *Blower* [1939] 2 All ER 406). A receipt signed by a vendor in return for the purchaser's deposit may also amount to a sufficient note of the contract (*Davies* v *Sweet* [1962] 2 QB 300) even if the vendor did not intend the receipt to have this effect. It is also possible to combine several related documents (e.g., a series of letters) in order to produce the necessary memorandum (*Griffiths* v *Young* [1970] Ch 675).

'Signed by the party to be charged or by some other person thereunto by him lawfully authorised'
This required that the document should be signed by the party against whom enforcement is sought, or by his agent. Thus if a purchaser alone signed a s. 40 memorandum, the purchaser could not later use the document to sue the vendor—for fairly obvious reasons!

An alternative to writing: part performance

The forerunner of LPA 1925, s. 40, was first introduced into English law by the Statute of Frauds, 1677, and was intended to combat the numbers of cases of perjured evidence in cases relating to land by requiring written, rather than oral, evidence of contracts. However, the 1677 statute soon caused its own problems since it became possible for a vendor to agree orally to sell land, allow the purchaser to move in and improve the land, and then claim the land back (plus improvements) on the ground that there was no contract enforceable at law. Not surprisingly at this point, equity, the guardian of conscience, intervened. To prevent the statute being used as an instrument of fraud, the equitable doctrine of part performance was developed. This doctrine provides that if a party to a contract has acted on the contract in reliance on the promise of the other party, then the contract will be enforced in equity, despite the lack of a written memorandum. One can see that this doctrine is linked to the concept of estoppel. It was specifically retained in relation to s. 40 cases by subsection (2) of that section.

The requirements for the operation of part performance
In order to use the doctrine of part performance, a plaintiff must show that acts have been done which point clearly to the existence of a contract. In essence the plaintiff is claiming that he would obviously not have acted as he did, had he not had a valid contract. This is a method of using actions as evidence of an agreement and thus those actions must be 'such as must be referred to some contract, and may be referred to the alleged one; that they prove the existence of some contract, and are consistent with the contract alleged' (Sir Edward Fry, *A Treatise on the Specific Performance of Contracts*, 6th ed. (London: Stevens, 1921), p. 278, approved by the House of Lords in *Steadman* v *Steadman* [1976] AC 536).

It is probably easiest to explain part performance by giving some examples of the operation of the doctrine. In *Rawlinson* v *Ames* [1925] Ch 96, the defendant had agreed to take a lease from the plaintiff but had asked the plaintiff to do some work on the land before the defendant moved in. The plaintiff did the necessary work under the defendant's supervision but the defendant then refused to take the lease, relying on s. 40 as there was no written contract. In this case the plaintiff was granted an order for specific performance of the oral contract. The court concluded that the plaintiff would not have carried out the improvements to the land at the defendant's direction had there not been a pre-existing contract. In *Wakeham* v *Mackenzie* [1968] 1 WLR 1175 the plaintiff moved out of her council flat and into the home of a widower in order to look after him. The plaintiff received no payment for her housekeeping services and contributed to the food and fuel bills. It was held that these actions were clear evidence of the existence of a contract between the plaintiff and the widower. The plaintiff succeeded in her claim that the widower had contracted to leave her the property in his will, because the actions were consistent with such a contract, and there was no evidence to rebut this claim because the widower had since died. From this it can be seen that, once sufficient actions are proved to establish the claim of part performance, oral evidence will be admitted in order to establish the exact terms of the contract. *Wakeham* v *Mackenzie* may be contrasted with the similar situation in *Maddison* v *Alderson* (1883) 8 App Cas 467 in which a housekeeper initially received wages but later worked for nothing because, she alleged, her employer had promised to make a will leaving the property to her. Here the court held that the part performance rule could not be applied because the housekeeper's actions could be explained in a number of ways and did not necessarily prove that there must have been a contract relating to the land.

An action which has often been said not to amount to an act of part performance is the payment of money. This may appear surprising but, of course, proving that A paid money to B does not prove that there must have been a contract relating to land made between them; the payment could be a simple loan or a gift. However, it now appears from *Steadman* v *Steadman* [1976] AC 536 that in some circumstances the payment of money may constitute an act of part performance. This case involved a matrimonial dispute in which a husband was in arrears with maintenance payments to his wife and in which he was seeking his wife's agreement to transfer her share of the matrimonial home to him. Mrs Steadman went to court over the maintenance arrears and at the door of the magistrates' court it was agreed that, if she waived her right to all but £100 of the arrears, her husband would pay her £1,500 for her share in the home. This agreement was placed before the magistrates and shortly afterwards Mr Steadman paid over the £100. However, Mrs Steadman later refused to transfer her share in the house to her husband, claiming that there was no enforceable contract. The House of Lords held that the payment of the £100, the notification of the agreement to the magistrates, and the preparation of the transfer documents by Mr Steadman's solicitors, together amounted to part performance. Accordingly Mr Steadman was entitled to enforcement of the contract.

In relation to s. 40 other problems have also cropped up in a number of cases. Most of these are more relevant to students of conveyancing but two examples may serve to illustrate the difficulties which did arise. In *Daulia Ltd* v *Four Millbank Nominees Ltd* [1978] Ch 231 the purchasers claimed that there was an oral agreement that the vendors would make a formal exchange of contracts if the purchasers attended at the vendor's offices with their part of the contract signed and with a bank draft for the deposit. When the purchasers did duly attend the vendors refused to exchange contracts. The Court of Appeal held that even in a case like this (a contract to contract) s. 40 had to be satisfied. Thus the agreement to exchange formal contracts if certain conditions were satisfied had itself to be evidenced in writing.

Another matter which was of particular interest to conveyancers was whether they could prevent their letters from constituting s. 40 memoranda by marking them 'subject to contract'. This problem was mentioned in *Daulia* and was considered further in *Cohen* v *Nessdale Ltd* [1981] 3 All ER 118. The rule was that, whilst a letter can constitute a sufficient memorandum, it will usually be prevented from having this effect if marked 'subject to contract'.

Acts amounting to part performance
The following are all acts which have been held to be sufficient acts of part performance.

(a)   The best example is the case in which the purchaser takes possession of the land with the consent of the vendor (or where a tenant goes into possession with the permission of the landlord) (*Bowers* v *Cator* (1798) 4 Ves Jr 91).

(b)   Remaining in possession of land may be an act of part performance if combined with other actions, such as payment of money (*Miller & Aldworth Ltd* v *Sharp* [1899] 1 Ch 622).

(c)   Payment of money may be sufficient if combined with other actions (*Steadman* v *Steadman* [1976] AC 536).

(d)   Frequently the making of alterations or improvements on the land has been held to be an act of part performance (*Broughton* v *Snook* [1938] Ch 505).

(e)   Performance of work on one's own land for another's benefit can amount to part performance (*McManus* v *Cooke* (1887) 35 ChD 681, and see *Rawlinson* v *Ames* [1925] Ch 96).

(f)   Leaving property may be an act of part performance (*Liddell* v *Hopkinson* (1974) 233 EG 512, in which a wife left the matrimonial home on an oral promise that her husband would pay her a portion of the proceeds of sale).

It should be noted that the acts relied on must have been done in performance of or in pursuance of a contract and must be more than pre-contractual acts. Thus making planning applications (*New Hart Builders* v *Brindley* [1975] Ch 342) would not amount to part performance. Nor can the doctrine be used to enforce a contract which is defective in some other way: the essential requirements of the law of contract must still be satisfied.

Since part performance is a creation of equity it is discretionary in its application (as are all equitable principles) and a court will decline to assist a party who relies on the doctrine if this would produce injustice, or if the party relying on the doctrine has 'dirty hands'.

Contracts which did not have to satisfy section 40
There were three occasions when LPA 1925, s. 40, did not apply:

(a)   If the sale was by the court, s. 40(2) provided that no written evidence of the contract was required. This is because the court record was itself sufficient evidence.

(b)   If the party who is relying on s. 40(1) had used fraud to prevent the contract being recorded he could not rely on the section as a defence, for to permit this would to be to allow the statute to be used as 'an engine of fraud' (*Viscountess Montacute* v *Maxwell* (1720) 1 P Wms 618.)

(c)   If a party forgot to plead s. 40(1) specifically he could not rely upon it (RSC Ord. 18, rr. 8 and 13; *Clarke* v *Callow* (1877) 46 LJ QB 53).

Contracts made on or after 27 September 1989

It can be seen from the description given above that over the years the rules relating to contracts had become extremely complex, not the least because LPA 1925, s. 40, did not prevent an oral contract from arising, it merely made it unenforceable. Accordingly, on the recommendation of the Law Commission, the law was changed in 1989. The rules which now apply to contracts are to be found in the Law of Property (Miscellaneous Provisions) Act 1989, s. 2, which replaces LPA 1925, s. 40. Unfortunately s. 2 appears to have some problems of its own, so it is not clear that all henceforth will be straightforward.

Section 2(1)–(3) is as follows:

(1)   A contract for the sale or other disposition of an interest in land can only be made in writing and only by incorporating all the terms which the parties have expressly agreed in one document or, where contracts are exchanged, in each.

(2)   The terms may be incorporated in a document either by being set out in it or by reference to some other document.

(3)   The document incorporating the terms or, where contracts are exchanged, one of the documents incorporating them (but not necessarily the same one) must be signed by or on behalf of each party to the contract.

As can be seen, this rule is very different to that contained in LPA 1925, s. 40: notably, now a contract for the sale of an interest in land must be *made* in writing. This change removes the old problems which arose from the fact that oral contracts were valid but unenforceable. Now if there is not a written agreement there is no contract at all. What is more, the document must contain all the terms that have been agreed between the parties. Under the old rules a party who had the benefit of a term of the contract could choose to waive that term, if it had not been recorded, and could enforce the balance of the agreement. The wording of s. 2 suggests that this is no longer possible because it requires that all the terms agreed be recorded before a valid contract can be made. In such a case it might however be possible to obtain rectification of the written agreement and s. 2(4) does make express reference to this possibility. It appears from *Joscelyne* v *Nissen* [1970] 2 QB 86 that, as long as there is a pre-existing agreement, it is not necessary to establish that there was a pre-existing contract in order to obtain rectification (which would be impossible due to the absence of a s. 2 document).

The new provision requires that both parties sign the written contract, not just the party against whom one is seeking to enforce. Until both sign no contract exists. However, subsection (3) does recognise that it is standard practice for two copies to be prepared and for these to be exchanged. In this case each party must sign his part of the contract and it is not necessary for both to sign both copies. (Problems may arise if the two copies are not identical in their terms.)

Obviously, because s. 2 is so new, very few cases have yet been decided that might help you understand it. One case that has reached the courts is *Spiro* v *Glencrown Properties Ltd* [1991] Ch 537. This case concerned an option to purchase and the issue was whether the notice exercising the option needed to comply with s. 2. Hoffman J held that, whilst the option agreement had to comply with the 1989 Act, the notice actually exercising the option did not have to do so. He said:

> Section 2 . . . was intended to prevent disputes over whether the parties had entered into a binding agreement or over what terms they had agreed. It prescribes the formalities for recording their mutual consent. But only the grant of the option depends upon consent. The exercise of the option is a unilateral act. It would destroy the very purpose of the option if the purchaser had to obtain the vendor's counter-signature to the notice by which it was exercised.

However, in reaching this conclusion Hoffman J, as he admitted, relied heavily on the purposive approach to statutory construction and did not follow authorities which indicated that the service of a notice under an option constituted the acceptance of an irrevocable offer to contract contained in the option agreement. Were that view of the mechanics of the option accepted, s. 2 would require the vendor's signature to the notice (and that the notice contained all the terms of the bargain).

The rules under s. 2 were also considered in *Record* v *Bell* [1991] 1 WLR 853. This case concerned a contract for the sale and purchase of a very expensive property in Smith Square, London. Contracts for the transaction were prepared in duplicate in the normal way (see below) and each part was signed by or on behalf of the parties and in due course they were exchanged with the intention of concluding a binding agreement. However, before the exchange took place the purchaser's solicitor had said that he would wish to see up to date copies of the entries at the Land Registry relating to the property, the title to which was registered. The vendor's solicitor was unable to produce the documents in time but assured the purchaser's solicitor that there would be no problems when the documents were revealed. The two solicitors therefore agreed (during a telephone call) that the exchange of contracts would go ahead but that the contract would be conditional upon the vendor's solicitor producing Land Registry entries which confirmed that the facts were as had been stated by the vendor's solicitor. When sending the vendor's signed copy of the contract to the purchaser's solicitor the vendor's solicitor mentioned the fact that the contract was conditional in his letter. The purchaser's solicitor sent the purchaser's signed copy in return but had attached to the document a signed note setting out the condition agreed between the solicitors. In due course the necessary Land Registry documents were produced and found to be entirely in order. However, when the time for completion of the whole transaction came the purchaser did not complete: it appears that he was prevented from doing so by financial losses caused by the war in the Gulf. The vendor sought to enforce the contract.

The problem in the case was, of course, whether on these facts there was a binding contract between the parties which satisfied s. 2 of the 1989 Act. Did the fact that the condition agreed did not appear in the contract documents mean that the agreement did not comply with s. 2? Section 2(2) clearly makes reference to some other document but the note of the agreement and the letter from the vendor's solicitor, which set out the term in question, were not mentioned *in* either contract. If the term formed part of the contract and was not mentioned or referred to in the contracts, the documents did not comply with s. 2 and thus no valid contract had been made. If this were true, the vendor could not enforce the agreement despite the existence of the documents which provided a complete record of the terms agreed and despite the fact that he had satisfied the specified condition.

It was held that whilst a letter of variation of a contract or a letter containing additional terms could be enforced if signed by both parties (or presumably if contained in two identical documents each signed by one party and exchanged) the facts of this case did not involve a later variation. The arrangement as to the condition was contemporaneous with the exchange of the parts of the contracts. One would accordingly expect that, due to the provisions of s. 2, the agreement would not have amounted to an enforceable contract. However, this was not the view taken by the learned judge, who concluded that in this transaction there had been two contracts: one for the sale of the estate in land and the other a collateral contract that the title to the property would be revealed as described when the necessary paperwork was produced. The collateral contract was not in itself a contract for the sale of an estate or interest in land and thus was not subject to s. 2 and could be concluded orally (as can any other contract if there is consideration). The collateral contract had been fulfilled and there was no defect in the contract for sale, which accordingly could be enforced.

In reaching this decision much reliance was placed upon the decision in *De Lassalle* v *Guildford* [1901] 2 KB 215 as to the occasions on which a collateral contract can arise.

If this case is extensively relied upon in the future it may produce a considerable flaw in the system introduced by s. 2, which was intended to ensure that disputes as to the terms of contracts largely became a thing of the past. It will also make it difficult to be sure when a s. 2 contract has been made as it appears that some additional terms will be covered by the collateral contract concept, whilst others presumably will not. Despite the fact that one may have considerabled sympathy for the vendor in this case, the result for land law may well be quite undesirable. Had s. 2 been rigorously applied, legal advisers would have known that they must ensure that all terms were included in the contract by some means (if necessary by express reference to another document) and parties injured by the failure of their advisers to ensure that this was done would have had a remedy in negligence.

The possibility of two separate contracts existing was also considered in *Tootal Clothing Ltd* v *Guinea Properties Management Ltd* [1992] 2 EGLR 80. Here the agreements were: (1) for the grant of a lease, and (2) that the tenant would carry out shopfitting works at the premises within 12 weeks and that for this work the landlord would pay £30,000. The contract to grant the lease was fulfilled by the formal grant of a lease and the tenant thereafter carried out the work. However, when the work was done the landlord refused to pay. In this case the Court of Appeal held s. 2 could not continue to apply to the agreement to grant the lease after the transaction had been completed by the making of the grant and that, in any event, there were two separate contracts here. Thus the agreement for the work did not have to be included in the same document as the agreement for the lease in order to be enforceable. Scott LJ said:

> If parties choose to hive off parts of the terms of their composite bargain into a separate contract distinct from the written land contract that incorporates the rest of the terms, I can see nothing in section 2 that provides an answer to an action for enforcement of the land contract, on the one hand, or of the separate contract on the other hand. Each has become, by the choice of the parties, a separate contract.

Part performance and estoppel

The new rules make no provision for the continuation of the doctrine of part performance; the Law Commission were of the view that those rules should be abolished. It was suggested that the doctrine of estoppel might be relied upon as an alternative:

> We see no cause to fear that the recommended repeal and replacement of the present section as to the formalities for contracts for sale or other disposition of land will inhibit the courts in the exercise of the equitable discretion to do justice between parties in individual otherwise hard cases.

(Law Com. No. 164 (1987), para. 5.5).

Has the doctrine of part performance in fact been abolished? What s. 40(2) said was:

> This section . . . does not affect the law relating to part performance . . .

Accordingly, to repeal s. 40 does not abolish the rule in itself. One must look to the origins of the equitable doctrine to see how it arose and whether it could apply to a case in which it is clear that no contract has been made (because the s. 2 formalities are not satisfied) but in which it is clear that a bargain had been made (which fell short of a contract only due to the absence of the required document).

We explained earlier that the original source of what became LPA 1925, s. 40, was the Statute of Frauds 1677. The first reference to the doctrine of part performance appears in 1686 (*Butcher* v *Stapley* (1686) 1 Vern 363) and it is clear that the doctrine was developed as a reaction to frauds perpetrated in reliance on the Statute of Frauds. As we have seen above, the whole point was to show that acts had been done which indicated the existence of a contract (see the remarks of Lord Selborne LC in *Maddison* v *Alderson* (1883) 8 App Cas 467, 476). The remedy given, if part performance was established, was specific performance of the contract. From all this it is clear that, where there is no contract, there is no room for the continued existence of part performance. After the 1989 Act, if there is a contract, that is only because s. 2 has been satisfied and in those circumstances there is no need for the doctrine.

The Law Commission were content to let hard cases be handled by the rules of estoppel. However, the category of cases assisted under that equitable principle is restricted by the need for some representation to have been made by one party and upon which the other had relied. In many of the part performance cases, no representation had been made by the vendor. In a case under s. 2, as a matter of law, there is no contract and accordingly if the purchaser believes that he has a right to the property he has made a mistake as to the law. For such mistakes he must suffer the loss. He cannot say: 'But I thought I had a right' because in doing so he is relying on his own ignorance. Accordingly, in the absence of an express promise that the property will be conveyed or transferred, it is difficult to see how an estoppel could be raised. However, the doctrine has changed over the years and it will be interesting to see what view the courts will take.

Contracts which do not have to satisfy s. 2
The contracts which may be made without a written contract are specified in s. 2(5).

Contracts to grant short leases are excluded altogether (leases for a term not exceeding 3 years—see below p. 99). This is because the old rule under LPA 1925, s. 40, was anomalous because a contract to grant a short lease had to comply with s. 40, whereas the actual grant of such a lease did not even require writing (LPA 1925, s. 54(2), provides an exemption to the general rule in s. 52). The new rule seems to be a decided improvement.

Also excluded are contracts made in the course of a public auction (which have always had their own rules) and contracts regulated under the Financial Services Act 1986. The Financial Services Act exclusion covers certain contracts for investments which happen to include an interest of some kind in land. An example might be a unit trust or a debenture (a debenture is a type of charge (mortgage) used over the property of a company and it will usually include a charge over any land which the company has).

Section 2(5) also expressly excludes 'the creation or operation of resulting, implied or constructive trusts'. This is in line with the rule under s. 40 and indeed, after the abolition of the doctrine of part performance, may be of even greater importance: now the constructive trust may be used more often in relation to bargains affecting land, provided that some element of trickery or bad faith can be established (see below p. 162).

The usual method of concluding a contract

Conveyancers have over the years adopted a particular method of concluding contracts for the sale of estates in land. The reason for choosing this method in the past was that it ensured that both parties to the contract had in their possession a document which satisfied LPA 1925, s. 40, and which therefore allowed either party to sue on the contract, should this prove necessary. The normal procedure was for two identical copies of the contract to be prepared. One copy was signed by the vendor and the other by the purchaser. When the time came to create a binding contract the parties exchanged their copies of the contract. As a result of the exchange of contracts each party held a record of the agreement signed by the other. In addition it is normal for the purchaser to pay a portion of the purchase price (usually 10% but lower percentages are becoming increasingly common as house prices rise) to the vendor, as a deposit. Section 2(1) of the 1989 Act expressly retains this method of concluding a contract, which will continue to be the normal method adopted by conveyancers.

Effect of the contract: passing the equitable interest

There is an important equitable maxim which says: 'Equity regards as done that which ought to be done'. In the case of a contract to sell an estate in land, 'that which ought to be done' is the completion of the sale by the execution of a deed which conveys the legal estate to the purchaser. Therefore, the application of the maxim means that, as soon as there is an enforceable contract, the purchaser is treated in equity as already having received the benefits of a conveyance. So, after the contract, the purchaser is treated as being the true owner of the property for all equitable purposes. This gives rise to a position in which there are two 'owners' of the property:

(a) The vendor remains the legal owner until a deed conveying the legal estate has been signed, witnessed and delivered (and registered in the case of registered land) (LPA 1925, s. 52(1)).
(b) The purchaser becomes the equitable owner as soon as the contract is concluded (*Lysaght* v *Edwards* (1876) 2 ChD 499, 506–10).

You will realise from chapter 1 that the result is to make the vendor a trustee of the legal estate and the purchaser a beneficiary owning the equitable interest. The vendor is, however, an unusual trustee because he has more rights than most trustees (e.g., the right to demand the purchase price), and in fact he usually retains personal use of the land until the sale is completed.

As the purchaser is already beneficial (equitable) owner, he should protect himself by insuring his interest in the property. It is the equitable interest which is the valuable interest in the land and its owner should insure. Indeed, should the house on the property burn down after contract but before conveyance, the purchaser is still bound to complete the purchase and pay over the purchase price (*Paine* v *Meller* (1801) 6 Ves Jr 349). Again, if the land should become the subject of a compulsory purchase order after contract, the purchaser must still proceed (*Hillingdon Estates Co.* v *Stonefield Estates Ltd* [1952] Ch 627). These rules may be regarded as unfair (particularly in relation to insurance) and it has been suggested that the rules on passing of risk should be amended. However, as yet there has been no change and thus the position can be summarised in the proposition that:

Risk passes to the purchaser on the conclusion of the contract.

All this is based on the proposition that the purchaser can insist on the performance of the contract by the vendor. This in turn depends on the availability of the equitable remedy of specific performance, which is discussed below.

Remedies

Once a contract has been concluded the parties are both legally bound to carry out their parts of the contract. Should either party fail to do this, a number of possible remedies are available to the other.

Damages
The common law remedy for breach of contract is damages. The usual measure of damages is the loss which the plaintiff has sustained as a result of non-performance. Accordingly it is usually possible for the wronged party to claim damages for the loss of the bargain. Liability in damages may arise in a number of ways, for example, refusal by either party to perform the contract or due to misrepresentation by the vendor. The Law of Property (Miscellaneous Provisions) Act 1989 has removed old rules which limited the measure of damages in certain cases and now ordinary contractual principles will be applied.

Specific performance
For many centuries equity has accepted that in cases concerning land the common law remedy of damages is likely to be inadequate. This is because each piece of land is unique in character, and a thwarted purchaser cannot take any damages that he might obtain and buy another identical property (as he might were the subject of the contract a car or a piece of furniture). Accordingly, equity provided the remedy of specific performance, which can be used to compel the recalcitrant party to carry out his promise. The remedy is available to either party, so a vendor may also use it to force a purchaser to complete (*Hope* v *Walter* [1900] 1 Ch 257). Being equitable this remedy is discretionary in nature and will be refused if the applicant has 'dirty hands', that is, if he is in some way at fault himself in relation to the obligations under the contract.

Rescission
Rescission is a remedy which either party may elect to use should the other party break a term of the contract which is a condition precedent. An example of this would be if the vendor were unable to prove that he had good title to the land; the purchaser would then normally choose to rescind the contract. Rescission is an optional remedy and the wronged party can choose to affirm the contract instead and to seek damages for breach. It is only available in cases in which *restitutio in integrum* is possible; that is, it must be possible to return the parties to their original position.

Rectification
This remedy is available to correct an innaccurate written record of an oral agreement. The remedy is difficult to obtain as the court will require very strong evidence that the document does not record the oral agreement (*Joscelyne* v *Nissen* [1970] 2 QB 86 at 98). This may become of greater importance now that the Law of Property (Miscellaneous Provisions) Act 1989 is in operation.

Injunction
This equitable remedy is available to restrain a threatened breach of contract.

Declaration
In certain cases a declaration of the court on an issue may be a useful remedy. It might, for example, be used if there were a dispute over the exact meaning of a term in the contract. Should the dispute be over a matter of proof of title this remedy is very useful and a simple procedure is provided by the use of a vendor and purchaser summons under LPA 1925, s. 49(1).

An illustration of the rules for contracts
We have seen that Barbara Bell is thinking of buying 3 Trant Way from Victoria Ventnor. We can illustrate the changes in the law produced by s. 2, Law of Property (Miscellaneous Provisions) Act 1989 by imagining that the two ladies have discussed the matter and that they are now both agreed that Miss Bell should have the property and have settled the price. Miss Bell, thinking she should have the matter set out clearly before she goes to see her solicitor, has written to Miss Ventnor setting out the terms that have been decided upon.

If these facts occurred before 27 September 1989 the parties would have concluded a contract at the time at which they made their oral agreement. However that agreement would not have been enforceable. When Miss Ventnor received Miss Bell's letter she would have come into possession of a document which satisfied LPA 1925, s. 40, provided that Miss Bell had signed her letter and that it was sufficiently detailed, which is probable. Thereafter Miss Ventnor could enforce the contract against Miss Bell. Miss Bell could not enforce against Miss Ventnor because Miss Ventnor had not signed a s. 40 memorandum.

If these facts occurred on or after 27 September 1989 neither lady would be able to enforce their bargain. The document that exists does not comply with the Law of Property (Miscellaneous Provisions) Act 1989, s. 2 because it is not signed by both parties. In addition it may only purport to record an existing agreement, whereas s. 2 requires that the contract be *made* in writing.

As you can see, the date of the contract will make a considerable difference to the result produced.

From contract to completion: investigating title

After the contract has been concluded, it is the job of the vendor to show that he does have the title to the land which he has contracted to sell to the purchaser. The means by which this is done varies depending upon whether the title to the land is registered or unregistered. Basically, if the title is registered the purchaser will investigate the register, whilst if the title is unregistered he will need to see the title deeds to the property. The methods used to protect third-party rights also differ between the two systems and the searches to be made by the purchaser will accordingly be different. The two systems are dealt with in detail below.

Completing the transaction

Once the purchaser is satisfied that the vendor has proved that he has good title to the land, the time will have arrived for the vendor to transfer the legal estate in the land to the purchaser. The vendor will also be obliged to give possession of the property to the purchaser. This transfer is usually called 'completion'. Obviously it requires a further document, and you will recall from chapter 1 that the document used to dispose of a legal estate must be a 'deed', a document which is signed, witnessed and delivered (Law of Property (Miscellaneous Provisions) Act 1989, s. 1). If the title to the land is registered the deed used is called a 'transfer', and it must be perfected by being registered at the Land Registry (see Registered Land below). If the land is unregistered the deed is called a 'conveyance' and it has the effect of conveying the legal estate to the purchaser without the need for further formalities (see Unregistered Land below).

Having completed an outline description of the procedure normally adopted for the sale of an estate in land, it is now time to look at the two systems of conveyancing.

REGISTERED LAND

The rules relating to registered land are nearly all to be found in the Land Registration Act 1925 and the Land Registration Rules 1925. The aim of the creators of the system was to simplify conveyancing by placing all the essential information about a piece of land on a register. Thereafter an intending purchaser would only need to look at the register in order to discover all that he needed to know about the land, including proof of ownership of estates in the land and details of any rights which third parties had in respect of it. Instead of producing a bundle of title deeds in order to prove his title to the land, a vendor would simply have to produce a copy of the details on the register which the purchaser would check against the register. In theory this is an excellent idea but, as we will see, the system in operation is not as watertight as the original concept. In fact the LRA 1925 contains several large holes and a number of small leaks.

The business of registration is conducted by the Chief Land Registrar under powers conferred by LRA 1925, s. 127. The registers are in fact maintained at a series of District Land Registries which have been created by the Lord Chancellor under s. 132 of the Act.

Form of the register

The register consists of three parts: the property register, the proprietorship register, and the charges register. An example of a register entry (a fictional entry relating to 1 Trant Way) as it appears on the land certificate is shown overleaf. These documents are now being computerised and a land certificate issued now would contain the same information but in a slightly different form as far as layout is concerned.

Property register
This part of the register describes the property and invariably refers to a *filed plan*. The filed plan is prepared from the largest size of ordnance survey map and on the register entry the land concerned is shown edged in red. Usually the description of the property is simply its postal address but a different type of description may sometimes be necessary (e.g., if the registration was of a field with no address). The property register also shows the *title number* which has been allocated by the registrar (e.g., ST1234 is the title number for 1 Trant Way). Accurately speaking it is not the land which is registered but estates in the land (see below). Since there may be more than one estate in one piece of land (e.g., a fee simple and a term of years) there may be more than one register entry for the same land. Each estate has its own entry and its own title number.

Proprietorship register
This part of the register shows the type of estate registered and the class of the title (see below). It also gives the name of the registered owner of the estate and his address. Such owners are described as 'registered proprietors'. The proprietorship register will also record any restrictions on the power of the proprietor to deal with the land, for example, if he is a trustee (see p. 38 below) or a bankrupt.

Charges register
The charges section carries the details of any encumbrances (i.e., third-party rights) registered against the estate. In the case of 1 Trant Way the property is subject to a notice that the land certificate has been deposited with a bank. A large number of other burdens on the land may also appear (such as restrictive covenants: s. 50(1)), which have been protected by entry as 'minor interests' (see below).

H.M. LAND REGISTRY

Edition **1.**   opened   1.3.1982   TITLE NUMBER ST1234   This register consists of   **2**   *pages*

A. PROPERTY REGISTER
containing the description of the registered land and the estate comprised in the Title

COUNTY	DISTRICT
STILTON	MOUSEHOLE

       The Freehold land shown and edged with red on the plan of the above Title filed at the Registry   registered on 1 March 1982 known as 1 Trant Way

B. PROPRIETORSHIP REGISTER
stating nature of the Title, name, address and description of the proprietor of the land and any entries affecting the right of disposing thereof

TITLE ABSOLUTE

Entry number	Proprietor, etc
1.	VICTOR VENN, Engineer, of 1 Trant Way, Mousehole, Stilton, registered on 1 March 1982.

Demand No 8304616 4/82 W & W Ltd. 1314

Model Ⅲ

Any entries struck through are no longer subsisting

TITLE NUMBER ST1234

	C. CHARGES REGISTER	
	containing charges, incumbrances etc., adversely affecting the land and registered dealings therewith	
Entry number	The date at the beginning of each entry is the date on which the entry was made on this edition of the register	**Remarks**
1.	1 March 1982-A conveyance of the land in this title dated 30 September 1934 and made between (1) Mary Brown (Vendor) and (2) Harold Robins (Purchaser) contains the following covenants: "The Purchaser hereby covenants with the Vendor for the benefit of her adjoining land known as 15 Trant Avenue observe and perform the stipulations and conditions contained in the Schedule hereto. THE SCHEDULE before referred to 1. No building erected on the land shall be used other than as a private dwellinghouse. 2. Nothing shall be done or permitted on the premises which may be a nuisance or annoyance to the adjoining house or to the neighbourhood. 3. The garden ground of the premises shall at all times be kept in neat and proper order and condition and shall not be converted to any other use whatsoever."	
2.	1 June 1984-NOTICE of Deposit of Land Certificate with Stilton Bank plc of 2 High Street, Mousehole, Stilton, registered on 1 June 1984.	

Any entries struck through are no longer subsisting

Land certificates and charge certificates

Once an estate has been registered, the registered proprietor will wish to have some documentary evidence of the condition of the register to replace his title deeds (which are no longer of importance). This need is satisfied by the provision of a 'land certificate', which is a copy, made by the registry, of the entries on the register. It should, however, be noted that it is the register itself which matters and so the land certificate should not be treated as absolute evidence of the position in relation to the land. Should the registered estate be subject to a registered charge (mortgage) the land certificate has to be returned to the registry and is retained there. It is replaced by a 'charge certificate', which is a similar document but which is normally in the hands of the owner of the charge (e.g., a mortgagee) rather than those of the estate owner.

Proving title to registered land

Between the contract and the transfer the vendor of registered land must prove his title; that is, he must show that he is capable of transferring what he has contracted to give. The purchaser needs to check that the vendor does own the estate in question and that it is free from any encumbrance, other than those already revealed to him by the vendor. We will look separately at these two aspects of proving title.

Ownership of the estate

The property and proprietorship registers, when read together, will tell the purchaser the nature of the property registered and who owns it. The type of estate is clear, since it will be described as either freehold or leasehold land, and rights which benefit the estate (such as easements over adjoining property) are also described. However, even if the benefit of such a right is not registered in this way, it may still be claimed by successive owners of the registered estate as long as it actually benefits the property (Land Registration Rules 1925, r. 251; LRA 1925, s. 72).

The register will also indicate how good the proprietor's estate is, by recording a 'grade' of title, awarded on first registration and showing how reliable the title is considered to be. When an estate comes into the registered title system for the first time (when a purchaser applies for first registration) the Registry will investigate the title to the land in the same way that an intending purchaser does. Indeed, the Registry may well be even more careful than such a purchaser, or his solicitor, would be, for the title once registered is guaranteed. Thus if the Registry makes a mistake it may have to compensate anyone who suffers a loss as a result. The Registrar will therefore wish to be satisfied that the title to the property has been proved in a manner which would satisfy a prudent purchaser but he does not have to demand a perfect title: LRA 1925, s. 13(c).

The quality of the titles investigated may vary considerably: one title may prove to be entirely sound; another might be based only on the rights a squatter has established by possession of the land for some years (title by adverse possession); and another may suffer from some technical defect. Accordingly the Act provides for seven classes of title: three for freehold estates and four for leasehold estates. These various 'grades' of title indicate the varying degrees of reliance which may be placed on the registered title.

Grades of freehold title

The classes of title which can be registered under LRA 1925 are:

(a) absolute freehold title (s. 5);
(b) possessory freehold title (s. 6);
(c) qualified freehold title (s. 7).

Absolute freehold title

Absolute freehold title is the best class of title known to the registered land system and it is very nearly indefeasible (though see the section on rectification of the register, below). Should the registrar decide that the title to an estate is not good enough to be placed in this class of title no appeal lies from his decision, though it may be possible to apply for judicial review (*Dennis* v *Malcolm* [1934] Ch 244; RSC, Ord. 53).

Under LRA 1925, s. 5, the effect of registration of a freehold estate with absolute title is to vest in the registered proprietor an estate in fee simple, together with all the rights, privileges and appurtenances belonging to the estate and subject to:

(a) encumbrances and other entries appearing on the register (this includes registered charges and other encumbrances protected by entry on the register); and
(b) overriding interests (a special class of third-party rights, see below p. 41)

A trustee who is registered as first proprietor is also bound by those rights of beneficiaries under the trust of which he has notice, even if they are not protected by entry on the register. A purchaser from the trustee would take free of them (unless they were overriding or had been protected by some entry on the register) but the trustee cannot free himself of his obligations to the beneficiaries merely by securing a registration which does not mention their interests (LRA 1925, s. 5).

Since the registrar may accept an imperfect title to an estate for registration with absolute title (s. 13), the registration can have a curative effect and prevent future purchasers concerning themselves with technical, but unimportant, defects. Once a title is registered it is the register alone which matters as evidence of title. (This is one reason why owners sometimes choose to register their estates voluntarily.)

C

Possessory freehold title
Possessory titles are less good than absolute titles but fortunately are fairly
rare, occurring in only about 1% of cases. Such titles are registered in cases
in which the ownership of the estate is evidenced purely by the fact that
the estate owner is in occupation of the land, or that he is in receipt of the
rents and profits from the occupant. This situation might arise if the deeds
to the property had been lost, or if the estate owner had acquired his rights
merely through long use of the land (title by adverse possession, p. 75). In
order to apply for possessory title, the estate owner must, under r. 37 of
the Land Registration Rules 1925, make a statutory declaration that he and
his predecessors in title have been in possession of the land for a stated number
of years. The declaration must also state that the applicant is not aware of
any third-party claims (other than any stated), that no one else is in adverse
possession of the property and that he is not aware of any doubt attaching
to his title. The applicant must also explain why he is unable to produce
the deeds. (See also r. 38 where deeds have been lost or destroyed.)

If the Chief Land Registrar receives the necessary information he will register
a possessory title, which has the same effect as registration with an absolute
title, save that it is subject to any adverse pre-registration estates, rights or
interests. Thus the danger of having a title which is possessory only is that
someone may appear who has a better claim to the estate (for example, the
original owner who has been dispossessed by the squatter). In time, any such
rights would be time-barred under the Limitation Act 1980 (p. 77) and so
the possessory title would become quite safe from disruption. To take account
of this the system allows the owner of a possessory title to apply to have
it upgraded to absolute title after it has been registered for 12 years: LRA
1986, s. 1(2). (Previously upgrading was possible only after 15 years: LRA
1925, s. 77(3)(b).)

Qualified freehold title
Qualified freehold titles are extremely rare. The effect of such a title is the
same as that of absolute freehold title, save that it is subject to an exception
in favour of interests arising before a specified date or arising under a specified
instrument. Such title is only granted if the Registrar decides that the title
is subject to some reservation and the details of the defect will be entered
on the register. Under LRA 1925, s. 7, this class of title can only be granted
at the request of the person applying for registration. An example of this
class of title might arise if a purchaser decided to take the risk of not
investigating the title to the property as thoroughly as is usual and did not
search as far into the past of the estate as is normal. In such a case the
registration would be made subject to any rights which predated the earliest
enquiries made by the purchaser. (It is normal to search back to a deed which
is 15 or more years old, as we will explain later. If a purchaser only searched
back for 10 years he would get a qualified title which was subject to any
earlier undiscovered rights.)

Grades of leasehold title

The classes of leasehold title which can be registered under LRA 1925 are:

(a) absolute leasehold title (ss. 8 and 9);
(b) good leasehold title (ss. 8 and 10);
(c) possessory leasehold title (ss. 8 and 11); and
(d) qualified leasehold title (s. 12).

Three of these titles are very similar to those discussed above in relation to freehold land; but one, good leasehold title, has no counterpart amongst the freehold titles.

Absolute leasehold title

As compared with the purchaser of a freehold estate, the purchaser of a leasehold estate has an extra dimension to consider when checking that the vendor can transfer the estate that he has contracted to give. Like the purchaser of the freehold estate, he will check the devolution of the title to the estate that he is buying, and will want to see that it has been correctly passed from one owner to another until it reached the vendor. However, in addition, the purchaser will often wish to be reassured that the landlord (lessor) who granted the lease was actually entitled to do so. Thus the purchaser really needs to investigate the landlord's title to the superior estate in order to check that he had a good title to that estate and therefore had the right to grant the lease which the purchaser intends to buy.

Under LRA 1925, s. 8, absolute leasehold title is granted only if the Registrar is satisfied both with the lease and with the superior title from which it is derived. Thus if X, a freehold owner, grants a lease to Y, Y can register with absolute leasehold title only if the Registrar is satisfied that the lease is good *and* that X's freehold title is good. In practice it is often not possible for the leaseholder (Y) to prove that the freeholder's title is good, since a leaseholder has no right to demand that his landlord proves that his title is good unless this was specifically provided for in any contract preceding the grant of lease (LPA 1925, s. 44). In practice where one buys a long lease (e.g., a 99-year term) the landlord will usually be prepared to prove his title. Moreover, if the superior estate is itself registered there is usually little problem and the Registrar will register an absolute title, even though the leaseholder may have no right to examine the superior title himself. Now that the register is open and no permission is required to inspect, it will be easier for the person acquiring a lease to check the position of the superior title, provided that it is registered.

Registration with absolute leasehold title vests the leasehold estate in the owner subject to the encumbrances described in the case of absolute freehold title and, in addition, to all express and implied covenants, obligations and liabilities imposed by the lease or incidental to the land.

The result of the registration is that the Registrar will guarantee that the lease was effectively granted and will also show on the leasehold title any covenants which bind the freehold estate and which therefore bind the lease as well as the superior title.

Good leasehold title
This class of title is granted when the Registrar is satisfied that the lease itself is good but where there is no evidence of the quality of the superior title. In such cases the registry cannot be absolutely sure that the lease was validly granted by a person with power to grant such an estate. Apart from the fact that the superior title cannot be guaranteed, good leasehold title has the same value as registration with absolute leasehold title (LRA 1925, s. 10). If the superior title is registered at a later date the Registrar has power to improve the good leasehold title to absolute leasehold title.

Possessory leasehold title
Possessory leasehold titles are very rare. They have the same qualifications as possessory freehold titles. In addition there is no guarantee of the superior title. This class of title may be converted to good leasehold title after it has been registered for 12 years (LRA 1986, s. 1(2)).

Qualified leasehold title
Qualified leasehold titles are practically unknown. They are similar to qualified freehold titles.

Unregistrable leases

There are two categories of leases which are never registrable even though they are legal estates (LRA 1925, ss. 8 and 19(2)(a)). They are:

    (a)   leases for not more than 21 years; and
    (b)   mortgage terms which are still subject to a right of redemption (see p. 249).

The reason for these exclusions is to prevent the register becoming cluttered with short leases and, in the case of mortgage terms, those which are otherwise adequately protected; and to save holders of such leases from the expense of registration.

    As a result of amendments to LRA 1925, s. 123, made by LRA 1986, s.2 all legal leases for *more than* 21 years must be registered. Shorter legal leases are dealt with as overriding interests (see below). Before the LRA 1986 there was an unnecessarily complicated system under which leases for more than 40 years had to be registered and those for more than 21 years could be registered. The simplification introduced by the LRA 1986 is much to be welcomed but there still exist leases in the 21 to 40 years category which have not been registered because they were created before the 1986 Act came into force and have not been transferred since.

Checking for encumbrances

Having seen what information about the ownership of the estate is provided for a purchaser by the register, we now need to consider how he will find out about any third-party rights in the property.

The prospective purchaser of an estate in registered land needs to know that, in the system provided by the LRA 1925, encumbrances are divided into two main categories: overriding interests, which will bind him although they are not mentioned on the register, and minor interests which will be void against him unless they are protected by some entry on the register. In addition, there are certain legal rights, known as 'registered interests', which we will consider after we have described overriding and minor interests.

Overriding interests

We began this account of registered title by saying that the original aim of the scheme was to enable a purchaser to learn all that he needed to know about the estate by looking at the register. We added that there were in fact several holes in the system and the category of encumbrances known as overriding interests is probably the largest of these holes.

When the registration system was created it was felt that certain third-party rights in land were of such great importance that they should bind a purchaser of an estate even if they were not mentioned on the register. The rights which are automatically binding in this way are called 'overriding interests' and they are listed in paragraphs (a) to (l) of LRA 1925, s. 70(1).

The list of overriding interests includes the following rights:

Easements and profits
'Rights of common, drainage rights, customary rights, . . . public rights, profits à prendre, rights of sheepwalk, rights of way, watercourses, rights of water, and other easements not being equitable easements required to be protected by notice on the register' (s. 70(1)(a)).

This makes all legal easements and profits overriding but does not cover equitable easements. However after *Celsteel Ltd* v *Alton House Holdings Ltd* [1985] 1 WLR 204 (see p. 42) it appears that some equitable interests may be overriding.

'Rights acquired or in course of being acquired under the Limitation Acts'
(s. 70(1)(f))
The effect of this provision is illustrated by *Chowood Ltd* v *Lyall* [1930] 2 Ch 156, in which a company was registered as the proprietor of an estate in a piece of land but later discovered that Mrs Lyall had already acquired title to a portion of the land as a squatter (see p. 75). Mrs Lyall's rights were rights obtained under the Limitation Acts and so were held to bind the company without the need for any entry on the register.

'The rights of every person in actual occupation of the land or in receipt of the rents and profits thereof, save where enquiry is made of such person and the rights are not disclosed' *(s. 70(1)(g))*
This is such an important category that it must be considered in some detail and therefore it will be dealt with separately after discussing the other overriding interests.

'In the case of a possessory, qualified, or good leasehold title, all estates, rights, interests, and powers excepted from the effect of registration' *(s. 70(1)(h))*
This category consists of rights which other people *may* have against a registered estate, the possible existence of which leads the Registrar to award one of the inferior 'grades' of title.

Local land charges (s. 70(1)(i))
Local land charges are made binding on registered estates by this provision and as a result it is still advisable to make a local land charges search before concluding a contract to purchase registered land.

'Leases granted for a term not exceeding 21 years' (s. 70(1)(k))
In order to prevent the register becoming cluttered with a large number of short leases, it is not possible to register those which are to last for 21 years or less. However, such leases are protected because they are all overriding under s. 70(1)(k). It should, however, be noted that because the word 'granted' appears in this provision it has been held that it will not apply to leases which are not legal and which accordingly cannot be regarded as being the subject of a grant (see *City Permanent Building Society* v *Miller* [1952] Ch 840. This paragraph was subject to a major amendment by LRA 1986, s. 4. Before that provision came into force a distinction was made between those short leases which had been granted at a rent without taking a fine (a premium, payable at the start of the lease), which were overriding, and other short leases which became minor interests. The LRA 1986 simplifies matters considerably and the old distinctions between short leases are no longer relevant. However, they may be encountered when reading cases and this alteration should be borne in mind. The change made by the LRA 1986 had the effect of converting some leases from minor interests to overriding interests overnight (see LRA 1986, s. 4(4)).

Other overriding interests
In addition to the categories we have mentioned, s. 70(1) also includes the following in the list of overriding interests: liabilities to repair highways, parts of churches and embankments, sea and river walls; fishing, sporting and manorial rights; and certain mineral rights.

Another overriding interest?
The case of *Celsteel Ltd* v *Alton House Holdings Ltd* [1985] 1 WLR 204 suggests that there may be overriding interests which are not included in the list in LRA 1925, s. 70(1). In this case the overriding interest claimed was an equitable easement. It could not therefore be an overriding interest under s. 70(1)(a),

which relates only to legal easements. Nonetheless it was held (at first instance) that the equitable easement was overriding because of the effect of r. 258 of the Land Registration Rules 1925 which declares that 'Rights, privileges, and appurtenances appertaining or reputed to appertain to land or demised, occupied, or enjoyed therewith or reputed or known as part or parcel of or appurtenant thereto' are to be overriding under s. 70. Accordingly the court appears to have accepted that there is power to create new overriding interests under s. 144 of the Act, which allows rules to be made for a number of specified purposes. Rule 258 was a rule made under this provision. It is perhaps worrying that r. 258 is so wide in its terms since it covers any rights which are openly enjoyed and which 'adversely affect registered land'.

Rights of a person in actual occupation

The overriding interest created by LRA 1925, s. 70(1)(g), is the interest which has given rise to the greatest number of problems in practice. Overriding interests under this provision consist of:

The rights of every person in actual occupation of the land or in receipt of the rents and profits thereof, save where enquiry is made of such person and the rights are not disclosed.

It should be noted that the paragraph does not create a right to occupy premises. What it does do is protect the rights of anyone who is in occupation at the time at which a purchaser acquires a registered estate. Thus if the occupier is a tenant under a lease who happens also to have an option to purchase the reversion (the right to 'buy out' his landlord's interest), the option and the lease are both capable of being overriding interests and would bind a purchaser even if there was no mention of them on the register (*Webb* v *Pollmount* [1966] Ch 584). Similarly the rights of a beneficiary arising under a trust of the land will be overriding if the beneficiary is in occupation of the land.

It is essential to realise that a person who is in occupation but who has no rights known to law or equity can get no benefit from s. 70(1)(g), nor can a person who has rights but who is not in occupation. These points are both illustrated by the leading case of *Strand Securities Ltd* v *Caswell* [1965] Ch 958. In this case Caswell had a lease of a London flat. He kept some furniture and clothing at the flat but did not live there. The property was occupied by Mr Caswell's stepdaughter who had moved in with his permission, because she was suffering matrimonial difficulties. She occupied the flat as a licensee (that is, as someone with permission—a licence—to do so). As we will see in chapter 4, the protection given by the law to licensees can vary considerably according to the individual circumstances, but the general principle, which applied in this case, is that this type of agreement can be terminated at any time and gives the licensee no rights in the land. The Court of Appeal held that Mr Caswell had no overriding interest in the property since, although he had rights (the lease), he was not in occupation. He was not in receipt of any rents or profits, because his stepdaughter was not paying him anything for her use of the property. The presence of his belongings at the property did not amount to occupation for the purposes of the Act. (See now *Kingsnorth Trust Co. Ltd* v *Tizard* [1986] 1 WLR 783, p. 71 below, an unregistered land case on occupation.) Of course the stepdaughter was in occupation of the property, but unfortunately she did not have any rights to the property which were capable of being overriding. The court did suggest that, had she occupied the property at the request of her stepfather and in order to look after the property for him, he might have been regarded as being in occupation through an agent. However, on the facts as they stood, she was clearly there because of her own needs and not as Mr Caswell's agent. (The issue of occupation through an agent was also considered by the Court of Appeal in *Lloyds Bank plc* v *Rosset* [1988] 3 WLR 1301 but, because they considered that Mrs Rosset had no rights in relation to the property, was not considered by the House of Lords, [1991] 1 AC 107.)

Another problem which can arise in relation to s. 70(1)(g) is the date at which the claimant must be in occupation of the premises, since there is often a delay between the creation of a right such as a mortgage and its registration. If, for example a wife claims an interest in a property registered in her husband's name does she have to show that she was in occupation on the date that any mortgage was created or on the date (often some time later) on which it was registered?

A slight variant of this typical story arose for consideration in *Abbey National Building Society* v *Cann* [1991] 1 AC 56. Mr George Cann purchased a property with the aid of a mortgage from the Abbey National, representing to the Society that the house was for his sole occupation. In fact when the purchase was completed George's mother and his uncle moved into the property with him. The evidence was that in fact their furniture arrived at the property some 35 minutes before the charge to the Society took place and that at that point there were also removal men on the premises moving in items on Mrs Cann's behalf. The charge was not registered until a month later and by that point it was quite clear that Mrs Cann and George's uncle, Abraham Cann, were both in occupation of the premises. Both Mrs Cann and Abraham claimed that they had interests in the property by reason of contribution and, when George defaulted on the mortgage payments, that their rights had priority to those of the Society. The House of Lords held that in a case such as this it was necessary to show actual occupation at the date the charge was created and not at the date at which it was registered. Furthermore it was said that Mrs Cann and Abraham could not have had any rights in relation to the premises until the transfer in favour of George took effect. Despite the commonly asserted theory that there must be a scintilla of time between the transfer being made and the charge taking effect (you have to own something before you can charge it), the two were to be regarded for this purpose as happening together and it could not be argued that Mrs Cann and Abraham had rights, and were in occupation, for one second prior to the grant of the charge. This amounts to a departure from the general principle under the LRA 1925, which is that it is the date of registration which matters.

The House of Lords also considered whether the moving in of furniture could amount to occupation of the premises but said that it did not: acts merely preparatory to occupation do not amount to occupation. Lord Oliver of Aylmerton said that occupation would 'involve some degree of permanence and continuity which would rule out mere fleeting presence' (at p. 855). It was however confirmed that, subject to the necessary permanence being shown, occupation through an agent was possible.

The extent of the occupation required for s. 70(1)(g) has caused considerable problems to the courts. In *Epps* v *Esso Petroleum Co. Ltd* [1973] 1 WLR 1071 the habit of parking cars on a piece of land was held not to constitute actual occupation of that land. In *Hodgson* v *Marks* [1971] Ch 892 it was held that an elderly lady was to be regarded as being in actual occupation of premises even though she shared the property with the registered proprietor. Mrs Hodgson's rights were those of a beneficiary under a trust. She had been the original owner of the estate and had transferred it to her lodger under an arrangement by which it was clear that she was transferring only the legal title and not the beneficial rights to the property, so that he held the legal estate on trust for her. When the former lodger sold the property to a third party (in contravention of his agreement with Mrs Hodgson), the purchaser was held to be bound by Mrs Hodgson's rights to the property. Since Mrs Hodgson was the true beneficial owner of the property, the purchaser was in the position of a trustee and was compelled to convey the legal estate to her. This case illustrates the dangers of the s. 70(1)(g) overriding interest, since the purchaser had bought an estate which in reality was worthless.

Another case concerning the position of a person sharing the property with the registered proprietor is *Williams & Glyn's Bank Ltd* v *Boland* [1981] AC 487. This case involved a wife who had acquired an interest in her husband's property by contributing to the purchase price, and so had become a beneficiary under a resulting trust of the land. She lived in the property with her husband, who was the sole registered proprietor. Mr Boland mortgaged the property to his bank and used the money raised in his business. Later, when he failed to make his mortgage repayments, the bank sought vacant possession of the premises, so that it could sell the estate in order to repay the loan. Mrs Boland then claimed that she had rights in the property and that, as she had been occupation of the premises when the mortgage was granted, the bank's rights as mortgagee were subject to her prior beneficial interest. The House of Lords upheld Mrs Boland's claim that she had an overriding interest which bound the bank.

The decision in *Boland* caused considerable concern at the time, especially amongst 'professional' mortgagees, such as the building societies and the banks. Against it must now be set the decision of the House of Lords in *City of London Building Society* v *Flegg* [1988] AC 54. We will consider this case when we come to deal with trusts (p. 208) but for the moment it is enough to mention that a procedure exists whereby land subject to certain trusts can be sold free of the beneficiaries' interests, provided that the purchase price is paid to at least two trustees, who hold the money upon trust for the beneficiaries in place of the land (this process is called 'overreaching', see p. 190). In *Boland*, the mortgage was made and the money received by the sole registered proprietor so that overreaching could not operate. However, in *Flegg* the mortgage money, which arose when a second mortgage was made, was paid to two legal owners who held the estate upon trust for themselves and the Fleggs. In these circumstances the House of Lords held that the interests of the Fleggs, who were merely beneficiaries under a trust, were overreached by that payment, even though the Fleggs had been in occupation of the premises at the date of the charge. The effect of that decision was to allow the mortgagee to get priority over the rights of the Fleggs and to be able to sell the property free of their interests. The Fleggs were left only with the right to sue their trustee legal owners for breach of trust, since the legal owners had used the mortgage money for their personal purposes. This decision is very hard for those placed in the position of the Fleggs since the legal owners who have entered into this kind of transaction are often bankrupt or have fled the country and it is often a matter of pure chance whether the property has one or two legal owners. However, the decision of the House of Lords is in harmony with the overreaching rules which are fundamental to much of the 1925 property legislation (contrast the view of the Court of Appeal, see [1986] Ch 605).

Against the decisions in both *Boland* and *Flegg* must be set that in *Paddington Building Society* v *Mendelsohn* (1985) 50 P & CR 244. There the competition was between a beneficiary under a resulting trust, who was in occupation of the property and who had known that a mortgage advance would be needed in order to purchase the property, and the building society which had granted that mortgage. In such a case the Court of Appeal held that the occupant had impliedly consented to the creation of the mortgage since the possibility of acquiring an interest in the property was dependent upon that mortgage. Thus the occupant could not claim an interest having priority to the rights of the building society. As a result of this case the *Boland* and *Flegg* issues will usually only arise in cases of second mortgages or sales. See also *Equity & Law Home Loans Ltd* v *Prestidge* [1992] 1 WLR 137, a case on unregistered land.

The result of these cases is that an intending purchaser or mortgagee should take great care to enquire of each resident what rights he or she has in the property. This seems to include any person who is in occupation, including any relatives of the proprietor, and even including any children (but on this see *Bird* v *Syme-Thomson* [1979] 1 WLR 440, 443). The difficulty of complying with this requirement has led to proposals that the law should be reformed but all attempts to do this have so far failed.

It should be noted that a person who is not in occupation will still have an overriding interest should he be in receipt of the 'rents and profits'. Oddly this seems to be true even if the person paying the rent is not in occupation. All this imposes a very heavy duty upon the intending purchaser to make enquiries and the courts have accepted that the imposition of such a duty is perfectly proper:

What is involved is a departure from an easy-going practice of dispensing with enquiries as to occupation. . . . To substitute for this a practice of more careful enquiry as to the fact of occupation, and, if necessary, as to the rights of occupiers, cannot, in my view of the matter, be considered as unacceptable. (Lord Wilberforce in *Williams & Glyn's Bank Ltd* v *Boland* [1981] AC 487 at p. 508.)

The law as it stands places the burden upon purchasers, mortgagees and other persons who are acquiring an interest in the property as part of a deliberate transaction. The only benefit of this arrangement is that such persons will usually have legal advisers to warn them of the risks, whereas the owners of overriding interests are frequently unaware of their rights and are therefore in no position to take steps to protect themselves. It is open to all intending purchasers to ask those occupying the property what rights they have and it is clear that any such rights will not affect a purchaser who enquires in this way, unless the occupier has told the purchaser about his claim. It is not sufficient, however, to ask the *registered proprietor* whether there are any such persons in occupation or whether anyone else has rights to the property (*Hodgson* v *Marks* [1971] Ch 892 per Russell LJ). It is also essential to note that a purchaser who makes reasonable inquiries but does not discover the overriding interest will nonetheless be bound by it. This is *not* a 'notice' rule.

In some instances persons have rights and are in occupation but nonetheless their rights are not overriding interests because of a specific statutory exclusion. Thus the right of a spouse to occupy the matrimonial home (see below chapter 6) is not capable of amounting to an overriding interest and must be protected by means of an entry on the register if it is to bind a purchaser (s. 2(8)(a) of the Matrimonial Homes Act 1983). Similarly by virtue of LRA 1925 s. 86(2), the rights of a beneficiary under a strict settlement (a type of trust governed by the SLA 1925 – see chapter 5 below) cannot be overriding. As a result it is necessary to check that there is no specific exlusion for the right that you are considering. The two mentioned here are the most common examples.

MINOR INTERESTS

This is the second main category of encumbrances on the registered estate. The class of minor interests is defined in LRA 1925, s. 3(xv), as consisting of those interests in registered land which are not substantively registrable and which are not overriding interests. We have already examined the nature of overriding interests. We will deal with those which are substantively registrable later but for the moment you should note that they consist of the two legal estates and the legal interests which are mentioned in LPA 1925, s. 1(2). If a right does not fall into one of these two categories, it must be a minor interest. To this extent, the class of minor interests may seem to be a kind of 'dustbin' category, though the rights which fall into it are by no means unimportant or 'rubbishy'! The class is wide and includes every type of interest, from restrictive covenants to the rights of a beneficiary under a trust as well as many other circumstances or obligations which affect the registered estate (see, e.g., *Clayhope Properties Ltd* v *Evans* [1986] 1 WLR 1223). We have seen that after exchange of contracts the purchaser becomes the equitable owner of the property and that the vendor becomes a type of trustee. The interest of the purchaser is that of a beneficiary and is therefore a minor interest.

LRA 1925, s. 2(1), states quite clearly that any interests in registered land which are neither substantively registrable nor overriding 'shall take effect in equity as minor interests'. Accordingly all minor interests are equitable only and have no effect at law.

Although we have spoken so far as though the classification of a right as overriding or minor is a permanent one, it should be remembered that there is an 'escape route' by which many minor interests may become overriding. This route is provided by LRA 1925, s. 70(1)(g); if the person entitled to the minor interest is in occupation of the land his right will become overriding. Conversely, it is possible for the owner of an overriding interest to protect it by entering it on the register as a minor interest (see below), and this will transform the overriding interest into a minor interest (see *Strand Securities Ltd* v *Caswell* [1965] Ch 958). In many situations this is the safest course to take.

A minor interest is unlike an overriding interest because it will be unenforceable against a later acquirer of the registered title unless it been protected by being noted on the register in one of the ways provided by LRA 1925. Section 3(xv) of the Act describes this process of an interest becoming unenforceable, due to lack of protection, as an interest being 'overriden'.

The Act provides four types of entry by means of which a minor interest may be protected:

(a)   notice;
(b)   restriction;
(c)   caution;
(d)   inhibition.

Notice
A notice is entered in the charges section of the register and, as such, any acquirer of the registered estate (or of another interest in the estate) will be bound by the interest so protected (LRA 1925, ss. 48–52). In particular, notices are commonly used to protect restrictive covenants. The difficulty with using a notice is that the notice must be entered on the land certificate as well as on the register (so that the certificate remains an accurate copy of the register) and therefore a person wishing to enter a notice is required to produce the land certificate to the Registrar (LRA 1925, s. 64(1)(c)). Although this may be possible in cases in which the registered proprietor agrees to the entry being made, it may be impossible in cases in which the proprietor is resisting the making of the entry. There are, however, exceptions to this requirement. When the right to be protected is the spouse's right to occupy the matrimonial home (Matrimonial Homes Act 1983, s. 2(8)) the land certificate need not be produced. This seems a reasonable exception since such rights are expressly made incapable of taking effect as overriding interests under s. 70(1)(g) even where the claimant is in actual occupation. By virtue of LRA 1925 s. 64 (as amended by LRA 1986) it is also possible to enter notice of a short lease without producing the land certificate. This exception is perhaps less important because such leases are overriding interests in any event.

Restrictions

A restriction prevents dealings with the registered property until a specified condition has been met. Typically, restrictions are used in cases in which the registered proprietor is a trustee of the estate, and in such cases a restriction is entered on the register to warn a purchaser that only dispositions permitted by the trust or under statute will be registered. Commonly it is provided that a receipt for any money paid must have been given by two trustees. However, applications to impose a restriction have to be made by the registered proprietor (LRA 1925, s. 58) and it is necessary to produce the land certificate.

Caution

In most cases in which the land certificate cannot be obtained the owner of an interest requiring protection will have to use a caution. This is described in LRA 1925, s. 54(1), as being a caution to the effect that the property cannot be dealt with unless notice of the intended dealing has been served on the cautioner. Section 55 provides that once such notice has been given to the cautioner no dealing shall be registered, without the cautioner's permission, within a prescribed period of days. The cautioner then has an opportunity to state his case before the Registrar, who decides whether the claim to the right is valid and whether it should be binding on the estate, or whether the proposed dealing should take free of it. The Registrar may, if he prefers, refer the matter to the court (Land Registration Rules 1925, r. 220; see, e.g., *Barclays Bank Ltd* v *Taylor* [1973] Ch 63).

It is also possible, under LRA 1925, s. 53, to enter a caution against a first registration of an estate. These cautions operate in a similar manner to those under s. 54 and ensure that a person with an interest in unregistered land has the opportunity of informing the Registrar of his rights before the estate is registered.

Inhibition

An inhibition is only placed on the register on the order of the court or of the Registrar (LRA 1925, s. 57). These orders are used to prevent any dealings with the land, either totally, or until the occurrence of a certain event or expiry of a certain time. Inhibitions are used most commonly in bankruptcy cases, in order to prevent the bankrupt proprietor disposing of his interest in the land to the detriment of his creditors.

Entry of a minor interest

In general therefore one requires the agreement of the registered proprietor to enter a notice or restriction, whilst cautions and inhibitions are more hostile entries and can be made without his cooperation.

It should be noted that one does not 'register' a minor interest: only legal estates and interests can be 'registered'. It is more accurate to describe a minor interest as being 'entered' or 'noted' on the register in one of the four possible ways.

Generally a minor interest which has not been entered on the register will not bind a person who later acquires an interest or estate in the property. However, in *Lyus* v *Prowsa Developments Ltd* [1982] 2 All ER 953 it was held that an unprotected minor interest (an agreement to sell the property) could bind a later purchaser of the property who had bought the estate expressly subject to the prior interest in a case in which the facts gave rise to a constructive trust. The court felt that, if this were not the case, the Act could be used as an instrument of fraud to allow the purchaser to resile from a positive obligation in the agreement under which he had acquired the property (but see the position in relation to unregistered land, p. 67). This case was discussed at length and approved by the Court of Appeal in *Ashburn Anstalt* v *Arnold* [1988] 2 WLR 706 but it was said (per Fox LJ at p. 728):

> The court will not impose a constructive trust unless it is satisfied that the conscience of the estate owner is affected. The mere fact that that land is expressed to be conveyed 'subject to' a contract does not necessarily imply that the grantee is to be under an obligation, not otherwise existing, to give effect to the provisions of the contract.

Registered interests

We must now make a brief mention of registered interests (sometimes also called 'registrable' interests).

This aspect of the system can appear a little confusing. LRA 1925, s. 2(1), provides that only legal estates are capable of substantive registration and that all other interests take effect as overriding or minor interests. However, s. 3(xi) defines 'legal estates' as meaning the 'estates, interests and charges' which exist at law under LPA 1925. Accordingly the legal interests in LPA 1925, s. 1(2), are also registrable. This is mainly of importance when one is dealing with mortgages, rentcharges and easements and involves registration of the *benefit* of these rights.

Mortgages
If the estate is registered then any legal charge (mortgage) of the estate should also be registered (LRA 1925, ss. 25 and 26). In fact it is very important to register such charges as they only take effect at law once they have been registered (s. 26) and until that point are equitable only (rules relating to the protection of mortgages are dealt with in more detail in chapter 7).

Legal rentcharges
Legal rentcharges should also be registered and, under LRA 1925, s. 19, they do not take effect at law until this has been done.

On registration of a legal charge or a legal rentcharge the land certificate must be sent in to the registry (Land Registration Rules 1925, r. 266). The registry will retain this document and will issue a charge certificate in its place (r. 262). The details of the charge will be entered on the charges section of the register and this information will be reproduced in the charge certificate.

Easements

Easements which benefit an estate are generally included in the registration of that estate. However, even if the benefit of an easement is not registered in this way it may still be claimed by successive owners of the registered estate as long as it actually benefits the property (Land Registration Rules 1925, r. 251; LRA 1925, s. 72).

Searching the register

Obviously the intending purchaser of registered land must make a search of the register in order to satisfy himself that the vendor is the registered proprietor of the estate and to check whether any legal interests have been substantively registered and whether any minor interests have been noted on the register. We must therefore consider how such searches are made.

First, the register is now open to inspection by anyone who cares to look. Copies of entries and certain documents may be obtained upon payment of a fee (LRA 1925, s. 112(2)). This is a change made by the LRA 1988: previously a search was possible only with permission or pursuant to a court order. This still does not mean that all the information at the Registry is available to the public, since information in the possession of the Registrar but which does not appear in a register entry, or in a document referred to in any entry, is not covered by s. 112(1) and some documents (leases and charges) are expressly excluded. However such other information is available at the discretion of the Registrar and, to some persons, as of right: s. 112(2). (See also the Land Registration (Open Register) Rules 1990: SI 1990 No. 1362.)

Secondly, the purchaser will normally need to obtain a complete copy of all the entries on the register. This is done by applying for 'office copy entries'. In practice the vendor will normally obtain and supply these copies to the purchaser as the means of proving his title to the estate he is selling. The office copy is dated and is guaranteed as being an accurate copy of the register on that date.

As office copies will normally have been supplied some time before the completion of the transaction by the registration of the new owner as proprietor of the estate, the purchaser will need:

(a) to check whether any alterations have been made to the register since the office copies were issued;

(b) to ensure that no further entries can be made after he has checked the register and before he has become the registered proprietor.

The purchaser satisfies these needs by making an official search to see whether the register has been changed since the date of his office copies (or since some other specified date, such as the date upon which the land certificate was last checked at the registry). The official search is guaranteed by the Registrar as being accurate and compensation is payable for any loss resulting from an error (LRA 1925, s. 83(3)). The official search has a second function: it will provide the searcher with a specified period during which any amendment made to the register will not affect him. This is called a 'priority period' and it lasts for 30 working days (Land Registration (Official Searches) Rules 1981 (SI 1981 No. 1135)).

How the priority period works
   (a)   The searcher receives an official certificate of search dated 3 February. The priority period of 30 working days ends on 17 March (usually this date is given on the certificate so that you do not have to work it out for yourself).
   (b)   On 12 March a charge (mortgage) in favour of the Red Leicester Building Society is registered against the estate.
   (c)   On 16 March the purchaser is registered as proprietor of the estate.

In this case the purchaser is not bound by the mortgage registered on 12 March because he has registered as the new proprietor within the priority period granted to him by his search certificate. If, however, he had been registered as proprietor on or after 18 March he would have registered outside the priority period and would have been bound by the charge registered on the 12th. Thus if it becomes likely that a purchaser will need extra time he should apply for an extension of his search certificate priority period. It is insufficient merely to make a fresh search since a new search certificate obtained after 12 March will reveal the registered charge which would therefore bind the purchaser.
   In our example it woud be likely that the building society would also have made a search before granting the charge. In such cases where there are overlapping searches the party who has the earlier search will get priority if the transaction is completed within the priority period. So, if the building society had made a search and had a certificate giving a priority period which expires on 15 March, the building society would get priority for the charge registered on the 12th. In such cases the second certificate, issued to the purchaser, mortgagee, or other person searching, would give notice that a prior certificate had been issued, so that the person concerned would be warned about the problem and would normally be entitled to refuse to complete the purchase or other transaction.

How safe is it to rely on the register?

We have now seen how the prospective purchaser of registered land can ascertain who owns the estate and obtains information about the encumbrances binding upon it. We now need to consider how safe it is to rely upon the register. As we have said, there are different grades of title, and if one buys an estate with less than title absolute there will obviously be a degree of risk involved. The purchaser will, however, want to know exactly how safe an absolute title is. Can he assume that the title is indefeasible and that he will not be disturbed at some date in the future by someone else claiming the estate? Unfortunately one would have to tell a purchaser that even an absolute title is not completely safe, for there are circumstances in which the register can be rectified, even against a registered proprietor with title absolute.

Rectification of the register

The statutory provisions for rectification are undeniably a further 'hole' in the registered land system. There is always a chance that the register is not an accurate reflection of the true position and that it may be rectified, and accordingly it is not true to say that one can depend absolutely on the accuracy of the register. In some cases a person who suffers loss due to a rectification of the register may apply for financial compensation from a central fund, and it is sometimes said therefore that in the case of registered land the State guarantees the title, because it provides a system of compensation for those who suffer from any deficiencies in the system. The 'State guarantee' concept is not altogether true, however, because, as we shall see, compensation is not available to every individual who suffers a loss.

Slips

Minor slips (e.g., the misspelling of a name) do not require a formal rectification of the register since r. 13 of the Land Registration Rules 1925 gives the Registrar power to correct 'any clerical error or error of a like nature'. Under r. 14 the Registrar may even cancel an entire registration if it has been made in error, but must usually obtain the consent of all the interested parties.

Rectification

Under LRA 1925, s. 82, the register may be rectified at any time pursuant to a court order, or by the Registrar in the following cases:

(a) where a court orders that a named person is entitled to an estate, right, interest or charge;

(b) where the court concludes that a person has been rightly aggrieved by an entry made, or not made on the register, or by a delay in making an entry;

(c) at any time with the consent of all interested parties;

(d) where an entry has been obtained by fraud;

(e) where by mistake two people have been registered as proprietors of the same interest or charge;

(f) where a mortgagee has been incorrectly entered as proprietor of the estate charged, rather than as proprietor of the charge;

(g) if a legal estate has been registered in the name of a person who if the land had not been registered would not have been the estate owner; and

(h) in any other case in which it is deemed just to rectify the register.

This process can be illustrated by the case of *Chowood Ltd* v *Lyall* [1930] 2 Ch 156 in which the registered proprietor of an estate was held to be bound by the prior rights of Mrs Lyall, who was a 'squatter'. In that case the register was rectified so as to remove Mrs Lyall's portion of the property from the registered title.

Read on its own, s. 82(1) gives extremely wide powers to rectify, and one can imagine that a purchaser might feel that the title that he proposes to buy is extremely insecure. However, the terms of s. 82(1) are somewhat curtailed by s. 82(3). This subsection (as amended by the Administration of Justice Act 1977, ss. 24 and 32) provides that:

> The register shall not be rectified, except for the purpose of giving effect to an overriding interest or an order of the court, so as to affect the title of the proprietor who is in possession—
> (a)   unless the proprietor has caused or substantially contributed to the error or omission by fraud or lack of proper care; or
> (Paragraph (b) has been repealed.)
> (c)   unless for any other reason, in any particular case, it is considered that it would be unjust not to rectify the register against him.

In *Chowood Ltd* v *Lyall* the rectification gave effect to Mrs Lyall's overriding interest (s. 70(1)(f)) and accordingly was not prevented by s. 82(3).

The amendment to the wording of s. 82(3) made by the 1977 Act prevents a registered proprietor from suffering loss in cases in which he has contributed to the erroneous registration but has done so innocently. Before 1977 even an innocent mistake by the proprietor made him liable to have the register rectified against him (*Re 139 Deptford High Street* [1951] Ch 884; *Re Sea View Gardens* [1967] 1 WLR 134). Now the proprietor's actions must have been either fraudulent or negligent.

Indemnity
A party who suffers loss either due to a rectification, or due to a refusal to rectify, may be able to claim compensation (an 'indemnity') under LRA 1925, s. 83. The payment will compensate for the actual loss suffered and is paid from a fund administered by the Registrar. The sums paid will include the value of the estate or interest lost and any reasonable costs and expenses (e.g., solicitors' fees). No compensation is payable where the claimant has caused or substantially contributed to the loss by fraud or negligence (s. 83(5)(a) as amended).

This appears to be a fairly generous provision for compensation, but there is a hidden limitation contained in the requirement that before an indemnity can be paid it must be shown that the loss which the applicant has suffered is due to the rectification, or due to the refusal to rectify. As a result of this provision it was held in *Re Chowood's Registered Land* [1933] Ch 574, *Hodgson* v *Marks* [1971] Ch 892 and *Re Boyle's Claim* [1961] 1 WLR 339, that where rectification is made to give effect to an overriding interest no compensation will be payable. In such cases the loss is caused by the proprietor acquiring an estate which is subject to an overriding interest. When the register is rectified the alteration gives effect to an existing state of affairs and does not cause any fresh loss (i.e. the loss is not due to the rectification). From this one can see just how dangerous overriding interests can prove to be for a purchaser of a registered estate, particularly where, as in *Hodgson* v *Marks*, the effect of the overriding interest is to deprive him of the whole estate.

Priorities: minor interests and overriding interests

So far in our account of registered title we have been concerned with the position of a purchaser who is buying a legal estate from the registered proprietor. However, it is necessary to consider as well the position of someone who acquires a lesser right in the land, e.g., a creditor who lends money on the security of a mortgage, or a purchaser who enters into a contract to buy the estate but who never completes the purchase, and who therefore holds only an equitable right under the contract. How will such persons be affected by the other encumbrances on the same estate?

The basic rule is that an overriding interest takes priority over any later estate or interest (LRA 1925, s. 70). Thus an overriding interest will bind anyone who later acquires an overriding or minor interest in the property.

A minor interest, if protected by entry on the register, will bind all those who acquire later estates or interests in the property. This includes anyone who acquires a registered estate, a registered interest, an overriding interest or a later minor interest (LRA 1925, ss. 20, 52, 55 and 102). Section 102 is amended by LRA 1986, s. 5, see p. 270.

Where the minor interest is unregistered and it is followed by a further minor interest, which is also unprotected, there appears to be nothing in LRA 1925 to solve the problem of which interest gets priority. This question arose in *Barclays Bank Ltd* v *Taylor* [1973] Ch 63 and the court held that in such a case, since the Act was silent, one had to revert to the old rule that 'Where the equities are equal the first in time prevails'. Thus the first-created minor interest retained its priority even though it had not been protected. If the unregistered interest is followed by the creation of a later minor interest which *is* protected by an entry being made on the register the same rule is applied: the first created minor interest retains its priority (*The Mortgage Corporation Ltd* v *Nationwide Credit Corporation Ltd, The Times*, 27 July 1992). A similar gap in the legislation appears to exist where an unprotected minor interest is followed by an overriding interest. Presumably in such a case the overriding interest would gain priority since its owner need take no action in order to protect himself. If an unprotected minor interest is followed by a fully registered charge (a legal interest) the later charge will gain priority because the 'where the equities are equal . . .' rule does not apply where one interest is legal.

The problem of priorities commonly arises in connection with successive mortgages of the property—that is, where the estate owner grants several mortgages of the same property—and is considered further in chapter 7.

First registration of title

Before completing this outline of the law relating to registered land we need to explain further the rules governing a first registration of an estate in registered land. Miss Bell, who is buying 3 Trant Way, will have to make such a first registration, because the estate that she is buying is not yet registered and the land now stands in an area of compulsory registration. In such a case the property will not be registered at the start of the transaction and Miss Bell will have to adopt the unregistered system of conveyancing (see below).

In such cases the legal title to the estate will pass to the purchaser as soon as the conveyance has been signed, sealed and delivered. It is only once the transaction has been completed and a conveyance made that she need concern herself with the provisions of the registered land system.

In order to compel purchasers to register their estates, LRA 1925, s. 123, provides that, if a registration is not made within two months of the date of the conveyance the legal title in the property will revert to the vendor. Thus, unless Miss Bell applies to have her title registered. she will, after two months, lose her legal title and will be left with only the equitable interest which she acquired when the contract for sale was concluded. This provision applies to all purchases of freehold estates and all purchases of leasehold estates where the lease has at least more than 21 years to run (LRA 1986, s. 2(2)). (Originally this only applied where there were 40 years to run: LRA 1925, s. 123(1).)

Once the title to the land has been registered in this way, all future dealings with the estate must be completed by being registered.

Completion of transfers by registration

Because it is the register which is crucial in registered land, LRA 1925 provides that all dealings with the land must be completed by being registered. Thus, until registration, a purchaser cannot obtain a legal interest in the property: he is an equitable owner from the date of the contract until the date of registration. Accordingly a transfer of a registered estate, unlike a conveyance of unregistered land, does not have the effect of conveying the legal title to a purchaser. The vendor remains the legal owner until the transfer has been registered (LRA 1925, s. 19). This rule also applies to the creation of legal interests in registered land (s. 19(2)) and in particular to legal charges (s. 26(1)).

UNREGISTERED LAND

As in the section of registered land, we will look separately at the two aspects of proving title: the ownership of the estate and the encumbrances upon it.

Ownership of the estate

Whereas with registered land an estate owner has only to point to the register in order to prove his title, an owner of an estate in unregistered land has to go to greater lengths. In this case title is proved ('deduced') by producing the title deeds to the property and by showing that the estate has been correctly conveyed from one owner to another over the years, and that it was last conveyed to ('vested in') the current vendor. Obviously one cannot hope to produce an unbroken chain of deeds stretching right back to the middle ages or beyond and so the habit began of accepting a title which had been proved for a certain long period of years. The parties to a contract for the sale of an estate may agree specifically on the length of the period which is to apply, but if no special agreement is made a standard provision is implied into the

Transfer of Whole [(1)]

HM Land Registry

Form 19
(Rules 98 or 115, Land Registration Rules, 1925)

Stamp pursuant to section 28 of the Finance Act 1931 to be impressed here.	*When the transfer attracts Inland Revenue Duty the stamps should be impressed here before lodging the transfer for registration.*

(1) For a transfer by a Company or Corporation form 19(Co) is printed. For transfer to joint proprietors form 19(JP) is printed.

County and district (or London borough)   STILTON

Title number(s)   ST 1234

Property   1 Trant Way, Mousehole /

Date   19   In consideration of   sixty-five

thousand ————————————————————————

(2) Delete the words in italics if not required.

pounds (£ 65,000—————————) *the receipt of which is hereby acknowledged* ([³])

(3) In BLOCK LETTERS enter the full name(s) postal address(es) (including postcode) and occupation(s) of the proprietor(s) of the land.

I/We([³]) VICTOR VENN of 1 Trant Way, Mousehole in the County of Stilton Antique Dealer————————

(4) If desired or otherwise as the case may be (see rules 76 and 77).

as beneficial owner hereby *transfer to*([⁴])

(5) In BLOCK LETTERS enter the full name(s) postal address(es) (including postcode) and occupation(s) of the transferee(s) for entry in the register.

([⁵]) ARNOLD ARMSTRONG (engineer) and ARRIETY ARMSTRONG (secretary) both of 11 THE CEDARS, MARDEN, STILTON, MA2 3AB

(6) On a transfer to a company registered under the Companies Act, enter here the company's registration number if entry thereof on the register is required.

([⁶]) (Company registration number—————————————)

(7) Enter any special clause here.

the land comprised in the title(s) above mentioned ([⁷])([⁸])

(8) A transfer for charitable purposes should follow form 36 in the schedule to the Land Registration Rules, 1925 (see rules 121 and 122).

(continued overleaf)

(9) *If a certificate of value for the purpose of the Stamp Act, 1891 and amending Acts is not required, delete this paragraph*

(²) ~~*It is hereby certified that the transaction hereby effected does not form part of a larger transaction*~~ *or series of transactions in respect of which the ~~amount or value or~~ aggregate amount or value of* ~~*the consideration exceeds £*~~

Signed as a deed by

...VICTOR...VENN........................   }   *Victor Venn*

in the presence of

Name **MICHAEL MOGGIE**   Signature of witness *Michael Moggie*

Address **14 THE BROADWAY, MOUSEHOLE, STILTON**

Occupation **RODENT OPERATIVE**

Signed as a deed by

....   }

in the presence of

Name   Signature of witness

Address

Occupation

The Solicitors' Law Stationery Society Ltd., Oyez House, 27 Crimscott Street, London SE1 5TS

1990 Edition
6 90   F17347
5061083
★ ★ ★ ★ ★

contract. Originally at common law the term implied was that one had to prove the devolution of the title for a period of at least 60 years but the accepted period is now 15 years by virtue of LPA 1969, s. 23. (Between 1874 and 1925 the period was 40 years, and from 1926 to 1969 it was 30 years.)

In order to deduce title one has to start with a 'good root of title'. This is a document which records a dealing with the whole legal and equitable interest in the land and which contains nothing to cast any doubts on the validity of the title. Usually a conveyancer will insist on a document which evidences a dealing for value, such as a conveyance on sale or a mortgage. The reason for accepting such a document is that one presumes that the purchaser in that transaction had himself investigated the title for the necessary period and that his taking the conveyance or granting the mortgage indicates that he found no defect. The document taken as a good root of title will be the first document which is older than the title period, that is, now, the first such document which is more than 15 years old. Accordingly, the good root of title might be a document which is 16, 30 or even 100 years old, depending on the dealings that have occurred in relation to the estate.

Once a good root of title has been shown, the vendor must produce every deed after the root of title which has affected the property. These deeds may include conveyances, wills and other deeds (e.g., a trust deed). If the vendor cannot prove an unbroken chain of title the purchaser may rescind the contract on the ground that the title is defective. The vendor usually proves his title by sending summaries or copies of the documents (an 'abstract of title') to the purchaser or his solicitor. These copies are then checked against the originals before completion.

Encumbrances: investigating third-party rights

As well as checking the title deeds to the property in order to ensure that the vendor is the estate owner, the purchaser will need to make enquiries in order to ascertain whether there are any third parties who have interests in the land. These enquiries fall into two categories:

(a)   searches for land charges under LCA 1972;
(b)   other enquiries about legal or equitable interests which are not land charges.

Land charges

Land charges consist of those interests in land which are set out in LCA 1972 (which replaced LCA 1925). Only interests which are included on the list in the Act are land charges. Interests which do appear on the list should be protected by registration at the Land Charges Registry, which is held on a computer at Plymouth. In fact the registry at Plymouth keeps five different registers (LCA 1972, s. 1) and the Land Charges Register is one of these five.

Classes of land charge

Land charges are divided by the 1972 Act into six classes (A to F) and certain of those classes are further subdivided.

Classes A and B   These are not particularly common. They consist of charges on land arising under statutory provisions.

Class C   This class is subdivided into four subclasses. Before considering these in detail it is important to note that rights of a type which fall within this class are registrable as land charges only if they were created on or after 1 January 1926 (the date upon which the 1925 legislation came into force) or, more unusually, if the right was created before that date but was itself transferred to some other holder at a later time.

Class C(i), the puisne mortgage   The puisne mortgage is defined in LCA 1972, s. 2(4), as a legal mortgage which 'is not secured by a deposit of documents relating to the legal estate affected'. Normally when lending money on the security of a mortgage, a mortgagee will take the deeds to the property away from the estate owner in order to prevent him dealing further with the property. If a legal mortgagee does take the deeds in this way, his mortgage is *not* a registrable land charge. It does not require registration, because the absence of the deeds is sufficient to alert any prospective purchaser to the possible existence of the mortgage. If the mortgagee does not take the deeds, the mortgage *is* a puisne mortgage and should be registered as a land charge. The puisne mortgage is slightly unusual because it is a legal interest in land, whilst most land charges are equitable or statutory interests.

Class C(ii), limited owner's charge   This is a land charge which arises when a tenant for life or statutory owner under the SLA 1925 (someone who has only a limited interest in the property—see chapter 5), or another person with a similar interest, has paid inheritance tax under the Finance Act 1986 (formerly capital transfer tax on the property under the provisions of Part III of the Finance Act 1975). Such persons may have a claim to charge the repayment of the tax against the land and that right is a land charge.

Class C(iii), general equitable charge   This class of land charge forms a kind of 'dustbin' category. Into this class fall all equitable charges on property which are not specifically excluded from class C(iii) by the Act itself. Section 2(4)(iii) excludes from this class:

(a)   any charge which is secured by a deposit of documents relating to the legal estate affected;
(b)   interests arising under trusts;
(c)   indemnity charges against rents apportioned or charged on land against the breach of covenants:
(d)   any charge which falls into another class of land charge.

Accordingly a beneficiary under a trust of a land cannot register his interest as a land charge. An equitable mortgagee who does not have the title deeds to the property can register a C(iii) land charge but an equitable mortgagee who has the deeds cannot.

Class C(iv), estate contract   An estate contract is any contract to convey or create a legal estate in land, or any option to purchase a legal estate or any right of pre-emption in respect of a legal estate (a right of first refusal). Thus a contract to buy a fee simple is a land charge, and so is a contract to grant a lease.

Class D   Class D is divided into three subclasses.

Class D(i), Inland Revenue charge   This is a land charge which arises in favour of the Inland Revenue when a liability to pay inheritance tax (formerly capital transfer tax) in respect of land has not been discharged.

Class D(ii), restrictive covenants   This class comprises any covenants or agreements which are restrictive of the user of land and which were created on or after 1 January 1926 (at which date the 1925 property legislation came into force). An example would be a covenant, entered into in 1940, not to keep pigs on a particular property. The same covenant would not be a registrable land charge had it been created in 1920.

Class D(iii), equitable easements   This class consists of any easements, rights or privileges affecting land which were created on or after 1 January 1926, and which are equitable only. Equitable profits à prendre fall within this definition. It should be noted that legal easements or profits are not registrable as land charges.

Class E   These are very rare and consist of annuities created before 1926 and which are not registered on the register of annuities (which is one of the other five registers maintained under the LCA).

Class F   These rights are very common and are of great importance in practice. The class consists of a right created by the Matrimonial Homes Act 1967 and now contained in the Matrimonial Homes Act 1983. The right in question is the spouse's right to occupy the matrimonial home. It applies only to couples who are legally married and will give a partner, who is not a co-owner of the matrimonial home, the right to occupy the home owned by the other spouse. This right is considered in more detail in chapter 6.

While all these classes of charge are important to a purchaser, who may find that the property which he is purchasing is less attractive because it is subject to any land charge, the ones that you will meet most commonly are classes C, D and F, and you should pay particular attention to these.

Registration of charges

In the case of land charges, registration is not made against the property but against the name of the estate owner of the burdened land (LCA 1972, s. 3). This choice of method for registration has caused a number of problems with the system.

Incorrect names
It is not uncommon for an estate owner to be known by a nickname or abbreviated name. If a registration is made against an incorrect version of a person's name, a search made against the true name may not reveal the entry. Or it may be that the registration has been made correctly but that the searcher searches an incorrect name. Once again such a search may well not reveal the relevant entry. These problems have produced a certain amount of litigation and it is useful to examine some of the cases in detail in order to appreciate the difficulties which may be produced.

In *Diligent Finance Ltd* v *Alleyne* (1972) 23 P & CR 346, land was conveyed to one Erskine Owen Alleyne. Later Mr Alleyne's wife registered a class F land charge against the name Erskine Alleyne. Following this registration Mr Alleyne negotiated a further mortgage advance on the property and the mortgagee checked that there were no unwanted encumbrances on the property by making a land charges search against the name Erskine Owen Alleyne. This search did not reveal the class F charge registered by Mrs Alleyne. When, later, Mrs Alleyne claimed that her registered charge bound the mortgagee she lost her case, because it was said that her registration had not been made against her husband's full correct name, whilst the mortgagee had made a search against the full name and had obtained a clean search certificate upon which it could rely (LCA 1972, s. 10(4)). It appears that the court took the view that it should assume that a person's correct names were those shown in the documents of title relating to the property. This interpretation relates badly to the general rule in English law that a man's name is the name by which he is known and that one may use any name, unless a fraudulent motive is involved.

The *Alleyne* case shows that even a wife may make a mistake about her husband's names. Often those wishing to register their interests will be in the position of Mrs Alleyne and will not know, or will have forgotten, the middle names of the estate owner. The problems which can arise when registrations and searches are made by persons who know the estate owner less well can be imagined! The difficulties are well illustrated by the leading case of *Oak Co-operative Building Society* v *Blackburn* [1968] Ch 730. In this case the estate owner's true name was Francis David Blackburn. The owner of a charge against Mr Blackburn's property registered a charge against the name Frank David Blackburn. Later Mr Blackburn granted a mortgage of the property to the building society which, in order to protect itself, made a search. Unfortunately the society searched against the name Francis Davis Blackburn and thus received a clear search certificate. In this case the Court of Appeal held that the registered charge bound the building society because it had been registered in a version of the true name, whilst the society's search had been made in an incorrect name. The court suggested that had the society searched in the full correct names and obtained a clean search then it would not have been bound by the registered charge. It should be noted that under the present system had a search been made in the name Frank Blackburn, it still would not have revealed the entry against the name Frank David Blackburn, but would reveal entries made against F. Blackburn, or just Blackburn (see Ruoff, *Searching without Tears*, pp. 49–55).

These cases indicate that if an estate owner has changed his name, then searches should be made against both names. This may be particularly relevant if the estate owner is a married woman.

Searching against the names of all past estate owners
The registration of a charge is against the name of the person who was the estate owner at the date that the charge was created. When the estate changes hands the registration is not altered but remains against the name of the original estate owner. Accordingly it is not sufficient to make a search simply against the name of the current estate owner. To be certain of finding all registered charges one must search against the names of all the estate owners since 1925. This is, however, impractical is most cases (though some conveyancers will still ask for the full list of names) because in proving his title a vendor is only obliged to go back to a good root of title, which may be only 15 years old.

The difficulties may be illustrated by referring back to the title to 3 Trant Way. The history of No. 3 since 1925 has been as follows:

1926	The estate owner at the date at which the 1925 legislation came into force was Bill Brie.
1928	Land charge class D(ii) registered against the name Bill Brie.
1935	Bill Brie sold legal estate to Cathy Camembert.
1945	Land charge class D(iii) registered against the name Cathy Camembert.
1965	Cathy Camembert sold legal estate to David Dolcelatte.
1975	Land charge class C(iv) registered against the name David Dolcelatte.
1978	David Dolcelatte sold legal estate to Victoria Ventnor.
1980	Land charge class C(i) registered against the name Victoria Ventnor.

You will remember that Barbara Bell is considering buying 3 Trant Way from Victoria Ventnor. If Miss Bell agrees to purchase the estate, Miss Ventnor will produce the 1965 conveyance made by Cathy Camembert to David Dolcelatte as the good root of title. The deeds since 1965 will also be produced. From these documents the purchaser will obtain the names of three past estate owners: Cathy Camembert, David Dolcelatte and Victoria Ventnor. If the purchaser makes land charges searches against these names, she will discover the charges registered in 1945, 1975 and 1980. However, the purchaser will have no means of knowing that the property once was owned by Bill Brie and so will not discover the class D(ii) land charge registered in 1928. This land charge is a restrictive covenant and it is quite likely that it will still

be capable of enforcement by a neighbouring landowner (see chapter 9).
Unfortunately for Barbara Bell, she will be deemed to have notice of this
charge and will therefore still be bound by it (LPA 1925, s. 198). This is
so even though Barbara had no means of discovering the registration.

This difficulty in the system was not originally envisaged as being of
importance, because in 1926 the statutory title period was 30 years and it
was expected that the registered title system, which does not use land charges,
would be generally in force quite quickly. Delays in the introduction of the
registered land system and the reduction of the title period to 15 years have
exacerbated the problem. As a result in 1969 the law was amended by s. 25
of the LPA 1969, which provides that, should a purchaser of an estate or
interest in the land suffer loss due to the existence of a registered land charge
prior to the root of title, he may obtain compensation from a central fund
administered by the Chief Land Registrar. However, in many cases this may
prove to be cold comfort to the purchaser, who may find the land less attractive
if subject to an unwanted encumbrance, and who may feel that money is
a poor compensation for what he has lost.

Effect of registration
Section 198(1) LPA 1925 provides that:

> The registration of any instrument or matter under the provisions of the
> Land Charges Act, . . . shall be deemed to constitute actual notice of such
> instrument or matter.

This refers back to the old equitable doctrine of notice (see p. 69) and has
the result of making any right protected by registration enforceable against
any later acquirer of an estate or interest in the property affected.

It should be noticed, however, that the fact that a charge appears on the
register does not in any way guarantee that it is an effective charge, for under
the Land Charges Rules 1974, r. 22, the Registrar is not concerned to check
the accuracy of an application to register a charge. It is also possible that
a charge may have been effective originally but is no longer so. Thus it may
be that a purchaser can be compelled to continue with a purchase even though
his searches reveal registered charges. All that is necessary is that the vendor
should show that the registered charge does not in fact affect his title (*Bull
v Hutchens* (1863) 32 Beav 615).

Searches

The practical consequence of LPA 1925, s. 198, is to ensure that a careful
purchaser makes a search of the Land Charges Register. Such searches may
be made at any time and they do not require the prior consent of the current
estate owner. The register is a public record, which is open to anyone who
is prepared to pay the search fee (LCA 1972, s. 9). Such searches are normally
made by post, but facilities are available for regular users of the system to
make searches by telephone if they wish. On receipt of a search requisition

a search is made and the result is communicated to the searcher in the form of a search certificate.

On receipt of a certificate a searcher is entitled to depend on its accuracy, since LCA 1972, s. 10(4), says that such a certificate 'according to its tenor, shall be conclusive'. Thus, if the certificate mistakenly fails to reveal a registered charge, the purchaser will take free of the charge (despite LPA 1925, s. 198), leaving the owner of the charge to sue the registrar personally for negligence (*Ministry of Housing* v *Sharp* [1970] 2 QB 223).

Protection under a search certificate

Section 10(4) of LCA 1972 says that a search certificate protects a 'purchaser'. For the purposes of the Act 'purchaser' is widely defined, and includes anyone who takes any interest in the land for valuable consideration (s. 17(1)). This would include mortgagees, lessees and the acquirers of other interests, both legal and equitable.

The protection given by s. 10(4) only extends to the actual result of the search and if other details on the certificate are inaccurate the registrar will not be responsible.

Once again, as with registered land, the purchaser will have to make a search some days before he completes the purchase of the property and he will wish to be sure that no fresh entries are made, after the date of the search and before completion, which could affect him. This is done once again by the use of a priority period, though in the case of land charges the period is only 15 working days from the date of the certificate. To be safe a purchaser must complete the transaction before the 15-day priority period expires. If he does so he is not affected by any charges registered between the date of the certificate and completion (LCA 1972, s. 11(5)).

Effect of non-registration of a charge

The effect of non-registration of a charge depends on the class of charge involved. Basically there are two rules: one for land charges of classes A, B, C(i), (ii) and (iii) and F; another for land charges of classes C(iv) and D(i), (ii) and (iii).

Classes A, B, C(i)–(iii) and F
The basic rule with these land charges (with slight variations for class A) is that, unless they are registered before his completion, a purchaser will take the property free of the charge (LCA 1972, s. 4(2), (5) and (8)). Such a purchaser may be either a purchaser of an estate in the land or a purchaser of any interest in the land. Thus even the purchaser of an equitable interest in the property can take an interest which has priority to an unregistered charge. Thus if A has a puisne mortgage (C(i)) over Blackacre, which he has failed to register, and later the fee simple owner grants an equitable mortgage to B, B's rights will take priority over A's. If the estate has to be sold to pay back the sums due under the mortgages, the debt owed to B will be paid

first and A may find that there is not enough money to pay him in full (see chapter 7).

Classes C(iv) and D(i)–(iii)

In these cases the rule to be applied is that contained in LCA 1972, s. 4(6). If the C(iv) or D land charge is not registered it cannot be enforced against the purchaser of a legal estate for money or money's worth. This is the only person who can take the land free of the charge and thus the purchaser of any lesser interest in the property will still be bound by the charge. Thus if an estate contract (C(iv)) has not been registered and later an equitable mortgage is created by the fee simple owner the estate contract can be enforced against the equitable mortgagee: the equitable mortgagee is not the purchaser of a legal estate.

The words 'money or money's worth' do require a certain amount of explanation, particularly as they appear in s. 4(6) but not in s. 4(5), which refers only to a purchaser for value. The effect is to exclude from the benefits of s. 4(6) certain persons who are purchasers for valuable consideration but who have not given a consideration in money or have given it in a form which cannot be computed in financial terms. An example of this is an agreement to convey land in consideration of a future marriage. This is regarded as valuable consideration but not money or money's worth since it is not possible to put a financial valuation on marriage.

In the case of *Midland Bank Trust Co. Ltd* v *Green* [1981] AC 513, the House of Lords considered the meaning of the words 'money or money's worth' in s. 4(6). Here a father had granted his son an option to purchase a farm for £22,500. This agreement came within the definition of estate contract given in LCA 1972, s. 2(4)(iv), and so was registrable as a land charge. The son failed to register his option. Later his father wished to avoid carrying through his promise and, acting on advice, he conveyed the legal estate in the property to his wife for £500. At the date of this conveyance the farm was actually worth £40,000. In the Court of Appeal, it was held that the sale at such a considerable undervalue was not a sale for 'money or money's worth'. However, the House of Lords reversed this decision and imposed the contractual rule that the court will not inquire into the adequacy of consideration, as long as the consideration is real. It would therefore appear that a sale for 1p would satisfy s. 4(6), providing that it was not made fraudulently.

Right still enforceable against original owner

Although the effect of non-registration is that the charge cannot be enforced against the new owner of the estate, the right does still remain enforceable against the original owner who granted it. This may not be so satisfactory for the person entitled; for instance, if he has failed to register an equitable right of way (D(iii)) he will no longer be able to use the right over the land, but he may well have a remedy in contract against the original owner and may be able to recover compensation. This is so even though it is he who is really at fault, through failing to register his land charge.

Knowledge is irrelevant
Midland Bank Trust Co Ltd v *Green* [1981] AC 513 also illustrates a second important point, that a purchaser can take an estate free of an unregistered land charge even if he *knows* that the land charge exists. It was clear that the mother had known about her son's interest, but she was still able to take the estate free of it because he had not registered it.

A similar point was made in *Hollington Bros Ltd* v *Rhodes* [1951] 2 TLR 691. There a purchaser bought the fee simple estate in a piece of land on the express understanding that the sale was subject to a prior agreement to grant a lease to a third party. This agreement was an estate contract but it had not been registered as a land charge. It was held that even though the purchaser had known of the land charge, and even though he had expressly bought subject to it, he was not bound by the charge because it was unregistered. These cases contrast oddly with the similar case of the unprotected minor interest in registered land which was held to bind a purchaser who expressly bought subject to it (*Lyus* v *Prowsa Developments Ltd* [1982] 2 All ER 953) but there the court felt able to impose a constructive trust. If the facts support a claim for a constructive trust then the same rule would be applied in unregistered land. If there is fraud on the part of the claimant he cannot, of course, rely on the statutory rules.

Priority notices

It sometimes happens that one knows in advance that several transactions relating to unregistered land will take place in such rapid succession that it would be impossible for the owner of a land charge to register it between its creation and a later disposition in respect of the same estate. A typical example occurs in the following set of circumstances:

(a) conveyance of estate by V to P;
(b) conveyance creates restrictive convenants on the use of land for the benefit of land retained by V;
(c) creation of a mortgage by P, who mortgages the estate to M in order to give security for a loan provided to enable P to pay for the estate.

In practice the conveyance, the creation of the mortgage and the payment over of the mortgage advance will all have to take place on the same day. If V does nothing before he conveys the property to P, he will be unable to register his covenant as a land charge before the mortgage in favour of M is created. Accordingly the covenant would not bind M. To deal with this problem V can register a 'priority notice' under LCA 1972, s. 11, which will entitle V to keep his priority to M. The formalities required are that the priority notice must be registered at least 15 days before the creation of the land charge. If then a land charge registration is made within 39 days of the entry of the priority notice, the registration is deemed to date from the date of the priority notice. In our example, if V had registered a priority notice M would be warned that V's interest would get priority, because when M makes a land charges search before granting the loan the search will reveal the priority notice. The same method should be used for the protection of any other type of land charge, when its future owner is aware that the estate owner intends to deal with the estate soon after the creation of the charge.

Other registers maintained by the land charges department

The Land Charges Register is only one of the five registers which are kept by the Land Charges Department under the provisions of LCA 1972. The other registers are also important to a purchaser of unregistered land, as they may reveal charges or obligations affecting the land which are of as much importance as those on the land charges register.

Register of pending actions
This is a register containing petitions in bankruptcy filed after 1925, and any pending actions in relation to land or any interest in or charge on land (s. 17(1)). The action concerned must involve some issue relating to the title of land or to some proprietary interest in land (e.g., *Greenhi Builders Ltd* v *Allen* [1979] 1 WLR 156). The aim of the register is to prevent the estate owner selling his estate before a dispute is resolved or at the expense of the interests of his creditors in the case of bankruptcy. Any purchaser of an estate or interest in the land will take the property subject to the result of the registered action. Probably the most important orders that appear on this register are bankruptcy orders (see Insolvency Act 1986).

Register of annuities
This register is no longer of great importance since it contains only certain annuities created before 1926.

Register of writs and orders affecting land
This is a register of court orders made in relation to land or of writs issued for the purpose of enforcing a court order (other writs come under the register of pending actions). This will include court orders appointing receivers in relation to land and any charging orders on land (which charge the payment of a judgment debt against property belonging to the debtor).

Register of deeds of arrangement
If a debtor makes a deed of arrangement (to settle his debts) with his creditors which affects land then that deed should be registered if made after 1925. A deed of arrangement is made when a debtor is insolvent but wishes to avoid going bankrupt, and a registration will warn any intending purchaser of the debtor's land that the property is subject to the prior agreement made in favour of the creditors.

Rules applicable to interests which are not land charges

It will be obvious from the account given above that there are many third-party rights to unregistered land which do not fall into any of the classes of land charge. Examples include the rights of beneficiaries under a trust of land, and legal and equitable mortgages which are protected by a deposit of the title deeds. In addition, all those rights which are registrable as land charges if created on or after 1 January 1926 are, in general, not registrable if created before that date. There are separate rules governing whether these interests will bind a purchaser, and these rules vary depending on whether the interest claimed by the third party is legal or equitable.

Legal interests

A purchaser will automatically be bound by all legal interests in the land which are not land charges (most legal interests are not on the land charges list). This rule is usually expressed by saying that 'Legal rights are good against the world'. The reason for this rule is that if common law recognised an interest in the land it was regarded as a right *in rem* ('in the thing') which therefore bound anyone who purchased an estate or interest in the burdened land. Accordingly, if an estate is subject to a legal mortgage which is protected by a deposit of the title deeds, then anyone who buys the estate will buy it subject to the mortgage. (In practice the purchaser would insist that the vendor repay the debt on completion of the sale so that the mortgage is discharged and the purchaser is not affected by it; but if the purchaser did not know about the mortgage, and so did not require that this be done, it would bind him.)

Equitable interests

The rule which applies to equitable interests is that they bind everyone except a bona fide purchaser for value of a legal estate without notice of the equitable interest. This rule is commonly referred to as the 'notice rule'. The reason for the rule is that equity will not allow a purchaser for value to ignore interests of which he had knowledge at the date of the purchase, since this is contrary to conscience, and so will enforce them against him in the same way as they are enforced against a volunteer (someone who does not give value).

Bona fides
The notice rule requires that the purchaser shall act in good faith and therefore that the purchaser should take all normal steps to discover any possible interests in the property.

Purchaser for value
It is necessary for the person who acquires the estate to give value if he is to rely on the notice rule. Thus a donee takes a gift of land subject to any equitable interests that there may be (which is quite fair). 'Value' includes money, money's worth and some other forms of consideration, such as a future marriage. It does not include a sale in consideration of mutual love and affection (even though this is good consideration) (*Goodright* d *Humphreys* v *Moses* (1774) 2 Bl R 1019).

A person who acquires an estate for value is described as a 'purchaser for value'. This may seem unnecessarily long-winded, since in ordinary speech

D

'purchaser' means 'buyer' and so includes the notion of taking for value. However, for the lawyer, 'purchaser' has the technical meaning of 'one who takes by act of the parties rather than by operation of law'. This means that he has had the property transferred to him in the appropriate way by the previous owner, rather than having it vested in him automatically by operation of some rule of law, such as that which vests a bankrupt's property in his trustee in bankruptcy or the deceased's property in his personal representatives. In this sense then, even a donee is a purchaser and so in a context like this it is necessary to state specifically that the person acquiring the estate is a purchaser for value.

Of a legal estate

The purchaser must buy a legal estate, rather than take an equitable interest in the land. Thus, if the purchaser is to be safe, he must have acquired the legal estate before he discovers the equitable interest. If he discovers the equitable interest after contract but before conveyance, he will be bound by it if he continues and takes the conveyance (*Wigg* v *Wigg* (1739) 1 Atk 382), although normally in such a case the purchaser will have a right to rescind the contract, because the vendor cannot give the unencumbered estate which he contracted to convey.

Without notice

There are three types of notice:

(a)   actual notice;
(b)   constructive notice;
(c)   imputed notice.

Actual notice   This is quite straightforward and requires that the purchaser should have actual knowledge of the existence of the equitable interest. It is not necessary for the purchaser to obtain this information from any particular source and he may even discover the truth from a complete outsider (*Lloyd* v *Banks* (1868) LR 3 Ch App 488). He is entitled, however, to ignore mere rumours (*Reeves* v *Pope* [1914] 2 KB 284).

Constructive notice   When the notice rule was first created by the courts of equity, clever purchasers soon realised that they could obtain an advantage if they declined to make any investigations which might lead to the discovery of equitable interests. Equity was quick to extend the rule to prevent purchasers deliberately 'turning a blind eye' in this way, as such behaviour was evidence of a lack of bona fides on the part of the purchaser. The means used was to say that the purchasers would be deemed to know of interests which they would have discovered if they had made the usual searches and so were bound by them. This rule is preserved in modern law by LPA 1925, s. 199(1)(ii). The 'usual searches' are of two types: first, the purchaser must investigate the vendor's title correctly by examining the title deeds, and secondly, the purchaser must inspect the land itself.

Constructive notice of matters revealed by examination of deeds A purchaser is bound by any right which he would have discovered had he inspected the vendor's title deeds for the statutory period (at present 15 years) (e.g., *Worthington* v *Morgan* (1849) 16 Sim 547, in which no investigation was made). The purchaser does not have to read or make enquiries about the earlier deeds, but if he does read such documents he will be bound by any interests which he discovers, for he then has actual notice (*Nottingham Patent Brick & Tile Co.* v *Butler* (1885) 15 QBD 261). As a result of this rule it is common for the owners of equitable interests to insist that a note of their rights is made on the deeds (e.g., on the back of a deed) so that future purchasers will have actual notice of their rights if they read the deeds and constructive notice if they omit to read them.

Constructive notice of matters revealed by inspection of land The rule that the purchaser must also inspect the land is commonly called the 'rule in *Hunt* v *Luck*'. In the case of *Hunt* v *Luck* [1902] 1 Ch 428, a purchaser was held to have notice of all the rights of a tenant who was in occupation of the land.

There are clearly similarities between this rule and LRA 1925, s. 70(1)(g), and both have given rise to similar problems. In particular, it has been doubted whether a purchaser of unregistered land has notice of the rights of a spouse of the estate owner, where that spouse lives in the property with the estate owner. It is now common for a wife to have an equitable interest in property which is owned by her husband (for example, she may have contributed to the purchase price). However, in the past, purchasers have not always made it their practice to enquire whether wives have such an interest. This attitude on the part of purchasers was accepted in *Caunce* v *Caunce* [1969] 1 WLR 286, in which it was held that a purchaser was entitled to presume that a wife lived in the property because of her relationship with the estate owner, and that her presence did not put the purchaser of the estate upon notice. However, this rule was heavily criticised by the House of Lords in the registered land case of *Williams & Glyn's Bank Ltd* v *Boland* [1981] AC 487 at p. 508 and in *Kingsnorth Trust Co. Ltd* v *Tizard* [1986] 1 WLR 783 a wife's occupation of unregistered land was regarded as being separate from that of her husband. Accordingly, the older rule in *Caunce* v *Caunce* should now be regarded as outdated and it is most unlikely that it would be applied in the future.

Kingsnorth Trust Co. Ltd v *Tizard* is a very interesting case and suggests that the rule in *Hunt* v *Luck* and LRA 1925, s. 70(1)(g), are growing closer to one another as time goes on. The case may accordingly also be of use, by analogy, when dealing with registered land. The facts were that Mrs Tizard had a beneficial interest in property which had been conveyed into the sole name of her husband. Accordingly Mr Tizard held the property upon trust for both himself and his wife. After some years the marriage failed and Mrs Tizard left the matrimonial home to live nearby. However the Tizard children remained at home with Mr Tizard and Mrs Tizard came to the house every morning, in order to get breakfast for the children and get them ready for school, and every evening, to see them to bed. Since she came to the house every day in this way, Mrs Tizard left most of her clothes and other personal belongings at the property. After the separation Mr Tizard decided to obtain a loan on the security of the house. An agent for the prospective mortgagee visited the house one Sunday afternoon by prior arrangement with Mr Tizard and in order to make an inspection. He looked about the premises but did not open any drawers or cupboards and thus did not discover Mrs Tizard's belongings. It was obvious that there were children living at the house and Mr Tizard explained to the agent that Mrs Tizard had left him, but lived nearby, and that their children still lived at the house. The mortgagee made an advance to Mr Tizard on this basis, taking a charge over the house as security. After some time the mortgagee found it necessary to enforce the charge against the property because sums due under the mortgage had not been paid. At this point Mrs Tizard heard about the charge and claimed that her interest in the property took precedence over the mortgage because the mortgagee had constructive notice of her rights. Judge John Finlay held that Mrs Tizard had been in occupation of the property at the date at which the agent made his inspection and later when the charge was granted. It was said that occupation need not be exclusive, continuous or uninterrupted. The learned judge did, however, agree that someone inspecting property under the rule in *Hunt* v *Luck* was not obliged to go as far as opening drawers or hunting in cupboards. However, since the agent had been told of the recent separation and the fact that Mrs Tizard still lived in the area, the judge felt that the mortgagee was put on notice and should have made further enquiries. The inspection of the property at a pre-arranged date did not amount to making sufficient enquiry (it appears that on the afternoon in question Mr Tizard had probably arranged that his wife should take the children out). This case, though only a first-instance decision, is of considerable importance because it widens the concept of occupation beyond its previously presumed limits and because it gives a detailed indication of the type of investigation which will be needed if a purchaser or mortgagee is to be safe from hidden rights. Certainly in cases in which it is known that a vendor or mortgagor is married it will be safest to insist on obtaining written approval from his or her spouse. (This case may be contrasted with the registered land case of *Strand Securities Ltd* v *Caswell* [1965] Ch 958 in which it was said that keeping your furniture and other belongings at a property did not constitute actual occupation for the purposes of s. 70(1)(g).)

Imputed notice   A purchaser is also deemed to have notice of an equitable interest if his agent has either actual or constructive notice of it. This rule is essential, since most purchasers do not conduct their own conveyancing. Thus if a conveyancer obtains actual notice of an equitable interest, his purchaser/client is also regarded as having notice of it (*Jared* v *Clements* [1903] 1 Ch 428). This rule seems not to apply, however, if the agent deliberately misleads or defrauds the purchaser, for one is not normally held liable for the fraudulent acts of an agent.

Equitable interests bind later acquirers of equitable interests

Thus far we have only considered the position of those who intend to buy the legal estates in their respective properties and, if they do so, will take the property free of those equitable interests (which are not land charges) of which they have no notice. However, it is possible for someone to acquire only an equitable interest in the property, for example, by entering into a contract (an estate contract) to buy the legal estate but never taking a conveyance of the legal estate. In such a case the intending purchaser has an equitable right to the land under the contract (see p. 29) and the question then arises of the extent to which he is bound by pre-existing equitable interests.

Obviously the bona fide purchaser rule does not protect the later acquirer of an equitable interest in the property. In this case the rule which applies is that 'Where the equities are equal the first in time prevails'. Thus a later acquirer of an equitable interest will take over an earlier equitable interest only where the 'equities' are not equal. This will only arise if the owner of the earlier equitable interest has been involved in a fraud on the later acquirer or possibly if the earlier equitable owner has been grossly negligent about protecting his interests (see further, p. 275).

Summary of searches to be made in relation to unregistered land

As a result of the foregoing, a purchaser of unregistered land must make the following enquiries in order to protect himself:

(a)   A local land charges search (made before contracts are exchanged).

(b)   A land charges search against the names of all the estate owners during the title period.

(c)   A thorough examination of the title deeds from the root of title onwards.

(d)   An investigation of the occupancy of the land including questioning any occupants as to their rights.

The conveyance

Once the purchaser is satisfied with his enquiries, the time will have arrived for the completion of the transaction. This, of course, requires a deed under LPA 1925, s. 52(1). This deed is called a 'conveyance' and it operates to convey the legal estate in the land to the purchaser. At the time of the conveyance the vendor will hand to the purchaser the title deeds to the property (unless he is selling only part of the land covered by the deeds, in which case the vendor will give the purchaser an undertaking to produce the deeds should the purchaser ever require them). The purchaser (or probably his legal adviser) should, of course, check the deeds to ensure that the copies that he has previously seen are true copies of the original documents. Thus whilst the owner of an estate in registered land usually has only to collect the land certificate, the purchaser of an estate in unregistered land may end up with quite a large pile of documents. This is the last stage in the transaction (apart from the payment of stamp duty, if payable) where the property does not stand in an area of compulsory registration. If the property is in a registration area the conveyance and the title deeds and details of the searches and enquiries made are sent to the Chief Land Registrar together with an application for first registration of title.

An example of a very simple conveyance is given on p. 76: Usually these documents are far longer and decidedly more complex than this example.

THE PURCHASE OF 1 AND 3 TRANT WAY

1 Trant Way: Registered Land

Since the title to this property is registered the conveyancing will be carried out in the following manner:

(a)   Mr Venn's solicitor sends a draft contract to Mr and Mrs Armstrong's solicitor.

(b)   The Armstrongs' solicitor raises preliminary enquiries with Venn's solicitor.

(c)   Local land charges search made.

(d)   Exchange of contracts—the Armstrongs become the equitable owners.

(e)   Supply of office copy entries of the register.

(f)   The Armstrongs' solicitor searches register.

(g)   Investigation of the land and questioning of any occupants about their rights (LRA 1925, s. 70(1)).

(h)   Transfer by Venn to Mr and Mrs Armstrong; land certificate handed to purchasers' solicitor.

(i)   Registration of the transfer—Mr and Mrs Armstrong become the legal owners.

3 Trant Way: Unregistered Land

The title to this property is unregistered and so the procedure is as follows:

(a)   Miss Ventnor's solicitor sends a draft contract to Miss Bell's solicitor.

(b)   Miss Bell's solicitor raises preliminary enquiries with Miss Ventnor's solicitors.

(c)   Local land charges search made.

(d)   Exchange of contracts—Miss Bell becomes equitable owner.

(e)   Abstract of title (summary of or copies of deeds) supplied to Miss Bell's solicitor.

(f)   Abstract copies inspected to ascertain whether the title is good.

(g)   Abstract copies examined for equitable interests which are not land charges—notice rules.

(h)   Occupancy of land investigated and any occupants questioned about their rights—rule in *Hunt* v *Luck*.

(i)   Land charges search made.

(j)   Abstract of title compared with original deeds (usually on completion day).

(k) Conveyance by Miss Ventnor to Miss Bell—Miss Bell becomes the legal owner of the estate and the title deeds are handed to her.

However an extra final step is required:

(l) Within two months of the date of the conveyance Miss Bell must be registered as the estate owner at Her Majesty's Land Registry (the registration is deemed to be made on the date on which the documents arrive in the registry, provided that they are all in order, so really all that is necessary is that the application to register should be made within two months).

ACQUISITION OF AN ESTATE BY ADVERSE POSSESSION

So far we have only been dealing with estates in land which have been acquired in a formal manner. However, as is mentioned above (p. 14), it is also possible to acquire an estate in land by adverse possession.

4 Trant Way

The current inhabitant of 4 Trant Way is Sidney Sorrell. Mr Sorrell moved into the property 15 years ago as a squatter, and has occupied it ever since. Fifteen years ago the house was in a bad state of repair and seemed to have been abandoned by its previous owners. Mr Sorrell has never received any complaints about his occupation of the premises and has made considerable improvements and alterations. He has had the electricity and gas supplies restored and has paid rates in respect of the property.

The original owner of the fee simple in 4 Trant Way was Oscar Oregano, who died six months ago at the age of 98. His entire estate was inherited by his nephew Nicholas Oregano, who has just discovered that his uncle had neglected the property and that it has been taken over by Mr Sorrell.

Title by adverse possession

There is an old English saying that 'Possession is nine points of the law'. In the case of title to land this saying is particularly true. Since the earliest times, title to land has been based on a form of possession, technically called 'seisin'. If two people had a dispute concerning the ownership of an estate in land the court would decide the case in favour of the person who could show that he had been seised of the land at the earlier date, or who could show that his predecessors in title had the earlier seisin. Thus prior seisin will decide the issue as between the two claimants.

Technically there is a difference between possession and seisin, but today this is of no real importance because possession is always regarded as clear evidence of seisin and therefore the two concepts are normally coexistent. A dispute about ownership will therefore be decided in favour of the party who can show prior possession of the property.

If we apply this basic rule to the position of 4 Trant Way we can see that both Sidney Sorrell and Nicholas Oregano have claims to the property.

THIS CONVEYANCE is made the   day of   BETWEEN

VICTORIA VENTNOR of 3 Trant Way Mousehole in the County of

Stilton (hereinafter called "the vendor") of the one part and

BARBARA BELL of Oak Tree Cottage Elmdale in Stilton aforesaid

(hereinafter called "the purchaser") of the other part.

WHEREAS the vendor is seised of the property hereinafter

described for an estate in fee simple absolute in possession free

from incumbrances and has agreed with the purchaser for the sale

thereof to her at a price of seventy thousand pounds (£70,000).

NOW THIS DEED WITNESSETH as follows:

In consideration of the sum of seventy thousand pounds (£70,000)

paid by the purchaser to the vendor (the receipt whereof the

vendor hereby acknowledges) the vendor as beneficial owner hereby

conveys unto the purchaser all that piece or parcel of land known

as 3 Trant Way Mousehole in the County of Stilton which for the

purposes of identification only is shown and delineated in red on

the plan attached hereto TO HOLD the same unto the purchaser in

fee simple.

IN WITNESS of which the vendor has executed this deed in the

presence of the attesting witness the day and year first before

written.

Signed and delivered   )
as a deed by   )   *Victoria Ventnor*
the said VICTORIA VENTNOR)
in the presence of:

Gerald Gerbil

GERALD GERBIL
THE LIMES,
HOLE HILL,
MOUSEHOLE, STILTON.

CIVIL SERVANT

Mr Sorrell is currently in possession of the property, and is accordingly presumed to be seised of an estate in fee simple. However, Nicholas Oregano also has a claim to the property because he can show that his uncle Oscar was once in possession of the property, and that accordingly his uncle was also seised of an estate in the property. That estate is, of course, an inheritable interest, and Nicholas can show that he has inherited the estate under the terms of his uncle's will. Accordingly Nicholas Oregano has an older estate in the property (and no doubt could produce his uncle's deeds to prove this). As a result one would presume that, in any dispute between Nicholas and Mr Sorrell about the ownership of the property, Nicholas would be regarded as having the better right to the property.

Thus far all seems fairly straightforward, but in fact the dispute between Nicholas and Mr Sorrell is likely to be affected by the provisions of the Limitation Act 1980, so that Nicholas's apparent rights prove to be worthless.

Effect of the Limitation Act 1980

To ensure that defendants are not harassed by stale claims, most legal systems provide that a plaintiff must commence his action within a prescribed time (the 'limitation period') or lose his right of action. In English law these provisions are contained in the Limitation Act 1980, s. 15 of which provides that the limitation period in respect of actions to recover land is 12 years. Thus generally if someone with a prior estate in land allows it to be occupied by a squatter for 12 years he will lose his right to recover the property from the interloper. So in our example, although Nicholas Oregano can prove that his uncle was in prior possession of the land, he may not be able to bring an action to recover the land from Mr Sorrell because the right to sue has been time-barred. Thus a layman will sometimes say that if a squatter remains in possession of land for 12 years the land 'becomes his'. It would be more accurate to say that the squatter is deemed to obtain an estate in the land as soon as he moves on to the property but that his estate is subject to attack by a prior owner until 12 years have elapsed. At one time the original owner's title continued even after the limitation period had elapsed, so that although he could not sue to recover the land he could rely on his title as a defence if he took possession again without a court action. However, today the rule is that at the end of the limitation period the original owner loses both his right to sue and his title to the property (Limitation Act 1980, s. 17).

This is the general background to the law on title by adverse possession. However, the detailed operation of the rules is quite complex and needs to be considered further.

Titles are relative

As we have seen the law is only concerned with competing claims and not with absolute rights. Thus if the following situation arises:

1969   A is the fee simple owner of property
1970   B takes possession of the land
1984   C takes possession of the land

and if B sues C in order to recover the land, C cannot defend the action by claiming that A, and not B, is the true owner of the estate. A court will consider only the competing claims of B and C, and will therefore regard B as being the better claimant because he has the prior estate (*Nicholls* v *Ely Beet Sugar Factory* [1931] 2 Ch 84 and *Mount Carmel Investments Ltd* v *Peter Thurlow Ltd* [1988] 1 WLR 1078). Interestingly, however, should A sue C, then C will be entitled to add together the time that he, C, has occupied the land and the time during which B occupied the land. Thus A will find himself time-barred against C, even though C has only been in occupation of the land for a few years. This is because time begins to run against A as soon as he is dispossessed and he therefore will lose his right to sue 12 years after B first took over the land (i.e., in 1982).

Possession must be adverse

It is obvious that sometimes when a person takes possession of land he does so with the authority of the true owner, and so it is not quite true to say that anyone who takes possession of land can be presumed to have an estate in fee simple. The time period under the Limitation Act 1980 begins to run once someone has taken possession in a manner which is inconsistent with the rights of the prior estate owner see Sch. 1, para. 8(1). The classic statement of this rule was always regarded as being that of Bramwell LJ in the case of *Leigh* v *Jack* (1879) 5 ExD 264, in which he said that for possession to be regarded as adverse to the rights of the prior estate owner, '[A]cts must be done which are inconsistent with his enjoyment of the soil for the purposes for which he intended to use it'. In *Leigh* v *Jack* the land involved had been intended by its owner to be used to build a highway but no action had been taken to start the construction of a road. From 1854 onwards a neighbouring landowner had used the property to store materials used in his factory and in 1865 and 1872 he had erected fences on the land. The Court held that none of these actions amounted to adverse possession of the disputed property, because the true owner of the property had no intention to build upon or cultivate the land and therefore the actions of the neighbouring owner were not inconsistent with the intentions of the prior owner. Cotton LJ said (at p. 274), '[T]here can be no discontinuance [of possession] by absence of use and enjoyment where the land is not capable of use and enjoyment'. However, the classic statement contained in *Leigh* v *Jack* has recently been distinguished by the Court of Appeal and, it appears, largely confined to its own facts. The criticism of the traditional view was first stated clearly by Slade LJ in

Powell v *McFarlane* (1977) 38 P & CR 452, where it was indicated that what mattered was not the intention of the prior owner but the nature of the land and the degree of control taken by the interloper:

> Factual possession signifies an appropriate degree of physical control. It must be a single and [exclusive] possession . . . thus an owner of land and a person intruding on that land without his consent cannot both be in possession of the land at the same time. The question what acts constitute a sufficient degree of exclusive physical control must depend on the circumstances, in particular the nature of the land and the manner in which land of that nature is commonly used or enjoyed.

That this analysis will be preferred for the future seems to have been put beyond real doubt by the latest and vitally important case on adverse possession in the Court of Appeal: *Buckinghamshire County Council* v *Moran* [1990] Ch 623.

Buckinghamshire County Council v *Moran* was a case in which the facts bore many similarities to those in *Leigh* v *Jack*. In 1955 the Council had acquired a plot of land, which appears to have been in the midst of a row of houses, for the purpose of constructing a road diversion. It was known that the road-works would not be carried out for many years and so the council merely fenced the plot from the road (but not from the neighbouring properties) and initially sent council workmen to cut the grass and keep the plot in order. From the late 1960s the owners of one of the neighbouring properties, to the knowledge of the council, began to cut the grass on the council's plot and keep it tidy. From that time on the council ceased to send its workmen to the plot. The neighbouring property changed hands several times and was bought by Mr Moran in 1971. Mr Moran knew that the title to the empty plot was vested in the council, which intended to use it for road-works. However, to look at the plot it appeared to form part of the garden of the property which Mr Moran had bought and was always maintained as such. The conveyance to Mr Moran expressly included all such rights as the vendors might have to the vacant plot. In 1976 the council wrote a letter disputing Mr Moran's rights to use the plot but thereafter took no action to recover it for at least nine years. Thus by the time that the action was brought Mr Moran and his predecessors in title had been using the plot as a garden for well over 12 years in total. The council argued, however, that as it had not had any use for the plot, other than to let it lie fallow until the road scheme could go ahead, the possession of Mr Moran and his predecessors had not been adverse to the council's rights. The Court of Appeal held, however, that Mr Moran had established a good claim to title by adverse possession over the plot of land, distinguishing *Leigh* v *Jack* on the ground that the acts of possession relied on in that case 'had been too trivial to amount to the taking of actual possession'. The court did accept that the standard of proof placed on the squatter in such a case would be high but that in a case such as this where Mr Moran had done all that was possible to take possession of the land that burden was satisfied. It was also established that the 'squatter' need not demonstrate an intention to acquire ownership of the property: the intention to possess it would suffice. This was of importance in this case since Mr Moran had always believed that the vacant plot was the property of the council and only appears to have intended to take the use of it.

As a result of the decision in *Buckinghamshire County Council* v *Moran* it will become far easier for squatters to obtain title to neglected pieces of land. Adverse possession is a matter of fact and the nature of the actions needed to establish it will vary as the character of the land varies. (See further *Wallis's Cayton Holiday Camp Ltd* v *Shell Mex & BP Ltd* [1975] QB 94 and *Williams Bros Direct Supply Ltd* v *Raftery* [1958] 1 QB 159.)

Although the possession taken must be adverse, this does not mean that it must be a source of inconvenience or annoyance to the prior owner. Indeed, as was remarked by Sir John Pennycuick in *Treloar* v *Nute* [1976] 1 WLR 1295, at p. 1302, it is usually only possible to obtain title by adverse possession to land which is neglected by its true owner. Possessory title would probably never arise if the actions of the 'squatter' counted as adverse possession only if they were an inconvenience to the true owner.

When does time start to run?

Time will start to run against a prior owner only once he has been dispossessed or has discontinued possession (Limitation Act 1980, sch. 1, para. 1) *and* when adverse possession has been taken by another person (para. 8). This requires that the true owner has either been forced out of possession or has abandoned possession. In the case of 4 Trant Way it would appear that at some date more than 15 years ago Oscar Oregano abandoned the use of the property. However the limitation period did not start to run against Mr Oregano, or his heirs, until a third party (Mr Sorrell) took possession of the property 15 years ago.

Knowledge is irrelevant

Since Oscar Oregano was aged 83 at the date at which Mr Sorrell took over 4 Trant Way, it seems to be quite likely that he knew nothing of what was happening on the property. However, it appears that Mr Oregano's ignorance of the truth will be of no assistance to Nicholas. This rule is usually said to arise from the case of *Rains* v *Buxton* (1880) 14 ChD 537 and was affirmed in *Powell* v *McFarlane* (1977) 38 P & CR 452. However, in fact in *Rains* v *Buxton* the issue did not arise because the court was of the opinion that the possession in that case was not concealed. It is certainly true, though, that the Limitation Act 1980 does not contain any provision requiring that the true owner must have known of the fact of adverse possession.

Adverse possession by tenants

It is not possible for a tenant to lay claim to the freehold title of the land which he occupies because clearly he occupies the land with the permission of the estate owner and in accordance with the terms of his lease. If the tenant fails to pay his rent this does not alter the position, although the landlord will lose his right to sue for the unpaid rent after six years have passed: this is a special limitation period under the Limitation Act 1980, s. 19. Usually leases also contain a right for the landlord to re-enter the land should any covenant in the lease be broken. These rights of re-entry are time barred after 12 years (Limitation Act 1980, s. 38(7)) but this causes no real problem since a continuing breach of covenant will give rise to a new time period on each occasion the covenant is broken. In addition a fresh right of re-entry will arise on the date on which the lease expires.

A tenant who holds the land under a periodic tenancy where there is no lease in writing is, however, in a special position. In the case of such oral tenancies the limitation period will run against the landlord as soon as the first period of the tenancy ends. However, should the tenant pay rent after this date the period will restart from the date that the rent was paid (Limitation Act 1980, sch. 1, para. 5). Thus if a periodic tenant with an oral lease fails to pay rent he may be able to obtain title to the leased property (*Moses* v *Lovegrove* [1952] 2 QB 533). Therefore, should a landlord in such a position wish to excuse his tenant from paying rent, he should require that the tenant give a regular written acknowledgement that the landlord is the true owner of the property. Such an acknowledgement will ensure that the tenant occupies the property with permission and that therefore his possession is not adverse to the landlord's title. It appears that an acknowledgement given after the expiry of the 12 year period will bar a claim to title by adverse possession (*Colchester Borough Council* v *Smith* [1992] 2 All ER 561).

Tenant dispossessed

So far we have been considering whether time runs in the tenant's favour against the landlord. Another situation to be considered arises where a tenant of land is dispossessed by a third party. Here the limitation period will begin to run only against the person who has a right to recover the land, that is, the tenant, but not against his landlord. The landlord has no right to recover the land until the end of the lease and so the limitation period will only run against the landlord once the period of the original lease has expired.

If:

in 1960 L granted a 25 year lease to T;
in 1965 T was dispossessed by S;

then as between T and S, T will be time-barred in 1977 but, as between L and S, S would have to remain in possession until 1997 in order to obtain a safe title.

Running of time against persons with future interests in the land

The usual rules are further modified in favour of persons who have future interests in land. If land is held upon trust for A for life and then for B, A has an immediate interest in the property and B has a future interest. If A was dispossessed by S in 1970 the usual rule applies to the running of the period against A and in 1982 his rights would be time-barred. However, the rights of B are further protected by s. 15(2) of the Limitation Act 1980. In the case of B the time period within which he must sue is either 12 years from the date of the adverse possession commencing *or* six years from the date at which he obtains an interest in possession in the property, *whichever is the greater*. B's interest will become an interest in possession when A dies and so, if A died in 1984, B's interest will only become time-barred in 1990, which is 20 years after S first obtained possession. (This rule does not apply, however, to a future interest under an entail. Entails are considered in more detail in chapter 4.)

Postponement of the limitation period

Fraud
If there has been fraud or fraudulent concealment of the fact of adverse possession, the time period does not begin to run against the prior owner until the date upon which he discovers the fraud or the concealment.

Mistake
In general a mistake of fact made by the prior owner will not stop the time period running, but under s. 32 of the Limitation Act 1980 in actions for relief from the consequences of mistake the time period commences when the mistake is discovered. Such actions are rare and only arise in cases in which the mistake itself is the ground upon which the action is brought (e.g., where someone has mistakenly paid too much for the land: *Phillips-Higgins* v *Harper* [1954] 1 QB 411).

Prior owner under a disability
If the prior owner is subject to a disability then the time period is *either* 12 years from the date of the dispossession *or* six years from the date at which the disability ends, *whichever is greater*, with a maximum available period of 30 years. If a person dies whilst still under a disability, then his estate will have a period of 12 years from the date of dispossession *or* six years from the date of the death, with a maximum of 30 years. For these rules to apply the disability must have existed at the date at which the cause of action arose. If the disability arises even a day later the ordinary 12-year period will apply. These rules are to be found in s. 28 of the Limitation Act 1980.

The states which amount to a disability for the purposes of s. 28 are (a) that the estate owner is an infant, and (b) that the estate owner is a patient under the Mental Health Act 1983.

Deciding whether an action is time-barred

Thus, in conclusion, it should be noted that there are a number of factors to be taken into account when deciding whether an action to recover land is time-barred. These include: the need for adverse possession; the possibility that the person who has been dispossessed is a tenant or is under a disability; and the chance that there are persons entitled to future interests in the land. It should not, therefore, be too readily assumed that occupation of another's land for a simple period of 12 years will necessarily allow one to obtain good title as against any prior owners.

Summary of limitation periods

Under the Limitation Act 1980 there are three main sets of time periods:

(a)   In the case of actions for the recovery of land, 12 years (s. 15).

(b)   For actions on simple contracts, in tort, or for arrears of rent, six years (ss. 2 and 19).

(c)   For actions on a speciality (e.g., a covenant under seal, which therefore includes covenants in conveyances or leases which are made by deed), 12 years (s. 8).

In certain cases special periods are used, thus in an action by the Crown for the recovery of Crown lands the period is 30 years, and in the case of an action by a charitable or spiritual corporation sole (e.g., a bishop), for the recovery of title to land belonging to the corporation sole, the period is also 30 years.

Adverse possession of registered land

It should be noted that the situation can be rather different in the case of registered land because the registered proprietor is the absolute owner of the estate and remains so until someone else is registered in his place. However, as we have already seen (p. 41), rights acquired or in the course of being acquired under the Limitation Act 1980 are overriding interests (LRA 1925, s. 70(1)(f)). Accordingly anyone who buys the registered estate from the proprietor will take the estate subject to the rights of the squatter, and time will continue to run against the purchaser. When the necessary limitation period has been completed, the registered proprietor is deemed to hold the estate upon trust for the squatter, and thereafter the squatter can apply to be registered as proprietor in place of the existing registered proprietor (LRA 1925, s. 75).

Applying the rules to 4 Trant Way

If one applies these rules to 4 Trant Way it would seem that Nicholas Oregano has little chance of recovering the property which once belonged to his uncle Oscar. Mr Sorrell's actions seem to be clear evidence of adverse possession commencing 15 years ago. Moving into a house, renovating it and going to the lengths of paying the rates are all actions which are inconsistent with the title of the prior owner.

Mr Sorrell may wish to consider making a voluntary registration of his title. If this is done he will be able in time to improve the registration into a registration with absolute title and it will facilitate the conveyancing should he ever wish to sell the land.

3 The Two Legal Estates

Having considered the general background to the modern law relating to land we must now examine in far greater detail the nature of the estates and interests in land. In this chapter we are concerned with the two legal estates; the legal and equitable interests will be considered hereafter.

You will recall that, under the provisions of LPA 1925, s. 1(1) there are two legal estates in land:

(a) the fee simple absolute in possession;
(b) the term of years absolute.

FEE SIMPLE

Factual background

The estate in fee simple in 5 Trant Way is owned by David Derby. He has decided to give the fee simple estate to one of his three nephews and is considering the following three possible dispositions:

(a) Giving the estate to his nephew Eric 'on condition that he does not marry'.
(b) Giving the estate to his nephew Frank 'until he finds full-time employment' (Frank is at present a student).
(c) Giving the estate to his friend George for life and then to his nephew Hal for life, 'provided that Hal marries before George dies'.

It is necessary to consider whether each of these three possible gifts would vest in the nephew or friend concerned a fee simple absolute in possession, or whether the gift would create an interest in land which is less than a legal estate.

The law

We have already seen in chapter 1 that a fee simple used to be an estate in land which was inheritable by the heirs general of its owner. This distinguished the fee simple from the life estate (which was not inheritable) and the fee tail (which was inheritable only by a restricted class of heirs, e.g., 'heirs of the body male'). When the rules of intestate succession were changed in 1925, the concept of 'the heir' became in the main obsolete, and it was no longer correct to define the fee simple as being inherited by the general heirs. It is, however, still true that the fee simple is an estate which lasts indefinitely, so long as there is anyone entitled to take the property under the will or on the intestacy of the previous owner. The other two freehold estates which used to exist (the life estate and the fee tail) do not come within the definition of legal estates in LPA 1925, s. 1(1), and, since they are not on the list of legal interests in s. 1(2), they therefore take effect as equitable interests under s. 1(3).

The word 'absolute' in s. 1(1) indicates that there must be no provision in the grant of the fee simple whereby it might end prematurely while there is still someone qualified to take it. Fees which are subject to such provisions are known as 'modified' fees, and can arise in two forms: (a) conditional interests, and (b) determinable interests. The disposition of 5 Trant Way to Eric Derby 'on condition that he does not marry' would be a conditional interest, whilst a disposition of the property to Frank Derby 'until he finds full-time employment' would be a determinable interest.

Conditional interests

A conditional interest arises where a fee simple is granted subject to a limitation which provides that the grantor will be able to re-enter the property at some date in the future on the occurrence (or non-occurrence) of specified events. In such a case the grantor appears initially to be giving a fee simple absolute, but then reserves the right to recover the land (right of re-entry). This type of arrangement is said to be an interest subject to a condition subsequent. Such interests do not comply with the requirements of LPA 1925, s. 1(1), and so, under the terms of that statute, could not amount to legal estates. However, this rule gave rise to immediate problems when the 1925 legislation came into force, because many estates were subject to rentcharges, which usually provided that the owner of the rentcharge would be entitled to re-enter the land if the payments secured by the rentcharge were not made. In certain parts of the country (e.g., Bristol and Manchester) most of the fee simple estates were then subject to rentcharges, and the effect of s. 1(1) was to turn all these estates into equitable interests, since they were all subject to a right of re-entry on occurrence of a specified condition. As a result, the Law of Property (Amendment) Act 1926 was passed, and the schedule to that Act amended LPA 1925, s. 7(1), to read:

[A] fee simple subject to a legal or equitable right of entry or re-entry is for the purposes of this Act a fee simple absolute.

This wording was, however, wider than was necessary to deal solely with the problem caused by rentcharges and produced the result that *all* fees simple subject to a right of re-entry became legal estates. Thus a conditional fee simple will be a legal estate within the meaning of LPA 1925, s. 1(1). Therefore, if 5 Trant Way is given to Eric Derby in fee simple on condition that 'he does not marry', Eric will receive a legal estate. The form of words used may, however, give rise to objections on the grounds of public policy (see p. 89).

Determinable interests

A determinable fee is one which according to its terms will last only until a specified event occurs, or does not occur. Thus a grant of the fee simple in 5 Trant Way to Frank Derby 'until he finds full-time employment' is a determinable fee. The fee lasts only until Frank gets a job. The fee would still be determinable even if it is very unlikely that the specified event will ever occur, because from the outset the period of the interest has been cut down. Such interests are not within LPA 1925, s. 1(1), and are not saved by s. 7(1) as amended. The grantor retains an interest in the land, known as the 'possibility of reverter', and when the determining event occurs, the property reverts automatically to him.

Differences between conditional and determinable fees

Whether a grant creates a conditional fee or a determinable fee may well be an accident of wording, and the grantor may not intend to create one rather than the other. The same arrangement can often be expressed in either way. Thus a grant 'to A on condition that he does not become a lawyer' is a conditional fee and creates a legal estate, subject to a right of re-entry; whilst a grant 'to A until he becomes a lawyer' is a determinable fee, which can only be an equitable interest. Because of this many students (and even courts, see *Re Moore* (1888) 39 ChD 116) find it difficult to distinguish between the two classes of right. The following lists of expressions which have been categorised as creating either conditional or determinable fees may help in identifying the nature of a particular grant:

CONDITIONAL   DETERMINABLE

'on condition that . . .'   'until . . .'
'providing that . . .'   'as long as . . .'
'but if . . .'   'for the duration of . . .'
                                    'while'

However, although the distinction between the two types of fee appears to be a matter of form, rather than of substance, the difference can be of considerable importance to the grantee. We have already seen that a conditional fee takes effect as a legal estate, while a determinable fee can exist only as an equitable interest. A further difference will be experienced if the specified event occurs, for in the case of the determinable fee the interest will immediately come to an end and the grantee has no further right to the land. By contrast, the fee on condition subsequent will in fact continue until the grantor or his successor exercises his right of re-entry, and so the grantor could find himself entitled to remain on the land almost indefinitely.

Thus a distinction which might seem to the grantor to be little more than a matter of style can have far-reaching consequences for the grantee and, as Parker MR said in *Re King's Trusts* (1892) 29 LR Ir 401, 410, the difference between the two produces a rule which is 'little short of disgraceful to our jurisprudence'.

Future interests

Conditional fees should not be confused with rights which are subject to a condition precedent, that is, a condition which has to be fulfilled before the grantee can enjoy the property. An illustration of such a condition is provided by the grant of 5 Trant Way to David Derby's friend George 'for life', and then to his nephew Hal for life, 'provided that Hal marries before George dies'.

If the gift was made in these terms, Hal would, at the outset, have no interest in the property, but merely a chance of acquiring one in the future. Rather confusingly, he is said to have a contingent, or conditional, interest, but in fact no interest in the land will arise until the condition is met. Should Hal marry before George's death, he will have satisfied the condition, and will then have a future interest in the property; that is, an interest entitling him to possession of the house at some time in the future. For two reasons, this interest would not be capable of being a legal estate: not only is it for life, but it also takes effect in the future, and so does not satisfy the requirement of LPA 1925, s. 1(1), that to be legal an estate must take effect in possession. Thus, under the Act, a future interest, even in fee simple, cannot be legal and takes effect only in equity.

We must now mention two technical terms used to describe future interests: 'remainders' and 'reversions'.

A 'reversion' arises where a grantor gives away an estate, or series of estates, which will last for a shorter time than his own estate. The gifts to George and Hal are an example of this, for David Derby has a fee simple, which is capable of lasting for ever, and would have given away, at the most, only two life interests. When they came to an end, the property would *revert* to Mr Derby, or, if he was dead, would form part of his estate and devolve according to the terms of his will, or by the rules of intestate succession. The grantor therefore has a future right to the property from the date of the gift, and that future right is called a reversion.

If, however, the grantor were to give away his full estate to a series of people, he will have kept no reversion in the property, and the future interests he has created will be called 'remainders'. Thus, if Mr Derby were to provide that, after George and Hal have died, the property should belong in fee simple to Ian, the grantor will have no reversion, and Hal and Ian would both be said to have remainders. George would have an interest in possession, and would be entitled to enjoy the property immediately the gift took effect.

We have seen that the full fee simple absolute in possession is the only freehold estate which can exist in law, and that all the other dispositions which David Derby wants to make (such as a life interest, a determinable fee simple and a future interest) can take effect only in equity. In order to give effect to his wishes, therefore, it would be necessary to make use of a trust, so that the legal fee simple would be held by a trustee and Mr Derby's nephews and friend would be entitled to equitable interests for the period and on the conditions stated in the grant (see further, chapter 5).

Intervention of public policy

It should not be thought from what has gone before that an estate owner is entitled to grant estates or interests subject to any limitations that he wishes. It is clear that the courts will intervene in cases in which a limitation is considered to be contrary to public policy. Thus in general a grant of an estate 'on condition that A does not marry' will be regarded as being contrary to public policy and the grant will take effect absolutely, and free of the objectionable condition (*Kelly* v *Monck* (1795) 3 Ridg Parl Rep 205). It is permissible, however, to make a provision the purpose of which is simply to provide for someone until he or she marries, rather than to prevent marriage (*Jones* v *Jones* (1876) 1 QBD 279). Thus normally an estate which is determinable on marriage is not so objectionable. David Derby, therefore would be well-advised to reconsider the proposed grant to his nephew Eric (p. 85), for the present wording could well result in a fee simple absolute free from condition.

It should also be noted that there are other cases in which public policy will intervene (e.g., where a disposition might have the effect of discouraging the religious education of a child (*Re Borwick* [1933] Ch 657) or preventing an adult taking public office or being employed in the armed services (*Re Edgar* [1939] 1 All ER 635; *Re Beard* [1908] 1 Ch 383), and that obviously the views expressed by the courts on such clauses are likely to vary with the times.

One class of conditions or determining events to which the courts have always taken strong exception is that by which the grantor tries to restrict the power of the recipient to dispose of the property freely. Ever since the statute *Quia Emptores* in 1290 it has been a principle of the law that generally an estate owner should have a free and unfettered power to alienate his property. Thus in *Hood* v *Oglander* (1865) 34 Beav 513, 522 it was said that a condition preventing alienation at any time would be void. The courts will, however, tolerate some restrictions on disposal of an estate which fall short of an absolute bar and indeed in some cases have been remarkably tolerant in dealing with restrictions which prevent disposal outside a particular family. Thus in *Re Macleay* (1875) LR 20 Eq 186 a disposition to someone 'on condition that he never sells it out of the family' was upheld. One cannot guarantee, however, that modern courts would be so generous and in any event this decision was rather more limited in its scope than may first appear: the recipient alone was bound by the condition, it did not bind anyone to whom he transferred the estate, and it only prevented a *sale* outside the family, the recipient could *give* the property to anyone. Despite this limited approval given to such a restriction upon disposal, it is best to avoid such arrangements for fear that they may be struck down, leaving the estate owner with a free power to alienate the property. (But in some cases a trust for sale may be used to allow the possibility of fetters on alienation, see p. 206.)

TERM OF YEARS ABSOLUTE

Factual background

You will recall, from chapter 1, that 2 Trant Way is for sale 'leasehold'.
The current fee simple owner of No. 2 is Fingall Forest, who is a widower
and who has no children. Mr Forest has decided that the property is too
large for his needs and he has had the house divided into three sections:
a flat, consisting of the second floor of the property, in which he lives; the
ground and first-floor maisonette, which is now for sale 'leasehold' (a 99-
year lease); and the basement which Mr Forest has let on a weekly tenancy
to an old friend, Gerald Gruyère, at a rent of £30 a week. Mr Forest's estate
agent has now found a prospective purchaser for the maisonette, Harry
Harding.

These two transactions, the sale of the maisonette on a 99-year lease, and
the letting of the basement on a weekly tenancy seem at first glance to have
very little in common. However, we shall see that although these rights to
use property appear very different from each other, they both fall into the
category of leases; that is to say, both are 'terms of years absolute'. The
lease of the maisonette for 99 years is an example of a lease for a 'fixed
term', that is, for one period which can last for weeks, months or years,
as the parties agree. At the end of the agreed period, the lease ends
automatically, without either side having to give the other notice. By contrast,
the letting of the basement on a weekly tenancy is an example of a 'periodic
tenancy'. It is not granted for a fixed number of weeks, but runs on indefinitely,
from week to week, until one of the parties wants to end the arrangement,
and therefore gives notice to the other.

The law

The technical name for the lease, 'term of years absolute', may seem less
strange at first sight than that used to describe the freehold estate, but
nonetheless it is necessary to consider carefully the terminology used.

The 'term'

The Law of Property Act 1925 requires that the leasehold estate should be
for 'a term', that is, for a fixed period rather than for an indefinite one.
Thus in *Lace* v *Chantler* [1944] KB 368, it was held that a lease 'for the
duration of the war' was not a legal estate because it was not for a fixed
term. A lease 'for 99 years', or other specified period, is therefore clearly
'a term' which satisfies the requirements of LPA 1925, s. 1(1); but is this
true of a weekly tenancy? One would imagine that a weekly tenancy (or any
other periodic tenancy, e.g., monthly, quarterly or annual) which runs on
indefinitely from one period to another could not be an estate in land, because
when it commences one does not know how long it will last. However, the
law does regard such tenancies as satisfying the requirement of a fixed term,
because they are regarded as being a lease for a week (fixed term), followed

by another lease for a week, followed by another lease for a week and so on until the lease is correctly terminated. Therefore even the tenant with a periodic tenancy does have a lease for a fixed term, which is therefore capable of being a legal estate. For a more modern application of this rule, see *Prudential Assurance Co Ltd* v *London Residuary Body* [1992] 3 WLR 279 which concerned a 'lease' granted until the landlord required the land itself for the purposes of widening a road (this case overruled the decision of the Court of Appeal in *Ashburn Anstalt* v *Arnold* [1989] Ch 1 in this regard). The *Prudential* case also laid to rest the different view, expressed by the Court of Appeal in *Re Midland Railway Co.'s Agreement* [1971] Ch 725, that the rule in *Lace* v *Chantler* does not apply to periodic tenancies and emphasised that the strict rule as to the requirement of certainty applied to all leases.

'Of years'

It is clear also that a 99-year lease is a term *of years* but a periodic tenancy will be for a period of a year, or less than a year. Nonetheless the periodic tenancy will still qualify as a legal estate, as would a lease for, say, a fixed period of three months, because LPA 1925, s. 205(1) (xxvii), provides that 'the expression "term of years" includes a term for less than a year, or for a year or years and a fraction of a year or from year to year'. Therefore, all that is necessary is a fixed period, and accordingly it must be possible to grant a lease for a very short period (e.g., two days) even though this is not likely to be common. In *Smallwood* v *Sheppards* [1895] 2 QB 627 it was held that a legal lease could be created for a period of three successive bank holidays, that is, for three separate days.

'Absolute'

The inclusion of this word in the definition of the leasehold estate causes some difficulty. When used to describe the fee simple it means, as we have seen (p. 86), that the estate is not liable to end prematurely, before the full period is up. However, leases often provide for determination before the term has run its full course; as we shall see, it is common practice to provide that the landlord may forfeit the lease for any breach of covenant by the tenant. Indeed some long leases even contain provisions allowing either the landlord or tenant, or both, the right to terminate the lease early on notice. Such clauses are often called 'break clauses'. However, there has never been any suggestion that such a provision prevents the lease taking effect as a legal estate, and yet that lease cannot be described as absolute in the same sense as the fee simple. It is in fact difficult to explain the use of the word 'absolute' in this context, and it may be instructive to note the view expressed by Megarry and Wade, *The Law of Real Property*, 5th ed., p. 129, that 'This word is here used in no intelligible sense'.

One further difference between the statutory definitions of the two legal estates may be noted here. We have seen (p. 3) that, in order to be legal, a fee simple absolute must take effect 'in possession', and that a future interest cannot be a legal estate. There is no similar provision in LPA 1925, s. 1(1), with regard to leases, and accordingly leases may be granted to take effect in the future and still have the status of legal estates. More information about future leases ('reversionary' leases) is given at p. 94.

We may now look at the nature of a lease in more detail.

Basic requirements for a lease

The lease has been defined (see *Woodfall's Law of Landlord and Tenant*, 28th ed. (London: Sweet & Maxwell, 1978, ch. 1) as 'the grant of a right to the exclusive possession of land for a determinate term less than that which the grantor has himself in the land'. This identifies three essential elements:

(a) exclusive possession,
(b) determinate term,
(c) term less than that of the grantor.

It should be noted that Woodfall's definition makes no mention of the payment of rent or premium as being an essential characteristic of a lease. It is true that leases are usually commercial arrangements, in which the tenant pays for the use of the land by regular instalments throughout the lease (rent), or by a lump sum at the start of the lease (premium or fine), or by a combination of both. However, there is no obligation on the landlord to charge for the use of his land, and valid leases may well be created without any provision for payment by the tenant (see further, p. 97).

Exclusive possession
Exclusive possession is an essential ingredient of a lease; without exclusive possession there can be no lease. What then is exclusive possession? Exclusive possession is the right to use premises to the exclusion of all others, including the landlord himself. In the words of Lord Templeman in *Street* v *Mountford* [1985] AC 809:

> The tenant possessing exclusive possession is able to exercise the rights of an owner of land, which is in the real sense his land albeit temporarily and subject to certain restrictions. A tenant armed with exclusive possession can keep out strangers and keep out the landlord.

If the occupier has not a right to exclusive possession of the premises then his right to use the premises cannot amount to a lease, a legal estate, but may be some lesser right in land, such as a licence or possibly an easement. However, the fact that a person has been given exclusive possession is not conclusive proof that he has a lease, for it is also possible to have a licence, or certain other rights in land, with exclusive possession (see, e.g., chapter 4). This point is also emphasised by Lord Templeman in *Street* v *Mountford*:

> There can be no tenancy unless the occupier enjoys exclusive possession; but an occupier who enjoys exclusive possession is not necessarily a tenant. He may be owner in fee simple, a trespasser, a mortgagee in possession,

an object of charity or a service occupier. To constitute a tenancy the occupier must be granted exclusive possession for a fixed or periodic term certain in consideration of a premium or periodical payments.

However, this case also emphasises that, normally, where there is exclusive possession, the courts will regard the arrangement as a lease (landlords often claim that the agreement creates only a licence, because in that case the occupant had only very limited protection under the Rent Acts). It should be noted that although exclusive possession normally gives the tenant the right to exclude everyone else, including the landlord, from the premises, the lease may reserve the right for the landlord to enter the premises on certain occasions (e.g., to inspect the state of repair of the property). Such a right must be exercised at reasonable hours and in a reasonable manner and does not prevent the tenant having exclusive possession, though a right for the landlord to come and go as he pleased, and without the tenant's permission, would have this effect. Thus in *Appah* v *Parncliffe Investments Ltd* [1964] 1 WLR 1064, in which the 'landlord' had reserved the right to come into the premises as and when he chose in order to empty meters and change linen, the arrangement was held to be a licence, since the occupier did not have exclusive possession.

The surrounding circumstances or the nature of the accommodation may also indicate whether the intention was to grant exclusive possession. Thus in *Camden London Borough Council* v *Shortlife Community Housing Ltd, The Times*, 12 March 1992, it was held that, where flats were occupied on the basis that they were intended to provide only short-life accommodation, this negatived any intention to confer exclusive possession on the occupants. This was true even though the premises in question were self-contained flats which had previously been let to council tenants. In *Westminster City Council* v *Clarke* [1992] 2 WLR 229 a similar principle was applied to a room provided by the Council in a hostel for single men. In this case the House of Lords took account of the intention of the Council in providing the accommodation and regarded a term allowing the Council to require a man to change rooms (which rebutted the claim to exclusive possession) as genuine and in accordance with the nature of the accommodation, rather than as a sham included for the sole purpose of avoiding the application of the Rent Acts.

These points may be summarised by saying that, in order for a lease to exist, the tenant must have exclusive possession, but exclusive possession is not in itself conclusive evidence of the existence of a lease. On this see further p. 151.

Determinate term

We have already seen from *Lace* v *Chantler* [1944] KB 368 that a lease must last for a fixed period, although a periodic tenancy will satisfy this test. In addition the commencement of the period must also be certain. Normally, if no mention is made in the agreement, it will be deemed to start immediately: *Furness* v *Bond* (1888) 4 TLR 457. If, however, one has only an agreement for a future lease, it will be void unless it is clear at what date the lease is to start, either from an express term in the contract or by inference (*Harvey* v *Pratt* [1965] 1 WLR 1025).

It is not infrequently the case that a landlord will nonetheless wish to permit the use of his property for an uncertain period. This can be done by using the process of granting a lease for a fixed period subject to earlier termination on the occurrence of an earlier event. Thus L can grant a legal lease to T 'for 99 years determinable if T leaves the country earlier', and it would have been possible to give effect to the wishes of the parties in *Lace* v *Chantler* if some similar device had been used.

Certain types of agreement give rise to particular problems which have been affected by statutory rules and these will now be considered.

Lease for life or until marriage   From what has gone before it will be clear that the grant of a lease 'for T's life' or 'until T marries' would not under the general rules be capable of amounting to a legal estate. However, it is not uncommon for such leases to be granted, and therefore the draftsmen of the property legislation provided a saving provision for such cases. Accordingly, by virtue of LPA 1925, s. 149(6), a lease for life, or until marriage, which has been granted at a rent or in consideration of a fine (premium) will be converted automatically into a fixed term of 90 years determinable on the tenant's death, or marriage. Such a fixed term is, of course, a legal estate within the meaning of s. 1(1). *Skipton Building Society* v *Clayton, The Times*, 25 March 1993 provides a recent example of the effects of s. 149(6). The section applies to such leases even if they were created before 1926. The term, it should be noted, does not terminate automatically on the death or marriage of the tenant. It terminates if thereafter either party to the agreement (including the tenant's personal representatives in the case of death) serves on the other one month's notice, expiring on a quarter day.

A lease comes within the section even if it is granted 'to T for the lifetime of X', so the life specified need not be that of the tenant but might be that of a third party, or of the landlord himself. The section applies to *all* cases of leases determinable on marriage or death (provided they are granted for value), so even if L, in an attempt to 'get it right', grants T a lease for '100 years determinable on T's earlier death' this will also be converted into a term of 90 years determinable on death. Similarly, a lease for '25 years if T remains a spinster' will also be converted into a lease for 90 years determinable on T's earlier marriage.

Where a lease for life or until marriage is granted without rent or fine, the lease takes effect only in equity and the tenant may have special powers under the Settled Land Act 1925 (see p. 185).

Leases to start in the future   As we have already seen (p. 92), a lease granting a term which does not start immediately but at some time in the future is called a 'reversionary lease'. In order to prevent the creation of such interests very far into the future, LPA 1925, s. 149(3), provides that any lease expressed to commence more than 21 years from the date of the instrument which creates it is to be void. This rule does not apply to agreements which were made before 1926. Similarly, a contract to grant a lease, which, when granted, will take effect more than 21 years from the date of the grant, is also void. On this latter point, it is important to note that the time-limit specified in s. 149(3) still relates to the period between the grant of the lease and the commencement of the term; the section does not impose any restriction on the length of time which may elapse between entering into the contract to grant a lease and actually making the grant. Thus it is possible, and, indeed, standard practice, for a landlord to covenant that he will, if the tenant wishes, grant him a further term when the present lease ends (option for renewal), and this option can be enforced at the end of the lease, however long the original term may be. It should be noted, however, that a contract to renew a lease for over 60 years after the termination of a current lease is void if the agreement was made after 1925 (Law of Property Act 1922, sch. 15, para. 7).

Perpetually renewable leases It is quite common for a lease to give the tenant a right to renew the lease for a further period on the expiration of the first term. As we have just seen, this is perfectly acceptable. However, such a provision in a lease can give rise to problems if it is badly drafted. In *Northchurch Estates Ltd* v *Daniels* [1947] Ch 117, a lease for a year contained a clause which gave the tenant a right to renew the lease at the end of the year 'on identical terms and conditions'. Unfortunately this clause, if interpreted literally, will mean that the second term will include an identical term allowing the tenant to call for a third term, the third term a clause providing for a fourth, and so on. As a result, the tenant would have a right to renew the lease perpetually. This caused considerable difficulties for the landlord, who would be able to terminate this perpetual lease only if the tenant broke a term of the agreement or forgot to give notice of his wish to renew the lease. The difficulty was increased by the fact that in the past the courts have construed such renewal clauses in a totally literal manner, even where it has been clear that the parties to the lease had not intended this result (*Caerphilly Concrete Products Ltd* v *Owen* [1972] 1 WLR 372).

Such perpetually renewable leases are now subject to s. 145 of and Sch. 15 to the Law of Property Act 1922 (which applies to all such leases created after 1925). These provisions convert the affected lease into a fixed term of 2,000 years, subject to a right of the tenant to terminate the lease on 10 days' notice in writing on any occasion on which the original lease would have expired had it not been renewed. The landlord has no similar right to terminate. Thus, in *Northchurch Estates Ltd* v *Daniels* the original lease for one year became a fixed term of 2,000 years and the tenant had the right to give 10 days' notice of termination at the end of each year, if he so chose. These leases are also subject to certain other special rules which are set out in Sch. 15 to the 1922 Act. These rules produce a result in which a landlord is heavily penalised for the careless drafting of the original lease. Usually it is quite clear that the original intention of the parties was that the tenant should have the right to renew the lease for a second term, with a further right to a third and final term at his choice. In *Northchurch Estates Ltd* v *Daniels* the real intention of the parties was that the tenant should have a lease for one year with a right to renew the lease twice if he so chose. The unfairness of transforming such an agreement into a 2,000-year term, when three years were intended, is obvious. Accordingly, recently, the courts have reversed their earlier tendency to enforce a literal interpretation of such leases and have indicated that a more liberal approach to interpretation will be adopted in the future, in order to prevent tenants obtaining an unjustified windfall because of poor drafting. Thus in *Marjorie Burnett Ltd v Barclay* (1980) 258 EG 624 it was held that a clause would only be construed so as to create a perpetually renewable lease if there is an express obligation for perpetual renewal. In this case a seven year lease contained a clause allowing the tenant to renew 'for a further seven years at a rent to be agreed', and 'such lease should also contain a like covenant for a further term of seven years on the expiration of the term thereby granted'. This arrangement was held not to create a perpetually renewable lease, since it was clear that the intention of the parties was to create a maximum of three terms.

Term less than that of the grantor
An owner in fee simple is able to grant a lease of his property for any term because the fee simple is itself effectively perpetual. Thus there is nothing to prevent a fee simple owner granting a lease to a tenant for 9,000, or even 90,000 years. In fact 99-year leases are common and 999-year leases, though hardly frequent, are to be found in practice.

However, the leasehold estate is unlike the fee simple for, whilst there can only be one fee simple estate in one piece of land, there can be more than one term of years. A tenant may himself grant a lease of the premises (a sublease) to a subtenant, as long as this sublease will last for a shorter period than the original ('head') lease. The subtenant may also grant a further lease of the same premises (an 'underlease') to an undertenant, as long as the underlease is for a shorter period than the sublease. Thus if L, the fee simple owner, grants T a 99-year lease of a property on 1 January 1980, T may grant a sublease to S for any shorter period (e.g., 25 years) and S may grant an underlease to U for any period shorter than the sublease (e.g., a monthly tenancy). This can be expressed diagrammatically as follows:

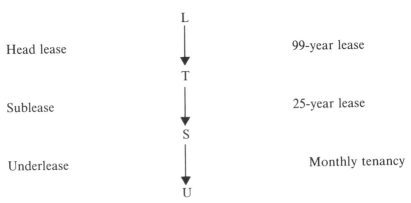

This process of creating further terms may continue almost indefinitely, as long as each subsequent lease will end before the end of the term of the person who granted the lease. In our diagram, L is a landlord, T and S are both tenants and landlords, and U is a tenant only. Each of these four people has a legal estate in the property concerned. S will recover the property by bringing U's tenancy to an end (this can be done by serving notice (see p. 108) but today this right to terminate such a lease may well be affected by the provisions of the Housing Act which give security of tenure to certain tenants). T will recover the use of the property when S's 25-year term expires. Thus S and T both have a right that the property will revert to them on the expiration of the terms which they have carved out of their own. This right is called a 'reversion', and since S and T are owners of leasehold estates they are each said to have a 'leasehold reversion'. Once T's 99-year lease expires, L (or his successors) will recover the property and thus L has a 'freehold reversion'.

Concurrent leases
At this point, a brief mention must be made of concurrent leases, or 'leases of the reversion' (not to be confused with reversionary leases, described at p. 94). When L has granted a lease to T, it is possible for L to grant another lease to A in respect of the same piece of land. A cannot take physical possession of the property, because T is already entitled to that, so the lease to A is regarded as a lease of L's reversion on T's lease. If the lease to A is longer than that to T, A will eventually be able to take physical possession of the property, but if it is for the same period, or a shorter one, he will never be able to enter, and he acts simply as T's landlord, collecting any rent due and enforcing covenants in the lease.

Concurrent leases are not likely to be met very often, except as a conveyancing device which permits the creation of successive mortgages of the same estate. We will explain how this works in the chapter on mortgages.

Is payment of rent an essential requirement?
Whenever we consider leases we tend to think of the term of years as being an arrangement whereby the tenant has the use of the land in consideration of a regular payment, called 'rent' (technically 'rent service'). In the case of a periodic tenancy this is likely to be a commercial estimation of the value of the property and to be payable weekly, monthly, quarterly or, more rarely, annually. With a long lease for a fixed period (e.g., a 99-year lease) it is more usual for the tenant to pay one large sum at the start of the lease (called a 'premium' or 'fine') and then to pay a small, nominal, rent on a yearly or half-yearly basis (usually called 'ground rent'). Normally therefore a tenant will pay some rent to his landlord, although in the case of ground rent it may be a trivial sum of money.

You will recall that in *Street* v *Mountford* [1985] AC 809 (see p. 93 above) Lord Templeman mentioned that a lease might be granted in consideration of rent *or* a premium. Thus it is possible to have a lease in consideration of one initial payment of a lump sum, rather than in consideration of the periodical payment of rent (see *Hill* v *Booth* [1930] 1 KB 381). In such a case there is a contractual obligation and the tenant obtains a legal estate, though no rent is involved.

Thus it is clear that the payment of rent, although usual, is not an essential characteristic of a lease; LPA 1925, for example, defines a term of years absolute as 'a term of years . . . (whether or not at a rent)' (s. 205(1)(xxvii)). The limitation of other provisions in that Act to leases at a rent or premium (for example, s. 149(3) and (6)) implies that a valid lease can exist where there is no provision for payment in either form, and such leases are likely to be found as a part of family settlements, or as conveyancing devices, for instance, in connection with mortgages.

Again, there have been cases in which rent was originally reserved, but problems have arisen because of badly drafted clauses for rent review. In both *Kenilworth Industrial Sites Ltd* v *E.C. Little & Co. Ltd* [1974] 1 WLR 1069, and *Beer* v *Bowden* [1981] 1 All ER 1070, the court accepted that it was possible for a lease to continue without any rent being payable at all. In the *Kenilworth* case, at p. 1071, Megarry J said:

> [T]he lease reserves no rent beyond the first five years . . .. If no new rent is ever ascertained, then as a matter of obligation under the terms of the lease, no rent at all is reserved for the last 16 years of the term.

(However, in both cases the tenants did admit that on the true construction of the lease they were liable to pay rent and the courts construed the leases in such a way as to allow the amount of the rent to be ascertained).

In *Ashburn Anstalt* v *Arnold* [1988] 2 WLR 706 the Court of Appeal confirmed that rent is not an essential requirement for a lease and said that the remarks in *Street* v *Mountford* were not to be read as introducing such a requirement. In this case a vendor of a leasehold estate had been given by the purchaser the right to exclusive possession of the premises rent-free until a specified date, the agreement to continue thereafter until terminated by a quarter's notice. This arrangement was held to be a lease and Fox LJ said, at p. 719:

> '. . . the reservation of rent is not necessary for the creation of a tenancy'.

This case was overruled on other grounds by the House of Lords in *Prudential Assurance Co Ltd* v *London Residuary Body* [1992] 3 WLR 279. However, the principle that it is possible to have a lease without payment of rent has been affirmed by the Court of Appeal in *Skipton Building Society* v *Clayton, The Times*, 25 March 1993.

Finally, it should be noted that although rent and premiums usually take the form of money payments, it is possible for payment to be made in kind or through the performance of services.

Types of lease

The types of lease most frequently encountered are leases for a fixed term and periodic tenancies. We will concentrate on these here, and leave until later any consideration of other forms, such as tenancies at will and at sufferance, and tenancies by estoppel (see p.113).

Fixed-term leases
These leases, as we have seen, may be of any period, ranging from a day (or presumably hours) to thousands of years. As long as the period is specified

these leases give rise to few problems. In general the courts seem willing to construe rather vaguely worded agreements in such a manner as to give rise to a certain term of years (see, e.g., *Re King's Leasehold Estates* (1873) LR 16 Eq 521). As we have seen (p. 94), some uncertain periods (e.g., a lease for life) are saved by statutory provisions.

Periodic tenancies

As we have already explained, these tenancies run on indefinitely from one period to another. The term is automatically renewed on each expiry date unless one party gives notice to the other, indicating either that the tenant does not require a further term or that the landlord does not intend to give one.

A periodic tenancy may arise either from an express grant or by implication of law. Such a tenancy will arise by implication where the tenant is in possession of the land and is paying rent which is calculated on a periodic basis. Where the tenancy is expressly granted, the grant will usually indicate which type of periodic tenancy is being created (e.g., yearly, quarterly, monthly or weekly). In the case of an implied grant, the period is usually determined by reference to the period for which rent is said to be due. For example, a yearly tenancy will arise by implication where the tenant is in possession of the land and is paying rent which is calculated as an annual sum, even if the payments are made at intervals of less than a year. Thus, if L grants T a lease 'at a rent of £2,000 payable in 12 monthly instalments', then T will have a yearly lease of the premises (*Shirley* v *Newman* (1795) 1 Esp 266 and *Ladies' Hosiery & Underwear Ltd* v *Parker* [1930] 1 Ch 304). However, it is also possible for the period of the tenancy to be determined by other terms of the agreement which indicate a particular period (e.g., reference to provisions for notice), or by local or business custom.

CREATION OF LEGAL LEASES

Express grant

Since a lease or tenancy creates a legal estate it is usually subject to the normal rule that a deed is required for its creation. This rule is now contained in LPA 1925, s. 52(1), which states that a grant is not effective to create a legal estate 'unless made by deed'. Normally, therefore, in order to create a legal estate, a lease should be signed, witnessed and delivered (at least by the landlord) if it is to create a legal estate. Further, if the landlord's title is registered, any lease for more than 21 years must itself be substantively registered if it is to take effect at law.

This rule is, however, inconvenient when one is dealing with a short lease, or a periodic tenancy, and accordingly the harshness of s. 52(1) is mitigated in the case of certain short leases by s. 54(2), which provides that s. 52(1) shall not

affect the creation by parol of leases taking effect in possession for a term not exceeding three years (whether or not the lessee is given power to extend the term) at the best rent which can reasonably be obtained without taking a fine.

Thus a lease for not more than three years (which includes periodic tenancies— *Hammond* v *Farrow* [1904] 2 KB 332 at p. 335) may be created by a simple oral or written agreement, as long as it is granted at the best rent which can be obtained (without a premium) and takes effect in possession. This last requirement means that the lease must begin at the date of grant, not at some time in the future, and as a result a reversionary (future) lease, even one for not more than three years, must always be granted by deed.

However, most short leases do take effect in possession, and accordingly are granted without a deed, in simple written form or by word of mouth. Thus many tenants have no written lease, though weekly tenants should normally have a rent book recording the basic agreement if the premises are domestic in nature (Landlord and Tenant Act 1985, s. 4). It is most unlikely that Mr Gruyère, the weekly tenant of the basement flat at 2 Trant Way, has a deed setting out his lease. Indeed, as he is a friend of the landlord, Mr Forest, he may well have no written document at all. Nonetheless, Mr Gruyère will have a legal lease, a legal estate, if his rent of £30 a week satisfies the 'best rent' test. The grant of the 99-year lease of the maisonette at 2 Trant Way will, however, have to be made by deed if it is to be a legal lease.

Implied grant

Because a lease for not more than three years may be created without any formalities, it is possible for certain leases to arise by implication, from the actions of the parties. The type of leases which arise in this manner will be periodic tenancies, which will be presumed to exist where it can be shown that a person is in possession of land with the owner's consent, and that rent has been paid and accepted (*Martin* v *Smith* (1874) LR 9 Exch 50). The type of periodic tenancy inferred (e.g., weekly, monthly, quarterly or annual) will depend upon the manner of calculation of the rent (or on some other term of the agreement—p. 97); where rent is expressed as a weekly sum a weekly tenancy will be inferred, and so on. The lease implied will be legal because such periodic tenancies may be created informally within the provisions of s. 54(2).

As we have seen, the implied grant is based on an inference drawn from the parties' behaviour, which suggests an intention to create a periodic tenancy. It is, of course, possible to displace this inference by showing that one or both of the parties did not have this intention: as, for example, where an express grant of a different type of lease was made (*Manfield & Sons Ltd* v *Botchin* [1970] 2 QB 612), or where the landlord is unaware that the person paying rent is not the person he had in contemplation (*Tickner* v *Buzzacott* [1965] Ch 426).

Contracts to grant leases

Although certain leases may be *granted* without formalities under LPA 1925, s. 54(2), in the past any *contract to grant* a lease had to satisfy the provisions of LPA 1925, s. 40 (see p. 19). Thus for any contract to grant a lease to be enforced, there had to be a written memorandum of the contract, satisfying s. 40(1), or a sufficient act of part performance. Normally, if the tenant had been allowed to enter into possession of the property and had paid rent, these actions amounted to sufficient acts of part performance by both parties and the contract would be enforceable in equity (see, e.g. *Wills* v *Stradling* (1797) 3 Ves Jr 378).

The rule that a short lease could be granted without formality but that a contract to grant the same lease required writing (in the absence of part performance) had long been the subject of criticism. In relation to contracts made on or after 27 September 1989 the rules were changed by the Law of Property (Miscellaneous Provisions) Act 1989, s. 2(5)(a). Now a contract to grant a lease for not more than 3 years may be made orally or by a written agreement which would not satisfy s. 2(1).

Contracts to grant longer leases do not fall within s. 2(1) and thus there must be a written contract incorporating all the terms of the agreement and signed by the parties. The doctrine of part performance can no longer apply. These rules should be kept in mind when one is reading older cases on contracts to grant leases. The change in the rules as to part performance may be particularly significant in the case of contracts for leases.

Provided these requirements are satisfied, either party to the contract may seek an order for specific performance of the contract. As this is an equitable remedy, it is subject to the usual equitable rules, and the party seeking to enforce the contract must not delay unduly and must 'come to equity with clean hands'. Accordingly, the party seeking to enforce the contract in this way must not himself be in breach of any of the terms of the agreement. Thus in *Coatsworth* v *Johnson* (1886) 55 LJ QB 220, in which the tenant was in continuing breach of an obligation to pay rent, the tenant was refused an order for specific performance. A similar position arose in *Cornish* v *Brook Green Laundry Ltd* [1959] 1 QB 394, in which the performance of certain works by the plaintiff was a condition precedent to the grant of the lease and those works had not been performed. Nor will specific performance be granted if the effect of granting the order will be to procure the breach of a term in a superior lease (*Warmington* v *Miller* [1973] QB 877). In such cases, accordingly, although a contract exists, it is of relatively little value, since the party seeking to enforce it cannot obtain performance, and the only remaining possibility for redress would be to seek damages at law for breach of contract.

Leases in equity: the doctrine in *Walsh* v *Lonsdale*

It is not at all uncommon for a landlord and tenant to attempt to create a legal lease but to fail to do so because the correct formalities have not been observed. In such cases one is dealing not with an express contract to grant a lease but with a failed attempt at an actual grant. However, for many years both law and equity agreed that such defective grants might be treated as contracts to grant the same lease, as long as LPA 1925, s. 40(1), was satisfied or there were sufficient acts of part performance (*Bond* v *Rosling* (1861) 1

E

B & S 371; *Tidey* v *Mollett* (1864) 16 CB (NS) 298). In addition equity would go further and would grant an order for specific performance in order to perfect the imperfect lease (*Parker* v *Taswell* (1858) 2 DeG & J 559). Of course, since 1989, for a court to find that a contract exists, it will be necessary to produce a document which satisfies the Law of Property (Miscellaneous Provisions) Act 1989, s. 2(1), unless the contract is one to grant a short lease.

The doctrine in Walsh v Lonsdale
The interaction of these various rules and of the provisions of the Supreme Court of Judicature Act 1873, s. 25(11) (now Supreme Court Act 1981, s. 49(1)), is clearly illustrated by the leading case of *Walsh* v *Lonsdale* (1882) 21 ChD 9. In this case, the landlord and tenant had entered into a written agreement (not under seal and so not a deed) under which a mill was to be let to the tenant for seven years. The rent was to vary according to the productivity of the mill and it was agreed that the tenant would pay the rent annually, in advance, if the landlord so demanded. The tenant thereupon took possession of the mill and paid rent at six-monthly intervals, in arrears, for a year and a half. At this point the landlord demanded the next year's rent in advance, in accordance with the written agreement. The tenant refused to pay rent in advance and the landlord accordingly distrained for it (a 'self-help' remedy, see p. 142). The tenant thereupon sued, claiming that the distraint was unlawful, and applied for an interim injunction to restrain the landlord.

It is clear from the rules set out above that the relationship between the landlord and tenant in this case differs depending upon whether one applies the legal rules or the equitable rules. At law, the tenant had an implied legal lease arising from his possession of the property and the payment of rent. Payment of rent at six-monthly intervals gives rise to an annual tenancy and, since rent had been paid and accepted in arrears, law would presume that it was a term of the legal lease that rent should be paid in this manner. In equity, however, the act of entering the property and paying rent merely supports the written agreement, which is an agreement for a lease of seven years with rent payable annually in advance. Provided that the party seeking to enforce had done nothing wrong, this contract would be enforced by equity with an order for specific performance (finally producing the lease originally intended). In the meantime, since 'Equity regards as done that which ought to be done', the parties would be regarded by equity as already having a seven year lease.

Which lease then prevailed, the annual legal lease or the seven year equitable lease? Only if the equitable lease prevailed would the landlord's action in distraining be proper. The court held that, due to the provisions of the Supreme Court of Judicature Acts 1873 and 1875, the equitable lease prevailed and that therefore the landlord's actions were lawful. (The 1873 and 1875 Acts required that, where the rules of law and equity conflict, the equitable rule should prevail—see now Supreme Court Act 1981, s. 49(1).)

Is an equitable lease as good as a legal lease?
Since normally an equitable lease can be converted into a legal lease by obtaining an order for specific performance, and since in the meantime equity will uphold the rights of the parties as though the legal lease had already been granted, it has often been said that 'A contract for a lease is as good as a lease' (see *Re Maughan* (1885) 14 QBD 956), However, this is not necessarily true, as an equitable right is invariably more precarious than a legal right. We have already seen that the force of a contract for a lease depends upon the availability of an order for specific performance. Whereas a legal remedy (e.g., damages) will be available without reference to the behaviour of the plaintiff, an equitable remedy is not available where the plaintiff has 'dirty hands'. Thus a contract for a lease is only 'as good as a lease' if the circumstances are such that an order for specific performance can be obtained.

Furthermore there are other difficulties when the position of third parties is involved. Let us assume that L1 agrees to give T a five-year lease of property and that this agreement is specifically enforceable (i.e. it is in writing). T will have an equitable lease of the property. If later L1 sells the fee simple of the property to L2, L2 may not necessarily be bound by T's lease because it is only an equitable interest in the property. In the case of unregistered land the contract for a lease will be an estate contract, a C(iv) land charge, under LCA 1972, s. 2(4) and will bind L2 only if it was registered as a land charge before the date of the conveyance to him. Even if L2 knew of the agreement he is not bound by it, as notice is irrelevant in the case of registrable but unregistered land charges (LCA 1972, s. 4(6)).

If title to the land is registered, the equitable lease will be classified as a minor interest and so must be protected by entry on the register if it is to bind L2 (unless T can establish the existence of a constructive trust as against L2). We have already seen (p. 42) that it was held in *City Permanent Building Society* v *Miller* [1952] Ch 840, that LRA 1925, s. 70(1)(k), is limited to legal leases, so that an equitable lease cannot obtain the status of an overriding interest under this provision. However, if, at the time of the transfer to L2, the tenant of the equitable lease is in 'actual occupation' of the property his right under the agreement will be an overriding interest by virtue of s. 70(1)(g) of the Act, and thus binding on L2. Nevertheless, as *Strand Securities Ltd* v *Caswell* [1965] Ch 958 shows, there are circumstances in which a tenant may not be in actual occupation at the relevant time, and a tenant with an equitable lease would therefore be well advised to protect his position by making an entry on the register.

Thus, while a legal lease will bind any purchaser, an equitable lease will only be binding in certain circumstances. Since such equitable leases usually only arise in cases in which the parties are unaware of the legal formalities for the creation of a lease, it is most unlikely that the tenant will know that he has to take further steps to protect his interest.

Where an equitable lease is not protected in the appropriate way, and so cannot be enforced against the purchaser for value, it is worth remembering that the tenant may also have a legal periodic tenancy, arising from his going into possession and the payment and receipt of rent. *Walsh* v *Lonsdale* (1882) 21 ChD 9 shows that where both legal and equitable rights are available, the equitable one prevails, and indeed the tenant may often prefer to rely on an equitable lease which gives him a longer term. However, if for some reason the equitable right cannot be enforced, either party may fall back on the protection of the legal lease.

A further defect of the contract for a lease arises in relation to the covenants in the lease. As we shall see later, each party to the lease will usually undertake certain duties, such as to pay rent or to keep the property in repair, by entering into covenants set out in the lease. Such covenants are not only enforceable between the original parties to the lease, but, provided the lease is legal, will normally run to bind and benefit both a purchaser from the landlord and a purchaser from the tenant (see p. 132). However, this depends on the purchaser acquiring an estate in the property; in the case of a purely equitable lease there is no legal estate in existence, and so the benefits and burdens of the covenants will not pass automatically to the new landlord or tenant.

The right to enforce a covenant may, however, be assigned, subject to the usual rules governing assignment of choses in action, and so if the landlord were to make some promise in the original agreement (e.g., to repair the structure) the benefit of that promise can be assigned to a purchaser from the tenant. Accordingly the purchaser would be able to sue the landlord, to enforce the landlord's part of the contract (*Manchester Brewery* v *Coombs* [1901] 2 Ch 608).

However, whilst the *benefit* of a chose in action may be assigned the *burden* is not transferable. Thus if the tenant agrees in an equitable lease to decorate the interior of the property the burden of this agreement cannot be transferred to a person purchasing the lease from the tenant. The original tenant will remain contractually liable for any breach of the agreement but the landlord will not be able to take action against the new tenant (*Purchase* v *Lichfield Brewery Co.* [1915] 1 KB 184; but see also *Boyer* v *Warbey* [1953] 1 QB 234).

If the landlord sells the fee simple reversion to a purchaser, that purchaser is in a stronger position than would otherwise be the case, due to statutory rules which apply equally to legal and equitable leases (LPA 1925, ss. 141 and 142; see further p. 137). The purchaser from the landlord will accordingly obtain both the benefits and the burdens of the original contract.

A further disadvantage of an equitable lease is that, whilst a legal lease comes within the definition of a 'conveyance' for the purposes of LPA 1925, s. 62, and so carries with it automatically certain rights enjoyed in connection with the land, a contract for a lease does not fall within s. 62 and so does not carry with it such benefits. (We will explain this more fully in the chapter on easements, see p. 296).

There are other ways in which an equitable lease is not the equivalent of a legal lease. Thus whilst certain 'usual covenants' (a term of art explained at p. 129) are implied into a contract for a lease, they are not implied into a full legal lease and the parties are bound by the stated terms only. In this case, the contract for a lease seems to have an advantage over a poorly drafted legal lease. A further difference, which is a disadvantage to the tenant, is that a purchaser of an equitable lease is not the purchaser of a legal estate and so will be bound by certain earlier equitable interests in the property.

He cannot claim to be a 'bona fide purchaser of a legal estate for value' in respect of earlier rights to which the notice rules apply, not can he claim the benefit of LCA 1972, s. 4(6), and so will be bound by unregistered class C(iv) and D land charges. He will of course be a purchaser within s. 4(5) of the Act and will take the property free of unregistered class C(i)–(iii) land charges (see p. 65).

From all this it can be seen that it is certainly not the case that a contract for a lease is as good as a lease. These rules provide a strong incentive for ensuring that leases are correctly granted, but unfortunately are not understood by many landlords and tenants. Accordingly, it is fortunate that the most common types of informal leases (periodic tenancies) are saved from this unsatisfactory position under the provisions of LPA 1925, s. 54(2).

DISPOSITION OF LEASES AND REVERSIONS

Both landlord and tenant have legal estates which may pass to others on sale, by way of gift or under the rules of testate or intestate succession. In what follows, we are primarily concerned with disposition on sale, but it must be remembered that there are other occasions besides sale on which leases and reversions may pass to newcomers.

Sale of the freehold reversion

It is always possible for the owner of the reversion in fee simple (the freehold landlord) to sell his estate in the land. This will be done in the normal manner by transfer and registration, in the case of registered land, and by conveyance, in the case of unregistered land (see chapter 2).

In the case of unregistered land, the purchaser will acquire the fee simple subject to any legal lease which exists, regardless of whether he knew of its existence, for 'Legal rights are good against the world' (see p. 64). Thus the purchaser of the fee simple becomes the tenant's new landlord, and, as we shall see later (p. 137), takes over most if not all of the original landlord's rights and duties under the lease.

Where the title to the fee simple is registered the position is more complicated, and the position varies according to the length of the lease.

Where the lease is granted for not more than 21 years it will be an overriding interest under LRA 1925, s. 70(1)(k), and so will bind the purchaser of the fee simple even if he did not know of it. (This is the rule since the amendments made by LRA 1986, s. 4.)

If the lease is for more than 21 years it must have been substantively registered in order to be created as a legal lease (LRA 1925, s. 123 as amended). This gives rise to a separate title number, register entry and land certificate for the lease, but as the lease is also noted on the charges register of the freehold title a purchaser will know of its existence (LRA 1925, s. 48). Under LRA 1986, s. 2, all leases for more than 21 years have to be registered. Prior to this Act only leases for more than 40 years had to be registered.

Sale of the lease by the tenant

A sale of his leasehold estate by the tenant is also possible (subject to any covenants in the lease restricting this right). The disposition of a lease is usually called an 'assignment'. Since this assignment is the conveyance or transfer of a legal estate it should be made by deed (LPA 1925, s. 52). This rule applies even to leases for not more than three years, because s. 54(2) provides an exception only for the original grant of such leases and does not apply to assignments (see *Crago* v *Julian* [1992] 1 WLR 372). However, a defective assignment will be regarded as a contract to assign in equity, provided that there is a written agreement or, perhaps, if an estoppel can be raised. Where such a contract arises, either party may then apply for an order for specific performance in order to effect a full legal assignment.

An exception to the requirement for a deed arises in cases in which the assignment takes effect due to operation of law. This can be important in cases in which a tenant purports to grant a sublease of the property but grants a term which is equivalent to, or greater than, the unexpired portion of his own lease. Such a disposition takes effect as an assignment of the lease rather than as the creation of a sublease. The reason for this is that a sublease can only be created if the tenant retains some interest in the property when he grants the sublease: he must be in such a position that he will recover the property at some point. In other words he must retain the leasehold reversion. If he parts with the property for the *whole* of the remainder of his head lease there is no leasehold reversion and the transaction can only take effect as an assignment of the head lease and not as a sublease (*Beardman* v *Wilson* (1868) LR 4 CP 57). If the purported sublease is for less than three years it is likely that the parties will not have concluded their agreement by deed (relying on s. 54(2)). If the effect of the agreement is to transfer the whole remaining term of the head lease to the 'sublessee' (in fact, the assignee) the result appears to be a valid legal assignment without the need for a deed. Lord Greene MR seems to have accepted this reasoning in the case of *Milmo* v *Carreras* [1946] KB 306 at p. 312, on the ground that such an assignment arose by operation of a rule of law. These remarks are, however, *obiter dicta* and the view could be challenged on the ground that the assignment in fact arises as a result of the actions and intentions of the parties. It does seem likely, however, that the *Milmo* v *Carreras* view would be adopted in any future case in order to prevent unnecessary further complications in this area of the law.

Sale of a leasehold reversion

We have already seen (p. 96) that the owner of a leasehold reversion performs two roles, being at the same time both the tenant of the head lease and the landlord of the sublease. Thus the sale of his estate must involve a consideration of the rules relating to both a lease and a reversion; the assignment of his lease must take the form described above, while the question of whether his purchaser takes subject to the sublease depends on principles similar to those outlined at p. 105.

DETERMINING A LEASE

Leases can be brought to an end in a very large number of ways. Some of these methods of determining a lease have a reduced effect today, however, due to the provisions of the Rent Acts, which may give the tenant of a dwelling a statutory right to continue with the tenancy even after it has been terminated under the contractual rules. Radical changes have now been made by the Housing Act 1988 to the position of tenants but considerable protection is still available. The older rules are still of importance, however, because in general the statutory provisions do not come into effect until after the contractual tenancy has been terminated. Accordingly a landlord who wishes to end a tenancy may first have to terminate the contractual tenancy and then take further action in order to bring to an end the statutory protection afforded the tenant.

Other statutory codes protect tenants of business premises and agricultural holdings, and again to a certain extent displace or modify the original rules. For these various statutory provisions, which are in general outside the scope of this book, reference may be made to Megarry and Wade, *The Law of Real Property*, 5th ed. (London: Stevens, 1984) or G.C. Cheshire and E.H. Burn, *Cheshire and Burn's Modern Law of Real Property*, 14th ed. (London: Butterworths, 1988) or to a suitable specialist text.

At law a lease may be determined in any of the following ways:

(a) expiry;
(b) notice;
(c) surrender;
(d) merger;
(e) enlargement;
(f) disclaimer;
(g) forfeiture.

It is also possible that the doctrine of frustration of contract may apply to leases, and this will be discussed after the other methods of determining a lease have been considered.

Expiry

A fixed-term lease gives rise to few problems, since it will expire automatically once the specified term comes to an end. In such cases it is not necessary for either party to the lease to take any action in order to terminate the lease. In addition, if a lease is granted for a fixed term but is subject to termination on the occurrence of a specified event, then the lease terminates automatically when the event occurs (see *Doe* d *Lockwood* v *Clarke* (1807) 8 East 185 and *Great Northern Railway Co.* v *Arnold* (1916) 33 TLR 114; though F.R. Crane (1963) 27 Conv (NS) 111 argues that the authorities are not clear and that notice is required). Leases determining on death or marriage are, however, affected by statutory provisions and do not terminate automatically (see the following paragraphs).

Notice

As we have already seen, periodic tenancies run on indefinitely, from one period to the next, until one party gives notice to the other that he wishes to end the arrangement. It was always open to the parties to make any agreement they pleased about the form and period of notice required. In the absence of such agreement, however, the common law would apply standard rules, and more recently the statutory codes designed to protect tenants have created a number of requirements which cannot be varied by agreement.

Form

In general there appears to be no requirement at common law that notice must be given in writing, at least in the case of tenancies created orally (*Timmins v Rowlinson* (1765) 3 Burr 1603). However, under s. 5(1) of the Protection from Eviction Act, 1977, notice to quit in respect of premises let as a dwelling must be given in writing. In addition any such notice must be given in a statutory form which draws to the attention of the tenant the fact that he may be entitled to security of tenure under statutory provisions. The provisions of Part I of the Housing Act 1988 thereafter generally prevent the landlord from recovering possession of such premises without a court order. Most business tenancies must also be terminated by written notice, in the statutory form, under the provisions of the Landlord and Tenant Act 1954. In the case of agricultural holdings, the rules relating to security of tenure and notice are now governed by chapter III of Part I of the Housing Act 1988, which generally brings such tenancies into line with other domestic leases.

Period

The correct period for notice will vary according to the type of lease or tenancy involved and these are considered separately below. However, there are certain statutory amendments to these rules which apply to leases of dwellings, business premises, and agricultural holdings, and to long tenancies at low rent. We do not have the space to describe all these here, but must mention that any notice to quit premises let as a dwelling must be given not less than four weeks before the date on which it is to take effect (Protection from Eviction Act 1977, s. 5(1)) unless the lease falls within one of the exempt categories under the Housing Act 1988. The exempt categories cover the sort of situation where the tenant has something more of the character of a 'lodger', rather than that of a normal tenant.

Notice periods for various leases and tenancies

Fixed-term leases   Some fixed-term leases contain clauses ('break clauses') allowing one party, or both, to determine the lease on notice before the term expires. The break clause may be exercisable on the occurrence of certain events, or at specified intervals throughout the term (e.g., at the end of the 7th or 14th year in a 21-year lease). Such a lease will usually provide for notice to be given before the break clause is exercised, and subject to the rules given above the correct notice period is that specified in the lease.

Yearly tenancies A yearly tenancy can be terminated by either party giving half a year's notice. Usually the notice should expire at the end of the first year or on its anniversary (*Doe* d. *Shore* v *Porter* (1789) 3 D & E 13). (The parties may of course agree to some other period of notice, subject to any statutory restriction.) The computation of the half year sometimes gives rise to problems, since the traditional quarter-days (Christmas Day, 25 December; Lady Day, 25 March; Midsummer Day, 24 June; and Michaelmas, 29 September) are not at regular intervals and yet were usually used as the dates on which the rent would be payable in a yearly tenancy. If the yearly lease ends on one of the quarter-days it seems that one should give two quarters' notice (*Morgan* v *Davies* (1878) 3 CPD 260). In the case of other yearly tenancies a true half year (183 days) should be used.

Other periodic tenancies Subject to the special cases mentioned above, the normal rule is that the correct period for notice is a full period under the lease. Thus for a quarterly tenancy one gives a quarter's notice; for a monthly tenancy, a month's notice; and for a weekly tenancy, one week's notice. (The day on which the notice is to expire is excluded in calculating the period.) The notice should expire at the end of one period of the lease.

Excluding the right to give notice
It is clear that the landlord's right to give notice does not have to be identical with that of the tenant (*Breams Property Investment Co. Ltd* v *Stroulger* [1948] 2 KB 1). However, it has been held to be contrary to the nature of a periodic lease to exclude a landlord's right to give notice altogether and such a term in a lease will be void (*Centaploy Ltd* v *Matlodge Ltd* [1974] Ch 1). Nevertheless, it has been suggested that a clause which postpones the landlord's right, is not void as long as it gives the landlord the right to give notice at some time, or on the occurrence of some event. In *Re Midland Railway Co's Agreement* [1971] Ch 725 a clause that the landlord company would not give notice until it required the land for its own use was upheld, even though evidence was given that the landlord would never require the land for its own use, at least in the foreseeable future. However, this decision has now been expressly overruled by the House of Lords in *Prudential Assurance Co Ltd* v *London Residuary Body* [1992] 3 WLR 279. In *Prudential* the original 'lease' was held to be void as not creating a term of years because the period of the supposed grant was 'until the . . . land is required by the Council for the purposes of widening of Walworth Road . . .' and was accordingly for an indeterminate term. However, the tenants had gone into possession and paid rent and thus sought to establish that they had a legal periodic tenancy (which was accepted) but which could not be terminated by the landlord until the road was needed for the specified purpose. Since it appeared that the road alteration would not now take place (the lease having continued already for some 60 years) the incorporation of such a term into the periodic tenancy would have given the tenant a lease, at a 1930 rent, which the landlord could never terminate. Lord Templeman concluded that the landlord's right could not be excluded in this manner: a periodic tenancy is saved from being an indeterminate term because each party has power to terminate on notice expiring at the end

of each period. Accordingly in *Prudential* the landlord could terminate the periodic tenancy by giving the appropriate notice (six months' notice in this instance). Therefore, any term which seeks to exclude the right to give notice, or to restrict it so that it cannot be used, will be disregarded and either party may give notice according to the usual rules.

Surrender

A surrender is the means whereby a tenant relinquishes his estate to his landlord, the reversioner, with the agreement of the landlord. A surrender releases the tenant from any future liability under the lease but does not release him from liability for past actions (e.g., past breaches of covenant) (*Richmond* v *Savill* [1926] 2 KB 530). Accordingly, the landlord would still be able to seek compensation for any past losses arising from such breach. It should be noted, however, that the circumstances of the surrender may be such that the landlord will be taken to have waived his right to compensation for past breaches (*Dalton* v *Pickard* [1926] 2 KB 545).

If the following situation exists:

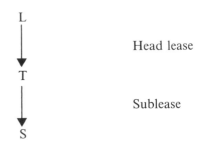

a surrender of the head lease by T will not end the sublease granted to S. The effect of the surrender will be that S will become a tenant of L, on the terms and conditions of the sublease. In other words, the surrender has no real effect on the subtenant, it merely alters the person to whom he is to pay his rent and to whom he owes a duty to observe the covenants in the sublease (LPA 1925, s. 150).

Since a surrender is a dealing with a legal estate in land, it should be done expressly and by deed. This is true even where one wishes to surrender a short lease, for the exemption in LPA 1925, s. 54(2), only applies to the grant of such leases and not to their surrender. A defective surrender (e.g., a surrender which, due to mistake, is unwitnessed) will operate as a contract in equity to surrender the lease, under the usual principles. No deed is required, however, in cases in which the lease is surrendered by operation of law (LPA 1925, s. 52(2)(c)). In practice this is quite common, since often the surrender is evidenced by the actions of the parties who would thereafter be estopped from denying the fact of the surrender (*Foster* v *Robinson* [1951] 1 KB 149). Such surrenders commonly arise when a landlord accepts back possession of the property and agrees that the tenant will be under no further liability. Thus in *Phené* v *Popplewell* (1862) 12 CB (NS) 334 a surrender was held to have been made without formalities when the landlord accepted back the premises, painted out the name of the former tenant on a signboard and put up a board advertising the property as being available to let. No such surrender will arise from a purely unilateral act, however, (e.g., the tenant returning the key, *Cannan* v *Grimley* (1850) 9 CB 634), and the other party to the lease may insist on the continued performance of the lease. A surrender requires the agreement of both parties.

Merger

A merger arises when the tenant acquires the immediate reversion to his lease or a third party acquires both the lease and the immediate reversion. In such an event the tenant would, in theory, become his own landlord. This is ridiculous, unless the tenant has some specific reason for wishing the lease and the reversion to remain separate, and so normally the lease will merge into the reversionary estate when they come into the hands of the same owner. However, this only occurs where it is the intention of the owner that the estates should merge, and LPA 1925, s. 185, preserves the equitable rule to this effect.

Since a merger involves the acquisition of the superior estate, the events which give rise to it can usually only be effected by deed (LPA 1925, s. 52(1)).

Enlargement

In practice this is very rare, because under the provisions of LPA 1925, s. 153, it can only be done in the case of a lease originally granted for 300 years or more and upon which no rent of any money value is payable. Where the numerous conditions of s. 153 are satisfied, the tenant may execute a deed of enlargement, which has the effect of increasing his interest to that of an estate in fee simple, and thereby extinguishing the title of the previous fee simple owner.

Disclaimer

A right to disclaim a lease normally arises by statute. The most common examples are the rights of trustees in bankruptcy and liquidators of companies to disclaim certain contracts under the provisions of the Insolvency Act 1986. A disclaimer releases the tenant from future liabilities under the lease.

Forfeiture

In certain circumstances it is possible for a landlord to forfeit a lease for breach, by the tenant, of one of the terms of the agreement. This method of determining a lease is considered in detail in the section dealing with enforcement of covenants (p. 142).

DOES THE DOCTRINE OF FRUSTRATION OF CONTRACT APPLY TO A LEASE?

In general, the doctrine of frustration applies in cases in which external factors prevent the parties to an agreement performing their obligations under the contract. A tenant who for some reason is unable to use the property may therefore claim that the lease is frustrated and he is freed from his obligations under it, but in general he will not succeed, for he still has an estate in the land and his duties under the lease continue. Thus, if the house on the property is destroyed by fire, the tenant must still pay any rent due under the lease, for he still has an estate in the land (*Matthey* v *Curling* [1922] 2 AC 180). In the famous old case of *Paradine* v *Jane* (1647) Al 26, a tenant was evicted from the property by the King's army during the Civil War. The tenant was held to be liable to pay the rent on the property, for the risk of such interference is that of the current legal occupier of the land. This rule is generally in the best interests of others who have an interest in the land which is based on that of the tenant (e.g., a mortgagee who has taken a mortgage of the tenant's estate), who would otherwise be deprived of their interest or security.

At the date of *Paradine* v *Jane*, the doctrine of frustration of contract had not been developed, and for many years there was considerable uncertainty whether that doctrine could ever apply to a term of years. Common sense suggested that it should be possible in cases in which the land itself or at least the subject-matter of the lease was destroyed. Thus in *Cricklewood Property & Investment Trust Ltd* v *Leighton's Investment Trust Ltd* [1945] AC 221 it was suggested, *obiter*, that the doctrine should apply in extreme circumstances 'if, for example, some vast convulsion of nature swallowed up the property altogether, or buried it in the depths of the sea'. Also, where an upper-floor flat is destroyed (e.g., by fire) and therefore the whole subject-matter of the lease disappears it had been argued that the doctrine of frustration should apply, though judicial opinion seemed to vary on this (see *Izon* v *Gorton* (1839) 5 Bing (NC) 501). Many long leases contain express provisions to cover this problem, usually, requiring one of the parties to the lease to insure the premises (often the landlord but at the tenant's expense) and requiring that any insurance moneys be immediately expended in rebuilding the property. This is useful where there is a long lease but may be little comfort to the tenant under a short lease if much of the lease period is taken up with rebuilding. However, if the tenant under the short lease has security of tenure under the Housing Act 1988 the continuance of the lease may still be a valuable right.

The issue of whether leases can ever be frustrated does seem to have been settled, at long last, by the House of Lords in *National Carriers Ltd* v *Panalpina (Northern) Ltd* [1981] AC 675. In that case the lease was of a warehouse. For some 20 months during the lease the street giving access to the premises was closed by the local authority, because a neighbouring derelict property was in a dangerous condition. The tenants were thus prevented from using the warehouse for that period. They failed to pay rent, and defended an action for its recovery by claiming that the lease had been frustrated. The House of Lords considered that, in the circumstances, the lease had not been frustrated because the interruption of 20 months (in a 10-year lease) did not destroy the entire contract. Their lordships did, however, accept the principle that in exceptional circumstances the doctrine of frustration could apply to a lease, despite the fact that a lease is more than a contract, since it creates an estate in land. Lord Wilberforce said (at p. 697):

> [T]hough such cases may be rare, the doctrine of frustration is capable of application to leases of land. It must be so applied with proper regard to the fact that a lease, that is, a grant of a legal estate, is involved. The court must consider whether any term is to be implied which would determine the lease in the event which has happened and/or ascertain the foundation of the agreement and decide whether this still exists in the light of the terms of the lease, the surrounding circumstances and any special rules which apply to leases or to the particular lease in question. If the 'frustrating event' occurs during the currency of the lease it will be appropriate to consider the Law Reform (Frustrated Contracts) Act 1943.

It was accepted that in reality the question is one of where the risk should fall: upon the tenant or upon the landlord.

SOME MORE TYPES OF LEASE

So far in this chapter we have concentrated on leases for a fixed term and on periodic tenancies, but it is now time to mention three more types of lease: tenancies at sufferance, tenancies at will and tenancies by estoppel.

Tenancies at sufferance

Tenancies at sufferance are rather peculiar in that they arise purely by operation of law and entirely without any form of agreement between the landlord and the tenant. They arise in cases in which the tenant originally had a valid tenancy but continues to occupy the property after the expiration of that term. This occupation must be without the landlord's consent, for if the tenant remains with the landlord's assent he holds as a tenant at will rather than at sufferance, while if the landlord dissents the former tenant is in the position of a trespasser.

Thus in *Remon v City of London Real Property Co. Ltd* [1921] 1 KB 49 in which a tenant remained in possession of the premises after a valid notice to quit had expired, the tenant was held not to be a tenant at sufferance since his landlords had taken action to endeavour to remove him from the premises. Scrutton LJ said (at p. 58):

> [T]enants by sufferance seem to have been confined to persons who held over without the assent or dissent of their landlords, and not to have included persons who held over wrongfully in spite of the active objection of their landlords.

In such a case there is no real tenancy, despite the name 'tenancy at sufferance' and no real relationship of landlord and tenant. The landlord cannot sue for rent (but may claim recompense for the use of the land — called 'mesne profits'). Should the landlord accept rent then this will normally give rise to a fresh periodic tenancy (*Mann* v *Lovejoy* (1826) Ry & M 355 and *Doe* d *Clarke* v *Smaridge* (1845) 7 QB 957). At common law the tenant at sufferance was in a very precarious position, because the landlord was able to recover possession of the premises, even by force. However, the landlord's rights are now subject to ss. 6 and 12(3) of the Criminal Law Act 1977 and s. 3 of the Protection from Eviction Act 1977.

Tenancies at will

The tenancy at will may arise in any case in which the tenant occupies the land with the permission of the landlord on the terms that the tenancy may be terminated by either party at any time. Parke B once described the tenancy at will as being the lowest estate known to the law (*Doe* d *Gray* v *Stanion* (1836) 1 M & W 700). Unlike the tenancy at sufferance it does give rise to a real relationship of landlord and tenant and rent may be payable (*Anderson* v *Midland Railway Co.* (1861) 3 E & E 614), although this is unusual.

The tenancy at will may be expressly granted (as in *Manfield & Sons Ltd* v *Botchin* [1970] 2 QB 612) or may arise by implication from the act of the parties. Thus a tenancy at will may be inferred where a former tenant continues to occupy the property with his landlord's consent after his lease has expired, and may also arise where the purchaser of a freehold or leasehold estate is allowed into possession of the property before the conveyance or transfer, or grant of the lease, has been concluded. Again, an owner may allow friends or members of his family to occupy his property for an indefinite period, and this arrangement may give rise to a tenancy at will. However, recent case law suggests that today the courts will be more inclined to regard some of these arrangements as licences, rather than as tenancies at will (*Heslop* v *Burns* [1974] 1 WLR 1241; *Street* v *Mountford* [1985] AC 809).

A tenancy at will may be brought to an end in a number of ways. On the one hand, it may be converted into an implied periodic tenancy, if rent is paid and accepted on a regular basis; while on the other hand, the whole arrangement may be determined at will by either side, without any period of notice. Moreover, the relationship is a personal one, so that it ends if either party dies, or assigns his interest to another.

Finally, it must be noted that a tenancy at will appears to fall outside the definition of 'term of years' provided by the 1925 legislation, and so it would appear that, since 1926, such a tenancy cannot amount to a legal estate. (But see Megarry and Wade, *The Law of Real Property*, 5th ed. (London: Stevens, 1984) p. 655.)

Tenancies by estoppel

So far, we have assumed that the leases we are considering have been created by a landlord who has a right to grant a lease of the property, either by virtue of being a fee simple owner or having a valid, superior lease. It may be, however, that the person granting the lease proves to have a defective title himself. He may be a squatter who has been in adverse possession of the land for less than 12 years and so be subject to a claim to recover the land by a prior owner, or, as in *Church of England Building Society* v *Piskor* [1954] Ch 553, he may be in the process of buying the property, but have not yet completed the purchase. As we have already seen, a prospective tenant has no right to investigate his landlord's title, unless provision for this is made in the preliminary contract, and thus a tenant may well take a lease in good faith and only later discover the truth. In such cases the tenant is not, however, able to repudiate his obligations under the lease, relying on the landlord's defective title, and indeed both parties are estopped from later denying one another's title (see *Industrial Properties (Barton Hill) Ltd* v *Associated Electrical Industries Ltd* [1977] QB 580). In this situation, there is said to be a tenancy 'by estoppel'. As between themselves, the parties have all the rights and duties of a landlord and tenant; moreover such a tenancy can be assigned just like any tenancy and, unless an owner with superior title intervenes, is generally as effective and binding as any other lease (*Gouldsworth* v *Knights* (1843) 11 M & W 337). If, however, at any time the superior owner does assert his claim to the property, then the tenant may become liable to the superior owner, to compensate him for the use of the land. In such a case, or if evicted by a superior owner, the tenant may then dispute his landlord's title and resist successfully a claim for rent. In the *Industrial Properties* case Lord Denning MR said:

> Short of eviction by title paramount, or its equivalent, . . . the tenant is estopped from denying the title of the landlord. It is no good his saying: 'The property does not belong to you but to a third person' unless that third person actually comes forward and successfully makes an adverse claim.. . . If the third person . . . makes no adverse claim or is debarred from making it, the tenant remains estopped from denying the landlord's title.

Finally it should be noted that this rule only operates if the landlord had no estate at all in the land at the date at which the purported grant was made, for if he had some legal estate, less in extent than that which he purported to grant, that whole estate would pass to the grantee and no tenancy by estoppel would arise. Thus if the landlord had, for example, a leasehold estate for five years and attempted to grant a sublease for a longer period than his own lease (for example, for 25 years) the purported grant of sublease would not create a lease by estoppel but would operate as an assignment of the existing five-year term (see p. 106).

Feeding the estoppel
If at any time during the continuance of the lease by estoppel the landlord obtains a full legal title to the land, this acquisition of title is said to 'feed' the lease by estoppel, which thereupon becomes a full legal lease (*Rawlin's Case* (1587) Jenk 254). Thus if a purchaser, before taking a conveyance of the fee simple estate, should purport to grant a lease of the property, that

lease will take effect only as a lease by estoppel, but will become a full legal lease as soon as the fee simple is conveyed to the purchaser. This can cause problems when the purchaser obtains a mortgage in order to finance the purchase of the estate but later fails to keep up his mortgage repayments. Both the lease and mortgage must have been created after title to the estate vested in the purchaser but in which order? If the first thing that happens is the feeding of the estoppel, the property over which the mortgage was granted was the estate subject to the lease and thus the mortgagee (the lender) is bound by the pre-existing legal lease. If however the mortgage is made before the legal lease is created, the result is different: the mortgage gets priority and the mortgagee could sell the mortgaged estate free of the lease. It has been said that, even if all the documents are prepared and signed in advance, there must be a moment between the vesting and the creation of the mortgage during which the estoppel could be fed (see *Church of England Building Society* v *Piskor* [1954] Ch 553) but in *Abbey National Building Society* v *Cann* [1990] 2 WLR 832 an argument based on the 'scintilla of time' argument was rejected (though not in relation to a case of estoppel).

COVENANTS IN LEASES

Every lease, even the most informal, contains covenants which define the obligations of the landlord and tenant under the lease. In a formally granted long lease (e.g., 99 years) it is likely that these obligations will be detailed and complex, and will be embodied in a long document. In the case of an informal periodic tenancy the obligations will be few, and will, in the main, be implied into the agreement by operation of law. The effect of these obligations is crucial to the operation of leases and gives rise to two main issues:

(a)   the nature of the obligations placed upon the original contracting parties (the original landlord and tenant); and
(b)   the effect of those original obligations on those who later acquire the lease or the reversion.

Before examining the law on covenants in detail let us first consider some practical examples of the formats used for various leases.

Factual background

You will recall from the earlier part of this chapter that the basement flat at 2 Trant Way has been let by Fingall Forest, the fee simple owner, to his friend Gerald Gruyère at a rent of £30 per week. This agreement was made orally and no further terms were specified. Mr Gruyère has been in possession of the flat for some time and pays his rent regularly.

The fee simple in 6 Trant Way is owned by Irene Ivy. On 25 March 1984 Mrs Ivy granted a 20-year lease of the property to John Jarlsberg. The lease was made by deed and is in the following form:

THIS LEASE made the 25th day of March 1984 between IRENE IVY of 15 Proudie Street, Grantchester in Stilton (hereinafter called 'the landlord') of the one part and JOHN JARLSBERG of 63 Upper Terrace, Mousehole in Stilton (hereinafter called 'the tenant') of the other part WITNESSETH as follows:

1.   The landlord hereby demises unto the tenant ALL THAT messuage or dwelling-house, together with the garden, offices and outbuilding thereto belonging, known at 6 Trant Way, Mousehole in the County of Stilton, which premises for the purposes of identification only are outlined in red on the plan attached hereto, TO HOLD the same unto the tenant from the 25th day of March 1984 for the term of 20 years YIELDING AND PAYING therefor the yearly rent agreed or determined in accordance with the provisions of clause 2 hereof by equal quarterly instalments in advance on the usual quarter-days (the first payment to be made on the date hereof).

2.   (a)   The rent shall be £3,000 per annum for the first five years of the said term.

(b)   [Rent review clause for later portion of term.]

3.   The tenant hereby covenants with the landlord as follows:

(a)   To pay the rent hereby reserved on the days and in the manner aforesaid without any deductions whatsoever.

(b)   To pay all rates, taxes and outgoings of an annual or recurring nature in respect of the demised premises.

(c)   Not to use or permit the use of the demised premises or any part thereof otherwise than as a private dwelling-house.

(d)   Not without the prior written consent of the landlord to assign, sublet or part with possession of the whole or part of the demised premises.

[Further covenants by the tenant.]

4.   The landlord hereby COVENANTS with the tenant as follows:

(a)   That the tenant paying the rent hereby reserved and observing and performing the covenants on his part herein contained shall peaceably and quietly hold and enjoy the premises hereby demised during the said term without any interruption or disturbance by the landlord or any person claiming under or in trust for the landlord.

(b)   That if at any time during the continuance of the term hereby created the tenant shall desire to purchase the fee simple reversion in the demised premises the landlord on receipt of six months' notice in writing from the tenant shall assure the demised premises unto the tenant in fee simple in consideration of a sum equal to 95 per cent of the market value of the premises, such value to be assessed as at the date upon which such notice shall expire.

[Further covenants by the landlord.]

5.   PROVIDED ALWAYS and it is hereby expressly agreed and declared as follows:

(a) That if at any time the rent hereby reserved or any part thereof is 21 days in arrears (whether formally demanded or not) or if the tenant has failed to observe or perform any of the tenant's covenants herein contained, the landlord may re-enter upon the demised premises or any part thereof in the name of the whole and thereupon the term hereby granted shall absolutely determine but without prejudice to any claim by the landlord against the tenant for any antecedent breach of the covenants herein contained.

IN WITNESS whereof the hand and seal of the landlord and of the tenant have been hereunto set the day and year first above-written.

SIGNED SEALED AND DELIVERED

by the said landlord   [Signature of Irene Ivy] SEAL

in the presence of:

[Signed by witness]

SIGNED SEALED AND DELIVERED

by the said tenant   [Signature of John Jarlsberg] SEAL

in the presence of:

[Signed by witness]

[There follows a plan of the property.]

(Note that this lease was made before the Law of Property (Miscellaneous Provisions) Act 1989 came into force and thus it complies with the old formalities for a deed and was signed, sealed and delivered.)

The ground and first-floor maisonette of 2 Trant Way is to be let by Fingall Forest to Harry Harding. The lease term is to be 99 years and Mr Harding is to pay a premium of £50,000 and a ground rent of £35 per annum, for the first 10 years, £45 for the second 10 years and so on, rising to £125 for the last nine years. The draft lease, which has been prepared by Mr Forest's solicitor for approval by Mr Harding's legal adviser, is a very detailed document, which is over 40 pages long. In this lease, which will be made by deed, the tenant will undertake a long list of obligations, ranging from a promise not to keep pets to a covenant to contribute to the cost of maintaining the structure of the premises. The landlord will also enter into a number of covenants, including a covenant to keep the building insured (though the tenant will pay a share of the insurance premium).

WHAT IS A COVENANT?

A 'covenant' is a promise made by one party (the 'covenantor') for the benefit of another party (the 'covenantee') which is contained in a deed signed, witnessed and delivered by the covenantor. As all leases for more than three years should be made by deed (LPA 1925, s. 52), normally the promises made in the lease will be covenants. However, there is a problem in the case of shorter leases, which can be created informally (s. 54(2)) and which therefore will not require a deed. It appears, however, that the promises in such leases are still to be regarded as enforceable covenants and may even pass to bind successive owners of the property (see *Boyer* v *Warbey* [1953] 1 QB 234 which involved a written lease for three years, and *Weg Motors Ltd* v *Hales* [1962] Ch 49).

Covenants must be distinguished from 'conditions', which may also impose obligations on a tenant. As will be explained further below (p. 142), if a tenant breaks a condition in the lease the landlord will have an automatic right to bring the term to an end, whilst the landlord does not automatically have such a right for breach of covenant and must make express provision for it in the lease. The question of whether a particular term in a lease is a covenant or a condition is a matter which is decided by reference to the intention of the parties. A condition arises in cases in which it is clear that the continuance of the term is conditional upon the fulfilment of his obligations by the tenant. Generally the courts presume that the terms of the lease are covenants unless clear words are used to show that the obligation is intended to be a condition. Thus in *Doe* d *Henniker* v *Watt* (1828) 8 B & C 308 it was held that a term in which the tenant 'stipulated and conditioned' that he would not assign or sublet the property, was a condition rather than a covenant. In fact most obligations, even the most fundamental (e.g., to pay rent) will be covenants rather than conditions.

Types of covenant

Every lease, however simple, contains some covenants, because certain basic covenants by both landlord and tenant are implied into every lease. Some leases, typically long leases, contain in addition to (or in substitution for) the implied covenants a very large number of express covenants. It is not possible to include here a list of all possible covenants because there are huge variations in such matters depending on the circumstances. We will accordingly deal only with the implied covenants and the common express covenants. In addition there is a list of covenants, called the 'usual covenants', which are important in cases in which the grant of a lease is preceded by a contract to grant the lease (as is normal conveyancing procedure in the case of long leases). In such cases it is an implied term of the contract that the lease, once granted, will contain at least the 'usual covenants'. Accordingly, we have divided our discussion of the types of covenants into three parts:

(a) implied covenants;
(b) express covenants; and
(c) usual covenants.

IMPLIED COVENANTS

Covenants by the landlord

It should always be remembered that a lease is a reciprocal arrangement which accordingly imposes obligations on the landlord, as well as upon the tenant. Some of these obligations are of such fundamental importance and are so much part of the landlord and tenant relationship that they are implied into every lease. These covenants will all be implied into the oral lease of 2 Trant Way, made between Fingall Forest and Gerald Gruyère.

Covenant to allow tenant quiet enjoyment
A covenant by the landlord that the tenant is to be allowed *quiet enjoyment* of the premises is implied into every lease which does not already provide expressly for this (*Markham* v *Paget* [1908] 1 Ch 697). The effect of the covenant is that the landlord must let the tenant into possession of the premises and that the landlord will be liable if the tenant's enjoyment of the property is substantially disturbed by any action of the landlord or by the action of someone deriving an interest in the property from the landlord. The landlord is not responsible for the actions of unrelated third parties.

It should be noted that the covenant for 'quiet enjoyment' is not concerned with noise made by the landlord. It involves acts which prevent the tenant from using the demised premises. The creation of considerable amounts of noise might, of course, have this effect, but the word 'quiet' in this context means 'uninterrupted', rather than 'noiseless', enjoyment of the property.

An obvious example of the breach of this covenant is the case of *Perera* v *Vandiyar* [1953] 1 WLR 672 in which the landlord tried to force the tenant out of the premises by continual harrassment of a serious nature, including having the gas and electricity supplies to the property cut off. Such severe breach of a landlord's basic obligations can also amount to a criminal offence under s. 1(3) of the Protection from Eviction Act 1977 if the landlord's intention is to force the tenant to leave the premises or under s. 1(3A) where relevant (see p. 141).

It has also been held to be a breach of the covenant to erect scaffolding which prevents the tenant gaining access to the premises (*Owen* v *Gadd* [1956] 2 QB 99). Other examples of breach of this covenant include: removing the windows and doors (*Lavender* v *Betts* [1942] 2 All ER 72); persistently threatening the tenant in an attempt to force him to leave (*Kenny* v *Preen* [1963] 1 QB 499); and causing the land to subside by carrying out mining activities beneath the surface (*Markham* v *Paget* [1908] 1 Ch 697). It should be noted, however, that acts which merely inconvenience the tenant do not amount to a breach of the covenant, particularly if the act complained of occurs outside the demised area. Thus in *Browne* v *Flower* [1911] 1 Ch 219 a landlord who erected an external staircase, outside the demised premises, was held not to have broken the covenant even though persons using the new staircase were able to look in through the windows of the demised premises and the tenant was thereby deprived of his privacy.

A landlord may be liable under this covenant even if the act amounting to a breach is committed by a third party. He will only be liable, however, for the lawful actions of those deriving their title under him, or for the actions of his servants or agents within the scope of their authority. The landlord is not liable for actions committed by persons deriving their title from him who are acting in excess of their own legal rights. In *Sanderson v Berwick-upon-Tweed Corporation* (1884) 13 QBD 547, a tenant complained that he was unable to use the demised premises (a farm) in a normal way because of flooding caused by drains on two neighbouring farms which were also owned by the landlord. Both the neighbouring farms were also let to tenants. On one farm the drains were in good order but the flooding was caused by the excessive use of them by the tenant: here the tenant was acting in excess of his lawful rights. On the second farm the tenant was using the drains perfectly properly, but flooding was being caused by a defect in the drain: here the tenant was acting within his lawful rights. The landlord was held not to be liable for the damage caused by the actions of the first tenant, but was liable for damage caused by the actions of the second. See also *Celsteel Ltd v Alton House Holdings Ltd (No 2)* [1987] 1 WLR 291.

The landlord is not responsible for acts committed by a person with a title which is superior to (rather than derived from) the landlord's title. Such a superior title is described as a 'title paramount'. This rule creates a substantial danger for the tenant, as is demonstrated by the case of *Jones v Lavington* [1903] 1 KB 253. In that case a tenant, who had only $8\frac{1}{2}$ years left to run on his own lease, purported to grant a sublease of the property for $10\frac{1}{2}$ years. (This in fact operates as an assignment of the lease—see p. 106.) In due course the freehold owner recovered the property from the 'subtenant' two years before the 'sublease' should have ended. The 'subtenant' could not resist the claim of the freehold owner because the original tenant had no power to give more than he had got (*nemo dat quod non habet*) and could only give an $8\frac{1}{2}$ year term. An action by the 'subtenant' against the tenant also failed because the tenant was not liable for actions by someone with title paramount (the freehold owner).Thus, if a tenant is to pay a large premium for a lease it is in his own interests to insist on investigating the proposed landlord's title.

Landlord must not derogate from his grant
It is a general principle of law that you must not take away with one hand what you have given with the other, because to do so is to derogate from your grant (*Palmer v Fletcher* (1663) 1 Lev 122). To a certain extent this covenant overlaps with the covenant for quiet enjoyment but, since this covenant not to derogate from the grant can be broken without there being a physical interference with the use of the premises, it is still worth considering it separately. A good illustration of the point is provided by *Aldin v Latimer Clark, Muirhead & Co.* [1894] 2 Ch 437, in which premises had been let to a tenant subject to a covenant that the tenant would use the property to run the business of a timber merchant. The demised premises included a wood-drying shed which depended on a natural flow of air passing on to the demised premises from neighbouring property, which also belonged to the landlord. Buildings were erected on the neighbouring property which prevented the

free flow of air to the drying shed and thereby rendered it useless. This did not amount to a breach of the covenant for quiet enjoyment because there was no physical interference with the demised premises. These facts did, however, amount to a breach of the obligation placed on the landlord not to derogate from his grant, because the action complained of prevented the very use for which the demised premises had been let. Another example is provided by *Harmer* v *Jumbil (Nigeria) Tin Areas Ltd* [1921] 1 Ch 200, in which land was let to store explosives. In order to store such items the tenant had to obtain a licence and it was a condition of the licence that there should be no other buildings within a specified distance. Accordingly the tenant was entitled to prevent the landlord from building on neighbouring land, which he also owned, because this would lead to the loss of the tenant's licence and prevent him from using the premises for the purpose for which they were let. However, the tenant who relies on this principle must make it clear to the landlord at the time of the grant what use he has in mind for the land (*Robinson* v *Kilvert* (1889) 41 ChD 88). Also the act complained of must actually interfere with the contemplated use and it is not sufficient to say that the landlord's actions have made the use more expensive or less profitable (*Port* v *Griffith* [1938] 1 All ER 295—business on demised premises became less profitable because neighbouring property used for a similar business). Once again the landlord is liable also for the actions of persons deriving title from him (*Aldin* v *Latimer Clark, Muirhead & Co.*).

Covenant that premises are fit for the purpose for which they are let or are habitable
Subject to the obligations imposed by the previous two implied covenants, there is in general no implied covenant that the premises will be fit for any particular purpose.

This is true even where the premises are domestic in character and yet prove to be unfit for human habitation (*Lane* v *Cox* [1897] 1 QB 415). This general rule arises because of the application of the principle of *caveat emptor*: it is for the prospective tenant to examine the property and decide whether it is fit for his purpose. However, the general rule is modified to a certain extent by statute and, in one instance, by common law.

Where a house is let furnished   It is clear from a number of authorities that if a house is let furnished then it must be fit for human habitation at the start of the term (*Smith* v *Marrable* (1843) 11 M & W 5). Thus when a furnished property was let after inhabitation by a tubercular patient without being disinfected, the landlord was held to be liable for breach of this implied obligation (*Collins* v *Hopkins* [1923] 2 KB 617). It should be noted that this implied condition only relates to the state of the premises at the commencement of the term, and the landlord is not liable under this heading if the premises become unfit during the lease term (*Harrison* v *Malet* (1886) 3 TLR 58; *Sarson* v *Roberts* [1895] 2 QB 395).

Where a house is let at a low rent   A covenant by the landlord that the premises are fit for human habitation is implied into certain leases of dwellings by the Housing Act 1985, s. 8. The provision applies only where the property is let at a low rent, and the maximum rent prescribed is £80 a year (with lower levels in respect of property outside London and leases granted before 1957). These levels of rent are derived from earlier statutory rent controls, but, as a result, it seems that today very few premises will come within the provisions of the Act, and accordingly we will say no more about them.

Where a dwelling is let for a short term   Under ss. 11–14 of the Landlord and Tenant Act 1985, certain covenants by the landlord are implied into all leases of dwellings for a term of less than seven years. This includes a lease for a longer term if the landlord can end the term on notice in under seven years. The covenants implied are:

(a)   To keep the structure and exterior in repair.
(b)   To keep in repair and working order the facilities for the supply of water, gas, electricity, sanitation (e.g., baths and w.c.'s), space heating and heating of water.

The landlord is liable only once he has notice of the defect. The 1985 Act provisions have proved to be of limited assistance in the cases of leases of flats in large blocks because the wording of s. 11 has allowed landlords to argue successfully that their repairing obligations arose only in relation to the demised flat and did not cover defects in other parts of the building (see *Campden Hill Towers Ltd* v *Gardner* [1977] QB 823). This can give rise to considerable problems for a tenant concerned about a hole in the roof (unless the lease is of the top-floor flat) or a central-heating boiler which is in a basement and not within the demised premises. This problem has been addressed by the Housing Act 1988, s. 116, which applies to all short leases entered into on or after 15 January 1989. Now where the demised premises consist of a dwelling forming *part* of a building the landlord also impliedly covenants:

(a)   to keep in repair the exterior and structure of the building itself; and
(b)   to keep in repair and proper working order the installations which are covered by the Housing Act 1985, s. 11, which serve the demised premises, directly or indirectly.

In both cases the landlord only covenants in relation to the parts of the building in which he has an interest or over which he has control. Also the tenant can only enforce this covenant if his enjoyment of his own flat or the common parts of the building is impaired.

General duty of care   In addition to the implied obligations to repair mentioned above, a landlord may be under a general duty to see that all persons who might reasonably be expected to be affected by defects in the state of the premises are reasonably safe from injury or damage to their property caused by such defect. This duty will be owed to the tenant, and to other persons coming on to the property. The obligation does not arise from a covenant implied into the lease but from the statutory liability imposed in tort by s. 4 of the Defective Premises Act 1972. However, this liability only arises where the landlord is responsible for repairs under the terms of the lease. *Barrett* v *Lounova (1982) Ltd* [1990] 1 QB 348 indicates that in some cases a covenant on the part of the landlord to repair at least the exterior of the building may be implied where this is necessary to give business efficacy to the lease.

Under s. 1(1) of the Defective Premises Act 1972, the landlord will also be liable to any person who acquires an interest in a dwelling which was built by the landlord, or where the landlord has done any work in connection with its provision. The obligations imposed upon the landlord are to see that the work is done properly and that appropriate materials have been used and that, as regards the work done, the premises will be fit for habitation.

Covenants by the tenant

Certain covenants by the tenant are implied into all leases. These are dealt with below.

To pay rent

As we have already explained, it is perfectly possible to have a lease without an obligation to pay rent. Accordingly a covenant to pay rent will not be implied automatically into every lease. However, the payment of rent is usual and it will normally be the intention of the parties that it should be paid.

To pay rates and other taxes on the premises

The tenant is under an implied obligation to pay all the rates and taxes for which the landlord is not made expressly liable, either by the terms of the lease or under a rule of law. Because tenants are impliedly liable for the rates and similar obligations, such as the new council tax, on a property, they should take care to ascertain whether their rent is inclusive or exclusive before they enter into the agreement, as fairly large sums can be involved.

Liability for damage or disrepair

A tenant's implied duties in respect of damage or disrepair are usually said to arise from his liability for 'waste'. Waste may be defined as an act or omission which alters the state of the land, and it can even include changes which *improve* the land ('ameliorating waste'). We are concerned here, however, with the sort of behaviour which may damage the property and it is usual to divide such waste into two categories: 'voluntary waste', which consists of doing something which should not be done (e.g., knocking down a wall), and 'permissive waste', which consists of leaving undone something which ought to be done (e.g., allowing a wall to fall down). The distinction is therefore between causing damage and failing to repair damage which occurs without the tenant doing anything. The extent of liability for waste depends on the type of lease involved and so we will consider the various leases separately.

Weekly tenancies Generally the rule is that a weekly tenant is liable for voluntary waste but not for permissive waste: in other words he may not knock a wall down but he can let it fall down (*Mint* v *Good* [1951] 1 KB 517). The duty is increased beyond this point, however, by the further rule that he must use the premises in a 'tenant-like manner' (*Warren* v *Keen* [1954] 1 QB 15). This means that the tenant must clean the premises, mend the electric light if it is fused, unstop blocked sinks and generally 'do the little jobs about the place which a reasonable tenant would do'. The exact duties of the tenant under this heading are not entirely clear, however, and each case must be judged on its facts.

Monthly and quarterly tenants The rules here seem to be the same as for a weekly tenancy.

Yearly tenants The position here is similar to that of other periodic tenants save that additionally a yearly tenant is deemed to be obliged to keep the premises wind and water-right (*Wedd* v *Porter* [1916] 2 KB 91). This obligation is, however, rather watered down by the further rule that the tenant is not liable for 'fair wear and tear' (*Warren* v *Keen* [1954] 1 QB 15). This means that he is not responsible for the gradual deterioration caused by normal use or by the normal action of the elements (*Haskell* v *Marlow* [1928] 2 KB 45), so that he does not have to replace stone steps which are worn down by use or tiles which are blown off the roof by the wind.

Tenants with fixed terms A tenant with a fixed term of years is certainly liable for voluntary waste and the better view seems to be that he is also liable for permissive waste (Statute of Marlborough 1267, c. 23; *Harnett* v *Maitland* (1847) 16 M & W 257; *Yellowly* v *Gower* (1855) 11 Exch 274. Thus it is an implied term that such a tenant should maintain the premises in the condition in which he received them at the start of the term.

Obligation to allow landlord entry In general, as the tenant has exclusive possession, he may exclude the landlord from the premises. However, a term will be implied that the landlord is to be allowed to enter the premises if the landlord is under a duty to repair (*Saner* v *Bilton* (1876) 7 ChD 815). This will give the landlord a right, to be exercised reasonably, to enter and inspect and carry out necessary repairs. A similar implied term is also included where statutory provisions require a landlord to repair.

EXPRESS COVENANTS

In most leases, the parties will not need to rely on the implied covenants because they will be supplanted or supplemented, by express covenants in the agreement. If, however, a lease contains express covenants but is silent on certain issues (e.g., contains no covenant referring to quiet enjoyment), the usual implied term will be added to the express terms in the lease. As we have already said, it is quite impossible for us to set out all the express covenants which may be included in a lease, and all we can do here is to mention the more important express covenants and discuss general matters of construction. One point which can be made about all express covenants is that usually covenants will be construed strictly against the landlord, since it is he who was responsible for the form of the lease.

Rent

Very few leases are concluded without there being an express agreement between the parties about the payment of rent. It is a general rule that the rent must be certain (a court cannot enforce an uncertain agreement) but this rule may be satisfied by providing a means whereby the rent is to be determined (e.g., rent to be set by a surveyor chosen by a named body—*Lloyds Bank Ltd* v *Marcan* [1973] 1 WLR 339, affirmed [1973] 1 WLR 1387). It is also common to include a clause whereby the rent is to be reviewed (usually with a view to increasing it) at intervals during the lease: see clause 2(b) in the lease on p. 117. (A great deal of case law on the interpretation of such rent-review clauses exists but this is beyond the scope of this text. For further information you should consult a specialist text on landlord and tenant law.)

Tenant's covenants not to assign, sublet or part with possession

A tenant is the owner of a legal estate in land and it is a basic principle of English law that an estate in land is freely alienable. However, the right to sell, or otherwise dispose of, an estate can be limited if the estate owner enters into a covenant to that effect. Most landlords take great care when selecting tenants (e.g., to ensure that they are of good character and can pay the rent) and, quite reasonably, will wish to ensure that the premises do not come into the hands of some less desirable person through assignment or subletting. Accordingly it is common to include in a lease a covenant which restricts the tenant's right to assign, sublet or otherwise part with possession of the demised premises. These covenants come in two forms:

(a) An absolute covenant against assigning etc.
(b) A covenant not to assign etc. without the landlord's consent.

In the case of the absolute covenant, it is, of course, open to the tenant to ask the landlord if he will allow a particular disposition, but the landlord is under no obligation to agree to this, even if he is acting quite unreasonably in refusing. However, if the covenant is in the second form (which is usual) that the tenant may not assign etc. *without consent*, the position is affected by s. 19(1)(a) of the Landlord and Tenant Act 1927, which implies into such a covenant the proviso that 'consent is not to be unreasonably withheld'. The burden of proving that the landlord has acted unreasonably in refusing his consent lies upon the tenant.

  Where the covenant is qualified in its form, s. 1(1) of the Landlord and Tenant Act 1988, imposes upon the landlord a statutory duty to make a decision, once his consent is requested, within a reasonable time of the tenant's application. This statute also provides that if the landlord's consent is sought in writing the landlord must either give consent or justify his refusal as being reasonable. Under the Act instead of the tenant having to establish that consent has been refused unreasonably, the burden of proof is shifted to the landlord, who must prove that the refusal was reasonable. Also the statute provides a statutory tort committed by the landlord who unreasonably will not consent. This will allow the tenant to obtain damages or to seek an injunction. In the past the only possible remedy was to obtain a declaration.

By virtue of the Housing Act 1988, s. 15, where a tenancy is an assured tenancy under that statute (and in future many leases will fall into this category) a covenant will be implied into the lease that the tenant may not assign the tenancy, or sublet, or part with possession of the whole or any part of the premises without the landlord's consent. Unfortunately for the tenant in such cases the Landlord and Tenant Act 1927, s. 19, is expressly excluded and accordingly the Landlord and Tenant Act 1988, s. 1(1), also will not apply. In such cases a tenant would be best advised to make an express provision in the contractual lease with the landlord but undoubtedly many will not.

The question then arises how one knows whether consent is being withheld unreasonably. The nearest approach to a general principle is to be found in the statement of the Court of Appeal in *Houlder Bros* v *Gibbs* [1925] 1 Ch 575: to be an acceptable reason for refusal of consent, an objection must relate to the personality of the intended assignee or to the use which he is likely to make of the property. This can be a helpful guide, but it does have the effect of excluding a number of reasons which, to the landlord at least, may well seem good. Thus in *Houlder Bros* v *Gibbs* the assignment was opposed because the proposed assignee already occupied other property belonging to the landlord, who feared that if the assignment was permitted, the assignee would give up the other property, which would be difficult to relet. This quite understandable reason was rejected by the Court of Appeal, which took the view that a refusal was not reasonable where 'the reason given is independent of the relationship between the lessor and the lessee, and on the grounds which are entirely personal to the lessor and wholly extraneous to the lessee' (at p. 583). This view has been criticised by the House of Lords in *Tredegar* v *Harwood* [1929] AC 72, but although their lordships were again considering what constitutes unreasonable refusal, they were not dealing with a covenant against assignment. Their views of *Houlder Bros* v *Gibbs*, although always referred to with respect, are no more than *obiter dicta*, and the Court of Appeal has continued to refer with approval to its earlier decision (see, for example, *Bickel* v *Duke of Westminster* [1977] QB 517 and *International Drilling Fluids Ltd* v *Louisville Investments (Uxbridge) Ltd* [1986] Ch 513).

In addition to applying the *Houlder Bros* principle, it is also often helpful to consider previous decisions on specific grounds of refusal. For example, it has been held unreasonable to refuse consent on the ground that a proposed tenant has diplomatic immunity (*Parker* v *Boggon* [1947] KB 346) or because the landlord wants to recover possession for himself (*Bates* v *Donaldson* [1896] 2 QB 241). It is also unreasonable to refuse consent on grounds of race, religion or sex, unless the landlord or his relative shares facilities with the tenant (Race Relations Act 1976, s. 24 and Housing Act 1988, s. 137; Sex Discrimination Act 1975).

Examples of acceptable reasons for refusal include: the unsatisfactory nature of the assignee's references (*Shanly* v *Ward* (1913) 29 TLR 714); the fact that the proposed assignment would interfere with the future development of the property (*Pimms Ltd* v *Tallow Chandlers Co.* [1964] 2 QB 547); and the proposed use of the premises in competition with the landlord's own business (*Premier Confectionery (London) Co. Ltd* v *London Commercial Sale Rooms Ltd* [1933] Ch 904).

Finally, it should be remembered that, although consideration of earlier decisions and of the views of the Court of Appeal in *Houlder Bros* v *Gibbs*, may help in predicting whether a refusal will be held to be reasonable, the question in each case is one of fact, and the court's decision must depend on all the circumstances of the particular case (*International Drilling Fluids Ltd* v *Louisville Investments (Uxbridge) Ltd*).

With a covenant not to assign etc. without consent the tenant should, of course, ensure that he does ask the landlord for permission. However, if the tenant asks for permission and it is refused there are two courses of action open to him:

(a)   He may seek a declaration from the court that the landlord's refusal is unreasonable and that he is therefore entitled to assign, sublet or part with possession or seek an injunction under the Landlord and Tenant Act 1988.

(b)   He may take the risk and make the disposition, which will be effective even if it is in breach of covenant (*Parker* v *Jones* [1910] 2 KB 32). If the tenant takes this second course it is then open to the landlord to take action against the tenant for breach of covenant, and the tenant will have a defence to the action if he can show that the landlord's refusal was unreasonable (*Ideal Film Renting Co.* v *Nielson* [1921] 1 Ch 575). It should be remembered, however, that the proposed assignee or subtenant may well refuse to proceed unless the landlord's consent has been obtained, as to do otherwise could well cause him problems in the future (see *Southern Depot Co.* v *British Railways Board* [1990] 33 EG 45).

It should be noted that covenants of this type are strictly interpreted. Accordingly a covenant forbidding 'assigning' does not prevent the creation of a subtenancy or a licence; similarly a covenant against 'subletting' does not prevent an assignment or the creation of a licence. Attention should therefore be given to the exact wording of the covenant in question (*Sweet & Maxwell Ltd* v *Universal News Services Ltd* [1964] 2 QB 699; *Re Doyle and O'Hara's Contract* [1899] IR 113). Similarly a tenant should take care when applying for a licence under such a provision, for should he obtain a licence to sublet the premises he will nonetheless be in breach of the covenant if thereafter he mistakenly assigns the property.

Covenants concerning repairs

Most leases for any period other than the shortest will contain detailed covenants obliging the landlord or the tenant to effect certain repairs. These covenants vary considerably with the circumstances, but in the case of a long lease (e.g., 99 years) it is quite normal for the tenant to be obliged to undertake all necessary repairs, including structural repairs to buildings. In shorter leases the burden may well be shared, with the tenant undertaking to decorate and to carry out internal repairs, whilst the landlord agrees to maintain the structure. Generally any liability of the landlord does not arise until he is given notice that the repair is required (*Makin* v *Watkinson* (1870) LR 6 Ex 25). Where he is obliged to repair, the landlord will have an implied right to enter the premises in order to inspect, but this right must be exercised reasonably. A covenant 'to repair' involves not only the maintenance of the existing property but will include replacement of parts which are irreparable (*Lurcott* v *Wakeley* [1911] 1 KB 905) and even complete rebuilding if the structure is destroyed, e.g., by fire (*Bullock* v *Dommitt* (1796) 2 Chit 608). Obviously it is wise to insure against such risks.

Covenants to insure

In some cases the landlord will covenant to insure premises (though the tenant may have to agree to pay some, or all, of the premium), whilst in others the tenant will undertake this obligation. Such covenants will be broken if the property is uninsured for any period, however, short, and even if no damage occurs during that time (*Penniall* v *Harborne* (1848) 11 QB 368).

Other covenants generally

The covenants mentioned above are only examples of the more common covenants. There are many other covenants in common use, e.g., covenants about noise levels, keeping animals, not erecting signs or other external additions (e.g., window-boxes) and many others. One common covenant is a covenant restricting the use of the premises, e.g., to use as 'a private dwelling only' or for a particular type of business. It is quite impossible to give a catalogue of all types of covenants because the covenants in common use will vary as the needs of modern life change. Covenants against the erection of satellite dishes to receive television broadcasts from other countries provide a new example and perhaps one day a covenant forbidding assigning or subletting to extraterrestial non-humanoids will appear! In the world of covenants anything is possible.

USUAL COVENANTS

We cannot end our general discussion of covenants in leases without mentioning the class of such agreements which is normally described as 'the usual covenants'. In any instance in which the grant of a lease is preceded by a contractual agreement, it is an implied term of that contract that the lease, when granted, will contain the usual covenants (*Propert* v *Parker* (1832) 3 My & K 280) and the lease may therefore be rectified if these are not included when it is granted. The class of usual covenants is not entirely fixed and will vary depending on the area in which the property stands or because of the nature of a trade run on the premises. In *Flexman* v *Corbett* [1930]

1 Ch 672, it was suggested that a covenant must be regarded as 'usual' if nine out of ten leases of the same kind would include the term. It was also pointed out that 'what is normal in Mayfair or Bayswater is not usual . . . in Whitechapel' (per Maugham J at p. 678). The following covenants are, however, always regarded as 'usual':

(a)   That the tenant will pay rent.
(b)   That the tenant will pay rates and taxes (other than those which must, by statutory provision, be borne by the landlord).
(c)   That the tenant will keep the premises in repair.
(d)   That, if the landlord has expressly covenanted to repair, he will be allowed reasonable access to view and repair the premises.
(e)   That the landlord will allow the tenant quiet enjoyment and that he will not derogate from his grant.
(f)   That the landlord will have a right to re-enter should the tenant fail to pay his rent (but not in the case of the breach of other covenants)

(For a more recent case on usual covenants, see *Chester* v *Buckingham Travel Ltd* [1981] 1 WLR 96.)

EFFECT OF COVENANTS ON THE ORIGINAL PARTIES TO A LEASE AND THEIR SUCCESSORS

Having identified the covenants which are in common use we need now to consider the question of the effect these covenants have on the original parties to the lease, their successors in title and persons who derive their title under such persons. These may conveniently be dealt with in two stages as follows:

(a)   The original parties to the covenant.
(b)   Persons other than the original parties to the lease.

Original parties to the lease

There is little problem when one is dealing with either of the original parties to a covenant contained in a lease, because between the original landlord and tenant there will be privity of contract, with the result that either party can enforce an obligation against the other, as is normal in the case of any contractual promise.

This contractual obligation will usually continue even if the covenanting party has disposed of his interest in the property, for generally covenants are so phrased that they relate not only to the covenantor's acts and omissions but also to those of his successors in title and persons deriving title under him. Even if the covenantor does not covenant expressly in these terms, they will be implied into the covenant by LPA 1925, s. 79, unless clearly excluded by the wording of the covenant. Accordingly, in normal circumstances an original tenant covenants not only about his own conduct, but also about that of his assignees ('successors in title') and subtenants ('persons deriving title under him'). Thus, if a tenant covenants that he will not do a specified act, he can still be sued by the landlord even after he has disposed of his whole estate and despite the fact that the act complained of is that of his assignee, for he is in breach of his covenant that neither he nor his successors will do that act (*Thursby* v *Plant* (1690) 1 Wms Saund 230).

Accordingly, the original tenant will remain liable throughout the whole term of the lease for any breach of covenant by his successors in title. This rule does produce unfair results in some cases and accordingly the Law Commission has recommended that the original tenant's continuing liability should be removed (Law Comm., Working Paper 95).

As we will see later, the burden of most covenants in a lease will pass on the assignment of the lease or the reversion, so that the new estate owner will become personally liable for any breach. This means that the covenantee often has a choice between suing the present estate owner, who has caused the breach, or proceeding against the original covenantor. It is usually more convenient to proceed against the present owner, if only because it is easier to find him, but if he should disappear, or be not worth suing, it may be better to try to recover from the original covenantor.

If the original covenantor does have to compensate for breach of covenant, he will naturally went to recoup his losses and may do so in one of two ways. To illustrate this, we will assume a series of assignments of a lease, which may be shown diagrammatically as follows:

L has recovered damages from T in respect of a breach of covenant by A3, and two courses of action are now open to T. He may seek to recover directly from A3, relying on the rule in *Moule* v *Garrett* (1872) LR 7 Ex 101 that 'where one person is compelled to pay damages by the legal default of another, he is entitled to recover from [that person] the sum so paid'. However, the fact that L preferred to sue T may suggest to T that it will not be worthwhile to proceed against A3 and so he may prefer the second choice, of going against his own assignee, A1. He is able to do this because, by virtue of LPA 1925, s. 77, any assignment of a lease includes an implied covenant by the assignee to indemnify the assignor for any breach of covenant in the lease.

Thus, T may sue A1, because A1 covenanted to indemnify T against such claims. Thereafter, A1 may sue A2 and A2 may sue A3, also on the basis of the s. 77 covenant which is implied into every assignment.

It is, of course, important to realise that in the situations we have just been considering, where a plaintiff has a choice of whom to sue, he can recover only one set of damages, and there is no question of his gaining double compensation by proceeding against two different defendants in respect of the same breach of covenant.

In the circumstances given in the diagram above, if the landlord, L, had been in breach of covenant during the currency of A2's tenancy, A2 may still sue L for damages even after he has assigned the lease to A3. This right may be valuable if A2 has spent money remedying a breach for which L was responsible and which had to be remedied before A3 would consent to purchase the lease (see *City & Metropolitan Properties Ltd* v *Greycroft Ltd* [1987] 1 WLR 1085). However, if in the example given, A1 and A3 were insolvent, it has been held that T cannot compel A1 to sue A2 in order to ensure that A2 pays the landlord. Thus in *In re Mirror Group (Holdings) Ltd, The Times,* 12 November 1992, it was held that in these circumstances T had to pay the landlord but had no means of recovering the cost because the right to sue the insolvent A1 for the sums so paid was worthless.

As we have seen, landlords also enter into covenants in leases. Once again the original landlord will be liable for breach of contract should he fail to meet his obligations. He also will be liable to the original tenant should an assignee of the reversion break a covenant.

Thus in the situation:

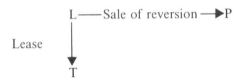

L will be liable to T for breach of contract if P (the purchaser of the fee simple reversion) breaks one of the landlord's covenants in the lease. Once again, the landlord is presumed to have covenanted for himself, his successors in title and those deriving title under him or them (LPA 1925, s. 79).

It should be noted, however, that when he assigns the reversion to P, the original landlord, L, will loose his right to sue the original tenant, T. At one time L could have sued T, even though L had ceased to have any interest in the property, because there was still a contractual obligation between T and L (although only nominal damages would be available as L would suffer little loss). However, due to s. 141 of LPA 1925 it now appears that on sale of the reversion the original landlord divests himself of all rights to enforce the covenant (*Arlesford Trading Co. Ltd* v *Servansingh* [1971] 1 WLR 1080 and *Re King* [1963] Ch 459). Thus in the example given L could no longer bring an action for breach of covenant against T.

Persons other than the original parties to the covenant

Although, as we have seen, the original covenantor remains liable for breach of covenant, most covenantees would in general find it more convenient to proceed against the person who has actually caused the breach. Accordingly, it is often essential to know whether an assignee or subtenant of a covenanting tenant, or a purchaser of a reversion from a covenanting landlord, can be made directly liable for breaches of covenant. Similarly such an assignee, subtenant or purchaser may well wish to know whether he has a right to enforce the original covenants in the lease. The problem here is that such a person is a later arrival on the scene, and is not a party to the contract between the original landlord and tenant. As it is a basic principle of contract law that a contract cannot be enforced against someone who is not privy to the contract, one might foresee difficulties arising. However, because of the unusual situation which arises in relation to leases, a second doctrine, that of 'privity of estate', has developed alongside the doctrine of privity of contract.

Privity of estate
There is said to be privity of estate when two persons, even though they have not contracted with one another, have a relationship of tenure with one another. In other words privity of estate arises when there is a relationship of landlord and tenant between the parties. If the following situation exists:

then there is both privity of contract and privity of estate between L and T. If T later assigns his lease to A there will be privity of contract between L and T (and between T and A because of the assignment) but privity of estate between L and A. After the assignment L becomes A's landlord and A becomes T's tenant.

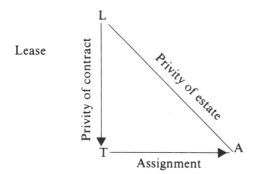

Similarly, if the landlord, L, sells the reversion to P, a purchaser, there will continue to be privity of contract between L and T (and between L and P because of the sale) but there will be privity of estate between T and P:

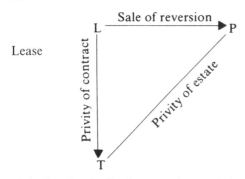

If the landlord sells the reversion and the tenant assigns the lease the situation illustrated below will arise:

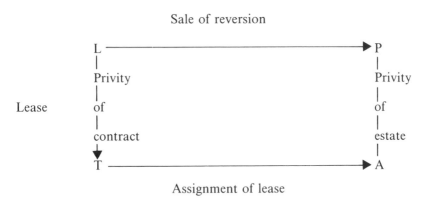

Thus there would be privity of estate between the purchaser of the reversion, P, and the assignee of the lease, A; they are, respectively, the new landlord and the new tenant.

If, however, T, instead of assigning, creates a sublease, we get a different situation. In such a case the subtenant, S, is the tenant of T and has no landlord and tenant relationship with L. Accordingly there is no privity of estate between S and L, but there is both privity of contract and privity of estate between T and S. This can be expressed in diagrammatic form as follows:

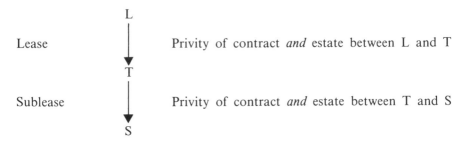

As can be seen, there is no direct relationship between L and S because T is in the way. If S assigns the sublease and L sells the fee simple reversion the following result is achieved:

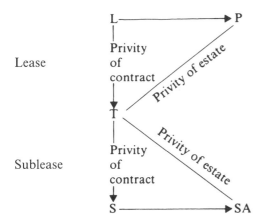

P has become T's landlord and there is privity of estate between them. SA has become T's tenant and there is privity of estate between them. There is no relationship between P and SA.

This pattern of privity of estate is important because, as we shall see below, certain covenants are enforceable between parties who are linked by privity of estate, as well as between parties linked by privity of contract. Save for the important exception of restrictive covenants, which are discussed in chapter 9 (see p. 319), covenants are not enforceable in the absence of privity of contract or estate. Therefore, in the diagram given above, P may well be able to enforce certain covenants against T but will be unable to enforce any covenants against SA, with whom he has no privity of contract or estate. SA will, however, be liable to T for breaches of certain covenants contained in the sublease because there is privity of estate between T and SA.

We must now consider which covenants can be enforced only between the original parties to the lease and which covenants will pass on assignment so that they will be enforced between the new landlord and tenant. It is convenient to deal with the assignment of the lease and the assignment of the reversion separately, as the rules which apply to each are slightly different.

Running of covenants on assignment of a lease

The rule which applies when a tenant assigns a lease is that the assignee will acquire the burden and the benefit of all covenants in the lease which 'touch and concern' the demised premises. This rule is derived from the venerable *Spencer's Case* (1583) 5 Co Rep 16a, in which it was held that a covenant made by a tenant to build a brick wall on the premises could be enforced against an assignee of the tenant. Thus for a third party to be affected by a covenant in a lease two things have to be established:

(a) that there is a privity of estate between the third party and the person seeking to enforce, or against whom enforcement is sought; and

(b) that the relevant covenant 'touches and concerns' the demised premises.

Thus it was said in *Spencer's Case* that if the tenant covenants to build a wall on other property belonging to the landlord, that covenant will not bind an assignee of the tenant because it does not 'touch and concern' the demised premises. In addition at the date of *Spencer's Case*, one had to establish that the original covenantor had covenanted on behalf of his assigns and successors in title, as well as for himself This requirement is now presumed by virtue of LPA 1925, s. 79, but may be excluded by clear words to the contrary. If for some reason (e.g., the covenant does not 'touch and concern' the demised property) the covenant cannot be enforced against the assignee, it can still be enforced against the original covenantor.

Under the rule in *Spencer's Case*, the assignee acquires not only the burden of certain covenants in the lease, but may also receive the right to enforce such of the landlord's covenants as 'touch and concern' the land.

Meaning of 'touching and concerning'
Unfortunately it is almost impossible to construct a simple test for covenants which will satisfy the *Spencer's Case* test of 'touching and concerning' the land. In *Breams Property Investment Co. Ltd* v *Stroulger* [1948] 2 KB 1 it was said that covenants fall into this class if they affect the landlord *qua* (as) landlord and the tenant *qua* tenant. It may be thought that this only substitutes one formula for another, and is not particularly helpful in practice. It does however draw attention to *Woodall* v *Clifton* [1905] 2 Ch 257, in which it was held that an agreement by the landlord giving the tenant an option to purchase the premises did not come within the rule in *Spencer's Case*, because the covenant does not affect the parties as landlord and tenant but as vendor and purchaser. (Such an option requires registration, where land is unregistered—see *Phillips* v *Mobil Oil Co. Ltd* [1989] 1 WLR 888). This certainly illustrates the point that not all covenants which appear to concern the land which is the subject of the lease will fall within the rule and pass on assignment. Non-competition clauses (*Congleton Corporation* v *Pattison* (1808) 10 East 130; *Thomas* v *Hayward* (1869) LR 4 Ex 311), covenants to keep other premises in repair (*Dewar* v *Goodman* [1909] AC 72), and covenants to repair chattels which are not fixed to the land (*Williams* v *Earle* (1868) LR 3 QB 739; *Gorton* v *Gregory* (1862) 3 B & S 90) are all covenants which have been held not to touch and concern the land. It would be impossible to compile a complete list of all covenants which do satisfy the rule in *Spencer's Case* but all the implied and common covenants which are set out in the earlier part of this chapter will do so.

Legal leases not made by deed
At the date at which *Spencer's Case* was decided it was clear that the rule, since it operates at law, only applied to legal leases made by deed. However, it was held in *Boyer* v *Warbey* [1953] 1 QB 234 that the rule could also apply

to a written lease for not more than three years which created a legal estate by virtue of LPA 1925, s. 54(2). Accordingly a covenant made by the tenant to pay £40 to the landlord at the end of the term (towards repairs) ran to bind an assignee of the legal written lease. It is probable that the same situation applies to oral leases within the s. 54(2) exception (but see *Elliott* v *Johnson* (1866) LR 2 QB 120). We have already seen that covenants do not run in the absence of a legal estate (p. 104).

Running of covenants on assignment of reversion

The rules which apply to a purchaser of the reversion from the landlord are similar to those which apply to the tenant's assignee, but are covered by statutory rules under LPA 1925, ss. 141 and 142. The rule here is that covenants run to bind and benefit a purchaser where the covenant 'has reference to the subject-matter of the lease'. (Since this is a statutory rule there is no requirement that there should be privity of estate: *Arlesford Trading Co. Ltd* v *Servansingh* [1971] 1 WLR 1080.) The statutory phrase 'having reference to the subject-matter of the lease' seems to be identical to the common law test of covenants 'touching and concerning the land' and the remarks made above on that test will also apply here. Due to the wording of s. 141, once the reversion has been transferred, the purchaser acquires the right to sue for breaches of covenant which were committed even before he acquired the reversion, and the previous owner of the reversion will lose the right to sue, since *all* benefits pass under the section to the acquirer of the reversion.

Position of subtenants

As we have seen, the rule in *Spencer's Case* (1583) 5 Co Rep 16a cannot apply to subtenants, because there is no privity of estate between a subtenant and the head landlord. Accordingly covenants in the head lease are not usually enforceable against a subtenant. However, since the tenant can be held liable for the actions of persons who derive their title from him (see p. 135), he will normally take the precaution of including in the sublease the same set of covenants which he himself has entered into in the head lease. This will allow the tenant to take action against the subtenant for breach of the covenant and thereby to protect himself against liability to his landlord (see p. 145).

The only occasion upon which a covenant can be enforced by the head landlord against a subtenant is where the covenant satisfies the rules in *Tulk* v *Moxhay* (1848) 2 Ph 774 which are dealt with in chapter 9.

A subtenant can receive the benefit of a covenant made by the landlord, because it is a general rule that the benefit, although not the burden, of a chose in action can be assigned. Such assignments should be made in writing and the person bound by the covenant (the landlord) should be notified (LPA 1925, s. 136(1)). Such express assignments will be very rare, as normally the tenant will wish to retain the benefit of the landlord's covenants himself (after all, he has to shoulder the burden of the lease and of the tenant's covenants).

Examples of application of the rules

Example 1
Some time ago, John Jarlsberg, the tenant of 6 Trant Way (see p. 116), obtained permission from his landlord, Irene Ivy, to assign his lease and thereafter assigned it to Keith Kale. Later, Irene Ivy sold the fee simple estate in 6 Trant Way to Liam Lyle, who has recently been registered as proprietor of the estate. Keith Kale has now decided that he would like to take advantage of the option to purchase which was given to the original tenant by the original lease made between Mrs Ivy and Mr Jarlesberg (clause 4(b), see p. 117). Mr Kale has served written notice on Mr Lyle of his intentions.
    In this situation we must consider:

(a)   which of the terms in the original lease bind or benefit Mr Kale, the tenant's assignee; and
(b)   which of the terms bind or benefit Mr Lyle, the purchaser of the freehold reversion.

The situation may be expressed diagrammatically as follows:

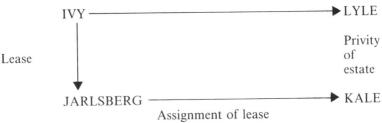

As a result of the transactions which have occurred, Mr Lyle is now Mr Kale's landlord. There is privity of estate between them. Mr Lyle will be bound by any of the landlord's covenants (LPA 1925, s. 142) and will benefit from any of the tenant's covenants (s. 141) in the original lease which have 'reference to the subject-matter thereof'. Similarly Mr Kale will automatically receive both the benefit and the burden of any covenants in the original lease which 'touch and concern' the land (*Spencer's Case* (1583) 5 Co Rep 16a).
    Accordingly Mr Kale is bound to pay the rent and to comply with the covenants preventing him from using the premises otherwise than as a dwelling and requiring him to obtain the landlord's permission before he assigns or sublets; he will also have the right to enforce the landlord's covenant for quiet enjoyment. All these covenants 'touch and concern' the land. Similarly Mr Lyle will be able to enforce the tenant's covenants against Mr Kale and will be bound by the covenant for quiet enjoyment, because the covenants have 'reference to the subject-matter' of the lease.
    The situation with regard to the option to purchase is not, however, the same, for it has been held that this covenant does not touch and concern the land; the option does not affect the parties *qua* landlord and tenant but *qua* vendor and purchaser (*Woodall* v *Clifton* [1905] 2 Ch 257). Accordingly, this right does not automatically benefit or burden Mr Kale and Mr Lyle.

The option did, however, give the original tenant, Mr Jarlsberg, an equitable interest in the fee simple estate. The benefit of that right can be assigned to Mr Kale, as can the benefit of any chose in action, but a clear assignment of the right will be required if Mr Kale is to establish a claim to it.

Even if Mr Kale can prove that the benefit of the right has been assigned to him he must still establish that the option is binding on Mr Lyle, who is a purchaser of the legal estate in fee simple. Mr Lyle will be bound by the equitable interest only if it has been protected as a C(iv) land charge before he purchased the fee simple (he will have used the unregistered conveyancing procedure and thereafter have made a first registration of title): see *Phillips* v *Mobil Oil Co. Ltd* [1989] 1 WLR 888. If the option has not been registered it will not bind Mr Lyle and cannot be enforced against him.

Finally, it may be helpful to mention that at one time the Rule against Perpetuities (see chapter 5) would have prevented the enforcement of the option by Mr Kale against Mr Lyle (*Woodall* v *Clifton* [1905] 2 Ch 257), but that this obstacle has now been removed by s. 9 of the Perpetuities and Accumulations Act 1964.

Example 2
7 Trant Way is owned in fee simple by Martin Mount. The property is divided into two flats, 7a and 7b. The entire property was let to Nigel Norman in 1982 for 99 years. The lease was made by deed and included a number of covenants on the part of Mr Norman, including covenants to pay rent, at present of £500 per month, to keep the property in good repair and not to use the premises for business purposes. Mr Norman has been registered as proprietor with leasehold title absolute. Immediately after completion of the lease, Mr Norman sublet flat 7a to Olav Orion and flat 7b to Paula Primrose. The two subtenants both have monthly tenancies, which were granted in writing and which contain covenants identical in form to those in the headlease. In 1984 Mr Norman assigned the head lease to Quentin Quick.

This situation can be expressed diagrammatically (see below).

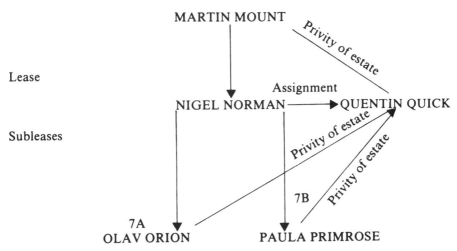

As a result, Mr Mount can enforce the tenant's covenants in the head lease against Mr Quick, because there is privity of estate between them. There is, however, no privity of estate between Mr Mount and Mr Orion, nor between Mr Mount and Miss Primrose, and so Mr Mount cannot take any action against either of the subtenants for breach of covenant (subject to the special rules in *Tulk* v *Moxhay* (1848) 2 Ph 774, for which see chapter 9). There is privity of estate between Mr Quick and Mr Orion, and Mr Quick and Miss Primrose, and so Mr Quick could enforce any of the covenants in the subleases against Mr Orion or Miss Primrose. Accordingly, should Mr Orion break a covenant, Mr Mount may sue only Mr Quick (who in the absence of any provisions excluding the operation of LPA 1925, s. 79, is responsible for the actions of persons deriving title under him) and Mr Quick should then sue Mr Orion.

Having considered the occasions upon which covenants in leases can be enforced we must now examine the methods which may be adopted to enforce such covenants.

ENFORCEMENT OF COVENANTS IN LEASES

Where a party to a lease is in breach of covenant, the usual battery of contractual remedies is available to the other party. Thus if a landlord is in breach of his covenant to repair, the tenant may seek an order for specific performance, although it should be noted that this remedy is not available if the party seeking to enforce is also in breach of covenant (*Jeune* v *Queen's Cross Properties Ltd* [1974] Ch 97) because specific performance is an equitable remedy and the person seeking it must have 'clean hands'. Similarly, if a tenant uses the premises to run a business, contrary to a covenant to use the premises only as a dwelling, the landlord could seek an injunction to restrain the breach. Further, either party might decide to claim damages for breach of contract as an alternative or additional remedy. However, in addition to these usual remedies there may be others available which are peculiar to leases. In particular, a tenant may be concerned to avoid a direct confrontation in the courts with his landlord (possibly because the tenant cannot afford the legal costs) and yet want to ensure that repairs to the property are made. Similarly, a landlord may wish to rid himself entirely of a tenant who has proved to be unreliable. We will accordingly consider here the special remedies available to landlords or tenants, though the availability of standard contractual remedies should not be forgotten.

Tenant's remedies against a defaulting landlord

Tenants' most frequent complaints against their landlords relate either to failure to comply with repairing covenants or, sometimes, to treatment which is calculated to drive the tenant out of the premises. The latter behaviour, whilst being breach of the covenant of quiet enjoyment, may also amount to the criminal offence of harassment. This offence is committed where acts are done which are likely to interfere with the tenant's peace or comfort or where services, reasonably required for occupation of the premises as a residence, are withdrawn (Protection from Eviction Act 1977, s. 1(3) as amended by Housing Act 1988, s. 29(1)). Only the local authority may institute proceedings for this offence. Section 1(3) has in the past often proved to be of little help to tenants because for the offence to be committed it had to be shown that the intention of the defendant was to cause the tenant to give up occupation or to refrain from exercising rights or seeking any remedy in relation to the premises. The requirement of evidence of intention on the part of the landlord sometimes makes it difficult to prove the case against the defendant (see *R v Phekoo* [1981] 1 WLR 1117). Also the section gave no real assistance to the tenant who wished to obtain a remedy in civil proceedings. The Housing Act 1988 has, however, made a number of amendments to the law in this area, one being the substitution of the word 'likely' for the word 'calculated' in s. 1(3). The 1988 Act introduced a further criminal offence which now becomes s. 1(3A) of the 1977 Act. This offence can only be committed by the landlord of a residential occupier (or the agent of such a landlord), whereas the s. 1(3) offence can be committed by 'any person'. Section 1(3A) is identical to s. 1(3) save that the required *mens rea* is lower in standard; for s. 1(3A) it is enough if the defendant knows *or has reasonable cause to believe that* the actions he had taken are likely to cause the tenant to give up occupation or fail to enforce his rights. It is a defence under s. 1(3B) for the defendant to prove that he had reasonable grounds for his actions. It should be noted that there is a third possible offence contained in s. 1(1) of the 1977 Act which is committed when any person unlawfully deprives a residential occupier of occupation of his premises. This offence is called 'unlawful eviction'. In order for the criminal offence to be established it is not however necessary to show that the tenant's contractual rights have been infringed: *R v Burke* [1990] 2 WLR 1313.

The Housing Act 1988, s. 27, also provides a tenant who is a residential occupier with a statutory cause of action should he be evicted by his landlord. The ingredients of this tort are the same as those of the criminal offences under the Protection from Eviction Act 1977 but it is not necessary for a criminal conviction to have been obtained before the tenant brings his action. The defences available to the landlord are similar to those available in criminal proceedings. In addition to this statutory right the tenant may also be able to found an action upon breach of contract, trespass, nuisance or even, if appropriate, assault. In a suitable eviction case the courts will even be prepared to make an award of exemplary damages against the landlord (see *Drane v Evangelou* [1978] 1 WLR 455 and the comments of Lord Hailsham of St Marylebone LC in *Broome v Cassell & Co. Ltd* [1972] AC 1027 at p. 1079).

Failure to repair can, in some circumstances, be dealt with by the local authority. If the premises are a statutory nuisance (e.g., are prejudicial to health) the local authority may apply to the magistrates for an order compelling the landlord to effect the necessary repairs (Public Health Act 1936, s. 92). In the alternative, the local authority may carry out the repairs and recover the cost from the landlord (Public Health Act 1961, s. 26). The local authority may also intervene where the property is unfit for human habitation (Housing Act 1985, ss. 189 and 264 as amended by Housing Act 1988, s. 130, or where substantial repairs are necessary to bring it up to a reasonable standard,

Housing Act 1985, s. 215). Certain tenants may also be able to request that a local authority serve notice to improve the demised premises (e.g., to provide a bathroom) under the terms of the Housing Act 1974, s. 89.

From this brief summary it can be seen that a tenant of residential premises may find it preferable to seek the protection of statutory rules, rather than attempting to enforce the landlord's covenants himself. It should, however, be noted that the statutory provisions concerning repair are only of assistance when the defects are serious in nature.

Landlord's remedies against a defaulting tenant

Distress
Distraint is an ancient remedy for non-payment of rent. It involves direct action by way of self-help. Put simply, the landlord will enter the demised premises and take possession of the tenant's belongings, up to the value of the unpaid rent. The goods are held for five days (usually they are left in place, the landlord taking what is called 'walking possession') and then may be sold if the rent is not paid. Certain goods are protected against distraint (e.g., clothing and the tools of the tenant's trade). The action must be taken by the landlord in person or by a certificated bailiff (you cannot 'send round the heavies') (Law of Distress Amendment Act 1888, s. 7). It cannot be used without leave of the court in the case of statutory tenancies (Rent Act 1977, s. 147).

The remedy of distress, although ancient, is still in use in this country. Frequently it can have serious consequences for the tenant since enforced sales of tenants' property rarely produce a high price for the goods sold. It has been recommended, both by the Law Commission and by the Committee on Enforcement of Judgment Debts (Cmnd 3909) that distress be abolished. However, the remedy remains available and appears to be reasonably popular with some landlords (particularly some local authorities). The rules regulating distress are complex and, at the least, some amendment to the existing provisions seems necessary.

Forfeiture
Usually, where a tenant has broken a covenant in a lease the landlord will wish to rid himself of the defaulter altogether. However, a landlord does not have an automatic right to forfeit the lease for breach of a covenant (though there is such a right in the case of breach of a condition, see p. 119). Before a landlord can seek to forfeit the lease he must show that the lease contained a clause permitting him to re-enter for breach of covenant. An example of a typical clause is given in clause 5(a) on p. 118. In the absence of such a clause the landlord will have no right to forfeit the lease and must fall back on the contractual remedies (e.g., injunction or damages) (*Doe* d *Wilson* v *Phillips* (1824) 2 Bing 13).

Waiver   Even where the lease contains a provision which gives the landlord a right of re-entry for breach, the landlord will be prevented from forfeiting the lease if he can be shown to have waived the breach. Waiver may be express (e.g., if the landlord states that he will ignore a breach) or may be implied. It is implied waiver which may cause difficulties to a landlord, since he may be taken to have waived a breach when he did not intend to do so. For an implied waiver to arise the landlord must first know that a breach has occurred and thereafter have acted in such a way that he has treated the lease as still continuing. The most common way of waiving a breach is found where the landlord claims or accepts rent from the tenant when he knows that a breach has occurred (*Segal Securities Ltd* v *Thoseby* [1963] 1 QB 887; *Davenport* v *R* (1877) 3 App Cas 115). However, any act which treats the lease as continuing will do (*Ward* v *Day* (1864) 5 B & S 359). If the breach is continuing in nature (e.g., breach of the covenant to repair), the waiver will not extend beyond the time during which the landlord knew that the breach would continue (*Segal Securities Ltd* v *Thoseby*). Nor does a waiver cover further breaches committed after the waiver was made (*Cooper* v *Henderson* (1982) 263 EG 592). These rules may cause problems for the landlord who, on discovering a breach of covenant, first ensures that he collects the rent before seeking to take further action against his tenant. This is particularly a problem because the landlord is also bound by the actions or knowledge of his servants or agents. Thus, should the landlord's agent accept rent at a date at which the landlord knew of a breach, this would amount to waiver.

Proceeding to forfeit   Once one has ensured that the landlord does have a right to re-enter in respect of the breach, and that he has not waived his right, a number of other provisions govern the procedure by which forfeiture may be obtained. Theoretically it is open to the landlord simply to take possession of the premises. However, this right is itself restricted, since any such entry must be peaceable and without force (Criminal Law Act 1977, s. 6) and cannot be used at all where the premises, or any part of them, are used as a residence by any person (Protection from Eviction Act 1977, s. 2). This rule is amended by the Housing Act 1988 in some cases. In particular it should be noted that peaceable re-entry may be made, without notice, where the tenant and the landlord share accommodation. However, the landlord must not use violence or force to obtain entry to the premises even in such cases. The Housing Act 1988 exceptions to the requirements for notice largely relate to persons whose position is that of, or akin to, a lodger. Such persons will still be entitled to any appropriate contractual period of notice. However, in the generality of leases it remains necessary to serve a formal notice to quit and to give at least four weeks' notice where the property is a dwelling. The normal mode of forfeiture is by application to the court under the rules given below. These rules differ depending on whether it is sought to forfeit for breach of the covenant to pay rent, or for breach of some other covenant.

Forfeiture for non-payment of rent   The first thing that the landlord must do, before he attempts to forfeit the lease for non-payment of rent, is to make a *formal demand* for the rent. The formal demand must be made by the landlord, or his agent, at the demised premises between the hours of sunrise and sunset on the day on which payment is due (see *Duppa* v *Mayo*

(1669) Saund 282 at p. 287 n 16). This performance is usually rendered unnecessary by a clause in the lease which specifies that the landlord may forfeit for non-payment of rent 'whether formally demanded or not' (see lease clause 5(a), p. 118). In any event, s. 210 of the Common Law Procedure Act 1852 dispenses with the need for a formal demand in cases where the rent is at least half a year in arrear and there are insuffucient goods on the premises to satisfy the debt should distress be levied.

Once the need for a formal demand has been dealt with, the landlord will normally (and must in the case of residential premises) proceed to court in order to obtain an order for possession. Even if at this stage the landlord proves that the rent is unpaid, the tenant may still be given a second chance before his lease is forfeited: the tenant is entitled to apply for *relief from forfeiture*. The rules on relief differ slightly depending on whether the action is to be heard in the High Court or a county court. In the High Court a tenant has a right to relief from forfeiture as long as he repays the arrears of rent and the costs of the action before the trial (Common Law Procedure Act 1852, s. 212). The court may even reopen matters after an order for possession has been granted as long as the application for relief is made within six months of execution of the judgment. If the action is heard in a county court then the action will be terminated if the arrears and the costs of the action are paid not less than five clear days before the hearing (County Courts Act 1984, s. 138(2)). The court may also make a suspended order should the tenant make a reasonable offer to pay and then, provided that payment is made within the specified time, the original lease will continue (s. 138(3)). (Tenants with tenancies which are protected under the Rent Acts may find that they have the advantage of further statutory provisions for their protection.)

Forfeiture for breach of covenants other than that to pay rent   Forfeiture of a lease for breach of covenants other than that to pay rent is governed by LPA 1925, s. 146. The aim of the procedure required by s. 146 is to allow the tenant a chance to remedy his fault before the ultimate sanction of forfeiture is imposed. Accordingly the section imposes a requirement upon the landlord to serve notice in the prescribed form. The s. 146 notice must:

(a)   specify the breach;
(b)   require that the breach be remedied, if it is remediable; and
(c)   require the tenant to pay financial compensation for the breach.

Item (a) must be contained in *all* notices; item (c) need not be included if the landlord does not require financial compensation (*Lock* v *Pearce* [1893] 2 Ch 271). It is item (b) which has given rise to the most problems, however, since it requires that the tenant be called upon to remedy the breach *if it is remediable*. If the breach is irremediable the notice need only specify the breach and the landlord may then proceed to forfeit the lease. It is therefore necessary to know whether a breach of covenant is remediable.

Older case law regarded the use of premises for immoral purposes (*Rugby School (Governors)* v *Tannahill* [1935] 1 KB 87) or for gambling (*Hoffman* v *Fineberg* [1949] Ch 245) as an irremediable breach of covenant, since the improper use would cast a stigma on the premises which could not be removed by merely ceasing the activity. Again, it has been held that if the breach consists of an assignment or subletting of the property, this breach cannot be remedied because the estate has been assigned or created and the situation cannot be reversed. This is so even if the tenant takes a surrender of a sublease which he has created in breach of covenant (*Scala House & District Property Co. Ltd* v *Forbes* [1974] QB 575, although the court did accept this as a reason for giving relief from forfeiture, under its statutory powers).

These particular decisions may well be justified, but they are sometimes used to support the wider principle that the breach of *any* negative covenant is incapable of being remedied. Like Humpty Dumpty, the covenant cannot be put back in its place once it has been broken; once the forbidden action has been done there is an irremediable breach. The same, it is said, is not true of the breach of a positive covenant (e.g., to repair), for the performance of that covenant, even if later than it should be, will fulfil the obligation. Thus if the property has been allowed to fall into disrepair one can still fulfil the obligation to repair by performing the necessary work.

This distinction, though theoretically neat, does not work very well in practice, and would seem to defeat the purpose of LPA 1925, s. 146, which is to encourage the tenant to act in accordance with the intention of the lease and thereby retain his estate, even if his performance is a rather 'last-minute' affair. Obviously, the breach of the covenant against assigning or subletting without consent is unusual, since the landlord, even once asked, may very well, and quite reasonably, refuse consent. With other covenants, however, one would think that the landlord should be satisfied as long as the tenant does in the end observe the covenants. Some of the case law on breach of negative covenants seems to suggest that this view is correct. For example, it is clear that in some circumstances in which a tenant's breach of covenant is due to the actions of his subtenant, the tenant may be able to remedy the breach by forfeiting the sublease and getting rid of the wrongdoer, even where the breach is such as to cast a stigma on the premises. Thus in *Glass* v *Kencakes Ltd* [1966] 1 QB 611, the tenant was held to have remedied his breach when he forfeited the sublease of his subtenant, who had used the premises for immoral purposes.

The question of which breaches are to be considered irremediable was considered by the Court of Appeal in the case of *Expert Clothing Service & Sales Ltd* v *Hillgate House Ltd* [1986] Ch 340, which suggests that now nearly all breaches of covenant are to be regarded as capable of being remedied. The covenants in question were both positive: (a) to give notice to the landlord of any charge created over the property and (b) to reconstruct the premises for occupation by a stated date, or as soon as possible thereafter. The tenant charged the premises without giving notice, and allowed the specified date to pass without making the reconstruction. A month later the landlord served a notice under LPA 1925, s. 146, which complained of the two breaches but did not require them to be remedied. The Court of Appeal held that both of these breaches were remediable and that accordingly the landlord's notice was defective. The relevant question appears to be whether compliance with the covenant (albeit late) together with financial compensation would 'have effectively remedied the harm which the lessors had suffered or were likely to suffer from the breach'. In certain cases, compliance would not be enough, and in those cases the breach, whether of a positive or negative covenant, would be irremediable. However, it was suggested that even negative covenants are very often capable of remedy by compliance, by ceasing to do the act complained of, so that if, for instance, a covenant has been broken by the erection of window-boxes, it may be remedied by removing the boxes and paying for the repair of any damage done. Thus it seems that in future it is to be regarded as a question of fact in every case whether a particular breach is remediable and that the issue cannot be decided solely by reference to whether the covenant is positive or negative in substance.

Once a notice requiring remedy has been served, the landlord must thereafter give the tenant a reasonable time in which to remedy the breach (LPA 1925, s. 146(1)). Obviously some breaches may be swiftly remedied (e.g., removing a window-box) whilst others, such as the building works in *Expert Clothing*, may take some time. Once a reasonable time has elapsed without remedial action by the tenant the landlord may then proceed to forfeit the lease.

Relief is also available in the case of breach of covenants other than that to pay rent. It is governed by LPA 1925, s. 146(2), which allows the tenant to apply for relief at any time up until the landlord has actually re-entered (a slightly shorter period than in the case of failure to pay rent). If relief is granted, the lease will continue as though proceedings had never been started, though it is open to the court to impose such terms as it thinks fit before granting relief (*Duke of Westminster* v *Swinton* [1948] 1 KB 524). In the case of a breach which denies the landlord's title, (*Warner* v *Sampson* [1958] 1 QB 404, reversed on other grounds [1959] 1 QB 297) and in certain cases specified in LPA 1925, s. 149(8) and (9)), relief is not available.

Although generally relief will not be available after a landlord has re-entered the property (see *Rogers* v *Rice* [1892] 2 Ch 170), it appears that relief will be available if the landlord has effected a peaceable re-entry after service of a notice under s. 146 without obtaining and enforcing a judgment. This was the view taken by the House of Lords in *Billson* v *Residential Apartments Ltd* [1992] 2 WLR 15, in reliance on the word 'otherwise' which appears in s. 146(2); relief is available where the landlord was proceeding by action 'or otherwise' and in the case in question the landlord was taken to be acting by entry after a s. 146 notice. Accordingly it appears to be safest in such cases for the landlord to obtain and then enforce a judgment. However, where this is done, the tenant will have the opportunity to seek relief when the case is heard.

Protection for subtenants when the head lease is forfeited
A subtenant may be very badly affected if the head lease is forfeited for a breach of covenant by the tenant, for the destruction of the head lease also destroys the sublease which is derived from it. This can be unfair to an innocent subtenant who has paid his rent and complied with the covenants in his lease. Today this situation is governed by LPA 1925, s. 146(4), which applies wherever a landlord seeks to enforce a right of re-entry or forfeiture,

even in those situations in which the tenant himself has no right to relief. Under this provision the subtenant may apply to the court for relief if the head lease from which he drives his title is forfeited. If relief is granted, the subtenant will become an immediate tenant of the head landlord, but for the period of the sublease, not for that of the head lease. The court may impose any conditions it sees fit upon the subtenant (e.g., compliance with covenants in the original head lease or payment of a higher rent).

Application of the forfeiture and relief rules

You will recall that the current situation with regard to 7a and 7b Trant Way is as follows:

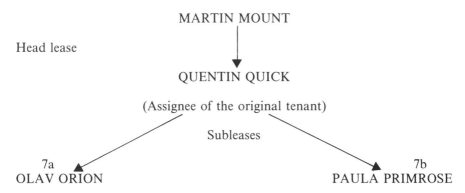

MARTIN MOUNT

Head lease

QUENTIN QUICK

(Assignee of the original tenant)

Subleases

7a
OLAV ORION

7b
PAULA PRIMROSE

You will also recall that the head lease and both subleases contain covenants (a) against using the property for business purposes and (b) t6 keep the premises in good repair. Quentin Quick is also bound by a covenant to pay rent of £500 per month. For the last five months, Mr Quick has not paid his rent to Mr Mount, even though both the subtenants, Mr Orion and Miss Primrose, have been paying their rent regularly to Mr Quick. In addition, for the last three months Mr Orion has been running a business from flat 7a. What can Mr Mount do to enforce the covenants which have been broken? As we have seen already, there is no privity of estate between Mr Mount and the two subtenants, so he cannot take direct action against either of them, on the basis of privity of estate, even though it is Mr Orion who is actually causing one of the breaches to which Mr Mount objects.

Mr Mount must instead take action against Mr Quick, who became his tenant on the assignment of the lease. (An action against Mr Orion may however, be possible under the rules relating to restrictive covenants, see p. 315).

Non-payment of rent
The head lease contains the usual clause which exempts the landlord from making a formal demand for the rent and also contains a clause allowing him to re-enter the premises if any covenant is broken. Accordingly, unless Mr Mount has in some manner waived the breach complained of, he may start proceedings to forfeit the lease for the non-payment of the rent. At

or before the hearing Mr Quick may ask for relief from forfeiture, and this will normally be granted as long as he pays the back rent and the costs of the action. In practice any offer of payment, as long as it is reasonable (e.g., by instalments over a prescribed period) will be accepted by the court. If, however, Mr Quick cannot make a reasonable offer, the lease will be forfeited for breach of the covenant to pay rent.

Using the premises for business purposes
Any attempt to forfeit the head lease for breach of the other covenants is subject to the LPA 1925, s. 146, notice procedure. Provided the operation of LPA 1925, s. 79, was not expressly excluded in the lease, Mr Quick will have covenanted on behalf of 'persons deriving title under him', and so will be liable for the breach, even though it has been caused by his subtenant. Accordingly, Mr Mount should serve a s. 146 notice on Mr Quick. It is likely that this breach will be regarded as remediable (see *Expert Clothing Service & Sales Ltd* v *Hillgate House Ltd* [1986] Ch 340) and so the notice should ask that the situation be remedied. After service of the notice, Mr Mount must allow Mr Quick a reasonable period in which to remedy the breach. On receipt of the s. 146 notice Mr Quick would be advised to serve a similar notice on Mr Orion, who is himself in breach of a covenant in the sublease of 7a. (In most cases, Mr Quick will have to proceed against Mr Orion under provisions contained in the Rent Acts or the Housing Act 1988 but the principle is the same.) The result will be, either that Mr Orion ceases to run the business, or that the sublease will be forfeited for the breach. Either result will have the effect of remedying the breach of the covenant in the head lease.

Position of Miss Primrose
If, for any reason, the head lease is forfeited, Miss Primrose is placed in a difficult position. Although she has behaved perfectly properly, she is in danger of losing her own lease because it is dependent upon the head lease from which it is derived. Accordingly Miss Primrose should apply for relief under LPA 1925, s. 146(4), and, as she is wholly innocent, it is very likely that if the head lease is forfeited, Miss Primrose will be protected by the court. If this happens she will become a direct tenant of Mr Mount, for the period and upon the terms of her sublease but subject to any altered terms imposed by the court. If, however, Mr Quick manages to avoid the forfeiture of the head lease, Miss Primrose has nothing to fear. As long as the head lease is valid the sublease will be safe, provided, of course, that Miss Primrose continues to observe the covenants in her own sublease.

4 Licences, Constructive and Resulting Trusts

Having considered the two legal estates in land, and before we turn to consider the legal and equitable interests in land, we must look at the law relating to licences. We will also at this point consider the effects of constructive and resulting trusts since these issues often arise in the same cases. Licences to use land are unusual since, although they are rights which concern the use of land, theoretically they create neither an estate nor an interest in land. Indeed the term 'licence' covers a diversity of rights to use land. Some of the problems which arise in this area are better illustrated if we look at some practical examples, before attempting to examine the law in detail.

Factual background

(a) Number 1 Trant Way has a small front garden with a short path leading to the front door, on which there is a door-knocker. Every day the postman, milkman and the paper-boy walk up to the front door in order to make deliveries.

(b) Barbara Bell has completed the purchase of 3 Trant Way and has moved into the property. Her father, Bob Bell, has come to live in the 'granny flat' on the top floor. Mr Bell has his own separate front door and Barbara has given her father the only set of keys to the flat. She never enters her father's flat unless he invites her in. When Mr Bell moved in Barbara told him, 'You need never worry again, you will have a home here with me for as long as you live'. Since moving in, Mr Bell has used some of his savings to make improvements to the flat.

(c) The fee simple estate of 8 Trant Way belongs to Mildred Mumps, who bought it in 1960. The basement of 8 Trant Way is a self-contained flat which has been occupied by Laura Lymeswold since 1985. Miss Lymeswold pays Mrs Mumps £40 a week for the use of the flat. However, Mrs Mumps is keen to ensure that Laura does not obtain the protection of the Rent Acts or now the Housing Act 1988 and has always refused to give her a written lease. She has always told Laura, 'You only have a licence, dear. You must go if I say so.' Mildred has kept a key to the front door of the flat (8A) and lets herself in once a month in order to empty the gas and electricity meters and in order to check that the flat is clean and in good order.

(d) Mrs Mumps occupies the rest of 8 Trant Way herself, together with

Henry Mumps. In fact Mildred and Henry are not married, but have lived together as husband and wife ever since Mildred first bought the property. They have two children aged 15 and 10. Mildred has a very highly paid job and so, whilst she has always worked (apart from brief maternity leave when the children were born), Henry has stayed at home to look after the children and does all the cooking and cleaning. Henry is very clever at 'do-it-yourself' and, whilst he has never contributed financially to the purchase of the property or to the family living expenses, he has made considerable improvements to the property. Recently Mildred and Henry's personal relationship has been under some strain and now Mildred appears to be having an affair with another man. Henry is very worried that soon Mildred may tell him that she wants to end their relationship.

These four situations are very different in nature, but each may well be regarded by a court as giving rise to a licence. One, the 'licence' of Laura Lymeswold, may cause considerable problems if considered by the courts, since it is likely that Laura will allege that the arrangement is not a licence at all but a lease which gives her extensive rights under the Rent Acts or now the Housing Act 1988. Two of the situations, those concerning the positions of Bob Bell and Henry Mumps, look like family arrangements which would only come before a court should the family relationships break down. The other situation, the front path, is one with which we are all familiar. Yet normally, when we walk on to someone else's land, we do not consider the nature of our right to do so. In addition to these examples there are many other types of rights which can amount to a licence to use land, for example, a licence to walk across another's property (which may look very like an easement) or a licence to run the sweet counter in a cinema foyer. These assorted rights give rise to three main problems:

(a)   What is the nature of a licence, and how can it be distinguished from other rights?
(b)   Are these licences enforceable against the original grantors, or may they be revoked at will?
(c)   Are these licences enforceable against successors in title of the original grantors?

NATURE OF A LICENCE

The starting-point for any consideration of the nature of a licence is the classic statement made by Vaughan CJ in *Thomas* v *Sorrell* (1673) Vaugh 330 at p. 351, that:

A dispensation or licence properly passeth no interest, nor alters or transfers property in any thing, but only makes an action lawful, which without it had been unlawful.

(Oddly enough this case concerned the granting of alcohol licences and had nothing to do with land law, yet ever since it has been regarded as crucial to any discussion of licences to use land). Put more simply, this means that a licence does not give the licensee an estate or interest in the land but does make his presence on the property authorised, so that he is not a trespasser. If we look at our four initial examples, it is clear that Bob Bell, Laura Lymeswold and Henry Mumps could not possibly be regarded as trespassers; obviously they have permission to be on the properties concerned. What about the postman, and others, who use the footpath leading to the front door of 1 Trant Way? In this case the owners of 1 Trant Way have not expressly given permission to each caller to walk up to the front door, but they have impliedly done so by providing the path and by putting a knocker on the door. Thus someone who walks up to the front door and knocks would not be a trespasser, though a visitor who went further and prowled about the rest of the garden would have gone beyond the limits of the implied licence and would be trespassing. It is also open to the estate owner to limit the implied licence, e.g., by putting up a sign saying 'No salesmen' at the garden gate, and then any person who is a salesman and who fails to observe the restriction would also be a trespasser.

Once one has established that a person who is on the land is not a trespasser, one then has to establish whether that person has an estate or interest in the land. If the person has no property ('proprietary') interest giving him the *right* to be on the land, then he is there *by permission* and is a licensee of some kind. The rights which are most commonly confused with licences are leases and easements and we will now consider these separately.

Distinguishing a lease from a licence

Sometimes it can be very difficult indeed to distinguish a lease from a licence. The agreement relating to 8a Trant Way is a good example of the type of arrangement which may give a considerable amount of difficulty to the lawyer who is asked to classify it. These arrangements have become very popular as tenants' rights have been increased by the Rent Acts and now the Housing Act 1988 and landlords/licensors have sought to avoid the application of these rules by ensuring that they grant licences (which have little protection) rather than leases (which are fully protected under the Acts).

As we saw in chapter 3, it is an essential requirement of a lease that the tenant should have exclusive possession of the demised premises. If the 'tenant' does not have this right then the arrangement *cannot* be a lease and must be a licence. Thus it becomes essential to be able to identify whether or not the tenant/licensee has exclusive possession. In *Appah* v *Parncliffe Investments Ltd*[1964] 1 WLR 1064 the plaintiff had an agreement under which she occupied a room in a house in which 17 such rooms were separately occupied. Each room had some cooking facilities but the bathroom was shared. The agreement provided that (a) no notice was required if an occupant wished to leave, (b) the fee simple owner retained the right to enter the room to empty gas and electricity meters and to clean; and (c) rules were made specifying that guests had to leave by 10.30 p.m. and otherwise regulating the use of the premises. The court held that this agreement must amount to a licence, since the licensee did not have exclusive possession of the room: she had no right to exclude the landlord, and the making of rules concerning her use of the premises indicated also that she did not have a proprietary right amounting to a lease.

As a result of this rule it is common for licensors to enter into agreements in which they reserve the right to use the premises themselves or to permit other persons to use the premises in common with the licensee. As long as the arrangement is not construed as being a lease masquerading as a licence, the effect will be to prevent the licensee obtaining exclusive possession so that the agreement *cannot* be a lease.

At one time it was true to say that if an agreement *did* give exclusive possession then it was necessarily a lease (see *Lynes* v *Snaith* [1899] 1 QB 486) but this is no longer true for, from the 1950s onward, there have been a number of decisions in which it has been held that, despite exclusive possession, the occupant is only a licensee. Accordingly, even when one has ascertained that an agreement does give exclusive possession, one still has to decide whether the arrangement amounts to a licence or a lease. Over the years exclusive possession of a room in an old people's home has been held to amount to a licence (*Abbeyfield (Harpenden) Society Ltd* v *Woods* [1968] 1 WLR 374), as were arrangements whereby a former agricultural worker remained in his property after his retirement but rent-free (*Foster* v *Robinson* [1951] 1 KB 149) and a homeless couple were given exclusive possession of a house rent-free (*Heslop* v *Burns* [1974] 1 WLR 1241). The common theme in most of these cases of licences with exclusive possession was summarised as follows by Denning LJ in the case of *Facchini* v *Bryson* [1952] 1 TLR 1386:

> In all the cases where an occupier has been held to be a licensee there has been something in the circumstances, such as a family arrangement, an act of friendship or generosity, or such like, to negative any intention to create a tenancy.

This statement draws attention to two issues: first, some act of generosity and, secondly, the intention of the parties to the arrangement. The importance of the intention of the landlord and tenant, or licensor and licensee, has been emphasised in other cases, such as *Marcroft Wagons Ltd* v *Smith* [1951] 2 KB 496. In that case the court took notice of the fact that it was clearly not the intention of the licensor to create a tenancy and that accordingly the agreement was a licence and not a lease. This can, however, give rise to difficulties, because in recent years landlords/licensors have always wished to grant licences in order to prevent the Rent Acts applying to the agreement. Thus in nearly every case the intention of the grantor will be to create a licence, whilst the recipient will probably wish to receive a lease. As a result it is clear that the courts will often hold an agreement to be a lease, even where it is expressly described as a licence. In this way, in *Addiscombe Garden Estates Ltd* v *Crabbe* [1958] 1 QB 513 an arrangement for the use of a tennis-court was held to amount to a business tenancy even though it purported to be a licence. In *Street* v *Mountford* [1985] AC 809 the House of Lords held that a written agreement which stated that it was a licence and which referred to the payment of a licence fee rather than rent, was nonetheless a lease. It was agreed by all concerned that the agreement gave exclusive possession to Mrs Mountford (the tenant) but that, when it was signed, both parties expressed the intention to create a licence (Mrs Mountford signed a declaration to this effect). Lord Templeman said, however (at p. 819):

If the agreement satisfied all the requirements of a tenancy, then the agreement produced a tenancy and the parties cannot alter the effect of the agreement by insisting that they only created a licence.

This decision seems to suggest that even the professed intentions of the parties cannot alter the effect of the agreement. However, it appears that a distinction must be drawn between the intention of the parties as evidenced by their conduct, and the apparent intention expressed by the words used. Thus the case emphasises the general rule that the court will look at the substance of the agreement rather than the form in which it is expressed. The case does, however, indicate that where exclusive possession is granted for a term at a rent (even if called a 'licence fee') the agreement will be presumed to be a lease, unless clear circumstances exist which negate that presumption. Presumably the type of circumstances which will destroy this presumption are those referred to by Denning LJ in *Facchini* v *Bryson*.

Leases v Licences since *Street* v *Mountford*

Normally one expects a decision of the House of Lords to have the effect of clarifying the law and laying to rest old controversies. The decision in *Street* v *Mountford* [1985] AC 809 appeared, however, to cause as many problems as it solved. Having emphasised that commercial arrangements which give exclusive possession will be construed as leases, the case has moved the problems in this area back to the field of what constitutes exclusive possession. 'Landlords' have gone out of their way to devise agreements which do not grant exclusive possession to the 'tenant' and which thus only confer licences and the status of licensor and licensee respectively.

In 1988 two cases which illustrate these issues reached the House of Lords. In *AG Securities* v *Vaughan* [1988] 3 WLR 1205 the landlord/licensor owned premises comprising a flat which had four bedrooms together with other normal living accommodation, such as a kitchen and bathroom. The flat was occupied by four people who were selected by the owner and who did not know one another. Each had arrived at a different time and each paid a different amount for the use of the rooms. Each had the use of one bedroom and the use of the other rooms in common with the other three. The owner did not dictate which room each occupier should have: that was agreed between the current occupiers. If an occupier left, the owner replaced him with a new occupier of the owner's choice but then left it to the four occupiers to settle between them the new room allocation. It was held that this arrangement constituted a licence because the occupiers did not (even jointly *inter se*) have exclusive possession of the property. Lord Oliver (at p. 1224) said:

The landlord is not excluded for he continues to enjoy the premises through his invitees, even though he may for the time being have precluded himself by contract with each from withdrawing the invitation.

In *Antoniades* v *Villiers*, also reported at [1990] 1 AC 417, a couple took a one-bedroom flat under written agreements which were described as 'licence agreements'. Each signed a separate agreement and each agreement provided that the 'licensor' might also occupy the premises or might license others to occupy jointly with the 'licensees'. The House of Lords held that this arrangement was clearly a lease and that the terms allowing for occupation by the landlord or others were simply shams. It would be ridiculous to contemplate that the landlord intended to share the young couple's bed or that he genuinely intended to send others to do this.

In *Hadjiloucas* v *Crean* [1988] 1 WLR 1006 an agreement similar to that in *Antoniades* v *Villiers* was made when a two-bedroom flat was let to two ladies. In *Villiers* it was said that the attempt to provide that the landlord might require the remaining lady to share with a stranger if the other left was 'a pretence'. Accordingly these cases draw a distinction between cases in which occupation by the licensor or others of his choice is possible within the terms of normal daily life and those others where the terms are merely inserted to avoid the statutory regime for the protection of tenants and cannot possibly reflect the true intention of the parties to the agreement. Unfortunately this is obviously a matter of degree and no doubt there will continue to be problems in distinguishing between leases and licences.

The factors to be taken into account when applying the decisions in *Vaughan* and *Villiers* were considered by the Court of Appeal in *Stribling* v *Wickham* [1989] 27 EG 81. The Court said that agreements for flat sharing of this type had to be construed in the light of all the surrounding circumstances, which would include the relationship between the sharers, the course of negotiations, the nature and the extent of the accommodation provided and the intended and actual mode of occupation. It was emphasised once again that it was the function of the courts to determine the true nature of 'the substance and reality' of the transaction.

Street v *Mountford* seemed primarily to be concerned with agreements for which money was being paid and which accordingly could be regarded as being commercial in nature. Usually where no rent is payable the circumstances will involve an 'act of generosity' which according to *Facchini* v *Bryson* [1952] 1 TLR 1386 will tend to indicate a licence. However, in at least one case since *Street* v *Mountford* an agreement for which no rent was paid has been construed as a lease. In *Ashburn Anstalt* v *W.J. Arnold & Co.* [1989] Ch 1 the purchaser of leasehold premises agreed to allow the vendor to remain in occupation rent-free until a specified date and thereafter until terminated by one quarter's notice. The Court of Appeal applied *Street* v *Mountford* and held that this gave rise to a lease, even though the arrangement was worded as a licence. Once again this was a commercial bargain, even though no rent was to be paid. This perhaps indicates that since *Street* v *Mountford* the courts have remained inclined to conclude that agreements create leases, for against the decision it can be said that this was an express agreement in a commercial context and that the intention of both parties, at least originally, was that the vendor should receive a licence. In this case it was clear that the tenant did have exclusive possession of the property but it seems odd that an agreement which appears to have been drafted after legal advice should in this way be construed as a lease even though expressly drafted as a licence and in circumstances in which it appears to have been quite reasonable for both parties to have intended to create a licence. It may be, however, that this is a case in which the court felt that the tenant had in some way been 'hard done by' and sought to provide what protection it could. It was also no doubt of relevance that the agreement was intended to allow the vendor of the property to remain at the premises until the purchaser was ready to proceed with an intended development. Once the development was completed it was expressly agreed that the original vendor should be granted a lease of shop premises 'in a prime position at the development'. It was obviously important for the vendor to remain at the premises, save whilst building work was in progress, in order to maintain the goodwill of its business. The decision was, however, worrying for those who do wish to create licences in similar circumstances and it is important to note that the decision has been overruled by the House of Lords in *Prudential Assurance Co. Ltd* v *London Residuary Body* [1992] 3 WLR 279 on the ground that the agreement did *not* give rise to a fixed term and thus could not amount to a lease.

Some small comfort for the landlord/licensor may also be gained from *Dresden Estates Ltd* v *Collinson* [1987] 1 EGLR 45. There the property concerned was a unit in industrial premises and the agreement provided that the licensor might move the licensee to another unit if he so chose. This arrangement had the effect of preventing the licensee from gaining exclusive possession of the unit which he had taken and thus could amount only to a licence. Although the Court of Appeal seems to have regarded such a term as unusual, it may well become increasingly popular, but if it becomes too common it will undoubtedly take on the look of a sham and thus cease to have its effect of preventing the protection available to a business tenant under Part II of the Landlord and Tenant Act 1954 from arising. It has also been accepted that in the case of some types of property used for trading, for example, stalls in markets and areas in stores, in which licences are common, licences are properly intended and will be construed as such (see *London & Associated Investment Trust plc* v *Calow* [1986] 2 EGLR 80, 84).

In *Family Housing Association* v *Jones* [1990] 1 WLR 779 the appellant, who was homeless, was given a flat in premises operated by a housing association in order to provide temporary accommodation. The agreement was described as being for the use of temporary accommodation and was expressed to be a licence. The association kept a set of keys in order to enter the premises to offer help to the 'licensee', to give her advice and to inspect the condition of the premises. A weekly 'charge' was payable for the use of the premises. The Court of Appeal held that this arrangement was a lease and not a licence. It was said that the retention of the key by the association was not decisive and that in this case it had been done in order to assist the tenant and not in order to allow the association to introduce a further occupant. However, in *Camden London Borough Council* v *Shortlife Community Housing Ltd, The Times*, 12 March 1992, in a similar case concerning short-term accommodation, the intention of the parties as to the brevity of the arrangment was taken to negate any intention to confer exclusive possession and a similar view was taken by the House of Lords in *Westminster City Council* v *Clarke* [1992] 2 WLR 229 (hostel for single men).

Another useful example is *Aslan* v *Murphy (Nos. 1 and 2)* [1990] 1 WLR 766. Here again the landlord had retained a key and, in the first case involved, had limited the hours of what was described as a licence to use a room, to exclude the time between 10.30 a.m. and noon each day. The agreement also said that a further occupant might be introduced at any time. Despite all these provisions the agreement was held to be a lease, the terms of the agreement not truly representing the intention of the parties. Where terms can be regarded as a sham or pretence they cannot be relied upon in order to establish that exclusive possession has not been granted. The court will seek to establish the nature of the 'true bargain' between the parties and here it was clear that the landlord had no intention of moving in another occupant to share the premises.

These are a few of the many cases which have come before the courts in the wake of the decision in *Street* v *Mountford*. For others see: *Brooker Settled Estates Ltd* v *Ayers* [1987] 1 EGLR 50 (right to a room in a larger flat); *Crancour Ltd* v *Da Silvaesa* [1986] 1 EGLR 80 (a right to use a room from midnight until 10.30 a.m. and from noon until midnight each day); *Wigan Borough Council* v *Green & Son (Wigan) Ltd* [1985] 2 EGLR 242 (the exclusive right to use a large stall in a covered market); *University of Reading* v *Johnson-Houghton* [1985] 2 EGLR 113 (use of gallops for racehorses) and *Ogwr BC* v *Dykes* [1989] 1 WLR 295 (former tenant allowed to remain after possession order on express terms that arrangement was a licence). These are merely a sample of the huge number of cases which have been before the courts and all should be seen simply as illustrations of the application of basic principles. It appears that the only conclusions that one can draw from the cases are that each case will be judged entirely on its own facts and that the courts will be very ready to regard attempts to create licences as amounting to a sham.

Distinguishing an easement or profit from a licence

If A walks across B's land and it is clear from the circumstances that A is not a trespasser, then one must establish whether A has an easement (a *right* to walk across the land—a right of way) or a licence (he has *permission* to walk across the land). A similar question arises when C fishes in D's lake: does C have a profit or a licence? Once again one has to distinguish between the ownership of a proprietary right and the existence of a permission which merely prevents A from being a trespasser. The distinction may well be very important, because an easement or profit grants a right which cannot be revoked whereas normally the permission given in a licence can be withdrawn. Unfortunately there is no simple method of distinguishing between an easement or profit and a licence. The only method of approach that can be adopted is to establish first whether the right claimed is capable of being an easement or profit (see chapter 8), for if not, it can be only a licence (*Hill* v *Tupper*

(1863) 2 H & C 121). Secondly, even if the arrangement is capable of giving rise to an easement or profit, it will amount to no more than a licence if the intention to create an interest in land is missing (see *Fitzgerald* v *Firbank* [1897] 2 Ch 96).

ENFORCEABILITY OF A LICENCE AGAINST THE GRANTOR

Originally, since a licence gave no right in law and was a mere permission, it could be revoked at any time at the will of the licensor (with one exception, see below). However, over the years a number of different types of licences have been recognised by the courts and it appears now that not all licences are so easily withdrawn. This has led some writers to consider whether it is really still true to say that a licence creates no interest in land (see further below). We will now consider the resulting issues in relation to each of the types of licence which are currently recognised.

Bare licences

In relation to the simplest form of licence the traditional rules apply and the licence is revocable at any time at the will of the licensor. This category is usually called the 'bare' licence and it is a residuary category: a licence is a bare licence if it does not fall into any of the other categories of licence mentioned in this chapter. A good example of a bare licence is the implied licence to walk up the garden path to the front door of 1 Trant Way. This licence is purely gratuitous and may be revoked at any time. Once the licence is revoked the former licensee must be given a reasonable period in which to leave and once that period has elapsed will become a trespasser if he remains on the property. In *Robson* v *Hallet* [1967] 2 QB 939 some police officers went up to the door of a house and knocked. In doing this they were licensees and within their rights. However, in the absence of a search warrant or other authority permitting the officers to insist on remaining, their licence could be revoked, although the householder had to give them reasonable time to leave the property. Most of us spend a large part of our lives as bare licensees, for every time we visit a friend's house or enter a shop we are acting as licensees (see *Davis* v *Lisle* [1936] 2 KB 434 at p. 440).

Licences coupled with a grant

Sometimes licences do not stand alone but are coupled to some other right. An example would be the grant of a profit allowing A to cut wood on B's land. Obviously a licence must be implied into this agreement as, unless A has permission to go on to B's land, A cannot exercise his right to cut wood. This type of licence is not revocable as long as the proprietary interest (the profit) continues. Otherwise the grantor, B, could derogate from his grant by saying to A, 'Yes, I know that you have a right to cut wood, but I will not give you permission to come on to my land in order to exercise your right'. This rule is very ancient (see *Palmer* v *Fletcher* (1663) 1 Lev 122) and can produce odd results in certain circumstances (see *Pwllbach Colliery Co.*

Ltd v *Woodman* [1915] AC 634). Another example of the operation of the
rule is given in *Doe* d *Hanley* v *Wood* (1819) 2 B & Ald 724, 738, in which
it was said that if a man sells hay standing on his land he cannot later prevent
the purchaser from entering the land to collect it. (see also *Wood* v *Manley*
(1839) 11 A & E 34 and *James Jones & Sons Ltd* v *Earl of Tankerville* [1909]
2 Ch 440).

Contractual licences

Originally the courts do not appear to have distinguished between bare licences
and those which were granted for consideration. In *R* v *Inhabitants of Horndon-
on-the-Hill* (1816) 4 M & S 562 a licence to build a cottage on a piece of
land, the licensee making an annual payment for the right, was held nonetheless
to be revocable at the will of the licensor. The same view was taken in the
famous case of *Wood* v *Leadbitter* (1845) 13 M & W 838, in which a racegoer
was ejected by force from a racecourse even though he had paid one guinea
(£1.05) for the right to enter the premises and view the racing. The racegoer
was unsuccessful when he sued the race steward for damages for battery and
false imprisonment, because the court said that his licence was revocable at
the will of the licensor. Since he had refused to leave when told to go, the
racegoer had become a trespasser and reasonable force could be used to remove
him. It was agreed (though of little comfort to the plaintiff) that he should
receive his guinea back as damages for breach of contract. This rigid view
of the inherent revocability of any type of licence continued at least until
the passing of the Supreme Court of Judicature Acts 1873 and 1875, after
which time the availability of equitable remedies in all courts appears to have
produced a considerable change in attitudes to the licence.

In *Hurst* v *Picture Theatres Ltd* [1915] 1 KB 1 a situation arose which
was very similar to that in *Wood* v *Leadbitter*. In this case a cinema-goer
was asked by the management to leave the premises because it was believed,
incorrectly, that he had not paid for his ticket. When he refused to leave,
the cinema-goer was ejected with the use of force and later sued for assault
and false imprisonment. In this case the court found for the licensee cinema-
goer. It was explained that since the licensee had a contract with the cinema
to watch the film, the equitable remedy of an injunction to restrain breach
or an order for specific performance of the contract would have been available
to prevent the breach of contract, had it been possible to obtain the remedy
in the short time before the breach actually occurred. Accordingly in equity
the licensee did have a right to remain for the whole contractual period; his
removal was unjustified; and he was entitled to damages for assault and false
imprisonment. Buckley LJ distinguished *Wood* v *Leadbitter* on the ground
that the case had been heard in a court of law before the Supreme Court
of Judicature Acts 1873 and 1875. According to this view of the contractual
licence, the licence is enforceable against the original grantor according to
its terms. Accordingly a contractual licence for a specified period cannot be
revoked by the grantor until the contractual period has expired (*Hounslow
London Borough Council* v *Twickenham Garden Developments Ltd* [1971] Ch
233). Should the licence be for an unspecified period, a term will be implied

that the licence can be terminated upon reasonable notice (*Winter Garden Theatre (London) Ltd* v *Millennium Productions Ltd* [1948] AC 173). Furthermore, *Hounslow London Borough Council* v *Twickenham Garden Developments Ltd* confirmed that a licence is a contractual licence if it is conferred by contract, and it is immaterial that the right to enter land may be only a secondary part of the contract.

Even where there is no express contract a court may be prepared to infer a contractual agreement giving rise to the licence. Upon occasion the courts have been prepared to read such a contract into a situation in order to protect the position of a deserted mistress. Thus in *Tanner* v *Tanner* [1975] 1 WLR 1346 a contractual licence was inferred in favour of a woman who had given up a protected tenancy in order to move into a home provided by her lover and there to care for the children of the relationship. Lord Denning MR said that the court should infer a contract that the mistress should remain in the property for so long as the children were of school age and accommodation was reasonably required. A contractual licence was similarly found in *Chandler* v *Kerley* [1978] 1 WLR 693 in which a man had bought a house from his mistress and her husband at less than the market price on the understanding that he would live there with his mistress and that eventually they would marry. When the relationship ended soon after the purchase, the Court of Appeal held that the mistress had a contractual licence to remain, which could be terminated only on reasonable notice (a year in this instance). A contractual licence was also inferred between a mother and daughter-in-law in *Hardwick* v *Johnson* [1978] 1 WLR 683. These decisions might be though to give some encouragement to Henry Mumps, who is resident at 8 Trant Way. However, other cases show that the courts will not always be willing to accept the existence of a contract in such cases. Indeed it seems unusual to construe arrangements of this nature as demonstrating the intention to create legal relations which is necessary in the law of contract. Thus in *Horrocks* v *Forray* [1976] WLR 230 a mistress failed to establish that a contractual licence existed on the basis of a claim that she had subordinated her choice of residence and mode of life to the will of her former lover in return for a promise that she should have a permanent home. The Court of Appeal rejected the lady's case on two grounds: first, the parties had no intention to enter into a legally binding agreement and, secondly, she had provided no consideration. (It should be recalled that the courts will not recognise consideration which they regard as being 'immoral' in character.) The situation in *Tanner* v *Tanner* was distinguished on the ground that in that case, '[T]he man and the woman were making arrangements for the future at arm's length' (at p. 745). The disparity between decisions in this area may make it difficult to advise Henry Mumps as to his rights but it is possible that he might be regarded as having a contractual licence which is to endure until the children of his relationship with Mildred leave school. (He may be able to establish other rights on the grounds of a resulting trust, see p. 171.)

Where a licence constitutes a 'periodic licence' of a dwelling, s. 5(1A) of the Protection from Eviction Act 1977 (inserted by the Housing Act 1988) requires that the licence may not be terminated otherwise than after four weeks' notice in writing, such notice to be in the prescribed form. In addition

s. 3(2A) and (2B) now provide that in the case of such licences the licensor may only recover possession of the property by court order. By these amendments the Housing Act 1988 has conferred a limited protection upon certain licensees and given them some of the rights enjoyed by tenants. The term 'periodic licence' is not defined but is likely to be construed as covering those licences which resemble periodic leases. It is not clear whether the term extends to cover bare licences or only relates to contractual licences. However, the provisions are likely to be used largely in relation to those contractual licences that closely resemble tenancies, save perhaps that the licensee does not have exclusive possession. As is the case with tenancies, neither s. 3 not s. 5 applies to 'excluded licences'. The largest category of these will be licences under which the licensee shares facilities with the licensor.

Licences by estoppel

The general doctrine of equitable estoppel has been applied extensively in the area of licences. The doctrine provides that where one party makes a representation to a second party, intending him to act upon it, and that second party acts upon it to his detriment, the person who made the representation will not be allowed to act inconsistently with it. The rule arises from the general jurisdiction of equity in cases in which the application of strict legal rules produces injustice. An old example of this approach, though not expressed to be decided on this basis, is *Dillwyn* v *Llewellyn* (1862) 4 De G F & J 517 in which a son was 'given' land by his father and thereafter built a house upon the land. No formal conveyance of the estate was ever made. Despite the usual rule that equity will not assist a volunteer (one who acquires property without giving value) and accordingly will not perfect an imperfect gift, the court held that the son was entitled to a conveyance of the fee simple because he had expended his own money on building, in reliance on his father's representation. A modern example of the same principle, and one which was expressly decided on the basis of estoppel, is *Inwards* v *Baker* [1965] 2 QB 29. Here a son, acting on a suggestion of his father, built a bungalow on his father's land (partly at his own expense). Thereafter the son occupied the bungalow in the belief that he would be able to remain there for his lifetime. However, when his father later died, the son discovered that the estate in the land had been left to other persons. The Court of Appeal held that the son had a licence entitling him to remain in the property as long as he wished, because he had altered his position to his detriment in reliance on a belief induced by his father's conduct. In this case Lord Denning MR suggested that the operation of the rules of estoppel gave rise to 'an equity' in favour of the son, and that this equity should be satisfied by the grant of any suitable remedy (in this case a licence for life).

In a number of cases not concerned with licences, a party is said to have a 'mere equity' when he has a right to some form of equitable remedy, which is enforceable not only against the other party to the transaction, but against that party's successors in title. The right to have a deed set aside for fraud or undue influence is an example of such an equity. Although enforceable against successors in title, such a right has in the past been regarded as falling short of an equitable interest in land, but it has to be said that in some of the decisions on licences it seems to have been treated as being similar in nature to an equitable interest (see *E.R. Ives Investment Ltd v High* [1967] 2 QB 379). The better view, however, seems to be that it still amounts simply to a right to a remedy (see Everton (1976) 40 Conv 209). However, it is clear and undisputed that an estoppel can be used to give rise to a licence which is enforceable against the original representor.

LICENCES, THE 'MERE EQUITY' AND CONSTRUCTIVE TRUSTS

The idea that an enforceable licence gives rise to a 'mere equity' has arisen chiefly in the case of licences by estoppel (see above) but has also been considered in relation to contractual licences. In some such instances the judges (particularly, in the past, Lord Denning MR) have adopted an elaborate analysis of the situation, holding that a contractual licence or licence by estoppel gives rise to an 'equity' and that once this has been established the court should seek any suitable method of satisfying the 'equity'. This complicated approach to the problem has not, however, been uniformly welcomed. In *Chandler* v *Kerley* [1978] 1 WLR 693 Lord Scarman seems to have accepted that the 'equity' analysis is possible but said that on the facts of that case its application was unnecessary: it was enough to say that Mrs Kerley had a contractual licence which would be enforced by the court (by injunction or specific performance like any other contract) according to its terms. In *Hardwick* v *Johnson* [1978] 1 WLR 683, whilst Lord Denning MR referred to the licence therein as an 'equitable licence', Browne and Roskill LJJ agreed that this analysis was completely unnecessary (and incorrect? — see Roskill LJ at p. 690) and that having decided that the agreement in question was a contractual licence its enforcement was as simple as the enforcement of any other contract.

The 'equity' analysis has proved rather more generally acceptable to the courts in the cases in which a licence has arisen by estoppel. As well as being extensively used by Lord Denning MR (see *E.R. Ives Investment Ltd v High* [1967] 2 QB 379 and *Inwards v Baker* [1965] 2 QB 29, amongst other cases), the 'equity' analysis was accepted in relation to a licence by estoppel by Scarman LJ in *Crabb* v *Arun District Council* [1976] Ch 179, by Cumming-Bruce LJ in *Pascoe v Turner* [1979] 1 WLR 431 and by Goff LJ in *Griffiths v Williams* (1977) 248 EG 947. In these cases the 'equity' has been satisfied in a number of different ways. Thus in *Pascoe v Turner* it was held that nothing less than a transfer of the entire legal estate to the licensee would so, whereas Scarman LJ in *Crabb* v *Arun District Council* indicated that in that case the grant of an easement or a licence (possibly irrevocable) would be sufficient. It should be noted, however, that Lord Denning MR and the other Lords Justice appear to be referring to different concepts when they use the term 'equity', for whilst Lord Denning appears to consider that the 'equity' is some kind of proprietary right (see *Errington v Errington* [1952] 1 KB 290), the other judges regard it rather as an occasion upon which a general equitable jurisdiction to redress a wrong should be exercised. The difference becomes crucial when one is led to consider whether a licence can be enforced against a third party (see below). It is certain that the result is to produce an uncertainty in an extremely important area of law, which can only be clarified by a thorough reconsideration of the issues in the House of Lords (the existing authorities all emanate from the Court of Appeal).

Constructive trusts

Before laying aside consideration of these rather thorny issues it is also necessary to consider the use of the constructive trust as a remedy in cases involving licences. In some cases the court has satisfied the 'equity' by imposing such a trust. An example of this is found in another decision of Lord Denning MR, in the case of *Binions* v *Evans* [1972] Ch 359. Here a widow had been given the right to live in a cottage for her lifetime. According to the express terms of the agreement, the widow was to be a tenant at will (see p. 114) and she agreed to take care of the premises while she had the use of them. The property was then sold to a purchaser, who agreed with the vendor that he would allow the widow to remain, and accordingly paid a reduced price for the cottage. Later, he sought to eject her, and the court had to consider the nature of her rights and whether they bound the purchaser for value. The Court of Appeal held, unanimously, that although the agreement described the widow as a tenant at will, its terms were inconsistent with such a tenancy. Lord Denning MR then considered whether the agreement conferred any estate or interest in land upon the widow and held that it did not. He concluded finally that the arrangement could therefore amount only to a licence and that the licence was contractual because the widow had given consideration when she agreed to take care of the premises. Thus far the analysis seems reasonable enough and one would expect the conclusion to be that the widow should be given an irrevocable licence for life (or perhaps that the court should recognise that this was the true nature of the agreement from its commencement). This was not, however, the line adopted by Lord Denning, who said that because the purchaser had bought the estate subject to the rights of the widow the court would impose a constructive trust upon him, since it would be inequitable to allow him to turn her out. This reasoning seems odd until one realises that it arises from the difficulties which would have beset the court in considering whether a contractual licence binds a third party (normally the rules of privity of contract will cause difficulties). The majority of the court did not, however, adopt Lord Denning's view, but held that the effect of the agreement was to give the widow an equitable life interest in the property under a Settled Land Act settlement. This result is even more surprising than that achieved by Lord Denning, both because it flies in the face of the express terms of the original agreement and also because the effect is to make the widow a tenant for life of the property (with the right to call for the legal estate to be conveyed to her and the power to sell it! — see chapter 5).

A SLA trust was also imposed by way of constructive trust in *Ungurian* v *Lesnoff* [1989] 3 WLR 840. The defendant was a Polish lady who agreed to leave Poland (with two children by a former marriage) in order to set up home in England with plaintiff. At one time there seem to have been plans to marry but for various reasons (the facts of this case are complicated and well worth reading) no marriage took place. The defendant gave up a secure home and good work prospects in order to leave her own country. A house was bought by the plaintiff and the defendant spent much time supervising repairs and alterations and doing some of the work herself. The court was satisfied that it was the intention of the parties when the house was bought that it would be used to provide a home for the defendant and her children. On the facts the court inferred that the common intention was that she should have a right to live in the house for life and that the plaintiff should hold the house on trust to permit such residence. The effect of this was to give rise to a settlement under the SLA 1925 and accordingly the property should be vested in the defendant as tenant for life of settled land. The result may arise from the unusual facts, which cannot be explored in any detail here, for it cannot be true that every case in which A provides a roof over the head of B can be construed as a declaration of trust. It was clear that the defendant had changed her position in reliance on the promise that a home would be provided but the facts were not such that a resulting trust could be found. This may be another example of a slightly odd result being produced by an attempt to ensure that justice has been done in a particular case.

The idea of the use of a constructive trust as a remedy was a departure from older theories in which it was a substantive institution (a trust arising by operation of law). *Eves v Eves* [1975] 1 WLR 1338 itself was a notable example of the elevation of the rights of a licensee to those of an equitable owner of a share in a property by the imposition of a constructive trust. Once again the case concerned an unmarried couple who lived together in a house owned by the man. He deceived the woman about his reasons for not having the house conveyed to them jointly. When later he deserted her, the Court of Appeal held that she was not a bare licensee, who could be ejected at will, but held a one-quarter interest in the property under a constructive trust. It should be noted in this case that there was no question of there being a resulting trust arising from contribution (see p. 172). The court imposed a trust because it felt that this was fair and just in the circumstances. As has been remarked (see, E.G.Hanbury and R.H.Maudsley, *Modern Equity*, 12th ed., by Jill E. Martin (London: Stevens, 1985), pp. 329–34) this use of the constructive trust as a remedy is as dangerous as it is beneficial in certain cases because it makes it extremely difficult to predict the outcome of a case and accordingly renders the law uncertain. The latest decisions suggest that in the late 1980s the courts will not be as ready to use the constructive trust in this manner as they were in the later 1970s and that a stricter view of the law is likely to be taken in future. For other examples of the use of constructive trusts in licence cases see *DHN Food Distributors Ltd v Tower Hamlets London Borough Council* [1976] 1 WLR 852 and *Re Sharpe* [1980] 1 WLR 219.

This is a complex and difficult area of the law and a detailed consideration of the problems properly belongs to a text on equity and trusts. However, constructive trusts have been used in such a large number of land law cases that it is desirable that we make some reference here to the nature of this type of trust. Unfortunately it is almost impossible to give a simple explanation of what constitutes a constructive trust or to explain when it will arise. In

Carl-Zeiss Stiftung v *Herbert Smith & Co. (No. 2)* [1969] 2 Ch 276, Edmund Davies LJ said, at p. 300:

English law provides no clear and all-embracing definition of a constructive trust. Its boundaries have been left perhaps deliberately vague, so as not to restrict the court by technicalities in deciding what the justice of a particular case may demand.

This difficulty is increased by the failure of a number of judges, and notably of Lord Denning who figured in many of the cases in this area, to distinguish clearly in their terminology between resulting and constructive trusts. Often the term 'constructive trust' is used where clearly the position should more properly be described as a resulting trust. It is perhaps most helpful to the student of land law to concentrate upon the circumstances in which a constructive trust will be imposed by the court. These are helpfully summarised by Oakley in his useful little book, *Constructive Trusts*, 2nd ed. (London: Sweet & Maxwell, 1987), as follows (see p. 17):

(a) 'where a person has obtained an advantage by acting fraudulently or unconscionably or (perhaps) inequitably';
(b) 'where a fiduciary has obtained an advantage as a result of a breach of his duty of loyalty';
(c) 'where there has been a disposition of trust property in breach of trust'.

Any of these can arise in the context of land law but it is the first category which is most often claimed and which gives rise to most problems. In the context of licences it is often argued that the facts are such as to justify the imposition of a constructive trust. The analysis that sometimes a licence can give rise to an 'equity', which should be satisfied by the court in an appropriate manner, has often given rise to the imposition of a constructive trust. The blurring of boundaries is particularly noticeable in cases in which the courts have concluded that an irrevocable licence exists. In some of these the further step has been taken and a constructive trust has clearly been imposed but in others that jump has not been made and the court's use of the concept of the 'equity' has been to conclude that the true nature of the licence granted is such that it is irrevocable. Confusions are caused because of the desire to approach each case upon its facts and reach a just conclusion, rather than to concentrate upon clear principles which will be capable of application in later cases.

What does now appear to be true is that the courts, having gone through a 'liberal' stage in the 1970s, in which the constructive trust was regarded more as a remedy to be imposed when justice required (see Lord Denning MR in *Hussey* v *Palmer* [1972] 1 WLR 1286, 1290), have reverted to the view that the constructive trust, though in a sense a remedy, should only be imposed in cases in which there has been some infringement of recognised rights.

In *Bannister* v *Bannister* [1948] 2 All ER 133 a lady sold her brother-in-law two cottages on the understanding that she would be allowed to live in one of them rent-free for the rest of her life. The understanding between the parties was not recorded in any document and appears to have amounted to the oral grant of a licence for life. When the brother-in-law tried to obtain possession of the cottage it was, however, claimed by the lady that the oral agreement amounted to an informal declaration of trust by the brother-in-law that he would hold the property upon trust for the lady for her lifetime. Such a declaration of trust normally requires writing under LPA 1925, s. 53(1)(b), but because of the unconscionable conduct of the brother-in-law in seeking to rely upon the absence of writing in these circumstances the court imposed a constructive trust upon him and declared that he held one of the cottages upon trust to allow the lady to occupy it during her lifetime. (Consider also *Binions* v *Evans* [1972] Ch 359, discussed above, which it has been suggested may be justified upon the alternative ground that Mrs Evans had a contract enforceable against the Tredegar estate and that the purchasers of the property, who knew of this, were therefore liable in tort for interference with the contract.)

The land registration case of *Lyus* v *Prowsa Developments Ltd* [1982] 2 All ER 953 is a case, unconnected with possible licence arguments, in which the imposition of a constructive trust was used to protect recognised rights and where once again the problem was the absence of the correct formalities, in this case the protection of a minor interest by entering it upon the register. Some writers have concluded that this extension of the constructive trust goes too far. In *An Introduction to the Law of Trusts* (1986), Paul Todd said of this case that it 'is a most extraordinary decision and is almost certainly wrong' (p. 112). Yet in *Ashburn Anstalt* v *Arnold* [1989] Ch 1, Fox LJ considered the case at length and said, 'This again seems to us to be a case where a constructive trust could justifiably be imposed'. The Court of Appeal did, however, emphasise that the courts should not be too eager to impose constructive trusts 'on inferences from too slender materials', and strongly criticised the decision in *Re Sharpe* [1980] 1 WLR 219. The test suggested by the court was 'whether the owner of the property has so conducted himself that it would be inequitable to allow him to deny the claimant an interest in the property'. (These comments in *Ashburn* were not discussed in *Prudential Assurance Co Ltd* v *London Residuary Body* [1992] 3 WLR 279 since they were *obiter dicta* and *Prudential* was concerned with the *ratio* in the earlier case. There is nothing to suggest that this analysis is defective and indeed it appears to be in line with recent authority concerning resulting trusts.)

The cases indicate that whilst the courts are no longer as willing to use the constructive trust in as liberal a manner as once was the case, the constructive trust will continue to grow and probably change its shape as time passes. At present one can only take each one separately and consider the extent to which it can be said to fall into one of the categories identified above. The fluidity of the law in this area should not be regarded as being too surprising because it is in their power to rectify unconscionable, or improper, behaviour that the modern courts come closest to the flexible character of the early courts of equity.

G

ENFORCEABILITY OF A LICENCE AGAINST THIRD PARTIES

As we have already seen in *Binions* v *Evans* [1972] Ch 359, it may well happen that a licensor will sell his estate to a third party, leaving the licensee with the problem of whether his licence can be enforced against the new owner, or whether he is likely to face eviction from the property. In the case of some of the various types of licence that we have described above, this question can be answered quite briefly. In the case of others the law does not provide such clear answers. Accordingly we will consider each type of licence separately.

Bare licences

With the bare licence there is no problem: since these licences can be revoked at will by the grantor they can certainly be revoked at any time by a successor in title of the licensor.

Licences coupled with an interest

These licences will bind a successor in title of the licensor if he is bound by the interest to which the licence is coupled. As long as the licensee can enforce his interest, he can insist on the continuance of his licence. Accordingly the enforceability of these licences depends on issues outside the scope of this chapter, and the rules applicable will vary as the nature of the coupled interest varies.

Contractual licences

Hurst v *Picture Theatres Ltd* [1915] 1 KB 1 established that a contractual licence was enforceable just as any other contract is enforceable. This suggests that a contractual licence would not bind a successor to the original licensor, because such a person would not be a party to the original contract. It is part of standard contractual principles that whilst the benefit of a contract can be assigned to a third party the burden, or obligation, under the contract cannot be transferred. Indeed in two cases this rule has been applied to contractual licences. In *King* v *David Allen & Sons, Billposting Ltd* [1916] 2 AC 54 the licensee had a contractual agreement under which it could display posters on the wall of a cinema. The House of Lords held that this contract could not bind a tenant who took a lease of the cinema from the licensor. In reaching this conclusion the court applied the normal rule that a contract creates a personal obligation enforceable only against the original parties. The Court of Appeal accepted the same principle in *Clore* v *Theatrical Properties Ltd* [1936] 3 All ER 483 and thus, whilst agreeing that the benefit of a licence could be assigned to a third party, said that the burden of the contract would not pass. Unfortunately for the licensee, this means that any contractual obligation to allow the licence to continue cannot bind a successor in title to the licensor.

This at least was the accepted position until the case of *Errington* v *Errington* [1952] 1 KB 290. A father bought a house in order to provide a home for his son and daughter-in-law. The property was conveyed to the father, but it was agreed that if the son and his wife paid all the mortgage instalments he would then convey the property to them. In due course the father died and the property vested in his widow as executrix (she was also beneficiary under the will). Thereafter the son went to live with his mother whilst the daughter-in-law remained in the property and continued to pay the mortgage instalments. At this point the mother attempted to revoke her daughter-in-law's licence. The Court of Appeal held that this licence was not revocable by the new owner, even though she was a third party to the original agreement. Denning LJ said that the original contractual arrangement gave rise to an 'equity' in favour of the daughter-in-law which was enforceable against a third party according to the notice rules (it certainly is not a land charge). Since the new owner was a volunteer, having acquired the property as a gift, she was bound by the contract. This decision can be criticised on the grounds that it flies in the face of normal contractual rules and is contrary to the decisions in two earlier, and binding, authorities. Furthermore, since at the date of the action the mother was still acting as executrix of her husband's estate and held the land in that capacity, she was *not* a third party at all but was bound as executrix by obligations which bound her husband's estate. The case, however, has been regarded as authority for the proposition that in certain circumstances a contractual licence will bind a third party who acquires as a volunteer, or even one who buys the property with notice.

Had *Errington* v *Errington* involved registered land (and a purchaser for value) then the question would arise of whether the daughter-in-law's 'equity' amounted to a 'right' capable of being an overriding interest under LRA 1925, s. 70(1)(g). Further, if the 'equity' was not capable of being an overriding interest, because the licensee was not in actual occupation, could it amount to a minor interest?

These issues were particularly important because of the proliferation of contractual licences used to avoid the application of the Rent Acts. Allowing that a contractual licensee can always be given reasonable notice (unless the terms of the licence specify otherwise) the licensee's situation would be even more precarious were a purchaser from the licensor not to be bound by the contractual terms.

The difficulties created by the decision in *Errington* v *Errington* were considered by the House of Lords in *National Provincial Bank Ltd* v *Hastings Car Mart Ltd* [1965] AC 1175 but sadly the House declined to express any final view upon the decision and thus the matter has remained unresolved for some considerable time.

The problems raised by *Errington* v *Errington* were however considered at some length by the Court of Appeal in *Ashburn Anstalt* v *Arnold* [1989] Ch 1. Unfortunately all the remarks of the Court upon this subject constitute *obiter dicta* because in the case the court in fact held that the agreement under consideration was a lease and not a licence and the *Ashburn* case has recently been heavily criticised (though not in relation to these comments) and the decision overruled by the House of Lords in *Prudential Assurance Co Ltd* v *London Residuary Body* [1992] 3 WLR 279. Nonetheless, in *Ashburn*, having heard lengthy argument upon the *Errington* problem the Court felt it proper to express its views upon this subject. After a detailed consideration of the authorities, Fox LJ concluded (at p. 725):

It must, we think, be very doubtful whether this court's decision in *Errington* v *Errington*. . . is consistent with its earlier decisions in *Daly* v *Edwardes* (1900) 83 LT 548: *Frank Warr & Co.* v *London County Council* [1904] 1 KB 713 and *Clore* v *Theatrical Properties Ltd* [1936] 3 All ER 483. That decision cannot be said to be in conflict with any later decision of the House of Lords, because the House expressly left the effect of a contractual licence open in the *Hastings Car Mart* case. But there must be very real doubts whether *Errington* can be reconciled with the earlier decisions of the House of Lords in *Edwardes* v *Barrington* (1901) 85 LT 650 and *King* v *David Allen & Sons (Billposting) Ltd* [1916] 2 AC 54. It would seem that we must follow those cases or choose between the two lines of authority. It is not, however, necessary to consider those alternative courses in detail, since in our judgment the House of Lords cases, whether or not as a matter of strict precedent they conclude this question, state the correct principle which we should follow. . . .

Before *Errington* the law appears to have been clear and well understood. It rested on an important and intelligible distinction between contractual obligations which gave rise to no estate or interest in the land and proprietary rights which, by definition, did. The far-reaching statement of principle in *Errington* was not supported by authority, not necessary for the decision of the case and *per incuriam* in the sense that it was made without reference to authorities which, if they would not have compelled, would surely have persuaded the court to adopt a different *ratio*. Of course, the law must be free to develop. But as a response to problems which had arisen, the *Errington* rule (without more) was neither practically necessary nor theoretically convincing.

As a result it seems most unlikely that in future it will be possible to argue that a contractual licence is binding on a third party to the contract and the contractual licence has been returned to its true place, which appears simply to be as part of the law of contract. The Court of Appeal did, however, accept that there might be cases in which the facts justified the imposition by the court of a constructive trust. It was emphasised that the courts will not take this step where the evidence is 'slender' and that the issue for the court in such cases is: 'whether the [third party] has acted in such a way that, as a matter of justice, a trust must be imposed' (p. 730).

The remarks of the Court of Appeal in this case, although theoretically only of persuasive authority, were a welcome clearing up of an untidy mess in this area of the law and it is hoped that these comments will not fall under the shadow of the decision in the House of Lords in *Prudential* to overrule the actual decision in *Ashburn* (which was made on entirely separate grounds). In cases where grave hardship is likely to be encountered the constructive trust is likely to provide an answer to the problem. Difficulties do, however, remain as a result of decisions upon licences enforceable by reason of an estoppel.

Licences by estoppel

The problems which have arisen in the case of the contractual licence have also caused difficulties with regard to the licence by estoppel. In some cases the courts have solved the problem by indicating that the circumstances had given rise to a constructive trust (see p. 162). When this occurs the licensee acquires an equitable interest in the land behind the trust and that equitable interest will bind third parties according to the usual equitable and statutory rules. In some cases, however, this path is not available and the court may be faced with the issue of whether a licence, which is not revocable by the licensor due to estoppel, can be revoked by a successor in title to the licensor. The leading case on this issue is *E.R.Ives Investment Ltd* v *High* [1967] 2 QB 379. A building company, whilst erecting a block of flats, mistakenly allowed the foundations of the new building to encroach on to land belonging to a neighbour. When the neighbour objected, he was persuaded to accept a right of way across the courtyard of the new block (allowing access to his back garden from the road) in compensation for the continuing trespass. Thereafter the neighbour built himself a garage, access to which was only possible via the courtyard. Later the owner of the block of flats sold the property to the plaintiffs, who bought it subject to the neighbour's right of way but who subsequently claimed that since this right amounted to an unregistered D(iii) land charge (an equitable easement) it was not binding on them. The Court of Appeal held that the neighbour's right to cross the courtyard did bind the plaintiffs (a third party to the agreement).

This decision appears to be reached on two separate grounds. The first ground is that it is a basic rule of law that one cannot take the benefit of such an agreement without accepting a related burden. (This principle is discussed further in relation to covenants relating to freehold land, see p. 319, and *Halsall* v *Brizell* [1957] Ch 169; *Hopgood* v *Brown* [1955] 1 WLR 213.) Thus as long as the plaintiffs wished to maintain their foundations on the neighbouring land they could not revoke the neighbour's right of way. This analysis causes few problems. It is the second reason given for the decision in this case which causes concern: that the actions of the original owner in allowing the neighbour to build his garage gave rise to an estoppel or, as Lord Denning MR put it, 'an equity arising out of acquiescence'. It was held that this 'equity', which is not a land charge and therefore was not void for non-registration, would bind a purchaser who bought with notice, as had the plaintiffs in this case. This second limb of the argument seems once again to create a type of licence which is binding on third parties, and the decision is a rare example of the enforcement of a licence against a purchaser for value. It seems to elevate the licence by estoppel into some kind of quasi-interest in land. Thus this case is a very strong example of the reasoning which says that some licences, and particularly licences by estoppel, give rise to an 'equity' which is capable of binding third parties. (See also *Inwards* v *Baker* [1965] 2 QB 29 and *Ward* v *Kirkland* [1967] Ch 194.) This departure from traditional ideas about licences has led to criticism (see Crane (1967) 31 Conv (NS) 332) and it must be said that since the dispute in *E.R.Ives Investment Ltd* v *High* could have been resolved on the point of the related benefit and burden alone, the discussion of the 'equity' arising from estoppel was quite unnecessary. The case, however, stands as authority for the proposition that licences can bind third parties, including a purchaser for value, and presumably will do so until these issues are further considered by the House of Lords. Since the retirement of Lord Denning MR, the Court of Appeal has been less likely to regard the licence as being capable of binding third parties save in those circumstances which justify the imposition of a constructive trust. The decision in *Errington* v *Errington* has already been the subject of attack (see p. 167) and that in *E.R. Ives Investment Ltd* v *High* may well follow.

If we apply the rules on licences to the Bells at 3 Trant Way it seems likely that Mr Bell has a licence by estoppel which can be enforced against his daughter, Barbara. Mr Bell has spent money on his flat in reliance on Miss Bell's statement that he has a home for life. It is likely that if a dispute arose a court could, at the least, hold that Mr Bell had an irrevocable licence for life.

The question of whether such a licence binds a third party might well become very important if Barbara wished to sell the property whilst her father wanted to remain there. The title to No 3 is registered, and there has as yet been no decision on the status of such licences in the case of registered title (title to the plaintiffs' land in *E.R. Ives Investment Ltd* v *High* was unregistered). If the court took the view that such a licence can bind a third party, it might take the further step of treating it as giving rise to an overriding interest, and Mr Bell, if in actual occupation, could rely on LRA 1925, s. 70(1)(g). If, however, it was held that such licences do not bind third parties or do not create rights which are capable of being overriding interests, Mr Bell would probably find himself being evicted by the new owner unless the facts justified the imposition of a constructive trust.

ARE LICENCES BECOMING INTERESTS IN LAND?

At the start of this chapter we referred to the traditional idea that licences are mere permissions and do not constitute interests in land. Having looked at the modern case law, it is worth considering whether this is still true, or whether modern decisions mean that the licence has become, or is becoming, an interest in land.

What is an interest in land?

The authorities seem to suggest that the crucial factor, in deciding whether a right amounts to an interest in land, is whether the right is enforceable against third parties. A right which cannot be enforced against a successor in title is clearly *not* an interest in land. However, since the answer to the question, 'What rights bind successors in title'?, appears to be, 'Those which are interests in land', this definition seems to be somewhat circular in nature. It is nevertheless the best that can be offered, and so, in considering whether a licence creates an interest in land, attention centres on whether it binds third parties, and in particular the purchaser for value.

What about licences?

In many of the cases which we discuss above, the claimants' rights were held to bind successors of the person who had originally created the right. In many instances the rights were held to bind the third party because the court felt that the particular circumstances of the case had given rise to a trust. Since beneficial interests under a trust are clearly rights which are capable of binding third parties in equity, the imposition of a trust allows one to avoid the thorny question of whether licences *per se* can affect successors. Despite a number of *obiter dicta* suggesting that licences do bind third parties, there are, it seems, only two cases (*Errington* v *Errington* [1952] 1 KB 290 and *E.R. Ives Investment Ltd* v *High* [1967] 2 QB 379) in which a licence has actually been held to be binding on a third party. However, as we have indicated above (pp. 167 and 170), both of these cases have been the subject of considerable academic and judicial criticism. Accordingly it might be thought that the doubts thus expressed would justify any later court called upon to consider this issue in disregarding or distinguishing these authorities. The suggestion that some licences may now amount to interests in land is accordingly only as reliable as are these two decisions and, since the remarks of the Court of Appeal in *Ashburn Anstalt* v *W.J. Arnold & Co* [1989] Ch 1, it seems unsafe to place too much reliance upon them. In appropriate cases the imposition of a constructive trust provides a claimant with a recognisable interest in land and resolves these difficulties.

A RELATED ISSUE: RESULTING TRUSTS

At this point we are going to consider the applicability of resulting trusts to land. We deal with this issue here, rather than in the chapter on trusts, because experience shows that the issues of licences and resulting trusts often arise from similar sets of facts.

In relation to land the resulting trust will arise in some cases in which one person has contributed towards the purchase of property which is conveyed into the name of another person. It may also arise where one party conveys an estate to another person for no consideration and in circumstances in which it is clear that a gift was not intended (see *Hodgson* v *Marks* [1971] Ch 892). It should be made clear from the start, however, that it is not in every case in which one person contributes to or improves another's land that a resulting trust will arise. Indeed the basic rule in English law is that such actions do not give one an interest in the property concerned.

The simplest cases to deal with are those in which a purchaser of property buys an estate using money belonging to another person. As long as it is clear that the other party was not providing the money by way of a loan or a gift, the purchaser will hold the property on resulting trust for the person who provided the money to buy it (*Dyer* v *Dyer* (1788) 2 Cox Eq Cas 92). If the other party provides only a portion of the purchase price he will obtain an equitable interest in the property which is proportional to his contribution (*Dewar* v *Dewar* [1975] 1 WLR 1532). In this context it should be noted that such financial assistance given to a wife or child will be subject to the principle of advancement, and a court will normally presume that it is made by way of gift unless there is clear evidence of a contrary intention (*Stock* v *McAvoy* (1872) LR 15 Eq 55).

The situation is more difficult where one party buys property but the other later improves it or pays mortgage instalments. This often arises with married couples or couples living together as husband and wife. In *Pettitt* v *Pettitt* [1970] AC 777, a house was vested in the name of a wife and had been purchased with her money. Over the years her husband had redecorated and improved the property, and claimed an interest in the house as a result. The House of Lords held that he had obtained no interest in the property as there was no agreement with his wife that he should obtain such an interest. (See also *Gissing* v *Gissing* [1971] AC 886.) Thus the rule was that to obtain an interest in property belonging to another by operation of a resulting trust two things must be established: (a) a contribution in money or money's worth, and (b) an agreement that the contribution would confer an interest in the property.

In the years following *Gissing* v *Gissing* the courts tended to extend the resulting trust principles considerably, so that it became easier and easier to establish a claim to a share in property by virtue of a contribution. The Court of Appeal (and particularly Lord Denning MR) was swift to extend the use of the resulting trust. Thus in *Hussey* v *Palmer* [1972] 1 WLR 1286 the Court of Appeal held that, when a mother expended money on property belonging to her daughter in order to provide an extra bedroom for the mother's use, she thereby obtained an interest in the property. This was so even though there was no real evidence that the parties had agreed that Mrs Hussey should obtain an interest in the land. In *Cooke* v *Head* [1972] 1 WLR 518 Lord Denning MR went so far as to suggest that wherever 'two parties by their joint efforts acquire property' then the court would hold that the property was subject to a trust. A similar position seems to have been adopted in *Eves* v *Eves* [1975] 1 WLR 1338, though the facts in that case were slightly unusual since one party had lied to the other in order to prevent the property being conveyed to them both as joint tenants in the first place. In *Hall* v *Hall* (1982) 3 FLR 379 Lord Denning MR said:

> If a man and a woman have been living together as husband and wife, and the woman has been contributing towards the establishment of the joint household, although the house is in the man's name, there is a resulting trust as a matter of ordinary common justice for her.

(See also *Tanner* v *Tanner* [1975] 1 WLR 1346.)

Over the years this question of whether, and how easily, one can obtain an interest in another's property has become less important in relation to married couples due to reforms of family law (see p. 238). However, these reforms do not apply to unmarried couples who must rely on the basic principles if one claims an interest in property belonging to the other.

The relaxation of the strict rules made over the years by the Court of Appeal was chiefly due to a wish to achieve a fair solution in such cases. However, since the case of *Burns* v *Burns* [1984] Ch 317 it appears that in future the courts will adhere rather more strictly to the two *Gissing* v *Gissing* requirements:

(a)   contribution;
(b)   an agreement that the contribution should give rise to an interest in the land.

Burns v *Burns* concerned an unmarried couple who had been living together as man and wife for 19 years. Mr Burns was the legal owner of the house in which they lived, and had provided the initial deposit and paid instalments due on the mortgage. For some time Mrs Burns stayed at home and cared for the children of the relationship. Later she undertook paid work and used her salary to pay some domestic bills and make minor improvements to the house (e.g., new doorknobs). When the parties' relationship collapsed, the Court of Appeal held that Mrs Burns had no right to a share in the house. This was because she had not contibuted to the purchase price of the property, directly or indirectly, and there was no agreement that she should obtain an interest. It was made clear that a resulting trust *can* arise from indirect contributions. Thus if Mrs Burns had paid all the household bills, and thereby released Mr Burns's income to pay the mortgage debt, this might count as an indirect contribution. Even once a contribution is made, though, one must still establish a common intention or agreement that the contributor should obtain an interest in the property. In *Burns* the court did indicate that such an agreement might occasionally be implied but only in the case of sizeable contributions. In general, though, the nature of the relationship between the parties will be such as to negative any suggestion that they intended to enter into a legally binding agreement (see May LJ at p. 335).

The case of *Grant* v *Edwards* [1986] 1 Ch 638 was similar to *Burns* v *Burns*. However, here the claimant mistress had made substantial contributions towards the purchase and improvement of the property and it was said that there was an oral agreement between the parties that she should thereby obtain an interest. The contributions made were both direct (£4,000 spent on repairs) and indirect (large sums spent on general household bills). The Court of Appeal held that in these circumstances the claimant had established a right to an interest in the property. The case does seem to give rise to a number of problems because the judgments in it appear to conflate two separate issues: those of resulting trusts and rights arising by estoppel.

This whole problem came before the House of Lords in *Lloyds Bank plc* v *Rosset* [1991] 1 AC 107. Here a property was purchased with money provided by a husband's family trust. On the insistence of the trustees the property was registered in the sole name of the husband. The house required a great deal of alteration and the necessary building work was paid for by the husband, with money obtained on an overdraft from his bank secured upon the property. Mrs Rosset was heavily involved in giving instructions to the builders and later did much of the needed decoration of the premises herself. It was held that Mrs Rosset's claim to a beneficial interest in the property failed. First, there had been no agreement that she should obtain such an interest. It was said that the intention to make the premises a joint venture is not enough, nor is the intention that the house should be occupied as a family home. It will be necessary to show that there have been express discussions about the interests between the partners. Secondly, the work done did not in itself suggest that there must have been some kind of agreement, so that the court might imply a bargain. It was suggested by Lord Bridge that the sort of work that Mrs Rosset had done was work which any wife might perform, even in the absence of an agreement that she was to have a share in the property.

In this case the court seemed to be influenced by the fact that the parties were married and the decision suggests that it may be easier to imply an agreement where an unmarried couple are involved. The case was not one covered by matrimonial law because the issue was whether Mrs Rosset had any claim with priority to that of the bank. Had a dispute arisen between Mr and Mrs Rosset it would be likely to arise on separation or divorce and as between the husband and wife the matrimonial courts may re-order the property holding.

In *Ungurian* v *Lesnoff* [1989] 3 WLR 840 Vinelott J was not prepared to infer an agreement that a lady should have an interest in property bought by a person she had hoped to marry and in order to provide a home for her and her children. However, in *Hammond* v *Mitchell* [1992] 2 All ER 109 (another case concerning an unmarried couple) Waite J accepted that, where a man had bought a property in his own name but had told his mistress (at the time his fiancée) that this was due to reasons connected with his divorce and that the property would be half hers once they were married, this was sufficient discussion and agreement to found a claim to a beneficial interest in the property. In this case the couple had remained together for some years and had two children, though they had never married. They had joined together in a number of commercial dealings and the decision seems to have been influenced by the couple's tendency to treat all their property as assets of a joint venture. It was also clear that at one point, when the property in question had to be mortgaged to raise further finances, the man had been present and had remained silent when a bank official asked the lady to sign a release of her rights in the property as against the bank (in connection with the grant of a loan secured on the property). Since here there had been discussions tending to suggest that the lady was intended to have a share in the property, Waite J was not concerned by the fact that no express agreement had been reached as to the extent of that share: this was to be decided on the basis of the contribution made. The case does however emphasise the problems which can arise where unmarried couples do not make clear arrangements as to the holding of any property.

The effect of these recent cases, especially *Burns* v *Burns*, is undoubtedly to place a number of people in weak positions and, bearing in mind that unmarried cohabitation is increasingly common, it may be that this is an area of law which requires consideration by the legislature.

If one applies these rules to Henry and Mildred Mumps one is forced to conclude that Henry may have some difficulty in establishing that he is entitled to an interest in 8 Trant Way. He has probably satisfied the test of making substantial contributions to the property, in this case indirectly by making improvements to the property. However, it may well be that he cannot show any agreement between himself and Mildred that he should obtain an interest in the house. Understandably, people in Henry's position rarely consider that they need to make formal agreements about such things until it is too late. It is clear from *Burns* v *Burns* that all Henry's years of devoted 'housewifery' will count for nothing in the issue. Perhaps these difficulties will encourage the use of pre-cohabitation contracts to clarify the position in such cases but this can only happen where, at the start of their relationship, the parties are cold-blooded enough to discuss what should happen should they part. In *Hammond* v *Mitchell* Waite J expressed some concerns at the problems which can arise in such cases and noted that the absence of the possibility of divorce proceedings can, due to property disputes, give rise to even greater stress than that which arises on the breakdown of a marriage.

5 Trusts

We explained briefly in the first chapter that the essential characteristic of the trust is the separation of title to property and the right to use and enjoy it. The trustee is the owner of the property, but he holds it not for himself but for the beneficiary, who is protected by equity and accordingly has an equitable interest in that property. In general, the trustee will have the *legal* title (in a trust of land, he will usually hold the legal estate). However, it must be realised that it is also possible to create a trust of an equitable interest; for example, a beneficiary under a trust may transfer his equitable interest to some other person and direct him to hold it on trust for some third party. Thus, the interest of the beneficiary under a trust is always equitable, but that of the trustee may be legal or equitable, according to the nature of the property which is subject to the trust.

A trust may be created expressly by the 'settlor' (the person who creates the trust), either during his lifetime (*inter vivos*) or by will. LPA 1925, s. 53(1), provides that 'a declaration of trust respecting any land or any interest therein must be manifested and proved by some writing' signed by the settlor, or by his will. Trusts are also imposed by statute in certain cases, some of which we will consider later.

In addition, as we mentioned in chapter 1 (p. 9), there are three categories of trusts which may arise without any express creation or statutory imposition, namely, implied, resulting and constructive trusts. We have already given some account of the last two of these (pp. 162 and 171), and all that needs to be said about the first category is that a trust will be implied by the court where it finds that there was an intention to create a trust even through no express words were used. The boundaries between implied, resulting and constructive trusts are not always clearly defined in modern decisions, and it seems that to some extent these categories overlap. Questions of the definition and scope of these types of trust are more appropriately dealt with in the textbooks on trusts, but mention has to be made of them here because of their use in recent decisions on licences, co-ownership and registered title.

One other type of trust must be mentioned briefly here: the trust for sale. This arises where the terms of the trust, however created, impose on the trustees the *duty* to sell the property, and to apply the proceeds as directed by the trust. This situation should be distinguished from that in which the trustees have the *power* to sell, for imposing the duty on them means that they must act, whereas a power merely enables them to do so if they think fit (i.e. 'You *must* sell', rather than 'You *may* sell'). The imposition of this duty on the trustees has a number of consequences, which we shall consider later (p. 208).

To a large extent, the same rules are applied to all trusts, irrespective of the nature of the trust property, and we assume that you will acquire a knowledge of such rules from your study of the law relating to trusts. We therefore propose to say very little about the most simple trust of land, in which trustees hold the legal estate for an adult beneficiary, who is entitled absolutely to the beneficial (equitable) interest. There are no special 'land law' rules relating to this situation, except that, in the case of registered title, the beneficiary should ensure that his interest is protected by the entry of a restriction or caution on the register. In the case of unregistered land, his rights against a purchaser for value of the legal estate have always depended upon the doctrine of notice, and this position was not changed by the 1925 legislation (see p. 69). There are, however, certain topics within the scope of this book which require a consideration of some form of trust. We have already seen that in certain cases concerning licences the courts have found it helpful to impose what they describe as resulting or constructive trusts (see p. 161) and in chapter 6 we shall see how Parliament has imposed statutory trusts for sale on most cases of co-ownership. For the rest of this chapter we shall be concerned with the forms of trust used to create settlements of land.

Settlements

A settlement may be defined as an arrangement whereby interests in a piece of property are given to a number of people in succession. Thus, in the most usual form, one person will have an immediate right to the enjoyment of the property, whilst other people will have rights to such enjoyment in the future. For example, a settlor may provide that A is to have the property during his life, but that on A's death it is to belong absolutely to B. This arrangement will constitute a settlement.

Factual background

The Thornes are looking for a home in Mousehole, and go to view two houses which are for sale in Trant Way. By a coincidence, both houses are occupied by elderly widows: Mrs Slope at No. 9 and Mrs Grantly at No. 10. Both women seem lonely and pleased to have someone to talk to, and tell the Thornes something about themselves and their families.

It appears that each of them is entitled, under her husband's will, to live for the rest of her life in the house she now occupies. Mrs Grantly, however, explains that she finds her house is too big for her now, and 'the trustees' have agreed to sell it and to buy a small flat for her with the proceeds. Mrs Slope, on the other hand, wants to sell because she is lonely living on her own, and has decided to move in with her sister. In conversation, she mentions that her husband's will provides that, at her death, the house is to go to her brother-in-law. This worries the Thornes, who wonder whether he will oppose her plans to sell the house. Mrs Slope also mentions that she has been registered as the owner of No. 9, and this puzzles the Thornes, because Mrs Grantly, whose position seems to them to be very similar to that of Mrs Slope, thinks that the trustees own her house.

Although the Thornes do not know it, the clue to the difference between the position of the two widows is contained in the following extracts from the wills of their respective husbands.

The will of Daniel Slope provided:

I give the house in which my wife and I shall be residing at the date of my death . . . to my trustees upon trust for my wife Catherine Ann Slope during her life and after her death upon trust for my brother Henry John Slope absolutely.

The will of Edward Grantly contained the following provision:

I give all my real and personal property . . . (hereinafter called 'my residuary estate') to my trustees upon trust to sell, call in and convert the same into money at such time or times and in such manner as my trustees shall think fit. . . .

My trustees shall stand possessed of my residuary estate upon trust to pay the income thereof to my wife, Margaret Jane Grantly, during her life.

After the death of my wife, and in the meantime subject to her interest, my trustees shall hold my residuary estate and the income thereof in trust for my nephew William Francis Grantly.

I direct that the house in which my wife and I shall be residing at the date of my death . . . shall not be sold during the lifetime of my wife without her consent in writing and that until the sale thereof my trustees shall permit my wife to occupy the same rent-free so long as she shall desire.

At the request of my wife my trustees shall sell this house (or any house purchased in lieu thereof in pursuance of a previous request) and apply the whole or any part of the net proceeds of sale in the purchase of another house selected by her . . . and shall hold the same upon the trusts declared by this my will.

As we shall see, each will does in fact give rise to a settlement, but the difference in the words used by the testators means that one settlement takes effect under the Settled Land Act 1925, while the other operates as a trust for sale. These two forms of settlement differ greatly in their machinery and administration, and we will have to consider each separately, but it may help to begin by explaining why it is that there are two ways of making a settlement. Although we are trying to avoid undue reference to history, it is necessary to refer briefly to it at this point, and in particular to explain the origin of the *strict settlement* which is the forerunner of the Settled Land Act settlement.

HISTORICAL BACKGROUND

Strict settlements

We must begin by emphasising that we are describing a process which began in the Middle Ages, and that we are talking about people who owned large amounts of land. The landowner who made the sort of strict settlement we will describe probably owned at least several large country estates, and at a later period may also have had a London town house, a hunting-box in the shires and a grouse moor in Scotland. The settlement in its developed form is designed to meet the needs of large landowners, like Trollope's Duke of Omnium, rather than those of small modern owner-occupiers, like the Slopes and Grantlys.

The purpose of making a strict settlement was in the main to ensure that the family estates remained in the family, passing intact to the heir, and that at the same time provision was made from the income of the estate for wives, widows and younger children. In a typical marriage settlement, made by a fee simple owner on his marriage, the settlor would deprive himself of his absolute title to the estate and create a mere life estate for himself, followed by a fee tail in favour of his eldest (probably yet unborn) son. He would also make a provision for the payment of a personal allowance to his wife ('pin-money') during the marriage, and a larger sum to support her during her widowhood, if she survived him, as well as providing 'portions' for the daughters and younger sons to support them in later life. The settlor had thus split the legal fee simple into several smaller estates (a life estate, a fee tail and a reversion in favour of his general heirs — see p. 88), which could be done at law before 1926.

An alternative way of making the same provision was to give the full fee simple to trustees, directing them to hold on trust for the family on similar terms, so that the settlor and his heir took equitable interests under the trust equivalent to the life estate and the fee tail, and money payments were provided for the rest of the family.

Whichever form was adopted, the result was the same, for, although the land could be sold or mortgaged if all those entitled under the settlement were of full age and agreed to act together, there was no one person who by himself could dispose of the whole legal and beneficial interest. Thus the chances of the property being lost to the family were greatly reduced.

There was one danger which threatened to interfere with the settlor's plans, for from the Middle Ages the common law had permitted a tenant in tail to 'bar' the fee tail and convert his limited estate into the full fee simple. We cannot give any details of this procedure here, but if you are interested (and it is a fascinating example of the use of legal fictions) you will find a full account in Megarry and Wade, *The Law of Real Property*, 5th ed., pp. 76–89.

This danger was, however, traditionally overcome by the settlor persuading his eldest son to bar the entail as soon as he came of age, and to resettle the resulting fee simple, giving himself a life estate and creating an entail in favour of his eldest son. This seems to have worked satisfactorily in most cases, and a process of barring the entail and resettling would go on for one generation after another, so that the current owners of the property never had more than a life estate.

Trusts for sale

As we have seen, the strict settlement was designed for landowners with a sentimental attachment to land which had probably been owned by their families for hundreds of years. It was not, however, particularly appropriate in the case of land which had been bought relatively recently, and as an investment rather than for occupation. Land on which housing estates or factories were built was of no sentimental value to its owners, and they usually intended to hold it as long as the yield was satisfactory but to sell and reinvest the proceeds when better bargains were available. Yet, all the same, such landowners might want to make settlements, in order to keep their capital intact for later generations and to provide for the present members of their families. Their needs were met by the use of the trust for sale.

Title would be vested in trustees, who would be under a duty to sell and reinvest, but who could postpone sale until the time was right (see p. 204). The income until sale, and the resulting capital, could be held in trust for a series of beneficiaries, as defined in the trust instrument, and so the settlor could provide an income for family members without dividing his capital between them.

Statutory powers of a tenant for life

Thus it is that the two methods of creating settlements developed; the strict settlement being used where particular land was to remain in the family, and the trust for sale being employed where the land was an investment which changed from time to time. There is only one further historical point to note, and that relates to strict settlements. In the 19th century, the restrictions on dealing with land which was subject to such settlements were seen to cause difficulty. Some settlements did permit limited sale and mortgaging, so that money could be raised to improve the rest of the estate; but, if such powers were not expressly provided, the current owner of the estate might well find himself unable to raise money for much-needed repairs and improvements, and as a result the property would deteriorate. A series of 19th century Acts, culminating in the Settled Land Act 1882, gave the current owner (the 'tenant for life') powers to deal with settled land, and even to sell it, despite the settlor's intentions. We shall return to this point in more detail when we come to look at the powers of the tenant for life under SLA 1925.

SETTLEMENTS UNDER THE SETTLED LAND ACT 1925

Basic form of a settlement

Before dealing with these settlements in detail it is as well to have a simple idea of their form. Accordingly we will look at 9 Trant Way and the position of Mrs Slope. Under her husband's will Mrs Slope has only a life interest in the property which, on her death, will pass to her brother-in-law, Henry Slope. Mrs Slope will therefore not be able to leave 9 Trant Way to anyone in her will: her interest in the property is limited and will die with her. As we already know, a life interest cannot be a legal estate or interest in land under the provisions of LPA 1925, s. 1, and Mrs Slope's interest in the land can therefore only amount to an equitable interest. On her death, Henry Slope will be entitled to the full fee simple and can expect to become the legal owner of No. 9. However, he has no right to immediate possession of the property, only a right to possession in the future, and so for the time being his interest does not satisfy LPA 1925, s. 1(1), and he too has only an equitable interest.

It is, however, a basic rule that land cannot be left without a legal owner. (The technical phrase which expresses this is that 'there can be no "abeyance of seisin"'.) Accordingly, someone must hold the legal estate upon trust for Mrs Slope and Henry Slope as beneficiaries. One might expect that the trustees appointed by the settlor would perform this function, but SLA 1925 does not adopt this method. Instead it provides that the person with the current interest (Mrs Slope) should hold the land as a type of trustee upon trust for herself and the other beneficiary. Mrs Slope is described as the 'tenant for life' and she not only holds the legal estate but also has a wide range of statutory powers to deal with the land, including the power to sell it. The trustees of the settlements do not hold the legal estate but they do have a number of functions, including the obligation to receive and invest the proceeds of any sale of the land. This explains why Mrs Slope is the registered owner of 9 Trant Way and why she has power to sell the property.

We will now look at the various types of arrangement which can give rise to a settlement under the Act, and consider the rules which govern its administration.

Types of settlement

The definition of a settlement is provided by SLA 1925, s. 1, which sets out the types of arrangement which make property settled land and subject to a trust governed by the provisions of that statute. The section provides that 'Any deed, will, agreement . . . or other instrument' under which land stands limited in certain ways will give rise to a settlement. We will consider each of the types of limitation in turn.

SLA 1925: s. 1(1)(i): Limited in trust for any persons by way of succession
This covers the position of Mrs Slope, for her husband has by his will created an arrangement under which she is to have a limited interest (for life) and will be succeeded in possession by his brother. This is the simplest, the classical, form of settlement and it arises whenever property is granted 'To A for life and then to B'. This paragraph of s. 1(1) of the Act is very widely drawn, and in fact the wording is wide enough to include several of the other specific arrangements set out in the later paragraphs.

SLA 1925, s. 1(1)(ii): Limited in trust for any person in possession:

(a) *For an entailed interest whether or not capable of being barred or defeated.*
Entails are no longer very common, though in the past they had some popularity
with the great landed families. An entail arises in a case in which land is
granted to 'A and the heirs of his body'. This phrase means that only a
particular class of heirs can inherit A's interest. Accordingly it cannot be
a fee simple estate and it does not come within LPA 1925, s. 1. Under such
a provision A's interest will pass only to his lineal descendants. Thus if A
dies childless without an 'heir of his body', the land will not pass to those
more remote members of his family (e.g., his brother or his father) who would
be entitled to take if he had held a fee simple. In such a case the entail
will cease and the property will revert to the settlor, or to his successors,
who accordingly are said to have a 'reversion' in the property.

At one time it was normal for an entail to be expressed in the form 'to
B and the heirs of his body male'. In such cases only the male lineal heirs
of B could inherit. If B died leaving two sons C and D, C (the elder) would
inherit. If C died leaving only a daughter, E, she could not inherit. However,
D could inherit because he is a direct male heir of B. If D were also dead
but had left a son, F, then F could inherit. Once again, F is the lineal male
descendant of B.

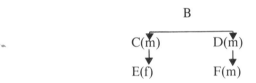

Jane Austen provides an excellent example of the problems which can result
from such an arrangement in her novel *Pride and Prejudice*. In modern times
the entail is not so much of a problem because it can be brought to an end
('barred') fairly easily and also because the current holder will have considerable
powers to deal with the property under SLA 1925.

(b) *For [a] . . . fee simple or . . . term of years . . . subject to an executory
limitation, gift, or disposition over.* This type of settlement is best explained
by an example. It would arise if a grant were made 'to A in fee simple but
to B when B is admitted as a solicitor'. In this situation A may lose his
interest in the property if B ever manages to qualify as a solicitor; only if
B predeceases A, without so qualifying, will A get an unconditional right
to the land. Accordingly one is again faced with the possibility of a succession
of interests and this creates a settlement.

(c) *For a base or determinable fee or any corresponding interest in leasehold
land.* The nature of the determinable fee has already been discussed (see p. 87).
The base fee is now extremely rare and a modern lawyer is most unlikely
ever to encounter one. It is an interest which would arise if someone with
an entailed interest sold that interest. He could not give the purchaser a greater

interest than he himself had, and so the purchaser would acquire an interest which could be inherited by any of his own heirs, but which would last only as long as the heirs of the body of the original entailed owner exist. These base fees are rare because entails themselves are now relatively uncommon and also because it is usually possible for the holder of an entailed interest to bar the entail completely and to convey a full fee simple to a purchaser under the provisions of the Fines and Recoveries Act 1833. (For more detail on the entail and the base fee see Megarry and Wade, *The Law of Real Property*, 5th ed. (London: Stevens, 1984), pp. 76–92.)

(d) *Being an infant, for an estate in fee simple or for a term of years absolute.* Any person under the age of 18 years is legally an 'infant' and is incapable of owning a legal estate. Obviously an infant might well be entitled to such an estate (e.g., under a will) and accordingly the land will be held by trustees upon trust for the infant, who will have an equitable interest in the property. Such trusts can be brought to an end when the infant reaches 18 and is capable of holding the legal estate for himself.

SLA 1925, s. 1(1)(iii): Limited in trust for any person for an estate in fee simple or for a term of years absolute contingently on the happening of any event. Such contingent interests arise when an ascertained person will obtain a legal estate at some point in the future if a specified event occurs (see p. 88). For example, parents, fearing youthful indiscretions, frequently provide that a young person is not to take property until he reaches an age greater than the age of majority, e.g. 21 or 25 years. Until that age, the beneficiary has only a contingent interest and this must be held behind a trust. If and when he reaches the prescribed age he will obtain a fully vested legal estate in the property. These contingent interests are often described as 'springing interests', because they will 'spring up' in the future, rather than following some earlier interest.

SLA 1925, s. 1(1)(iv):
This paragraph was repealed in 1949.

SLA 1925, s. 1(1)(v): Charged . . . with the payment of any rentcharge for the life of any person, or any less period, or of any capital, annual, or periodical sums for the portions, advancement, maintenance, or otherwise for the benefit of any persons . . .
This paragraph covers arrangements of a family nature, where a settlor attempts to give one person a legal estate but at the same time charges the property with the payment of sums of money for the maintenance of other persons (e.g., younger children). It is intended that these sums should be paid from the income of the estate, which in general goes to the tenant for life. It should be noted that not all land subject to a rentcharge thereby becomes settled land; the paragraph only covers payments for portions, advancement and maintenance of another person. Accordingly land subject, for example, to a rentcharge to pay for the maintenance of a road would *not* fall within this

provision, and so the existence of estate rentcharges (see p. 328) does not make the property into settled land.

Moreover, even where the rentcharges do fall within this paragraph, it may be possible to deal with the land without using Settled Land Act machinery. This is because it was realised, after the Act was passed, that a number of purchasers had in the past bought land subject to such rentcharges, on the vendors' undertaking to indemnify them against the charges. These owners now found themselves subject to Settled Land Act provisions, requiring complicated documents and the appointment of trustees. The Law of Property (Amendment) Act 1926, s. 1, therefore provided that such land could still be dealt with as if it were not settled land, and thus its owner now has a choice. He may sell the land without going through the Settled Land Act formalities, provided the land is sold *subject to* the charges (probably with a provision for the vendor to indemnify the purchaser). However, if the purchaser wishes to buy the land *free of* the charges the Settled Land Act machinery must be adopted: a vesting deed (see p. 187) will be required and trustees must be appointed to receive the purchase money. The purchaser will then take the land free of the charges, which will attach instead to the purchase money (see p. 190). The reduction of the number of rentcharges by the Rentcharges Act 1977 makes these situations more unusual.

These then are the types of arrangement which will give rise to a settlement. It is, however, possible to create similar interests but behind a trust for sale. Such arrangements are operated solely as trusts for sale and are exempted from the provisions of the Settled Land Act 1925 (SLA 1925, s. 1(7)).

Tenant for life

The Settled Land Act 1925 gives day-to-day control of the settled land to the tenant for life, and it is accordingly essential to identify this person. Section 19 of the Act says that the tenant for life is 'The person of full age who is for the time being beneficially entitled under a settlement to possession of settled land for his life'. Thus in the case of 9 Trant Way, Mrs Slope, who has a life interest in possession (i.e., not a future life interest), will be the tenant for life.

Obviously in a number of the forms of settlement no one has a life interest in the property. For example, the owner of an entailed interest has an inheritable interest and not one which will last for his lifetime only. Accordingly s. 20 of the Act provides that other 'limited' owners shall have the powers of a tenant for life. The effect of s. 20 is to give the person who is currently entitled to an estate or interest in possession the powers of the tenant for life, as long as that person is of full age (over 18). This will include a person who is entitled only to the income of the property for his life, or for the lifetime of another (s. 20(1)(viii)), even though such a person appears to have only an interest in money rather than in the land. It also includes a tenant under a lease for life, provided he is not holding at a rent (s. 20(1)(iv) to (vi)), so that such a tenant, whose lease is not converted into a fixed term by LPA 1925, s. 149(6), can exercise the powers of a tenant for life.

Sometimes there is no person who qualifies as tenant for life, either under s. 19 or s. 20. This is most commonly the case when the person currently entitled to the land is an infant (see s. 26). In such cases the powers of the tenant for life will be exercised by the 'Statutory owner' (see definition of this phrase in SLA 1925, s. 117(1)(xxvi)). The statutory owner will be:

(a) any person upon whom the settlement confers the powers of the tenant for life; or
(b) in any other case, the trustees of the settlement.

Thus the settlor may make an express appointment of the statutory owners under (a); but if he does not do so, the trustees will assume that role.

TRUSTEES

First trustees

Although the tenant for life deals with the day-to-day management of the property, the trustees of a settlement are still extremely important, as we will see in due course. It is accordingly also important to be able to identify the trustees correctly. For this purpose reference should be made to SLA 1925, s. 30, which lists the possibilities in order of preference.

(a) The first choice for trustees are those persons who under the settlement have power to sell the land or who have power to consent to or approve the exercise of the power of sale. (In fact the trustees will have no power to sell for this right is given to the tenant for life by the statute, but the fact that the settlor had tried to give them the power leads to their being identified as trustees under this head.)
(b) The second possibility, and the most common, is the persons named as trustees of the settlement in the deed by which it was created.
(c) The third possibility is those persons who are trustees with power of sale or with power to consent to or approve of sale of any *other* land which is held on the same trusts under the same settlement.
(d) Fourthly come any persons who have a future power to sell or to consent to or approve sale. Thus if land is conveyed 'to A for life and then to Tim and Tom upon trust for sale', Tim and Tom will become trustees of the settlement since they are persons who will have the right to sell the land in the future.
(e) If none of the four previous methods produce the necessary trustees then all the beneficiaries acting together may by deed appoint trustees. This can only be done if the beneficiaries who appoint can between them dispose of the *whole* equitable interest in the property and, of course, if they are all of full age. If the settlement arises under a will or on intestacy then the deceased's personal representatives will be trustees until other trustees are appointed (SLA 1925, s. 30(3)).

In the case of compound settlements, that is, where the settlement is created by several separate documents, the trustees should be ascertained by reference to SLA 1925, s. 31.

If there are no trustees, or in any case in which it is expedient, the court can appoint trustees under s. 34 on the application of any beneficiary under the settlement (or, in the case of an infant beneficiary , his guardian or next friend). A settlement should not be left without trustees, as they have important duties and powers in relation to the settled land and this provision ensures that, whatever the difficulties, trustees can be appointed.

New, or additional, trustees

It is essential that the settlement should have the services of the correct number of trustees throughout its existence. The Trustee Act 1925, s. 34, provides that the number of trustees should never be increased above four. The same Act, by s. 39, provides that no trustee may retire so as to reduce the number of trustees below two, unless the remaining trustee is a 'trust corporation' (defined in SLA, s. 117(xxx), as including 'the Public Trustee or a corporation . . . appointed by the court in any particular case to be a trustee' and including other bodies recognised under the Public Trustee Rules 1912 or s. 37, Law of Property (Amendment) Act 1926). Where it is necessary to appoint a new trustee this must be done under the provisions of s. 36 of the Trustee Act. A new appointment should be made by a person who was given the power to appoint by the settlement, or, if there is no such person, by the remaining trustee or trustees (or the personal representatives of the last surviving trustee if all have died). An appointment under s. 36 should be made in writing and, once made, a deed of declaration should be executed under SLA 1925, s. 35(1). Later this deed of declaration can be used to prove to a person required to pay capital money to the trustees that the current trustees are in fact entitled to give a good receipt for the money. If, for some reason, new trustees cannot be appointed under s. 36 of the Trustee Act the trust still need not be left without them, for under s. 41 of the same Act the court may also appoint new trustees where 'it is found inexpedient, difficult or impracticable so to do without the assistance of the court'.

CREATING A SETTLEMENT

Settlements created *inter vivos*

The basic procedure for the creation of a settlement *inter vivos* is governed by SLA 1925, s. 4. This requires that the settlement should be effected by two deeds:

(a)   a trust instrument; and
(b)   a vesting deed.

Trust instrument

The trust instrument is the document which sets out in detail the intentions of the settlor. Under SLA 1925, s. 4(3), it should contain the following information:

(a) a declaration of the trusts affecting the land;
(b) the appointment of trustees;
(c) a statement of who is to have the power to appoint new trustees (if any);
(d) any extra powers to be given to the tenant for life or trustees, in addition to those conferred by the Act.

It can be seen from this that the trust instrument may be a very long document, particularly if the settlor chooses to extend the statutory powers, and that it will include all the personal details of the trust, including the names (or descriptions) of all the beneficiaries and the nature of their interests in the property. Some of this information may well be of a private nature and be such that the beneficiaries would not wish it revealed to an outsider, such as an intending purchaser of the settled land.

Vesting deed

It is the second document, the vesting deed, which provides all the necessary public information about the trust. The contents of the vesting deed are set out in SLA 1925, s. 5(1):

(a) a description of the settled land (e.g., its address);
(b) a declaration that the land is vested in the person to whom it is conveyed, or in whom it is declared to be vested, upon the trusts affecting the land;
(c) the names of the trustees;
(d) any powers, additional to the statutory powers, conferred by the settlement; and
(e) the name of any person who is entitled to appoint new trustees.

The details contained in this document provide all the information that a purchaser of the settled land needs to know. It is not necessary for him to know anything of the details of the beneficial interests in the settlement and so this information does not appear in the vesting deed. Section 4(2) requires that settled land should be legally vested in the tenant for life or statutory owner, and it is the vesting deed which performs this function in the case of unregistered land. The wording of s. 5(1)(b) on this point may seem a little confusing and in order to understand it one has to realise that it is designed to cover two possible situations. In the first, the settlor gives himself an interest under the settlement, for instance keeping a life interest for himself and providing that other interests should take effect on his death. In such a case, he is the first tenant for life and so should hold the legal estate. In fact, that estate is already vested in him, for he owned the legal estate absolutely before making the settlement. The vesting deed therefore merely declares that he holds the legal estate, for it is not necessary to convey it to him.

In the other possible situation, the settlor divests himself of all interest in the property and the first tenant for life is therefore someone other than the settlor. In this case, the legal estate will actually be conveyed to the tenant for life by the vesting deed.

The vesting deed should be executed by the settlor at the same time as the trust instrument. If he does not do so, the trust is only partially constituted, and the tenant for life or statutory owner has a right under SLA 1925, s. 9(2), to demand that the trustees of the settlement execute the necessary vesting deed. Should they refuse to do so, the court may make an order which operates as a vesting deed (s. 9(2)).

Where title to the land is registered, the procedure for creating a settlement follows the same pattern, except that a prescribed form of vesting transfer must be used in place of the vesting deed (Land Registration Rules 1925, r. 99) and, most importantly, the legal estate will not vest in the tenant for life until the transaction is completed by registration. The tenant for life will be registered as the sole proprietor, and the interests of the beneficiaries should be protected by the entry of a restriction, which in general terms will provide that no future dealing with the land is to be registered unless any capital money arising from the transaction is paid to two named persons (the trustees of the settlement). This serves the purpose of alerting intending purchasers to the fact that this is settled land, and also should ensure compliance with the overreaching procedure (see p. 190). If for any reason the Registrar is unaware of the need to enter the restriction, a beneficiary may protect his or her interest by means of a caution. This might, for example, be necessary where the tenant for life, being also the settlor, was registered as proprietor before he made the settlement, and then does not apply for entry of the restriction.

Settlements created by will

Where a settlement is created by will, SLA 1925, s. 6, provides that the will itself shall fulfil the functions of the trust instrument. The estate will of course pass on a grant of probate or letters of administration to the personal representatives of the settlor. In such cases, the trust is completed by the execution by the personal representatives of a 'vesting assent' in favour of the tenant for life or statutory owners. In the case of registered land, the transfer should be completed by registration, as explained above.

The curtain principle

We have seen that the vesting deed (or transfer or assent, as the case may be) should contain all the information required by a prospective purchaser, without revealing to him any confidential or unnecessary information contained in the trust instrument. SLA 1925, s. 110(2), provides that, subject to certain exceptions, the purchaser is neither entitled nor bound to see the trust instrument, but may rely on information contained in the vesting deed. This rule is commonly described as 'the curtain principle', for the trust instrument and the information it contains is concealed from the purchaser by the 'curtain' of the vesting deed. However, in certain cases set out in the proviso to s. 110(2), the purchaser is required to satisfy himself of certain matters, including the fact that the person in whom the settled land is vested by the vesting deed is the person in whom it ought to be vested. In other words, the purchaser should check that the apparent tenant for life is really entitled under the settlement, and this will involve lifting the curtain and looking at the trust instrument. Reference should be made to the proviso for the circumstances under which this is necessary, but they may be summarised very generally by saying that they are all cases in which the vesting deed has been made after, rather than contemporaneously with, the trust instrument. Thus where a new settlement is made as prescribed by the Act, the curtain should remain intact.

The paralysing section

In order to ensure that the structure required by SLA 1925 is adopted, s. 13 contains a provision which paralyses certain transactions until the trust is fully constituted. The section provides that once a tenant for life or statutory owner has become entitled to the execution of a vesting deed in his favour and until such a deed is executed, any purported disposition of the settled land by the tenant for life or statutory owner is void. Thus any attempt by the tenant for life to convey the land to a purchaser would be ineffective to pass the legal estate. Such a transaction, however, operates as a contract to transfer the estate once the necessary vesting instrument has been made.

Since this provision might unfairly disadvantage an innocent purchaser, s. 13 does provide protection for a 'purchaser of a legal estate without notice of such tenant for life or statutory owner having become . . . entitled . . .' to the execution of a vesting deed. Thus the paralysing provision does not operate where an innocent purchaser acquires the legal estate.

The provisions of s. 13 are most likely to be relevant in those settlements where the tenant for life is also the settlor, for, in other cases, the tenant for life will normally be unable to prove his title to the land until the legal estate has been vested in him by the vesting deed. Section 13 could, however, produce difficulties where a tenant for life purports to grant a short lease before a vesting deed is made, for in such cases it is not normal for the tenant to demand evidence of the landlord's title.

Finally, it should be noted that it is unnecessary to execute a vesting deed in the rare situation in which the settlement comes to an end before the deed has been made (*Re Alefounder's Will Trusts* [1927] 1 Ch 360), and in such a case the owner can dispose of the land without being affected by s. 13.

POWERS OF A TENANT FOR LIFE

One of the main purposes of the Victorian reforms of the law on settled land was to ensure that such land could be dealt with when necessary. This is an advantage to the tenant for life who might otherwise find himself burdened with land which he could not afford to maintain but which he could not mortgage or sell. Accordingly SLA 1925 gives a tenant for life or statutory owner extensive rights to deal with the land, which may allow him to act in a way completely contrary to the wishes of the settlor. In particular, the tenant for life has the power to sell the land, despite the fact that the settlor's main purpose in making the settlement may well have been to keep the land in the family.

We will look at these powers in detail later on, but first we must explain a procedure known as 'overreaching'.

Overreaching

In the second chapter in this book, we explained the general principle that if trustees sell property which is subject to a trust the purchaser will take subject to the beneficiaries' rights, if he knew (or ought to have known) of them. He will, in fact, become no more than a trustee, holding the property for the beneficiaries. In order to give effect to the policy of making settled land readily sellable, it was necessary for the legislature to amend this principle in some way, for no purchaser would be willing to buy land which might be subject to a trust. Accordingly a series of Acts, culminating in the 1925 legislation, have established the process of 'overreaching' the rights of the beneficiaries. Put simply, overreaching is a process whereby the beneficiaries' interests are lifted from the trust property and are attached instead to the capital money (for example, the price paid by the purchaser). The purchaser takes the estate free from all the beneficiaries' rights, even if he has actual notice of them, and the money is held by the trustees for the beneficiaries (see *City of London Building Society* v *Flegg* discussed at p. 208). The principle of overreaching applies both to settlements under SLA 1925 and to trusts for sale. Different statutory provisions apply to each, and there may be differences in what the trustees are required to do with the capital money, but one essential requirement is the same in both cases: the overreaching provisions will operate to protect the purchaser only if the capital money is paid to not fewer than two trustees (or to a trust corporation (see p. 186)). In no circumstances should the purchase money be paid to any of the beneficiaries. This point cannot be overemphasised, and accordingly we will continue to stress it throughout the rest of this chapter.

So far, the only sort of capital money we have mentioned has been the purchase price arising on outright sale, but it should be realised that capital money can be created by other dealings with the land. A premium paid for the grant of a lease amounts to capital money, and so does money lent on the security of a mortgage. Accordingly, these sums too must be paid to the trustees, and not directly to any beneficiary.

Overreaching under SLA 1925

In the case of land settled under SLA 1925, the overreaching provisions will operate provided the transaction is carried out correctly and in accordance with the Act: that is, if the transaction is within the powers of the tenant for life and any capital money is paid to two trustees or a trust corporation (s. 18(1)). If these requirements are met, the overreaching provisions in s. 72

will apply. Under this section, with certain exceptions, an authorised transaction is effectual to pass the estate or interest 'discharged from all the limitations, powers, and provisions of the settlement, and from all estates, interests, and charges subsisting or to arise thereunder' (s. 72(2). Accordingly, should Mr and Mrs Thorne decide to buy 9 Trant Way from Mrs Slope, they will obtain a fee simple estate free of the equitable interests of Mrs Slope and of her brother-in-law, Henry Slope, *as long as* the formalities required by the Act are observed. In particular, they must pay the purchase money to the trustees. The interests of Mrs Slope and Henry Slope will become interests in the purchase price, which will be in the hands of the trustees of the settlement. Mrs Slope, as tenant for life, will have the power to direct how the money is to be invested, and will enjoy the income from it for the rest of her life. When she dies, Henry Slope will become absolutely entitled to the property in which the money has been invested.

Finally, it should be noted that s. 72(2) sets out a list of interests which are *not* overreached on a dealing by the tenant for life. The position may be summarised briefly by saying that the overreaching provisions do not affect estates or interests which were created before the settlement was made, nor those created during the settlement in exercise of the tenant for life's powers. All these bind the purchaser according to the usual principles of registered or unregistered title, as the case may be. Thus if Mr Slope had mortgaged 9 Trant Way before his death, the settlement made by his will would be subject to the prior interest of the mortgagee. If Mrs Slope sells the property to the Thornes, the conveyance would not overreach the mortgage and the Thornes would take the house subject to it unless, as will undoubtedly be the case, they insist that she repays the debt and redeems the mortgage before passing the property to them. Similarly, if Mrs Slope has let part of the house in exercise of her powers as tenant for life, the Thornes will take the property subject to that lease, in the same way as a purchaser from an absolute owner would take subject to any legal lease.

It is now time to look in detail at the powers of the tenant for life.

Power to sell

The most important of the rights of the tenant for life is the right to sell the settled land or to sell any easement or other right over the land. This right is granted by SLA 1925, s. 38, which also allows the settled land to be exchanged for other land or rights (though exchanging is rare). The tenant for life is under no obligation to sell the property; the section merely gives him the right should he choose to exercise it. Any sale made under s. 38 must be made in accordance with s. 39. Most importantly the sale must be 'made for the best consideration in money that can reasonably be obtained'. The sale may be by auction or by private contract, as the tenant for life wishes. The conveyance will be executed by the tenant for life, since the legal estate in the land is vested in him. However, in order to prevent the tenant for life selling the land and then making off with the proceeds of sale (a fraud on the other beneficiaries) the proceeds of sale ('capital money') must be paid to two trustees or into court under s. 18(1)(b).

Power to lease

The power of the tenant for life to grant leases arises under SLA 1925, s. 41. Leases so granted may continue after the death of the tenant for life, and so fetter those next entitled under the settlement, and so the period for which a tenant for life may grant leases is limited. Normally, they may be granted for any period not exceeding 50 years, with special provisions for mining leases (100 years) and building or forestry leases (999 years). Today, because of the Rent Acts, these rules can produce a lease which in fact lasts for more than 50 years, since a protected tenant will be able to remain in possession of the premises even after the contractual tenancy has come to an end.

Any lease granted under SLA 1925, s. 41, must comply with the requirements of s. 42. It must be made by deed (s. 42(2)(i)) unless the lease is for not more than three years, in which case it can be created by any written instrument (s. 42(5)(iii)). The lease must take effect in possession not later than 12 months after the date of the instrument by which it is created or in reversion after an existing lease having not more than seven years to run at the date of the new lease. The lease must reserve the best rent that can reasonably be obtained (though a fine (premium) may be taken) (s. 42(1)(ii)) and must contain a covenant by the tenant that he will pay the rent, and a provision for re-entry should the rent remain unpaid for a specified period not exceeding 30 days.

A tenant for life who is contemplating granting a lease of the settled land may well wish to know whether it is in his best interests to grant the lease at a high rent or to take a lower rent and a fine. Any rent paid will amount to income arising from the land and will accordingly be payable entirely to the tenant for life. A fine, however, amounts to capital money (s. 42(4)) and so must be paid to the trustees (s. 18(1)). The trustees will invest the capital money (see below) and the income arising from such investment is payable to the tenant for life. When granting the lease the tenant for life will need to consider which possibility is in his best interests and the best interests of the trust as a whole.

Power to grant options

The tenant for life has power to grant options to purchase, to take a lease or to take any other interest in the settled land under SLA 1925, s. 51. Such options must be exercisable within an agreed period not exceeding 10 years (s. 51(2)).

Power to mortgage

SLA 1925, s. 71, gives a tenant for life the power to mortgage the settled land but only to raise money for specified purposes. These purposes are set out in s. 71(2) and include the right to mortgage in order to pay for those improvements which are authorised by the Act. The authorised improvements are set out in Sch. 3 to the Act and fall into three categories, divided according to who is to meet the costs. In all cases, the settled land may be mortgaged to provide the money needed for the work, but the tenant for life must repay the cost of improvements listed in Part III of the schedule (for example, the installation of central heating) and may be required to pay for those in Part II (such as structural alterations of buildings). Part I, however, contains long-term improvements (including drainage, irrigation and the provision of labourers' cottages) which benefit the remainderman as much as the present tenant for life. Such improvements should be paid for out of capital, and the trustees cannot require the tenant for life to meet such costs.

It should be noted that these provisions cover improvements and not *repairs*. Normally, with some exceptions relating to agricultural land, repairs to the settled land must be paid for by the tenant for life at his own expense.

Other statutory powers

In addition to the major statutory powers mentioned above, SLA 1925, ss. 52 to 70, include a number of other rights which are not used so commonly. In addition s. 64 confers a general power for the tenant for life to effect any transaction under an order of the court.

Extra powers conferred by the settlor

The settlor is free to grant any extra powers which are not included in SLA 1925 and this is commonly done. Obviously such powers will vary from trust to trust, but in many cases the tenant for life will be given the same rights 'as a beneficial owner'. In such cases the discretion of the tenant for life is only restricted by his duties towards the other beneficiaries and the trust as a whole.

GIVING NOTICE AND OBTAINING CONSENT

Giving notice

In a number of cases the tenant for life is not entitled to exercise his powers unless he gives notice to the trustees of his intentions. This does not mean that the tenant for life must obtain the consent of the trustees, and normally they will have no right to prevent the tenant for life entering into the proposed transaction. The purpose of these provisions is to keep the trustees informed about the property and also to warn them of occasions on which they will be required to receive capital money. SLA 1925, s. 101, requires the tenant for life to give notice to the trustees when he intends 'to make a sale, exchange, lease, mortgage, or charge or to grant an option'. A person dealing in good faith with the tenant for life is not, however, required to ensure that proper notice has been given (s. 101(5)). Whilst notice is generally required for the grant of a lease, one for not more than 21 years which otherwise complies with the Act may be granted without notice being given (s. 42(5)).

Obtaining consent

In general it is not possible for a settlor to provide that the tenant for life may exercise a statutory power only with the consent of some other person (e.g., the trustees or another beneficiary), since such a provision would amount to an attempt to restrict or fetter the tenant for life's powers (see below). There are, however, certain limited exceptions to this rule:

(a)   The settlor may provide that the tenant for life must not make any disposition in relation to the principal mansion house on the settled land without the consent of trustees (or an order of the court dispensing with such consent) (SLA 1925, s. 65). A requirement for consent is implied into settlements created before 1 January 1926 but must be included expressly in settlements created after that date. This rule will apply relatively infrequently, for a 'principal mansion house' is a house where the grounds and lands normally enjoyed with the house exceed 25 acres, and which is not a farmhouse (s. 65(2)).

(b)   SLA 1925, s. 66(1), provides that in certain restricted cases, the consent of the trustees or a court order is required to cut and sell timber (for this is an act which decreases the capital value of the property).

(c)   The compromise of claims and settling of disputes by the tenant for life is subject to the consent of the trustees (SLA 1925, s. 58(1)) as is the power to release, waive or modify rights (s. 58(2)).

Apart from these specific cases the tenant for life does not require consent before he exercises his powers.

Attempts to fetter or restrict the powers of the tenant for life

Whilst it is open to the settlor to extend the power of the tenant for life, he has no right to cut down the statutory powers. SLA 1925, s. 106, says that any provision which forbids the exercise of a statutory power or which attempts or tends to prevent the exercise of any such power is void. This section is very wide and renders void any provision in the trust which discourages the use by the tenant for life of his powers. Thus in *Re Ames* [1893] 2 Ch 479, a provision that the tenant for life lost the right to a monetary benefit should the land be sold was held to be void since it discouraged sale. A common restriction, which has given rise to much judicial consideration, is a provision that the tenant for life should lose his interest in the property should he cease to reside in it, or alternatively that the interest is given to him while he lives there. This restriction, if fully operative, would discourage the exercise of the powers to sell or let the property, because on selling or letting the tenant for life would be required to leave the property and would thereupon forfeit his interest. As a result of SLA 1925, s. 106, the courts have held that should the tenant for life in such a case leave the property in furtherance of the exercise of his statutory powers he will *not* lose his interest in the estate (*Re Acklom* [1929] 1 Ch 195), for such a forfeiture is void under the section. Should, however, the tenant for life leave the premises for some other reason (e.g., his own convenience) then the forfeiture clause is valid (see *Re Haynes* (1887) 37 ChD 306 and *Re Trenchard* [1902] 1 Ch 378). Accordingly it should be regarded as a question of fact in each case whether the provision to which objection is taken does in fact amount to a fetter under s. 106.

SLA 1925, s. 104(1), provides that the powers given to the tenant for life are not assignable by him. Thus, even though the tenant for life is free to sell his equitable life interest to another person, he is not able to vest his statutory powers in that purchaser. In addition any contract by which a tenant for life agrees not to exercise any of his statutory powers is completely void (s. 104(2)).

TENANT FOR LIFE IS TRUSTEE OF HIS POWERS

A tenant for life is in a rather unusual position because, whilst he has the legal estate of the settled land vested in him, he only has a partial beneficial interest in the property. Accordingly the tenant for life holds the legal estate as trustee upon trust for himself and the other beneficiaries. In addition, by virtue of SLA 1925, s. 107, the tenant for life is a trustee of all the powers granted to him by the Act, and when exercising them must 'have regard to the interests of all parties entitled under the settlement'. The result is that to some extent the other beneficiaries are protected against an abuse of power by the tenant for life.

It appears, however, that the court will not force a tenant for life to exercise any of his powers, such as to improve the settled property or to sell it (*Re 90 Thornhill Road* [1970] Ch 261), for these are powers, rather than duties. It is also clear that the court will not intervene if the proposed transaction is for a fair price and is otherwise proper, even though the tenant for life has decided to enter into the transaction for some malicious purpose. Thus in *Weelwright v Walker* (1883) 23 ChD 752, the court refused to intervene when a tenant for life proposed to sell settled land in order to prevent the remainderman, whom he disliked, ever residing in the property. Since the sale was at a fair price and complied with the Act the court would not prevent it, even though the tenant for life's motivation for sale was malice towards the remainderman. The court will, however, intervene where the tenant for life seeks to use his powers in a way which would be prejudicial towards other beneficiaries (*Hampden v Earl of Buckinghamshire* [1893] 2 Ch 531). An exercise of a power in an attempt to evade the terms of the settlement will also be objectionable. In *Middlemas v Stevens* [1901] 1 Ch 574 the tenant for life was the widow of the settlor, and according to the terms of the settlement had an interest terminating on her death or remarriage. The tenant for life wished to remarry and, in order to ensure that she could continue to live on the settled land after their marriage, granted a 21-year lease of the property to her future husband. The court held that the lease had been granted in bad faith and, since the grantee was aware of the circumstances, the lease was void. This does not mean, however, that any grant of a lease to a spouse of the tenant for life is necessarily bad; there must be something further in the circumstances to suggest *mala fides* (bad faith) (*Gilbey v Rush* [1906] 1 Ch 11).

DEFECTIVE DISPOSITIONS

Although the powers of the tenant for life or statutory owner are considerable, they are by no means unlimited. Accordingly it is necessary to consider the position should these powers be exceeded. What, for example, would happen if Mrs Slope purported to grant a 99-year lease of 9 Trant Way (contrary to SLA 1925, s. 41) or mortgaged the property to buy a new car for herself (contrary to s. 71)?

Defective or improper dispositions are covered primarily by SLA 1925, s. 18(1), which provides that any disposition by a tenant for life or statutory owner in excess of his powers shall be void. (It may, however, affect the tenant for life's own equitable interest.)

It is necessary to protect the interests of those who, in good faith, are the recipients of an estate or interest granted in excess of powers. This protection is provided by s. 110(1), which provides that on any disposition the purchaser (which includes tenants, mortgagees etc.: s. 117) shall 'be conclusively taken to have given the best price, consideration, or rent . . . that could reasonably be obtained . . . and to have complied with all the requisitions of' the Act, provided that the purchaser was 'dealing in good faith with a tenant for life or statutory owner'. This provision can be of considerable help to a purchaser under an authorised transaction, if the trustees or remainderman later suggest that the price paid was inadequate. An example of this is found in *Hurrell* v *Littlejohn* [1904] 1 Ch 689. In this case, a purchaser had bought settled land from the tenant for life at £2,000 and immediately resold it for £3,000. In an action brought against him by the remainderman, the purchaser relied successfully on s. 110(1), and was held to have given the best price reasonably obtainable.

The section is, however, perhaps of less use in the case of unauthorised transactions, because before entering into a transaction the purchaser will investigate the title to the property and discover that the land is settled. Once this discovery is made, the purchaser cannot 'in good faith' rely on a transaction which is in breach of the Act. The problem may arise, however, if the transaction is one for which no proof of title is normally required (e.g., some leases) or where the tenant for life has some means of establishing his title which conceals the existence of the trust. This can occur when the settlor is also the first tenant for life under the settlement (see p. 187) and has retained the original conveyance to himself as absolute owner. This will enable him to conceal the settlement and represent himself as absolute owner to a purchaser who would then deal with him in good faith.

Another illustration of how this can occur is found in the rather unusual facts of *Weston* v *Henshaw* [1950] Ch 510. Here a father conveyed land to his son as absolute owner in 1921. In 1927 the son reconveyed the property to his father, and the father later settled the estate upon his son as tenant for life. The legal estate was conveyed to the son by a vesting deed, but he also retained the 1921 deed of conveyance, and later used this as evidence of his title when mortgaging the settled land to raise money for purposes not authorised by the Act. On the death of the son the truth was discovered and the remainderman claimed that the mortgage was void under SLA 1925,

s. 18, and did not bind him as beneficiary under the trust. The mortgagee, however, claimed to be a bona fide purchaser and therefore protected by s. 110(1). One would imagine that this is a clear example of a case in which s. 110 should apply, but the court held that it did not, because the mortgagee did not *know* that he was dealing with a tenant for life. The court therefore decided in favour of the remainderman and against the mortgagee. This decision has been heavily criticised, for it seems to deprive the purchaser of any protection in the case of unauthorised transactions. We have already seen that he is not protected if he knows he is dealing with the tenant for life, because he is taken to know too that the transaction is outside the SLA provisions; and *Weston* v *Henshaw* then excludes him in just those situations where he does appear to be acting in good faith. Accordingly, in *Re Morgan's Lease* [1972] Ch 1 the court held that s. 110(1) applied even where a purchaser was not aware that he was dealing with a tenant for life. Both cases were heard at first instance only and are accordingly only persuasive authority. Generally *Re Morgan's Lease* is regarded as being the better authority, particularly as the court there was able to base its decision on an earlier case (*Mogridge* v *Clapp* [1892] 3 Ch 382) which was not considered by the court in *Weston* v *Henshaw*.

Even if s. 110(1) applies where the purchaser acts in good faith not knowing that he is dealing with a tenant for life, there may still be difficulties. The section says that the purchaser is deemed to have complied with the 'requisitions' of the Act. Obviously this protects a purchaser who has failed to comply with, for example, the requirement that capital money be paid to the trustees. However, what of the 'purchaser' who has been granted a 99-year lease? Under the Act normally only 50-year leases can be granted. The requirement that longer leases be not granted is a requirement placed on the tenant for life and not on the purchaser (as, too, is the requirement that mortgages should be made for authorised purposes only). It could be argued that unauthorised transactions lie outside the scope of s. 110(1), not because of the state of the purchaser's knowledge, but because the subsection is concerned with the purchaser's conduct and is not phrased in such a way as to protect him against bad faith on the part of the tenant for life. This might have been a better reason for the decision in *Weston* v *Henshaw*, but it is not a point which has received much consideration. In any event, it seems that there is so far no decision on the position of a lease granted for more than the prescribed period.

Finally, we must mention that none of these problems about unauthorised dispositions should arise in the case of registered land. The restriction or caution (see p. 188) should make it clear to any prospective purchaser that he is dealing with settled land, and, indeed, the standard form of restriction directs that no disposition is to be registered unless authorised by SLA 1925. If no restriction or caution is entered, the purchaser should be protected in his dealings with the registered proprietor, and it is thought that SLA 1925, s. 18, and *Weston* v *Henshaw* could not prevail over the general provisions of LRA 1925.

H

ROLE OF TRUSTEES OF SETTLEMENTS

We have already mentioned that, although the tenant for life holds the legal estate and has wide powers of management, the trustees of the settlement are extremely important. It is now time to look at their duties and functions; some of these have already been described, and we will refer to them only briefly, but others require more detailed consideration here.

Duties where settlement defectively created

Where a settlement has been created but no vesting deed has been executed, the trustees should perfect the settlement by themselves executing a vesting deed.

Functions where there is no tenant for life, or where the tenant for life has ceased to have a substantial interest in the property

We have already seen that where the person currently entitled under the settlement is an infant, the trustees will be required, in the absence of any express provisions by the settlor, to exercise the tenant for life's powers as statutory owners (see p. 185).

The trustees also act as statutory owners in any other case where there is no tenant for life (SLA 1925, s. 23). This situation would arise, for example, in the sort of settlement envisaged by SLA 1925, s. 1(1)(iii), where an interest is to 'spring up' in the future, with no preceding earlier interest (see p. 183). Until the interest arises, there is no tenant for life, and the legal estate will be held and the powers exercised by the trustees as statutory owners.

The trustees may also be called upon to exercise the statutory powers if the tenant for life has ceased to have a substantial interest in the property (e.g., because he has sold his equitable interest or has become bankrupt) *and* has unreasonably refused to exercise his powers *or* has consented to the change (SLA 1925, s. 24). However, before the powers can be transferred to the trustees in this way a court order must be obtained.

Functions in connection with dispositions of settled land

As we saw earlier, the trustees must be given notice before a tenant for life or statutory owner makes certain dispositions of settled land. In certain cases, moreover, the consent of the trustees may be required.

The major function of the trustees is, however, to receive any capital money which arises from the transaction, since under SLA 1925, s. 18(1)(b), the overreaching provisions can only operate where capital money is paid either to the trustees of the settlement or into court (see also s. 75). Accordingly no disposition which gives rise to capital money can be completed where the trust lacks trustees.

Should the tenant for life wish to acquire the estate for himself, the trustees take on a special importance. The tenant for life is himself a trustee and as such, under general equitable rules, would be unable to acquire the settled land or any interest in it for his own benefit (*Keech* v *Sandford* (1726) Ca t King 61). SLA 1925, s. 68, however, makes such transactions possible by temporarily (and only for the purpose of the particular disposition) transferring the powers of the tenant for life to the trustees. This avoids the tenant for life being placed in a position in which his interests as purchaser and trustee conflict.

Powers of investment

Since one of the main functions of trustees is to receive capital money, they are given statutory powers in relation to the investment of that money (SLA 1925, s. 75(1)). Some capital money, for example, mortgage advances will, of course, simply be applied for the purpose for which it was raised, but in general capital money must be invested and the income obtained paid to the tenant for life.

The statutory powers of investment are set out in SLA 1925, s. 73 and include powers to purchase certain securities (s. 73(1)(i)) and to purchase land in England and Wales (s. 73(1)(xi) and (2)). It is normal, however, for most settlors to extend these powers of investment, and frequently as a result the trustees will have unlimited powers (s. 73(1)(xxi)).

Under s. 75(2) the tenant for life has the right to choose the investments to be made, and to direct the trustees accordingly, although if he does not do so the trustees are to exercise their own discretion. This means that the tenant for life who lives on the settled land, but finds it unsuitable for his purposes, may sell it and require the trustees to use the proceeds to buy some other property for him. It seems unlikely that this will happen with Mrs Slope, because she intends to move in with her sister, and presumably the capital money will be invested to provide additional income for her. However, if living with her sister proves unsatisfactory in some way, the money can, in the future, be used to provide her with her own house again.

Duties when the interest of the tenant for life comes to an end

Depending on the terms of the settlement, the interest of a tenant for life may come to an end during his lifetime, or at his death. For example, an interest given to a widow 'until remarriage' will end during her lifetime if she remarries; but if she does not remarry, or if the interest given to her is simply for life, with no restriction, the interest will end at her death.

Where the interest ends during the tenant's life, it is the responsibility of the tenant to convey the legal estate to the person next entitled under the settlement, and the trustees are not concerned with the matter. If the land continues to be settled, so that the person next entitled takes only a limited interest, the transfer should be made by vesting deed (SLA 1925, ss. 7(4) and 8(4)), which will contain all the information needed by a prospective purchaser. This would be appropriate where, for instance, the widow's interest is followed under the settlement by an entailed interest. However, where the settlement in fact comes to an end, and the person receiving the estate is absolutely entitled, the estate should be passed to him by an ordinary conveyance and not one containing all the details prescribed for a vesting deed (SLA 1925, s. 7(5)). If, in either case, the tenant for life fails to execute the required deed, the court may make a vesting order (SLA 1925, s. 12).

Where the tenant for life's interest comes to an end with his death, the trustees may have a role to play. If the land remains settled (as above), the estate does not vest in the deceased's ordinary personal representatives, but instead vests in the trustees as special personal representatives (Administration of Estates Act 1925, s. 22(1), in the case of a will; Supreme Court Act 1981, s. 116, in the case of intestacy). The trustees are then required to convey the estate to the next tenant for life by a vesting deed or vesting assent, which again will contain all the information a purchaser would need to know. (An assent is a written document not under seal which may be used by personal representatives to transfer an estate.)

If, however, the settlement has come to an end, the estate vests in the deceased tenant for life's ordinary personal representatives, and they will transfer it to the person who is absolutely entitled by an ordinary conveyance or assent (*Re Bridgett & Hayes's Contract* [1928] Ch 163).

Functions when settlement ends

Normally the trustees' functions end when the settlement ends, but, in certain cases in which it would not be clear to an intending purchaser that the trust has ended, the final function of the trustees will be to execute a deed of discharge which declares that the trust has come to an end (SLA 1925, s. 17).

A practical example may serve to explain this further. A settlor settles land 'upon A for life and then to B absolutely'. The land is vested in A as tenant for life. Thereafter A buys B's equitable interest in the property. A thus becomes solely entitled to the property, but must ask the trustees to execute a deed of discharge so that he can prove to any intending purchaser that the trust has indeed ended.

The purpose of the deed of discharge is thus to cancel the effect of the earlier vesting deed, which tells a prospective purchaser that the land is subject to a settlement. If no vesting deed has been executed before the settlement ends (as in *Re Alefounder's Will Trusts* [1927] 1 Ch 360), no deed of discharge is required to neutralise it, and similarly such a deed will not be needed if there are other documents in the title which show that the settlement has come to an end. Thus the ordinary conveyance by a tenant for life or his ordinary personal representatives to the person absolutely entitled (see below) is sufficient evidence that the settlement has come to an end, and there is no need for a deed of discharge.

General functions of trustees

As well as exercising their specific powers, trustees must also have regard to their general fiduciary relationship to the trust. Accordingly the trustees should keep a general 'watching brief' over the trust and ensure that all is proceeding properly. In *Re Boston's Will Trusts* [1956] Ch 395 at p. 405, Vaisey J said that the general duty of the trustees is to 'conserve the settled property'.

Accordingly the trustees should intervene should it come to their attention that the tenant for life intends to act in excess of his powers. Also the trustees must be parties to any action in respect of the land. Therefore, Mrs Slope's trustees cannot prevent her selling 9 Trant Way, but could intervene if it became clear, for example, that she intended to sell the property at a gross undervalue.

END OF A SETTLEMENT

A settlement lasts as long as (SLA 1925, s. 3):

(a)   any limitation, charge, or power of charging under the settlement subsists or is capable of being exercised; or
(b)   as long as the person who would otherwise be owner of the legal estate is an infant.

Thus if a grant is made 'to A for life and then to B absolutely', the settlement will end on A's death unless, at that date, B is under 18, in which case it will end on B's 18th birthday. If the settlement is, 'to C for life and then to D in tail male', the settlement will end when there are no more lineal male heirs of D. At that point the estate will revert to the settlor or his heirs. In Mrs Slope's case the settlement will end upon her death, and Henry Slope will then be entitled to have the fee simple of 9 Trant Way vested in him. On Mrs Slope's death the estate will pass first to her ordinary personal representatives who will then be obliged to vest the estate in Henry Slope (i.e., it does not pass to him automatically). Should Mrs Slope have sold 9 Trant Way, on her death Henry Slope will be absolutely entitled to all the capital money (probably represented by investments) held by the trustees and he can call for this to be placed in his own hands.

TRUSTS FOR SALE

Our description of a settlement under the Settled Land Act 1925 may well have given rise to a general feeling that 'all this is rather old-fashioned'. This is certainly true, for today such settlements are rarely created deliberately. Many modern examples of settled land are created accidentally in 'home-made' wills (e.g., where the testator gives his house 'to my son Fred and when he dies it is to be divided between his children'). The modern method of creating a settlement of land is to use the second available form, the trust for sale, because such trusts are far more flexible than SLA settlements. For a variety of reasons, however, the material given above should not be ignored. One may well come across SLA settlements in practice when investigating title; and one also needs to know why such settlements should not be created and which form of words will give rise to them. Further, as we shall see, LPA 1925 applies some of the SLA rules to trusts for sale.

The position of Mrs Grantly in relation to 10 Trant Way (see p. 177) demonstrates that it is perfectly possible to have an interest for life behind a trust for sale. In this case, however, the legal estate is vested in the trustees, and we shall see that the operation of the trust will differ in a number of ways from that applicable to 9 Trant Way.

DEFINITION OF A TRUST FOR SALE

The trust for sale is defined by LPA 1925, s. 205(1)(xxix), as:

> an immediate binding trust for sale, whether or not exercisable at the request or with the consent of any person, and with or without a power at discretion to postpone the sale.

Accordingly, in order to show that an arrangement is a trust for sale it is necessary to interpret the words 'an immediate binding trust for sale'.

'Immediate'

It might be wondered whether the trust relating to 10 Trant Way is an immediate trust for sale, because Mrs Grantly appears to have a life interest in the property, in which she has a right to reside and which cannot be sold without her consent. However, it appears from *Re Herklot's Will Trusts* [1964] 1 WLR 583 that even in such a situation there can be an immediate trust for sale, since LPA 1925, s. 205(1)(xxix), expressly contemplates that the *sale* may be postponed: it is the trust which must be 'immediate' and not the sale. Thus *Re Hanson* [1928] 1 Ch 96 provides an example of a case in which the trust itself was not immediate, because the settlor had provided that money (his residuary estate) should be used to buy a house for his widow, and that after a specified period (when his son reached 25 or his widow remarried before that date) the property was to be held by trustees upon trust for sale. In this case it was held that the property would be settled land until the specified period expired, at which point an immediate trust to sell would arise. From this it is clear that it is really the form chosen to express the terms of the trust which is crucial. In Mrs Grantly's case the general aim of the trust is the same as that in *Re Hanson*, but nonetheless 10 Trant Way is subject to a trust for sale during Mrs Grantly's life because her interest is expressly made subject to the immediate trust to sell. *Re Hanson* also shows that it is possible for a trust for sale to follow a settlement.

'Binding'

The interpretation of this word has unfortunately led to a number of conflicting views. In *Re Parker's Settled Estates* [1928] Ch 247 Romer J seems to have interpreted the word as meaning that the trustees are under an absolute obligation to sell (as opposed to having a power to sell) and that the obligation is not revocable. This is in fact already implied by the phrase 'trust for sale'. However, in *Re Leigh's Settled Estates* [1926] Ch 852 and *Re Norton* [1929] 1 Ch 84 it was suggested that the word indicates that the whole legal estate must be subject to the trust to sell and that there are no prior encumbrances which are not overreachable on a sale by the trustees. Fortunately this is no longer a serious difficulty, because LPA 1925, s. 2(2) (as amended in 1926), provides machinery for solving the difficulty which arose in *Re Leigh's Settled Estates*, and in any event prior settlements are now rare. However, although no practical difficulty is caused, it is still not altogether clear what meaning is to be given to the word 'binding' in this context.

'Trust for sale'

We have already explained that, in order for a trust to be regarded as a 'trust for sale', the trustees must be under a *duty* to sell, and not merely have a *power* to do so. A problem used to arise with a phrase favoured by settlors, who would provide that the trustees should 'sell or retain' the land. This would appear to create a power to sell, rather than a duty, but the matter is resolved by LPA 1925, s. 25(4), which provides that 'a trust either to retain or sell land . . . shall be construed as a trust to sell the land with power to postpone the sale'. This statutory intervention has the purpose of giving effect to the presumed intention of the settlor.

Doctrine of conversion

This seems a suitable place to mention an important consequence of the duty to sell, namely that the land which is subject to the trust is notionally converted to personal property by the equitable doctrine of conversion.

The whole basis of the trust for sale is that the trustees are under a duty to sell the land. It is a general rule of equity that 'Equity regards as done that which ought to be done'. In the case of a trust for sale, 'that which ought to be done' is the selling of the property and so *from the day on which the trust arises* equity will regard the property as being already sold, so that notionally the land has been converted into money. As a result, the equitable interests of the beneficiaries are not regarded as being interests in land. They are deemed to be interests in money and accordingly amount to personal property not real property (see p. 13 and chapter 10). We will consider some of the difficulties caused by this notional conversion later in the chapter (see p. 208).

CREATION OF A TRUST FOR SALE

A trust for sale may be created expressly *inter vivos* (during the life of the settlor) or by will. Unlike a Settled Land Act settlement a trust for sale may be created by using only one document, since nothing in the statutes requires that two should be used. It is, however, quite common for two documents to be employed, one declaring the trusts and the other vesting the property in the trustees. However, even where only one document is used, any intending purchaser need not concern himself with the beneficial interests under the trust, since he will obtain a good legal title free of the trusts, as long as the statutory requirements for overreaching are observed (see p. 207).

In addition to express creation, trusts for sale are imposed by statute in a number of situations. In the next chapter, we shall look in detail at the statutory trusts imposed on most forms of co-ownership, but it should be noted that similar trusts will operate in the following circumstances:

(a) In cases of intestacy, the deceased's property is held by his administrators on trust for sale (Administration of Estates Act 1925, s. 33(1)).

(b) Where trustees lend trust funds on the security of a mortgage and then foreclose (i.e., take the property in satisfaction of the debt, see p. 257), they hold the property on trust for sale (LPA 1925, s. 31).

(c) Where trustees of a trust of personal property or of a trust for sale of land invest the trust funds in the purchase of land, they hold that land on trust for sale (LPA 1925, s. 32(1)).

Trusts for sale of registered land

In the case of registered land, the trustees are registered as proprietors, and a restriction is entered on the register which will provide that no disposition of the land by one surviving proprietor under which capital money arises is to be registered, except on the order of the Registrar or the court. If the consent of certain persons is required before the property can be sold (see p. 206), a special restriction must be entered naming those persons.

ROLE OF TRUSTEES

Legal estate vested in trustees

In the case of the trust for sale there is no statutory provision requiring the legal estate to be vested in a beneficiary, and accordingly in this case the property will be vested in the trustees upon the trusts of the settlement. Hence Mrs Grantly has no right to have the legal estate in 10 Trant Way vested in herself. Under the Trustee Act 1925, s. 34, there may not be more than four trustees. The powers to appoint trustees are contained in the Trustee Act 1925, s. 36, and are similar to those which apply to settled land. It is usual for the settlor to name the original trustees but if he does not do so he may give some specified person the power to appoint; if neither of these courses is adopted, the statutory rules should be followed.

Trustees' duties and powers

Obligation to sell and power to postpone
The effect of a trust for sale is to impose upon the trustees an obligation to sell the land. However, this obligation may be subject to a power to postpone sale or to a requirement that the property be not sold without the consent of certain persons (LPA 1925, s. 205(1)(xxix)). Even if the settlor does not expressly give a power to postpone sale, it will be implied in all cases unless the settlor clearly shows a contrary intention in the document creating the trust (LPA 1925, s. 25(1)).

It is a general rule of equity that trustees must exercise their powers unanimously. Accordingly, should a disagreement arise between the trustees over whether or not the land should be sold, then the result will be that the land *must* be sold, for as soon as the power to postpone can no longer be exercised unanimously, the trustees must give effect to their primary obligation, which is to sell (*Re Mayo* [1943] Ch 302). This is still the case even where a majority of the trustees do not wish to sell, with the result that the land must be sold even if only *one* trustee wants this. As we shall see later (p. 207), this rule is affected by the provisions of LPA 1925, s. 26(3), but that section applies mainly in cases of co-ownership and is accordingly dealt with in chapter 6 (p. 234).

Other statutory powers
Under LPA 1925, s. 28, the trustees for sale are given 'all the powers of a tenant for life and the trustees of a settlement under the Settled Land Act 1925', including the powers conferred by SLA 1925, s. 102, to manage the property during a minority.

Additional powers
It is always possible for the settlor to confer additional powers upon the trustees and it is normal for this to be done. In particular the trustees' powers of investment are normally extended.

Delegation of powers
The trustees do have a limited right to delegate their powers under LPA 1925, s. 29. This allows the powers of leasing and general power of management of the land to be delegated to any person of full age who is 'beneficially entitled in possession to the net rents and profits of the land during his life or for any less period'. This delegation lasts only for as long as the property remains unsold, and in any event is revocable at any time at the wish of the trustees. The trustees' power to delegate means that where the beneficiary is permitted to live in the trust property (either under the express terms of the trust, as in Mrs Grantly's case, or at the discretion of the trustees) the trustees can leave the day-to-day management of the property to the beneficiary, so that, for example, alterations and repairs can be undertaken by the occupant, as though it was his or her 'own' house. Thus the trustees of Mrs Grantly's trust could give her many of the powers which Mrs Slope enjoys in relation to 9 Trant Way. However, the trustees cannot delegate their power to decide upon sale and so control of sale by a beneficiary must be dealt with in other ways (see p. 206).

Enforcing sale or exercise of trustees' powers

It is not altogether uncommon for disputes to arise between trustees for sale, or between trustees and their beneficiaries. Most commonly this occurs where there is a dispute over whether the land should be sold or not. In such a case 'any person interested' may apply to the court for an order for sale (or other relevant order) under LPA 1925, s. 30. This allows trustees or beneficiaries to make an application. On hearing the application the court has a very wide discretion, for the section says that it 'may make such order as it thinks fit'. Subject to the rule in *Re Mayo* [1943] Ch 302, the courts do not usually interfere with the decisions of trustees who have considered the matter carefully and reached a reasoned conclusion (*Re Blake* (1885) 29 ChD 913; *Re Kipping* [1914] 1 Ch 62). The most common use of this power by the courts is made in relation to cases of co-ownership which are dealt with in more detail in chapter 6.

Limitation on trustees' powers: duty to obtain consents and to consult the beneficiaries

We have seen that the powers of a tenant for life of settled land cannot be fettered in any way. The position of trustees under a trust for sale is, however, very different, for the trust may provide that they must not sell without the consent of certain named people, and additionally they are required in certain cases to consult the beneficiaries and give effect to their wishes (LPA 1925, s. 26(3)).

Consents
The statutory definition of the trust for sale (LPA 1925, s. 205(1)(xxix)) expressly contemplates that the trustees' obligation to sell may be made exercisable only 'with the consent of any person'. Thus in the trust relating to 10 Trant Way, Mr Grantly has provided that his trustees shall not sell the property 'during the lifetime of my wife without her consent in writing'. It would equally have been open to him to provide that the property should not be sold without the consent of his nephew William (the remainderman), or indeed without the consent of any other person whom he cared to name.

The requirements for consents might have proved to be of concern to intending purchasers of the land. Were the settlor to require a large number of consents before sale, the purchaser might find himself embarrassed by the delay and expense involved in checking that all necessary consents had been obtained. Accordingly LPA 1925, s. 26(1), provides that, where the trust requires that the consent of more than two persons be obtained, the consent of any two of them shall be deemed sufficient in favour of the purchaser. Thus, provided the purchaser satisfies himself that two of the named persons have consented, he need not enquire about the others. Also the purchaser need not worry about the absence of the consent of any person who is subject to a disability (e.g., is under 18 or is a patient under the Mental Health Act (LPA 1925, s. 26(2)). Consent may be obtained on behalf of such persons from a parent, guardian or receiver. It should be noted, however, that s. 26 protects only the purchaser; should the trustees proceed without all the necessary consents they may still be liable for breach of trust. This reduces the utility of these provisions, since the trustees will not wish to take the risk involved in proceeding without a consent. They may, however, gain assistance from LPA 1925, s. 30 (see p. 205), which applies not only to refusals by the trustees to use their powers but also to any case where 'any requisite consent cannot be obtained'. The court may make such an order as it thinks fit, which would include authorising sale without the required consents. This procedure may be used either where the consent cannot be requested (e.g., where the person concerned has disappeared) or where consent has been requested and refused (*Re Beale's Settlement Trusts* [1932] 2 Ch 15). The clever use of consents can produce the peculiar result that a settlor, by creating a trust for sale, can prevent the sale of that land for an indefinite period. This result appears even stranger when one considers that a settlor who creates a Settled Land Act settlement cannot prevent the tenant for life from selling the land (although traditionally this was one of the main reasons for creating a strict settlement). The case of *Re Inns* [1947] Ch 576 illustrates exactly how the obligation to sell in a trust for sale can effectively be frustrated. In this case a testator had left a large house upon trust for sale for his widow during her lifetime and thereafter for the district council (for use as a hospital). The trust was so arranged that should the council use the property as the testator wished, it would receive an additional gift of £10,000 to pay for equipment. It was provided that the property could not be sold without the consent of the widow *and* the council. The house had become too expensive for the widow to run, but the council would not consent to sale since if it did so it would lose its remainder in the property and the additional £10,000. The court held that these provisions were valid, even though the effect was to ensure that the property would never be sold because the council would never give consent.

Consulting the beneficiaries (LPA 1925, s. 26(3))
Where the trust for sale is a statutory trust, or where in an express trust the settlor so requires, the trustees must consult the beneficiaries before sale and should give effect to the wishes of the majority by value (LPA 1925, s. 26(3)). (This is mainly relevant in the case of co-owned land and is dealt with further in chapter 6). The section protects anyone who may buy from the trustees, by providing that the purchaser shall not be concerned to see that the requirements of the section have been complied with.

POSITION OF A PURCHASER

We have already seen that there are special statutory provisions designed to reduce the burden on the purchaser where the trustees are required to obtain consents or to consult the beneficiaries.

More generally, the purchaser can take advantage of the overreaching provisions. We have already described these in general terms at p. 190, and merely need to add that the specific provisions referring to trusts for sale are contained in LPA 1925, ss. 2(1)(i) and (ii) and 27. Thus, providing the purchaser pays the proceeds of sale or other capital money to two trustees or a trust corporation, he will take the legal estate free of the beneficiaries' interests, even if he has notice of them.

The Law of Property Act 1925 does not say what the position would be were a purchaser not to comply with s. 27. Accordingly one must in such a case consider the ordinary rules which determine whether a purchaser is bound by an equitable interest in land. Normally he will take free of such interests in unregistered land where he is a bona fide purchaser for value without notice. Therefore it is possible to obtain a legal estate free of the beneficial interests, even where capital money is not paid to two trustees: *Caunce* v *Caunce* [1969] 1 WLR 286. In registered land normally the purchaser will have notice of the trust and the rights of the beneficiaries because a restriction will have been entered on the register. Accordingly the purchaser would be warned to insist on the appointment of a second trustee for his own protection. If the interests of the beneficiaries have not been protected by such an entry the beneficiaries may nonetheless be protected because they are in actual occupation of the land: see *Williams & Glyns Bank Ltd* v *Boland* [1981] AC 487. However, if money is paid to *two* legal owners, the overreaching provisions operate even where a beneficiary is in actual occupation (*City of London Building Society* v *Flegg* [1988] AC 54).

Finally, what should a prospective purchaser do if the vendor tells him that the trust for sale has already come to an end and he does not, therefore, need to pay the purchase price to two trustees? Under LPA 1925, s. 23, a trust for sale, as far as an intending purchaser is concerned, lasts until the land has been conveyed to or under the direction of the persons who are interested in the proceeds of sale. Thus if it is clear that the property has been subject to a trust for sale, a purchaser should insist on paying his purchase money to two trustees (and thus overreaching), unless the vendor can prove that one of the situations specified in s. 23 has arisen or unless the provisions of the Law of Property (Joint Tenants) Act 1964 can be used (see p. 238).

NATURE OF THE BENEFICIARY'S INTEREST UNDER A TRUST FOR SALE

We have already explained that the trustees' duty to sell brings into play the equitable doctrine of conversion, so that from the creation of the trust the land is notionally converted into money (see p. 203). Unfortunately a large number of statutory provisions (including some sections of the property legislation) refer solely to interests 'in land' and accordingly pose problems of interpretation in their application to trusts for sale. Frequently an illogical result is produced if the doctrine of conversion produces the result that a particular statutory provision applies to the equitable interests under a SLA settlement, but not to those arising under a trust for sale. Accordingly in *Cooper* v *Critchley* [1955] Ch 431 a beneficial interest in a trust for sale was held to be an interest in land for the purposes of LPA 1925, s. 40; and a beneficiary under such a trust was held to be 'interested in land' for the purpose of lodging a caution under the provisions of LRA 1925 in the case of *Elias* v *Mitchell* [1972] Ch 652. In *Irani Finance Ltd* v *Singh* [1971] Ch 59, however, an interest in a trust for sale was held not to be an interest in land for the purpose of s. 35 of the Administration of Justice Act 1956 (which allowed courts to impose 'charges on land', see now Charging Orders Act 1979, ss. 1 and 2). Nor was it held to be an interest in land in *Cedar Holdings Ltd* v *Green* [1981] Ch 129. The same issue was considered by the House of Lords in *Williams & Glyn's Bank Ltd* v *Boland* [1981] AC 487, where the court had to decide whether the beneficial interest under a trust for sale could be an overriding interest under LRA 1925, s. 70(1)(g). It was held that the interest did fall within s. 70(1), but this did not require the court to regard the interest as an interest in land, since the section refers only to interests 'subsisting in reference' to land.

In *Bull* v *Bull* [1955] 1 QB 234, the beneficiaries under a trust for sale were a son and his mother, who were co-owners of the equitable interest. On his marriage the son tried to prevent his mother from continuing to live in the property. The court held that until sale each beneficiary was entitled equally to possession of the land. This seems to suggest that the interests were in some way interests in land, since if they were solely interests in money neither beneficiary would have rights in respect of the land itself.

It is not really possible to produce a logical rationalisation of all these cases on the effects of conversion. It is of course true that in these cases the courts were required to interpret several different statutory provisions, and that an interest under a trust for sale may well fall within some of these but not within others; but having given this explanation one may still conclude in the end that in general the courts will choose whichever interpretation produces the fairest result on the facts.

COMPARISON OF THE TWO FORMS OF SETTLEMENT

We have previously said that today the strict settlement is rarely used and that almost inevitably the trust for sale is preferred. It is well worth summarising the reasons for this choice. The first point to note is that the trust for sale can be used to achieve any of the types of interest specified in SLA 1925. As we have seen, Mrs Grantly has a life interest in 10 Trant Way but her interest was expressly created behind a trust for sale, and an entailed interest may be created in the same way. The beneficiary can be given the right to live in the property, and in any other property bought with the proceeds of sale, and powers of management can be delegated to him or her, so that in practical terms the beneficiary's way of life should not be affected by the creation of a trust for sale rather than a SLA settlement. Secondly, a trust for sale may be created using simpler documentation, though in practice this is often not the case. Thirdly, should a settlor wish to ensure that the land cannot be sold, he cannot do this if he uses a SLA settlement. It is, however, possible to go at least some way to achieving this result in the case of a trust for sale, by the careful use of requirements that the land be not sold without the consent of certain persons. Fourthly, frequently it is desired to apply the same trusts to chattels as well as land (e.g., the settlor wishes to give a life interest in a house *and* its contents). This can be done with a trust for sale but not with a settlement. Finally, there have often been tax advantages in using a trust for sale rather than a settlement, although it is beyond the scope of this book to do more than mention the point and this is not now an advantage. Put simply, a trust for sale can be used to do anything a settlement will do, *and more besides.*

STATUTORY TRANSFORMATION OF CERTAIN ACCIDENTALLY CREATED SETTLEMENTS

As we have said, Settled Land Act settlements today most commonly arise by accident, and due to badly drafted (often 'home-made') wills. An example of such an accidental settlement is found where the testator leaves his house by will: 'to my wife and then when she dies it is to be divided between the children'. Under the SLA 1925 rules, this will produce a settlement in which the widow becomes tenant for life, even though it is likely that the real intention of the testator was that the widow should be a full beneficial owner (so that she could sell the house and use the proceeds of sale as she wished instead of having only a life interest in them). Accordingly a limited amendment to the law has been made by s. 22 of the Administration of Justice Act 1982. The effect of this provision would be to transform the example given above into an *absolute* gift to the widow. This deprives the children of any interest, but this may not matter too greatly, as normally they will obtain an interest in the property on their mother's death, unless she has exhausted the property or left it by will to others. Section 22 is very limited in effect, however, and only applies where the testator first purports to give an absolute gift to his or her spouse, but later by the same instrument purports to give an interest in the property to his or her issue. Thus the provision does not apply to an *inter vivos* gift nor to gifts to persons other than the testator's spouse. Nor will s. 22 apply if the gift in remainder is to someone who does not fall into the class of the testator's issue. Accordingly all the following dispositions will still give rise to SLA settlements:

(a) A disposition *inter vivos* 'to my wife and then on her death to our children'.

(b) A devise (disposition by will) 'to my sister and then when she dies to my children'.

(c) A devise 'to my husband and then on his death to my friend X'.

(d) A devise: 'I give my wife my house for her lifetime but when she dies it is to be divided between our children'. (This is not a devise in terms which would give the widow an absolute interest were the children not mentioned.)

The effect of s. 22 will accordingly be to reduce cases in which settlements are created accidentally, but will not prevent such cases altogether.

THE RULE AGAINST PERPETUITIES

Before we leave the subject of settlements, we must give a brief account of the rules which govern the kind of future interests which can be created under settlements, and so the last part of this chapter will be concerned with the 'rule against perpetuities'.

Common law has always disliked uncertainty in relation to future interests in land, for such uncertainty tends to make the property inalienable for some time, and common law has always opposed any arrangement which restricts free alienation. For example, should a settlor, who as yet has no children, wish to settle land upon 'the first of my great-grandchildren to obtain a law degree', it could easily be 70 or 80 years before the great-grandchild who is to take the gift can be ascertained. For that period of time there would be no one absolutely entitled to the property, and therefore no one with a power to dispose of it. As a result, the courts developed rules ('against perpetuities') which invalidated certain objectionable future interests. Unfortunately, the rigid application of these rules frequently led to ridiculous results (as we will see below), and finally statutory amendments were made by the Law of Property Act 1925 (to a limited extent) and the Perpetuities and Accumulations Act 1964. As the changes are only modifications of the earlier rules, it is still necessary to understand those rules, and accordingly we will consider them first. For convenience, we will call them the 'common law rules', but throughout this section that phrase denotes the rules applied in both law and equity, in contrast to the later amendments by statute.

The common law rules

Contingent and vested interests
The common law rules against perpetuities are concerned only with *contingent* (or conditional) future interests. Such an interest is a gift under a settlement which is to take effect in the future, but is conditional either because the person who is to take it has not yet been identified or because some other requirement has to be fulfilled before he is entitled to the interest. Thus, in the example 'to the first of my great-grandchildren to obtain a law degree', there is no way of knowing who, if anyone, will eventually qualify for the gift. Even when several great-grandchildren have been born, the interest will remain contingent until one of them is awarded the necessary degree. When the person who is to take the future interest has been identified and all necessary conditions fulfilled, he will be said to have a future interest which is 'vested in interest'. He now has an interest in the property, an immediate right to future possession, and he can sell or mortgage that right, and pass it to his successors on his death. By contrast, a contingent future interest, though called an 'interest', does not give any right to the property: even if the person who may be entitled can be identified, he has nothing more than a hope or chance of acquiring an interest if the condition is fulfilled.

In the settlements we have considered earlier in this chapter, both Henry Slope (No. 9) and William Grantly (No. 10) have future interests which are vested in interest, for each is identified and does not have to perform any condition before taking his interest. All each has to do is to wait for the end of the previous interest (which will occur on the deaths of Mrs Slope and Mrs Grantly respectively). When that happens, the interest of each will be said to be 'vested in possession', and each one will at last be entitled to the actual enjoyment of the property. Some further examples may help to clarify the point. If a settlor grants land *inter vivos*:

to A for life, then to A's first child to reach 21 for life, then to B absolutely

the interests of A and B are not covered by the rule, for they both have interests which have vested. Their interests are vested, because the person who is to obtain an interest is *ascertained* and no condition which has yet to be fulfilled is attached to the gift. A's interest is vested in possession, entitling him to immediate enjoyment of the property, and B has a future right, vested in interest. However, the gift to A's child has not vested, unless A already has a child who is aged 21 or more. Even if A has a younger child (e.g., aged 5) the gift is still contingent upon that child reaching 21. It is quite possible that this child may yet die, and that another child of A will be the first to reach 21, or, a further possibility, that no child will ever qualify. If a grant is made:

to C but if C ever becomes a doctor then to D

C has a vested interest but D has a contingent interest, because he will get the property only if C becomes a doctor.

The rule
As we have said, the rule against perpetuities is concerned with contingent interests and with the period of time within which they vest in interest. The rule is sometimes described as a rule against remoteness of vesting, for it prescribes a limited period within which a contingent interest must vest (in interest, not in possession) and invalidates any interest which may vest outside that time.

The rule is that: *a contingent interest is void unless it must vest in interest, if it vests at all, within the perpetuity period.* The period consists of the lifetime of a life or lives in being at the date at which the disposition takes effect, plus 21 years (plus any necessary period of gestation).

When applying the rule, you will need to know when the disposition you are considering took effect. Settlements made *inter vivos* take effect from the date of the grant, and those made by will take effect from the death of the testator (*not* from the date when he made the will).

The period
The rule against perpetuities operates by invalidating contingent future interests which may fail to vest in interest within a prescribed period. This period is expressed by the formula: 'A life in being plus 21 years'. The 21-year requirement is quite straightforward, and has its origin in the days when one reached majority at that age and accordingly became capable of holding a legal estate in land. It has not been amended even though the age of majority has now been reduced to 18. It is the first portion of the formula which tends to cause difficulties.

A life in being   The 'life in being' may be that of any human being who is alive at the date at which the grant becomes effective. The use of the lives of animals has been ruled out (*Re Dean* (1889) 41 ChD 552; *Re Kelly* [1932] IR 255), which is eminently sensible when one considers the great age which some beasts (e.g., tortoises) can attain. Because it is impossible to ascertain the names and dates of death of all human beings who were alive on a particular date, the common law rule requires that the persons who are to be regarded as the relevant 'lives in being' should be identifiable from the grant. They may be identified expressly, or by implication. Thus should I make a gift to:

the first child of my son A to reach the age of 21,

A would be a relevant life in being. A settlor might, however, choose to identify a particular group of people (preferably those who are expected to be long-lived and easy to identify), solely to serve as lives in being. Such people need not have any connection with the trust. Thus often a 'royal lives clause' may be used which (today) might identify as the class of lives in being 'all the lineal descendants of George V' who are living at the date of the grant. Such clauses provide a large group of persons to act as lives in being, who are sufficiently in the public eye to be readily identified (see *Re Leverhulme (No. 2)* [1943] 2 All ER 274; also, on 'descendants of Queen Victoria', *Re Villar* [1928] Ch 471.)

Some examples may illustrate:

To A for life and thereafter to the first child of A to reach 21.

In this example A is a relevant life in being. The perpetuities rule is satisfied, for the gift to A's child must vest, if it vests at all, within 21 years of the death of A.

To B (who is not married) and then to any widow of B.

In this case B is a relevant life in being and the gift to his widow will be valid, for it must vest, if it vests at all, within 21 years of B's death.

A gift by will to such of the settlor's grandchildren who reach 21.

In this case the settlor's children will be relevant lives in being, for even if he had no children when he made the will, any child he may have in the future must have been born by the date of his death, which is when the gift takes effect. The grant is valid if the gift must vest within 21 years of the death of the settlor's last living child (which it must).

Addition of a period of gestation   It may have occurred to you that in the last example it is not quite true to say that all the settlor's children must be lives in being at his death, for it is possible that the settlor's wife was pregnant at his death and gave birth to his last child after his death. Similarly, the last of the settlor's children to die might be a son who dies leaving a pregnant wife. The child thus born would reach the age of 21 more than 21 years after his father's death. As a result of such possibilities, the common law has always accepted that any relevant gestation period should be included in the perpetuity period. Thus the settlor's posthumous child is regarded as a life in being, and the last grandchild also is regarded as receiving a vested gift in time, because his period of gestation is added to the 21-year period. Any foetus in this position of being between its conception and birth at a relevant time is commonly referred to as being *en ventre sa mère* (in his mother's womb).

It is perhaps worth mentioning that the development of methods of freezing semen, ova and embryos could cause considerable difficulties for the law in the realm of perpetuities. Thus far no case has been brought which depends on the possibility of a 'test-tube baby' forming a relevant life in being, but one can imagine the problems that might result. (Sections 27–30 of the Human Fertilisation and Embryology Act 1990 illustrate the problems of defining 'father' and 'mother' today and there have been instances in which children have been born several years after their father's death, as the result of the use of frozen sperm.)

A rule about possibilities not probabilities   The common law rule renders void any gift which might vest outside the period, however unlikely it is that this will occur. An example may illustrate the problem: assume a gift to:

The first child of X to become an accountant.

In this example X is a life in being. The gift is invalid, because it is possible that X may have a child born after the date of settlement (and who is not therefore himself a life in being) who may qualify as an accountant more than 21 years after the death of X. It is not relevant that, at the date of the grant, X has a son Y, who is due to qualify as an accountant in a year's time. The common law will not wait and see whether the gift does in fact vest within the perpetuity period. It insists on considering the position at the date of the grant. If at that date there is *any possibility*, however remote, that the gift could vest outside the period, it will be void. It is possible that Y might die before qualifying as an accountant, that X might then have a further child, Z, who would not be a life in being, and that Z might become an accountant more than 21 years after X's death. Thus there is a remote possibility that this gift may vest outside the perpetuity period, and accordingly *the grant will be void.*

A favourite illustration of this difficulty is that of the 'unborn widow', which arises in the following grant:

To A for life and then to any widow of A for life and thereafter to the eldest of A's children then living.

If A is unmarried at the date of the grant, it is fairly easy to see what difficulties might arise, because there is a possibility that he might not marry for some time, and might then marry a woman who was not born when the gift took effect. For example, if A were 25 at the date of the grant and 20 years later, at the age of 45, married a woman of 18, Mrs A would obviously not have been a life in being at the date of the grant. The grant to A's widow would still be valid, because it must vest within 21 years of the death of A, the life in being. The problem arises with regard to the gift to the eldest of A's children living at the date of the death of A's widow. Imagine that Mr and Mrs A have a child, B, two years after their marriage and that one year later A dies. At the date of A's death, Mrs A will be 21 and B will be 1. If Mrs A lives until she is 43 (22 years after A's death) the gift to B will vest more than 21 years after A's death. (The gift cannot vest in interest before Mrs A's death, because B might die before his mother and therefore would not qualify as the eldest child of A 'then living'.) Accordingly, because events *might* fall out this way, the remainder to A's eldest child is void.

It might be thought that the position would be different if A were married at the date of the grant, for Mrs A would be a life in being. In fact, this would make no difference at all, for it is still possible for Mrs A to die before her husband, and for him to remarry, taking as his second wife a woman who was not born at the date of the gift. The difficulties we have considered above, on the assumption that A is a bachelor, would then arise, and therefore the gift to the eldest child is void at the outset, even if A had a wife at the time of the grant.

All these 'but what if' forecasts may seem very far-fetched, but the common law regards the unlikelihood of the events occurring as irrelevant. The remotest possibility of the gift vesting outside the perpetuity period will render it invalid.

Fertile infants and ancients at common law The nightmarish and nonsensical quality of the common law rules on perpetuities is exacerbated by a number of decisions which establish that, at common law, a person is deemed to be fertile however young or old he or she may be. Thus in *Re Dawson* (1888) 39 ChD 155, Chitty J insisted that a woman aged 60 years and 3 months was to be regarded as still being capable of bearing children (see also *Jee v Audley* (1787) 1 Cox Eq Cas 324 and *Re Sayer's Trusts* (1868) LR 6 Eq 319). In *Re Gaite's Will Trusts* [1949] 1 All ER 459 a gift was held to be valid, not because a five-year-old could be presumed incapable of bearing a child but because a five-year-old could not marry and therefore could not bear a *legitimate* child. (For dispositions after 1 January 1970 illegitimate children are deemed to be included in the term 'children' but before that date could be ignored: Family Law Reform Act 1969, s. 15.)

Class gifts

It is quite common for settlors to make gifts to groups or classes of people rather than to a single person: e.g., to A's daughters. These class gifts can give rise to particular problems, for in their case there is a further requirement for vesting, namely, that the share to be taken by each person must be identified. This of course cannot be done until it is known how many people there are in the class, and in the example given above one cannot know with any certainty how many daughters A will have until he is dead. In this particular case, there should be no danger of the gift being void for remoteness, for A will be a life in being and so his daughters' interests must all vest within the perpetuity period. However, difficulties could be caused by the following gift:

To A for life and then to B's grandchildren.

Here the gift in remainder is to a class of people, B's grandchildren. The problem in this case is that, in order for the gift to B's grandchildren to be valid, it must be shown that the interest of each grandchild must vest, if it vests at all, within the perpetuity period. If the interest of any one grandchild could vest outside the period, the gift to the whole class is void, because it is impossible to determine within the perpetuity period how much each member should take. Obviously it is quite possible that one of B's grandchildren may be born more than 21 years after the deaths of A and B (lives in being) and therefore this gift gives rise to difficulties, and one might think that the whole gift to the grandchildren will be void.

In such cases the gift may, however, be rescued by the 'class closing rule'. This rule was not invented to save gifts which might be void for perpetuity, but rather to solve the problem of the size of share each member of a class is to receive. In our example it may be that on A's death there are living two children of B, one of whom has two children. Accordingly there are in existence two members of the class, 'B's grandchildren', but it is possible that more may be born later. If the gift is otherwise valid, B's two existing grandchildren are entitled to demand their shares immediately A dies, but if *all* B's future grandchildren are to share in the gift it is not possible to calculate at A's death the amount which each should take. This would prevent any distribution being made until B's children had both died, for until then there is still a possibility of further grandchildren being born. This is so even if B's children are both daughters, and clearly past the age of child-bearing (see above).

Common law recognised the undesirability of this position, and accordingly, in *Andrews* v *Partington* (1791) 3 Bro CC 401, introduced a rule by which the list of possible members of a class is closed when the first member of the class is able to claim his interest in possession. In our example, B's two existing grandchildren will take interests in possession on A's death. Accordingly the rule in *Andrews* v *Partington* closes the class of 'B's grandchildren' at A's death, and B's two existing grandchildren will each receive a half share in the property. Any later grandchildren are excluded from the gift and receive nothing.

If a gift is contingent on members of the class reaching a certain age, e.g.:

To such of B's grandchildren as reach 21,

the class closes when the first of B's grandchildren reaches that age. Any other grandchildren existing at that date are presumed to be potential members of the class and a share should be allocated for them, but they only receive that share when they reach 21. If any one of them should die before reaching that age, his or her notional share will be distributed between those members of the class who do reach the qualifying age. Thus *Andrews* v *Partington* enables a distribution of a minimum share to be made as each one qualifies, with a possibility that the size of the share may increase in future.

Any grandchildren who are born after the date on which the first grandchild reached 21 are excluded from the class by the rule in *Andrews* v *Partington*.

The operation of the class closing rules is very important because it can save a gift which might otherwise have offended the perpetuity rule. In the case of the gift:

To C for life and then to D's grandchildren

the class will close when C dies, if at that date D has at least one grandchild. You will recall that, unfortunately, common law will never wait to see what happens, and so here it is not possible to wait until C dies in order to see whether the class closing rule will save the gift. The issue must be decided finally at the date of the grant. However, if at the date of the grant D already has a grandchild, E, it is clear that on C's death the class of 'D's grandchildren' will close immediately and that the interests of those grandchildren alive at C's death will vest in possession. This *must* be within the perpetuity period (C's life plus 21 years), and so in this case the class closing rule saves a grant which would otherwise be void.

The rule still works even if E dies before C, because E's successors will be entitled to E's share on C's death. This is because E has a future right which vested in interest as soon as he was born, and this is property which can pass under E's will or on intestacy. His position is different from that of B's grandchildren in the previous example, who have only contingent interests until they qualify by reaching 21. Although a notional share is allocated to them as soon as they are born, their interests do not vest in interest until they reach the specified age. Until then, they have no right to the property and therefore if they die before meeting the condition they have nothing to pass to their successors, and their notional share enhances the amount taken by those who do qualify.

If, however, D has no grandchild at the date of the grant, one cannot be sure that such a child will be born before C's death so as to enable the class closing rule to operate. Thus in such a situation the grant will be void under the perpetuity rule. By the same principle if the gift is:

To F for life and then to such of G's grandchildren as reach the age of 21,

then the gift will be saved if G already has a grandchild who is aged 21 at the date of the grant. Otherwise the entire gift to G's grandchildren is void.

Reforms made in 1925

The 1925 property legislation introduced limited reforms in relation to grants made in an instrument executed on or after 1 January 1926, or contained in the will of a testator who died on or after that date (LPA 1925, s. 163(2)). The reform introduced was aimed at the following kind of disposition:

To A for life and then to the first of A's children to reach the age of 25.

If A has no child aged 25 at the date of the grant this disposition would be void at common law, because A might die leaving a child aged 2 who would not reach the age of 25 until 23 years after A's death and outside the perpetuity period (A's life plus 21 years). The alteration made by s. 163 is that where a limitation is void because of an excess in the age of a beneficiary, or class of beneficiaries, then one may reduce the stipulated age to 21. Accordingly, the gift given above will be saved, because the age requirement will be reduced to 21 and obviously any child of A must reach 21 within 21 years (plus any gestation period) after A's death. Not only does this validate an otherwise invalid gift; it also will give A's child an interest vested in possession four years earlier than the settlor intended, so that the child will begin to enjoy the property at that earlier date.

The statutory amendment does not alter a disposition which was valid under the common law rules. Thus a gift to:

The first child of B to reach 25

produces different results depending on whether B is dead or alive at the date of the grant. If B was dead at the date of the grant all his children are identifiable, and can themselves operate as lives in being. In such a case the disposition would be valid at common law, since it must vest, if at all, during the lifetime of a life in being, and so would vest in possession in the first child to reach 25.

However, if B is still alive at the date of the gift, there is a possibility that all his existing children might die, and that B would then produce a further child, who would not be a life in being and who would reach 25 more than 21 years after his father's death. The gift would therefore be void at common law, and s. 163 accordingly reduces the specified age to 21.

Perpetuities and Accumulations Act 1964

The perpetuities rules were given a rather more thorough overhaul by the Perpetuities and Accumulations Act 1964. However, this Act only applies to dispositions which come into effect after 15 July 1964 and so one must still apply the common law rules to earlier settlements. Furthermore the Act amends rather than replaces the old rules and so the common law rules are still of importance to the draftsman of a modern settlement. We will consider the principal changes introduced by the Act.

Power to specify fixed perpetuity period
One of the problems of the common law rules is that one has a variable and therefore unpredictable perpetuity period, since calculation of the length of time involved will depend upon the imponderable question of how long the 'lives in being' will live. Accordingly s. 1 of the 1964 Act gives the settlor the alternative of stating a fixed period, which must not be more than 80 years, as the perpetuity period for his settlement. This fixed period is generally used as a substitute for the old 'royal lives' clauses. Such clauses may still

be used if the settlor so chooses, but the fixed period provides a neater and more convenient alternative.

Introduction of a 'wait and see' rule
As we have seen already, one of the major problems with the common law rule is that one is obliged to judge the issue of perpetuities at the outset and this leads to a consideration of every possibility, however far-fetched. This unsatisfactory position is altered by s. 3(1) of the 1964 Act. This section provides that where a disposition is void under the common law rule, it should be treated as though it was not subject to that rule, until such time as it bcomes clear that it will vest, if at all, outside the perpetuity period. In other words, one can wait through the perpetuity period to see what really happens, rather than basing the decision on what *might* happen. Accordingly, the only type of disposition which is void *ab initio* is one which clearly *must* vest outside the perpetuity period and cannot possibly vest within it. If we consider again the grant:

To the first child of X to become an accountant,

we will see that under the 1964 rule all we have to do is to wait and see whether any child of X does ever become an accountant within the perpetuity period. Similarly in the case of the grant:

To A for life and then to any widow of A for life and thereafter to the eldest of A's children then living,

we simply wait to see what happens. If A dies, leaving a widow who was alive at the date of the gift, she does constitute a life in being and it becomes clear that the eldest child's interest will vest, if at all, during the perpetuity period. If, however, A has married the 'unborn widow' (i.e., someone who was not alive at the date of the gift) then one waits again to see whether she dies within 21 years of A's death, leaving a child in whom the property can vest. If she outlives A by 21 years it then becomes clear that the gift must vest outside the perpetuity period. No more can be done to save the gift under the 'wait and see' provisions, but all is not lost, for there are special statutory provisions designed to rescue such a disposition which we shall describe later (p. 221).

It is important to note that s. 3(1) applies only where the disposition would be void at common law. Therefore, when dealing with perpetuity problems, one must first apply the common law rule, and explain why it invalidates the gift, before going on to apply the provisions of the section: it is not enough to adopt a general approach of 'wait and see' with regard to all contingent interests.

If the 'wait and see' principle does not save a gift, it may nonetheless be saved by one of the other amendments made by the Act, as we will see below.

Introduction of statutory 'lives in being'
A further amendment to the common law rules is that when we 'wait and see' we do not apply the same test for 'lives in being' as under the earlier rules. Thus the 'wait and see' perpetuity period is calculated by reference to the lives which are prescribed by the statute for this purpose. These rules are contained in s. 3(4) and (5) of the 1964 Act. They provide that one calculates the period by reference to any of the following who are in being and ascertainable at the *start* of the perpetuity period:

(a)   the person making the disposition (settlor);
(b)   a person in whose favour the disposition is made (in the case of class gifts this includes all members and potential members of the class);
(c)   the parents or grandparents of any person in whose favour a disposition is made (basically any parent or grandparent of someone who falls into category (b));
(d)   any person on the failure of whose prior interest the disposition is limited to take effect.

It is thought that by increasing the categories of people who can be lives in being, a greater chance is given of the interest vesting in time.

No other persons may be used as lives in being for the 'wait and see' provisions. If there are no persons falling into this category at the date at which the disposition takes effect, then a fixed period of 21 years is imposed (s. 3(4)(b)).

Reduction of age
The 1964 Act repealed s. 163 of the LPA 1925 (but only in respect of dispositions made after 15 July 1964), and provided new age reduction rules, which apply where 'a disposition is limited by reference to the attainment by any person or persons of a specified age exceeding 21 years' (s. 4). These new rules apply only where the interest would be void at common law, and one should not apply them until one has waited (under s. 3(1)) to see whether the interest will vest within the period. Thus, if we take a disposition made after 1964 to:

The first child of B to reach 25,

our first reaction must be to wait and see whether the gift vests within the common law period (B's life plus 21 years). If B dies leaving one child, C, aged 2, it will be clear that C can never hope to reach the age of 25 within 21 years of B's death. At this point we know that the 'wait and see' provisions have not helped. The next step will therefore be to apply s. 4, which requires that an age reduction should be applied in order to attempt to save the disposition. However, we do not simply reduce the qualifying age to 21 (as was the case under the 1925 Act). Instead we have to apply a two-stage process:

(a)   we decide whether the gift would be valid were the qualifying age 21; if yes, then

(b) we reduce the age 'to the age nearest to that age which would, if specified instead, have prevented the disposition from being . . . void'.

If we apply this rule to our example we will see that the disposition would have been valid had the age limit been 21. C will reach 21 within 21 years of B's death. However, since C was 2 at his father's death, it is not necessary to reduce the qualifying age to 21 in order to ensure that the disposition vests in the period, for C will become 21 only 19 years after his father's death. The effect of s. 4 is therefore to reduce the qualifying age to 23, because that is the age closest to the specified age of 25 which is capable of satisfying the perpetuity rule. Accordingly, if C lives until he is 23 he will obtain an interest vested in possession under the 1964 Act.

Introduction of presumptions about fertility
As well as allowing us to 'wait and see', the 1964 Act introduced certain presumptions about fertility, which help to remove some of the more ridiculous problems caused by the common law rules. Under s. 2 of the Act the following presumptions apply:

(a) a male cannot be a father if he is aged under 14;
(b) a female cannot be a mother if she is aged under 12 or over 55.

There is no upper age limit presumed in respect of a man's fertility. It is obvious that these presumptions are not an entirely accurate reflection of physical possibilities, particularly as far as the lower age limits are concerned. As a result, s. 2(2) allows the court to make such order as it thinks fit to readjust the position should it later be discovered that a birth has in fact occurred outside the presumed fertility periods. In addition to making use of the statutory presumptions described above, it is also open to the court to receive evidence that a particular male over 14 or female aged 12–55 is in fact infertile (s. 2(1)(b)). This is most likely to be of assistance in the cases of women who have undergone hysterectomies. More care would have to be taken in the case of evidence relating to sterilisation operations (e.g., vasectomy) as these can sometimes be reversed, rendering the individual fertile once more.

Amendment of rules on the 'unborn widow'
You will recall from p. 214 above that a disposition:

To A for life and then to any widow of A for life and thereafter to the eldest of A's children then living,

gives rise to considerable problems at common law, because of the possibility that the future Mrs A might not have been born at the date of the disposition and so is not a life in being. We have seen (p. 219) how, under the 1964 Act, it is possible to 'wait and see' whether Mrs A is a life in being, and if she is not, whether she does in fact die within 21 years of A's death, leaving a child of A in whom the gift can vest. However 'wait and see' will not help in that case, if Mrs A survives her husband by more than 21 years. Accordingly, in such cases, s. 5 of the 1964 Act provides that the disposition 'to the eldest of A's children' shall be treated 'as if it had instead been limited by reference to the time immediately before the end of [the perpetuity] period'. Thus, in our example, if Mrs A is not a life in being and outlives her husband by more than 21 years, the eldest child of A who is living at the end of the period (A's life plus 21 years) will obtain a vested interest at that date. If A dies leaving two children, B and C (B being the elder), and a widow who outlives him by 21 years, B will obtain a vested interest 21 years after his father's death. Should B then die *before* the widow, B's estate will retain a vested interest, and C will *not* obtain any interest in the property, even though this is contrary to the express wishes of the settlor. Although the result is to alter the intended outcome slightly, this rule does have the merit that it prevents the gift over to A's eldest child being wholly void.

Options relating to land
If you looked at the report of *Woodall* v *Clifton* [1905] 2 Ch 257, which was mentioned in the section about covenants in leases (p. 136), you will know that an option to purchase an interest in land is subject to the perpetuity rule, and is void if it could be exercised outside the period.

The 1964 Act contains two provisions about options:

(a)   Section 9(2) provides that the perpetuity period in respect of options is 21 years, and that the statutory period of 80 years shall not apply here.
(b)   Section 9(1) provides that the rule against perpetuities shall not apply to an option to purchase the reversion on a lease, provided that the option is exercisable only by the tenant or his successors in title, and must be exercised, if at all, no later than one year after the expiry of the lease.

In conclusion

In conclusion, we must remind you that most of the statutory provisions are designed to rescue dispositions which are invalidated by the rule against perpetuities, and do not, apart from the statutory 80-year period, provide any alternatives to it. This means that, when drafting a settlement, regard must be had to the common law rules, and no modern settlement should ever be drafted in such a way as to be void under those rules. However, mistakes will no doubt continue to be made and discovered, and accordingly the student may find the following summary useful.

(a)   *Dispositions coming in to effect before 1 January 1926.* Apply common law rules only.
(b)   *Dispositions coming into effect between 1 January 1926 and 15 July 1964.* Apply common law rules but with the modification of the age reductions provided by LPA 1925, s. 163.
(c)   *Dispositions coming into effect on or after 16 July 1964.* Apply common law rules, but with the modifications imposed by the Perpetuities and Accumulations Act 1964, and in particular:

(i) in drafting a settlement, take into account the availability of an 80-year fixed period;

(ii) in interpreting a settlement, take into account:

(1) 'wait and see' (including statutory lives in being);
(2) age reductions under s. 4;
(3) presumptions about fertility in s. 2;
(4) special 'unborn widow' rules in s. 5.

Finally, we must mention that we have concentrated on stating the general principle and giving a few examples of its application. Those who want information about the authorities from which the principle is derived, or the many other detailed rules which we have not mentioned, should refer to the appropriate chapters in Sir Robert Megarry and H.W.R. Wade, *The Law of Real Property*, 5th ed. (London: Stevens, 1984) or G.C. Cheshire and E.H. Burn, *Cheshire and Burn's Modern Law of Real Property*, 14th ed. (London: Butterworths, 1988) or to J.H.C. Morris and W.B. Leach, *The Rule against Perpetuities*, 2nd ed. (London: Stevens, 1962).

6   Co-ownership

At one time the normal pattern of land ownership in Britain was that the estate in land, unless subject to a trust, was vested in one person as sole beneficial owner. Changes in social conditions, and in particular the alteration in the status of women, have meant that today sole ownership has become far more rare and that it is normal for domestic property to be the subject of co-ownership. This co-ownership may arise deliberately, because the property is conveyed to two or more person as co-owners, or by operation of law (e.g., as the product of a resulting trust).

Factual background

Mr and Mrs Armstrong have now completed the purchase of the fee simple estate in 1 Trant Way. The property was transferred 'to Arnold Armstrong and Arriety Armstrong' and they have now been registered as proprietors at the Land Registry.

The fee simple estate in 11 Trant Way is vested in Mark Mould, who bought the property in 1979. The property is also occupied by Sally Mould, Mark's wife, and their two children. Mrs Mould has not worked outside the home during the marriage, but has been engaged full time in bringing up the children.

You will recall that the position of Henry Mumps at 8 Trant Way is similar to that of Mrs Mould at No. 11, but with two notable differences:

(a)   Henry and Mildred Mumps are not married; and
(b)   Henry has made improvements to Mildred's property.

12 Trant Way was bought a year ago by six friends who are all studying Outer Mongolian history at Mousehole University and who expect to graduate in two years' time. The friends each contributed one-sixth of the purchase price and, because they were short of money, one of their number did the conveyancing himself. The property was conveyed to all six: i.e. to Alice, Brian, Colin, David, Eric and Fanny. At the date of the conveyance Alice was 17 and all the others were 18. The intention was that the house was to be kept until all six graduated and that it should then be sold.

13 Trant Way belongs to a firm of chartered surveyors. The partners in the firm are Sidney Search and Frederick Find and the legal estate, a 99-year lease, has been conveyed into the names of the two partners.

TWO TYPES OF CO-OWNERSHIP

In modern law there are two types of co-ownership: (a) the *joint tenancy*, and (b) the *tenancy in common*. It is essential to be able to distinguish between the two and so we will first look at the characteristics of each, before going on to consider how they arise.

Joint tenancy

The joint tenancy is in a way the more perfect of the two types of co-ownership. It is a method of ownership in which the co-owners are *not* regarded as having "shares" in the land but as together owning the whole estate. It is as though the co-owners are not really treated as separate owners but as an inseparable group owner. Thus if Arnold and Arriety Armstrong are joint tenants in respect of 1 Trant Way, we cannot say that Arnold owns half and that Arriety owns half. We must say that Arnold and Arriety *together* own the whole estate. In the notation used in this chapter we will place joint tenants inside parentheses:

(Arnold and Arriety)

to indicate this relationship.

For this 'perfect' relationship to exist one must establish first that what are traditionally called the 'four unities' exist. These unities are essential to the joint nature of the ownership, in which no co-owner has a share distinguishable from that of the other co-owners. The unities are:

(a) time;
(b) title;
(c) interest; and
(d) possession.

Time This unity requires that the interests of all the co-owners should vest at the same time. Thus in a disposition, 'to A for life and then to B and C', B and C have the unity of time because the interest of each vests on the death of A. In the case of Mr and Mrs Armstrong this unity exists because the interest of each vested when 1 Trant Way was transferred to them as co-owners.

Title This requires that the co-owners should all have acquired their title by the same means, e.g., all from the same document. In the case of Mr and Mrs Armstrong they both derive their title from the transfer which, on registration, vested the legal estate in them. This unity would also be satisfied if two or more persons together took land by adverse possession. In this case, title is derived from the action of taking possession of the land, and if this action is taken by persons acting jointly the unity of title would be present. (*Ward* v *Ward* (1871) LR 6 Ch App 789).

Interest   For a joint tenancy to exist, the interests of all the co-owners must also be identical. Each interest must be of the same duration, and of the same nature and extent. Thus if one co-owner has a life interest and the other an interest in fee simple, they cannot be joint tenants because this unity is not present.

Possession   Finally the co-owners must be equally entitled to the possession of the whole land (see *Bull* v *Bull* [1955] 1 QB 234). If one could point to a portion of the land and say, 'That portion is mine and is not yours', then there would be no co-ownership. In such a case each would be a sole owner of a smaller part of the land.

Words of severance

Even where all four unities are present it is still possible for the arrangement not to satisfy the requirements for a joint tenancy. This will happen where it is clear that the parties are to be regarded as having separate shares in the property (even though they may not wish to partition the land). Any words suggesting that the co-owners are to be regarded as owners of shares, rather than as a kind of group sole owner, will prevent the ownership being a joint tenancy. This will happen in particular if the conveyance or transfer to the co-owners contains 'words of severance'. These are words such as 'in equal shares' (*Payne* v *Webb* (1874) LR 19 Eq 26), which show that the co-owners do not have the indivisible relationship which is necessary for the joint tenancy. Words which have been held to produce this result include:

'equally' (*Lewen* v *Dodd* (1595) Cro Eliz 443);
'share and share alike' (*Heathe* v *Heathe* (1740) 2 Atk 121);
'to be divided between' (*Peat* v *Chapman* (1750) 1 Ves Sen 542);
'between' (*Lashbrook* v *Cock* (1816) 2 Mer 70).

Right of survivorship

One crucial aspect of joint tenancy is the 'right of survivorship' or *jus accrescendi*. Since a joint tenant is not regarded as having a distinct share in the co-owned land, he is not able to dispose of his interest by will on his death, nor will it pass on intestacy if he fails to make a will. Instead on the death of one joint tenant the remaining joint tenants obtain the interest of the deceased. This is the natural result of regarding joint tenants as a kind of unified and indivisible group. The last survivor of the group will of course become a sole beneficial owner and will be able to dispose of the property as he pleases on his death. With the joint tenancy it pays to be long-lived! This rule may prove to be a nuisance in some types of co-ownership and may encourage the choice of the tenancy in common instead. However, in some cases, for instance, between husband and wife, it may be very convenient and avoid unnecessary dispositions on the death of one co-owner.

Tenancy in common

The tenancy in common is not such a 'perfect' relationship of co-ownership. For such a tenancy to exist, only one unity is required, that of possession. This is, however, essential for, as we have already seen, if it did not exist there would be no co-ownership but merely individual ownership of separate portions of land. The tenant in common, unlike the joint tenant, is entitled to a notional share of the property (e.g., a half or a quarter), which he can dispose of during life or at death, but this is an 'undivided share', and until partition or sale occurs all the tenants in common are entitled to possession of the whole. Thus, provided unity of possession is present, a tenancy in common will arise in any case of co-ownership where the other unities are absent, and the arrangement cannot therefore give rise to a joint tenancy.

However, it must be remembered that often all four unities may be present, but there will still be only a tenancy in common because of the clear intention of the parties that they should hold in this way, or because of the presence of words of severance in the document creating their interests. Further, even where such intention or words are not present, there are some very important cases in which equity will presume that a tenancy in common has been created.

Thus, if the co-owners have contributed in unequal portions to the purchase price, equity considered it unfair to impose upon them the equality of the joint tenancy, and the effects of the right of survivorship, for it might be that the tenant who had contributed least might prove to be the longest lived, and thus become the sole owner of the whole property. Accordingly in such cases equity has always presumed that unequal contributors hold the property as tenants in common, each co-owner having a share in the property proportional to his contribution to the purchase price. (*Lake* v *Gibson* (1729) 1 Eq Rep 290; and , in modern law, *Bull* v *Bull* [1955] 1 QB 234). This presumption could of course be rebutted by clear evidence of an intention to the contrary: either that the parties should after all hold as joint tenants, or that as tenants in common the size of their shares should not correspond to the amount of their respective contributions. Again, where the co-ownership is of a commercial character the right of survivorship appears to equity to be inappropriate. Thus in the case of partnership property, equity also leans in favour of the tenancy in common, and so would assume that the type of co-ownership applicable to 13 Trant Way (owned by the chartered surveyors) is the tenancy in common (*Re Fuller's Contract* [1933] Ch 652). Another example of this principle is found where two people lend money on mortgage (joint mortgagees): they are presumed to hold the estate which they receive by way of security as tenants in common (*Morley* v *Bird* (1798) 3 Ves Jr 628). See also *Malayan Credit Ltd* v *Jack Chia-MPH Ltd* [1986] AC 549, PC.

Different positions in law and equity

Whilst equity has always preferred the tenancy in common, law leaned in favour of the joint tenancy. The reason for this was that with the joint tenancy the number of co-owners always decreases (because of the right of survivorship). This facilitates dealings with the legal estate, by concentrating the title to it into fewer hands, rather than by increasing the number of owners, as can happen when the share of a tenant in common passes on his death to several people. Thus it has always been true that whilst equity might regard a set of co-owners as tenants in common, law might regard the same persons as joint tenants. It is useful therefore always to think of co-owners under two separate headings thus:

13 Trant Way

LAW	EQUITY
(Search and Find)	Search and Find
Joint tenancy	Tenancy in common

In this example Search and Find are legal joint tenants, but are tenants in common in equity. To put it another way, they hold the legal estate as joint tenants but the beneficial interest (the equitable interest) as tenants in common. We will adopt this standard diagrammatic form hereafter and you will note that joint tenants appear together in parentheses, whereas tenants in common appear without parentheses.

It may be thought at first that considerable difficulties would be caused if law and equity regarded one arrangement as giving rise to different forms of co-ownership. Are the owners to be regarded as joint tenants, subject to the right of survivorship, or as tenants in common? The difficulty may be illustrated by considering the position of A and B, who hold the legal estate as joint tenants but who, because of unequal contributions, are regarded by equity as tenants in common. During their lifetime, this may cause no great difficulty, but what happens when B dies, having made a will by which he leaves his interest in the property to C? At law, A will become solely entitled to the property, and C will take nothing, but in equity B's share under his tenancy in common passes under his will, and C is therefore entitled to that share. What will happen?

Fortunately, the apparent difficulty has always been resolved by the use of the trust. From the outset, equity accepted that at law A and B were joint tenants, but required that they should hold the estate in trust for themselves as tenants in common in equity (or, in other words, as tenants in common of the beneficial interest). When B dies, A is left holding the legal estate, not for himself alone, but in trust for himself and C, again as tenants in common.

LAW	EQUITY
(A and B)	A and B
A	A and C

No legal tenancies in common

A further occasion for a divergence between law and equity came with the modern rule, introduced by the 1925 legislation, that there cannot be a tenancy in common of the legal estate. This change was one of many designed to facilitate conveyancing; as we have already seen (p. 226), the joint tenancy offers considerable advantages in this regard.

The new rule is to be found in LPA 1925, s. 34(1): 'An undivided share in land shall not be capable of being created . . .'.

This does not prevent the creation of tenancies in common in equity because, as we shall see very soon, these are regarded as interests in money and so do not fall within the wording of this section. Nowadays, therefore, if a conveyance of a legal estate is made 'to A and B as tenants in common', or if words of severance are used ('to A and B in equal shares'), this will not affect the legal estate, which will pass to them as joint tenants, but effect will be given to the intention by treating them as tenants in common in equity.

Imposition of statutory trusts

We have seen already that when law and equity differed over the nature of the tenancy created, any apparent conflict was resolved by the use of a trust (p. 227). The 1925 property legislation went further than this and imposed statutory trusts on most forms of co-ownership (see LPA 1925, s. 34(2) (tenancies in common) and s. 36(1) (joint tenancies)). The 'statutory trusts' are defined in LPA 1925, s. 35, and consist of a trust for sale. Thus the co-owners hold the legal estate upon trust for sale for themselves as beneficiaries. As a result of the doctrine of conversion (see p. 203), this means that the equitable interests of the co-owners will be interests in money and not in land.

This imposition of the statutory trust for sale must be related to the overall policy of the 1925 legislation: to simplify conveyancing and to make it easier for a purchaser to buy land. The fact that any property subject to co-ownership is also subject to a trust for sale enables the purchaser to take advantage of the overreaching machinery (LPA 1925, ss. 2(1) and 27; see p. 207): providing he pays the purchase money to two trustees he takes free of the beneficial interests and need not concern himself with questions of who is entitled in equity and whether they agree to the sale (see, e.g. *City of London Building Society* v *Flegg* [1988] AC 54). He is concerned only with title to the legal estate.

So far, we have spoken as though the trust for sale is imposed in all cases of co-ownership, but we must mention briefly that there appear to be certain gaps not covered by the provisions of LPA 1925, ss. 34 to 36. One example may suffice: it seems that the wording of s. 34 does not apply to tenancies in common which arise otherwise than expressly (e.g., on a resulting trust). However, this gap appears to have been filled by the court in the case of *Bull* v *Bull* [1955] 1 QB 234, in which the trust for sale was imposed in these circumstances.

Finally, it should be noted that the imposition of the statutory trust is limited to cases where there are several beneficial owners (i.e., in equity).

J

It does not apply where there are several joint tenants of the legal estate holding as trustees for a sole beneficiary.

Maximum of four trustees

In order to prevent a trust having an inordinate number of trustees, the Trustee Act 1925, s. 34(2), limits the number of trustees to a maximum of four. Where more than four are named the property vests in the first four who are of full age. Where land is simply conveyed to a group of persons as tenants in common, LPA 1925, s. 34(2), provides that the first four of full age will take the legal estate as joint tenants and hold it upon trust for the whole group as tenants in common in equity. As a result the conveyance of 12 Trant Way to the six students will vest the legal estate in the first four who are over 18 (Brian, Colin, David and Eric) and these four will be registered as proprietors on first registration. Alice, who was only 17 at the date of the conveyance, and Fanny will be owners in equity only. The legal estate *must* be held by the trustees as joint tenants but the nature of the equitable ownership will depend on the presence or absence of the four unities and words of severance. We know that all six contributed equally to the purchase price, so there is no question of equity presuming a tenancy in common. Assuming that there are no words of severance, the result is as follows:

LAW	EQUITY
(B, C, D and E)	(A, B, C, D, E and F)

There is a joint tenancy in both law and equity but with six equitable owners and only four (the maximum) at law.

SEVERANCE OF A JOINT TENANCY

A relationship which begins as a joint tenancy need not remain so, for, in certain circumstances, it is possible for a joint tenant to sever his interest and thereby to convert it into a tenancy in common. A primary reason for severance may be to avoid the effects of the right of survivorship. Of course, it is *never* possible these days to sever a joint tenancy of the legal estate, for to do this would be to create a legal tenancy in common, which is prohibited by LPA 1925, s. 34(1). Accordingly LPA 1925, s. 36(2) provides that: 'No severance of a joint tenancy of a legal estate, so as to create a tenancy in common in land, shall be permissible . . .'.

Severance of an *equitable* joint tenancy is, however, still possible (and frequent in practice) and may be effected in a number of ways, which are set out in the proviso to s. 36(2):

Provided that, where a legal estate (not being settled land) is vested in joint tenants beneficially, and any tenant desires to sever the joint tenancy in equity, he shall give to the other joint tenants a notice in writing of such desire or do such other acts or things as would, in the case of personal estate, have been effectual to sever the tenancy in equity.

When the equitable joint tenancy is severed the joint tenant severing will take an equal portion of the interest as a tenant in common. Thus if the property was expressly conveyed to two persons as joint tenants, on severance each will acquire a half share as tenants in common (*Goodman* v *Gallant* [1986] Fam 106).

We will now look in detail at those methods of severing.

Notice in writing

This is probably the simplest way today of severing a joint tenancy. The notice, if posted, should be served on all the other joint tenants in a registered letter at their last known place of abode or business (LPA 1925, s. 196(4)). Provided that this method of service is adopted it is irrelevant that the co-owner does not in fact receive knowledge of the notice. In *Re 88 Berkeley Road NW9* [1971] Ch 648 the two joint tenants both occupied the premises. One co-owner served notice of severance on the other joint tenant by registered post to the property. It later became clear that when the letter was delivered it was received and signed for by the person who had sent it and that it was never handed to the addressee. This was held nonetheless to amount to good service and the joint tenancy had accordingly been severed. (Recorded delivery is also acceptable: Recorded Delivery Service Act 1962, s. 1 and Schedule, para. 1). Instead of posting the notice it will also be enough to address it to the other joint tenants and leave it at, or affix it to, their last known abode or place of business (LPA 1925, s. 196(3)).

'Such other acts or things as would, in the case of personal estate, . . . sever the tenancy in equity'

It may seem strange that methods of severing appropriate to personal property are prescribed here, but you will remember that the statutory trust for sale has the effect of notionally converting the beneficiaries' interest into an interest in money (i.e., personal property).

Next, one has to consider what 'acts or things' bring about severance in equity. The classic statement, to which later decisions usually refer with approval, is that of Sir William Page Wood V-C in *Williams* v *Hensman* (1861) 1 John & H 546 at p. 557:

A joint tenancy may be severed in three ways: in the first place, an act of any one of the persons interested operating upon his own share may create a severance as to that share . . . Each one is at liberty to dispose of his own interest in such manner as to sever it from the joint fund — losing, of course, at the same time, his own right of survivorship. Secondly, a joint tenancy may be severed by mutual agreement. And, in the third place, there may be a severance by any course of dealing sufficient to intimate that the interests of all were mutually treated as constituting a tenancy in common.

We will look at each of these three methods in turn.

'An act . . . operating upon his own share'.
The example given of this method is that of disposing of one's own interest in such a way as to sever it from the joint fund — for example, on sale. This creates severance because it has the effect of destroying one of the unities essential to the joint tenancy: that of title. The purchaser does not share the unity of title with the other co-owners, for he takes under a different document, and so cannot be a joint tenant with them. In law, severance would occur when the estate was conveyed to the purchaser; but in equity it takes place as soon as there is a specifically enforceable contract to sell. It will be remembered that equity recognises the purchaser as owner from the date of the contract, and the change of equitable ownership is enough to destroy the unities.

Where severance is effected by sale of the beneficial interest, it must be realised that the joint tenant cannot transfer his interest in the *legal* estate to the purchaser, for to do so would amount to severance of the legal joint tenancy, which is forbidden (LPA 1925, s. 36(2)). So, even after he has disposed of his beneficial interest, he continues to hold the legal estate as a trustee, and can give it up only by releasing his interest to his fellow joint tenants or by retiring from the trust (Trustee Act 1925, s. 39).

Another way of disrupting the unities and therefore of severing a legal joint tenancy before 1926 occurred when one joint tenant acquired a greater interest than his fellows and thereby destroyed the unity of interest. Thus if A, B and C were equitable joint tenants for life and A acquired the interest in remainder, this would transform A's interest into a tenancy in common. Although not specifically mentioned in *Williams* v *Hensman*, it could perhaps be described as an act which operates on one's own share, and therefore may come within this first category.

Mutual agreement
Severance can be effected by the agreement of all the joint tenants. The agreement may, of course, be express, but can also be inferred from the conduct of the parties. The leading modern case which illustrates this method of severance is *Burgess* v *Rawnsley* [1975] Ch 429. Here it was held that an oral agreement by one joint tenant to purchase the share of the other had effected a severance (because the parties were thinking in terms of 'shares'), even though such an agreement would not be legally enforceable because there was no written memorandum or part performance to satisfy LPA 1925, s. 40. We have seen that a contract must be specifically enforceable if it is to constitute severance under the first rule in *Williams* v *Hensman*; but the Court of Appeal emphasised that this requirement 'only applies where the suggestion is that the joint tenancy has been severed by an alienation by one joint tenant to a third party, and does not apply to severance by agreement between the joint tenants' (per Browne LJ, [1975] Ch 429 at p. 444).

'Any course of dealing [which shows] that the interests of all were mutually treated as constituting a tenancy in common'
In *Burgess* v *Rawnsley*, members of the Court of Appeal expressed views on this third category, although they emphasised that as the decision was based

on the second ground (mutual agreement), these views were necessarily *obiter dicta*. Thus Sir John Pennycuick explained that it includes 'negotiations which, although not otherwise resulting in any agreement, indicate a common intention that the joint tenancy should be regarded as severed' (at p. 447). It should be noted that Lord Denning MR gave a slightly wider interpretation (at p. 439), which seems to cover a unilateral declaration by the party wishing to sever:

It is sufficient if there is a course of dealing in which one party makes clear to the other that he desires that their shares should no longer be held jointly but be held in common.

This does not seem to fit too well with the requirement of *mutual* behaviour stated in *Williams* v *Hensman*, and it should be noted that Sir John Pennycuick expressly states that in his view a mere verbal notice by one party to the other cannot operate as severance (p. 448).

Forfeiture
One final method of severance, not covered by LPA 1925, s. 36(2) or *Williams* v *Hensman* (1861) 1 John & H 546 must be noted briefly. Should one joint tenant kill the other (which is not altogether unknown), it seems that the right of survivorship cannot operate because this would allow the homicide to benefit from his criminal act. The general principle that this is not permitted is to be found in *In the estate of Hall* [1914] P 1, and some recent decisions in Australia and New Zealand have applied this to cases of joint tenancy, although it seems there is as yet no English decision on the point.

Example of the operation of the severance rules

Let us take the position at 12 Trant Way (the six students) and assume that the following events occur:

(a) A serves notice of severance on B, C, D, E and F;
(b) B sells his interest to X; and
(c) C dies.

This produces the following devolution of title to the legal estate and the equitable interest:

EVENT	LAW	EQUITY	EXPLANATION
	(B, C, D and E)	(A, B, C, D, E and F)	At start all are joint tenants.
(a)	(B, C, D and E)	A (B, C, D, E and F)	Position at law not affected. A becomes tenant in common in equity with one-sixth share, but others remain joint tenants *inter se* ('between themselves').
(b)	(B, C, D and E)	A, X (C, D, E and F)	Position at law not affected. In equity, severance by destruction of unities. X becomes tenant in common with one-sixth share. C, D, E and F remain joint tenants *inter se* of four-sixths.
(c)	(B, D and E)	A, X (D, E and F)	Right of survivorship operates in law and equity. D, E and F now jointly own four-sixths of equitable interest.

RELATIONSHIP BETWEEN CO-OWNERS

It is not uncommon for co-owners of property to have differences of opinion about the management of their property and accordingly we need to consider the legal position in relation to the common areas of dispute.

Selling: consultation and consents

Because all co-owned property is subject to a trust for sale, disputes about whether the estate should be retained or sold need careful consideration. The basic principle in the case of any trust for sale is that once one trustee will no longer agree to postpone sale the property must be sold (*Re Mayo* [1943] Ch 302), because the primary obligation is to sell. In the case of co-ownership this rule is, however, subject to the provisions of LPA 1925, s. 26(3). This provides that where land is subject to a *statutory* trust for sale the trustees:

> shall so far as practicable consult the persons of full age for the time being beneficially interested in possession . . . and shall, so far as consistent with the general interest of the trust, give effect to the wishes of such persons, or, in the case of dispute, of the majority (according to the value of their combined interests).

The effect of this provision is that when deciding on sale the trustees should be guided by the wishes of the majority of the beneficiaries, unless this produces an effect which is clearly contrary to the general interest of the trust. This overrides the *Re Mayo* principle, so that if, in the case of 12 Trant Way, Eric, a trustee, wishes to sell, the property should not be sold if the other equitable co-owners wish to retain the land.

If the trustees do not consult as required by s. 26(3), or ignore the results of consultation, the beneficiaries may seek an injunction to restrain any intended breach of trust by the trustees, or may claim compensation should the objectionable transaction have been completed.

A purchaser of land held on the statutory trusts is not required to ensure that the trustees have in fact complied with the consultation procedure. As long as the overreaching provisions are satisfied the purchaser gets a good title free of the beneficial interests, even if the beneficiaries have *not* been consulted. The trustees would, however, be liable to the beneficiaries for breach of trust.

The description we have just given makes it sound as though deciding whether or not to sell is relatively simple, the decision being taken by a majority of the beneficiaries who will direct the trustees what to do. In real life, however, it is likely to be a much more complicated matter, because usually in cases of co-ownership the same people are acting as both trustees and beneficiaries; they are very often connected by marriage or family relationship; and the property in question is their only home. The majority decision to sell may deprive the minority of a home, and the proposal to sell may be only part of a larger dispute about the parties' future together. It therefore must not be assumed that having 'consulted the beneficiaries', the 'trustees' can always readily give effect to the wishes of the majority, and a particular problem arises where the minority refuses to move out so that the house can be offered for sale with vacant possession.

It was this problem which was considered by the Court of Appeal in *Bull* v *Bull* [1955] 1 QB 234, a case to which we have already referred in connection with trusts for sale (p. 202). Here a financial contribution by the mother to the purchase price of a house conveyed to her son created a resulting trust, in which the son held the legal estate in trust for himself and his mother as tenants in common. The house was bought to provide a home for both of them, but after his marriage the son wanted his mother to move out, and finally sought a possession order against her. The Court of Appeal held that such an application against a fellow tenant in common was completely inappropriate: as we have seen, each tenant in common has a right to possession of the whole of the property (unity of possession — p. 226) and one cannot therefore evict another. The only way to proceed, even for those who, like the son, have a majority holding, is to seek an order for sale under LPA 1925, s. 30 (see p. 205).

Thus it appears that LPA 1925, s. 26(3), which displaces the rule in *Re Mayo* in the case of statutory trusts, is itself overlaid by the decision in *Bull* v *Bull*. Where the minority is in occupation, and cannot be reconciled to the decision, it seems that the trustees cannot simply disregard the minority's wishes and give effect to those of the majority, but must in fact obtain a court order before they can sell the property.

Further, it must be noted that the courts will not normally make an order for sale under s. 30 where the property was acquired for a particular purpose and that purpose is still continuing. An early application of this principle is found in *Re Buchanan-Wollaston's Conveyance* [1939] Ch 738. There a group of neighbours had jointly bought a piece of land adjoining their properties with the intention of keeping it as an open space and thereby preventing further building. Later one neighbour sold his house and wished also to realise the money he had tied up in the open land. His application for an order for sale of the co-owned property was rejected on the ground that the land had been bought for a particular purpose and that purpose was still being satisfied by the retention of the property. Other examples of the idea of the continuing purpose are found in cases about the matrimonial home. In *Jones* v *Challenger* [1961] 1 QB 176 a husband and wife jointly acquired leasehold premises as a matrimonial home. After divorce proceedings the wife sought an order for sale. The court granted the order because the purpose for which the property was bought had ended on divorce. The position might, however, be different in a case where there are children, and a home is still being provided for one partner and the children. In *Rawlings* v *Rawlings* [1964] P 398 Salmon LJ indicated that in such cases an order for sale should be delayed until the children 'are grown up'. (See also Goff J in *Mayes* v *Mayes* (1969) 210 EG 935 and *Re Evers' Trust* [1980] 1 WLR 1327.) However, a contrary view was taken in *Williams* v *Williams* [1976] Ch 278. Normally such disputes in the case of married couples will be resolved by the courts as part of divorce proceedings (see p. 242) but these considerations may still be relevant in the case of unmarried co-owners.

A right to occupy the land?

Since, due to the imposition of the statutory trust for sale and the doctrine of conversion (p. 203), the interest of a co-owner is theoretically in money and not land it may seem to be a matter of doubt whether a co-owner can claim any rights in relationship to the land itself. However, as we have seen, the Court of Appeal in *Bull* v *Bull* held that one tenant in common could not evict another, because each had the same right to possession of the land. This would, of course, have been the position before the imposition of the statutory trust by the 1925 property legislation. Although these trusts are of value when the property comes to be sold, enabling the purchaser to take advantage of the overreaching machinery, they would, if interpreted strictly, produce very inconvenient results during the period of co-ownership. In *Bull* v *Bull*, and in the decisions which have developed the idea of the continuing purpose, it seems that the courts have been primarily concerned with the needs of the co-owners and have not pressed the concept of the statutory trust to its logical conclusion.

Liability for rent to other co-owners?

Before 1926 the right to occupy the land existed equally in favour of all the co-owners, and presumably continues to do so today, in so far as it exists at all (see above). In practice, however, it may be unlikely or impossible that all should in fact occupy the premises. In such cases, will the occupier be liable to pay rent or compensation to the other co-owners on the basis that his occupation prevents them exercising their own similar right? The general rule in such cases is that co-owners are not liable to one another for an occupation rent, for there is no right to exclude the other co-owner who might still, if he so chooses, exercise his rights in relation to the premises (*Henderson* v *Eason* (1851) 17 QB 701). In rare circumstances, however, rent may be payable. Thus in *Dennis* v *McDonald* [1982] Fam 63, in which one tenant in common, by his violence towards the other owner, prevented her from occupying the premises, it was held that rent was payable. The sum payable was assessed at half the fair rent which would be payable in respect of the property were it subject to a protected tenancy.

Partitioning

Where the land is sufficiently extensive it may prove convenient for the co-owners to decide to partition the premises between themselves. In this way each becomes a sole beneficial owner of a portion of the land. Such partition can always be effected by agreement between all the co-owners. Under LPA 1925, s. 28(3), trustees for sale may, with the consent of the beneficiaries, partition the land and convey the portions thus created to the co-owners.

POSITION OF A PURCHASER

A primary purpose of the 1925 property legislation was to simplify conveyancing. The rules of land law were accordingly altered in order to facilitate this process. The main aim in the case of co-ownership was to ease the burden placed upon the intending purchaser, by making the investigation of title more simple, and enabling him to take the property free of the beneficial interests. Investigation of title has been simplified by the abolition of legal tenancies in common, and the imposition of the trust for sale enables the purchaser to take advantage of the overreaching provisions. This means that the purchaser need not concern himself with the position in equity. There may be 20 co-owners in equity and considerable disagreement between them about what should be done with the land. This need not trouble the purchaser at all. He will have a maximum of four legal owners with whom he must deal and need not concern himself with the opinions of the other co-owners, nor with whether the statutory duty of consultation, imposed by LPA 1925, s. 26(3), has been performed.

There used to be, however, one problem which the purchaser might encounter in the case of unregistered title, and this arose when property held originally by joint tenants in law and equity finally vested in one sole surviving tenant. In such a case, the documents showing title would inform the purchaser that the land had been held by joint tenants, and accordingly he would know that the property had been subject to a trust. Was it safe for him to accept a conveyance from the sole survivor or should he demand the appointment of a second trustee? On the face of it, the survivor, through the right of survivorship, was solely entitled in law and equity and could dispose of the whole legal and beneficial interest. However, there was the danger that one of the deceased tenants might have severed his joint tenancy during his lifetime, creating a tenancy in common and thus having a share in the property which at his death would vest in someone other than the remaining original co-owner. Usually, when severance is made, a note (a 'memorandum of severance') is endorsed on the original conveyance to the joint tenants, so that any later purchaser will know that a tenancy in common has been created. Nevertheless, the severance is valid even if this is not done, and so its absence is no guarantee to the purchaser that severance has not occurred. Thus the apparent 'sole survivor in law and equity' might really be holding in trust for himself and another, and if the purchaser did not pay the purchase money to two trustees the overreaching provisions would not operate and he would take the land subject to the right of any beneficiary of whom he could be said to have notice. To guard against this danger, purchasers would insist on the appointment of a second trustee, even when in fact this was not necessary.

The matter was finally resolved by the Law of Property (Joint Tenants) Act 1964. This statute provides that as long as the remaining joint tenant describes himself in the conveyance to the purchaser as 'beneficial owner', the purchaser will obtain good title free of any equitable interests and need not concern himself about the possibility of an earlier severance. Accordingly if a joint tenant does sever and wishes to avoid the possibility of the 1964 Act being used by a sole survivor of the original co-owners he should ensure that a memorandum of severance is endorsed on or annexed to the document which vested the land in the co-owners.

It should be noted that the 1964 Act does not apply at all to registered land (s. 3). The Registrar will remove the name of a joint proprietor from the register on production of his death certificate, and such other evidence as he may require (Land Registration Rules 1925, r. 172).

CO-OWNERSHIP AND MATRIMONIAL PROPERTY

We must now briefly consider the special rules which exist in relation to matrimonial or quasi-matrimonial property. These rules are not limited to cases of co-ownership, but because matrimonial property is often subject to co-ownership it seems appropriate to deal with the subject in this chapter. The special rules we have to consider have arisen because the legislature has considered that, at certain points, the general law should be modified in order to produce a fairer disposition of property and rights between couples. Most of the legislation was created in order to protect married women who had made no financial contribution to the family but who had spent their time caring for the home and their children. At one time, and not so far in the past, it was possible for a husband who was a sole legal owner of the matrimonial home to leave the property and then to sell it 'over the head' of his wife. The wife often had no means of preventing herself being rendered homeless. This situation has led to a number of alterations to the law, which we will now consider in more detail. Although we tend to think of these rules as being for the benefit of wives, it should be remembered that they will apply equally well to a husband, where the property is vested in his wife. As we shall see, a number of the provisions apply equally to unmarried couples, living together as man and wife.

Spouse's right to occupy the matrimonial home

In 1965 the House of Lords held in *National Provincial Bank Ltd* v *Ainsworth* [1965] AC 1175 that a wife who had no proprietary interest in the matrimonial home had no right to reside in that property which could be enforced against a purchaser. She did at common law have a right to be supported and to be provided with a home, but this was a personal right enforceable against her husband only. Thus a husband could desert his wife and family, and sell or mortgage the house in which they lived, leaving them homeless. Following the House of Lords' decision, a new statutory right was created in 1967; the relevant provisions are now contained in s. 1(1) of the Matrimonial Homes Act 1983. This statute applies only to married couples (including parties to polygamous marriages, s. 10(2)) and applies to husbands and wives equally.

Where one spouse is entitled to occupy a dwelling because he or she has an estate or interest, or for any other reason, the other spouse has the following rights (s. 1(1)):

(a) if in occupation, a right not to be evicted or excluded from the dwelling-house or any part thereof by the other spouse except with the leave of the court . . .;

(b) if not in occupation, a right with the leave of the court . . . to enter into and occupy the dwelling-house.

Either spouse may apply to the court under s. 1(2) for an order declaring or enforcing the rights granted by this section. The provision applies *only* to property which has been the matrimonial home of the couple in question and the rights last only as long as the marriage subsists (s. 1(10)). It should be noted also that a spouse who has a beneficial interest in the property but who is not a legal co-owner may also rely upon the right conferred by s. 1(1).

The interest created by s. 1 operates by virtue of s. 2 of the Act as a charge on the estate or interest of the other spouse. This charge should, in the case of unregistered land, be registered as a class F land charge, and if so protected will bind any purchaser who acquires the estate from the legal estate owner. In the case of registered land this right should be protected by entry on the register as a minor interest. The right *cannot* amount to an overriding interest (e.g., under LRA 1925, s. 70(1)(g)) because this possibility is expressly excluded by s. 2(8)(b). The entry made on the register must be by way of notice (s. 2(8)(a)) and not caution (s. 2(9)). However, it is not necessary to produce the land certificate to the registry, and this means that one spouse can make the entry without the consent, or even the knowledge, of the other.

In the case of Mark and Sally Mould at 11 Trant Way, Sally has a right of occupation of the property under the provisions of the 1983 Act. As Mark bought the property in 1979, the title is unregistered and accordingly Sally should protect her interest by entering a class F land charge, at the Land

Charges Registry, against the name 'Mark Mould'. She may make this entry at any time and does not have to wait until problems over the property arise, although, as you will appreciate, a spouse will normally only think of doing this when matrimonial difficulties have arisen. The right under s. 1 arises on marriage or acquisition of the property, whichever is the later. Thus, if Sally and Mark had married in 1970, Sally's right under s. 1 arose as soon as Mark acquired the property. If, however, they were married in 1980, after the acquisition of the property, Sally's right arose at the date of the marriage. The right ends when the marriage ends but this should not be a problem as on a divorce the Court will consider what property arrangements are appropriate.

Right to exclude the other partner from the home

The jurisdiction given to the court by s. 1(2) and (3) of the Matrimonial Homes Act 1983 is very extensive and even permits an order which excludes the owner-spouse from the property. In making an exclusion order the court may have regard to the 'conduct of the spouses in relation to each other and otherwise, to their respective needs and financial resources, to the needs of any children and to all the circumstances of the case'. In considering these matters the court will give equal weight to all the issues mentioned in the section and will regard as paramount the need to make an order which is 'just and reasonable' (see *Richards* v *Richards* [1984] AC 174). Since the court is expressly empowered to consider conduct when making an order, the provisions of the 1983 Act can be used to obtain an injunction excluding a violent spouse from the matrimonial home.

Kashmir Kaur v *Gill* [1988] 3 WLR 39 illustrates that s. 1(3) may also be used against a purchaser from the owning spouse. In that case the wife, having left the matrimonial home, registered her right to occupy a few days before her husband transfered the property to a purchaser. The purchaser accordingly had acquired subject to the wife's right. The Court of Appeal held, however, that when deciding whether to make an order allowing the wife back into the property any special circumstances of the purchaser should be taken into account (he was blind) as s. 1(3) required them to consider *all* the circumstances of the case.

In addition to these provisions there are two other Acts which enable a violent partner to be excluded from the home.

Domestic Violence and Matrimonial Proceedings Act 1976
Unlike the Matrimonial Homes Act 1983, the Domestic Violence and Matrimonial Proceedings Act 1976 applies both to married couples and to 'a man and a woman who are living with each other in the same household as husband and wife' (s. 1(2)). Accordingly if Henry Mumps should require protection from violence by Mildred, he would be entitled to use the provisions of this statute even though he is not legally married to her. The 1976 Act will not, however, assist homosexual partners since the Act specifically requires that the parties be 'a man and a woman'. The Act allows the court to make an order restraining one spouse (or person in the position of a spouse) from molesting his or her partner, or any child living with the partner, and also

excluding the violent spouse from the matrimonial home (and its environs). In addition, a spouse who has been forced to leave the property by the violence of his or her partner may obtain an order for re-entry to the premises, together with an ouster injunction requiring the violent party to leave (see *Davis* v *Johnson* [1979] AC 264). The effect of an order is not to confer any rights in the property on the partner seeking it, but exists merely for the personal protection of the applicant. Accordingly it has been said that where the applicant has no proprietary interest in the property the order should be made for a short period only (e.g., three months) (*Davis* v *Johnson*). Generally, where the parties are married, *Richards* v *Richards* [1984] AC 174 suggests that proceedings should be brought under the Matrimonial Homes Act 1983 or as part of divorce proceedings rather than under the Domestic Violence and Matrimonial Proceedings Act 1976, so the 1976 Act will probably in future be used mainly by unmarried couples.

Domestic Proceedings and Magistrates' Courts Act 1978
Under s. 16 of the Domestic Proceedings and Magistrates' Courts Act 1978 a magistrates' court may make an order requiring a violent spouse to leave the matrimonial home or prohibiting such a spouse from entering the home. The Act applies only to married couples, and this provision seems likely to be used less frequently in future, as greater use is made of proceedings under the Matrimonial Homes Act 1983.

Right to a beneficial interest in property belonging to the other party

We have already seen (p. 171) that where one person contributes to the purchase or improvement of a property which is vested in another, the contributor may obtain an interest in the estate by way of resulting trust. In general an agreement that the contribution should give rise to an interest will be required. The need for such an agreement is frequently a source of difficulty when one is dealing with couples (whether married or not) because one does not normally make such an agreement when one trusts one's partner. The difficulty emerges when the relationship breaks down, at which point the parties will undoubtedly differ as to their original intentions. In *Grant* v *Edwards* [1986] 2 All ER 426 Nourse LJ accepted that the necessary common intention could be inferred from the conduct of the parties, although in this particular case there was thought to be an oral agreement between them. In *Ungurian* v *Lesnoff* [1989] 3 WLR 840, Vinelott J was not prepared to infer a common intention that a woman should acquire an interest, when the arrangement had been that she should live with a man in a house which he had provided.

The advantage of the resulting trust rules is that they are applicable to married and unmarried couples (including homosexual couples), to other family members and to friends.

In addition to these rules, married persons may also rely on s. 37 of the Matrimonial Proceedings and Property Act 1970 in order to claim a share, or to increase their share, in property belonging to their spouses. This provision applies where 'a husband or wife contributes in money or money's worth to the improvement of real or personal property in which or in the proceeds of sale of which either or both of them has or have a beneficial interest'.

The contributions must be 'of a substantial nature'. Note that this section only applies to contributions to improvements and *not* to purchase. Where such a contribution is made it will be presumed that the parties intended the contributor to obtain a share, or an enlarged share, in the premises. (This presumed intention may be displaced by express agreement to the contrary.) The court is given a general discretion to assess the amount of the share thus obtained. The improvements which Henry Mumps has made to 8 Trant Way would have allowed him to claim under s. 37 were it not for the fact that he is not married to Mildred. This emphasises once again that unmarried couples are at a disadvantage in this type of situation. Henry's improvements might, however, be relevant to any claim he might make on the basis of a resulting trust. However, he must prove in any such proceedings that there was an agreement that he would obtain an interest in the property. Were he married that intention would be implied.

Rights on divorce

One can see that the current law on family property is becoming inadequate due to changes in social conditions during recent years. The couple who live together without marrying will find that the law is inadequate to achieve a fair resolution of any disputes between them should their relationship later fail. In the case of married couples, however, the law has moved very far from its original strict approach to ownership. On divorce the court has a wide jurisdiction under the Matrimonial Causes Act 1973 (as amended by the Matrimonial and Family Proceedings Act 1984) to make orders adjusting the ownership of property between the divorcing parties. In making any order the court will consider a wide range of issues including the needs, earning capacity and, sometimes, conduct of the parties. In reaching a decision concerning the division of property it was held by the Court of Appeal in *Wachtel* v *Wachtel* [1973] Fam 72 that one should concentrate on the needs of the parties and *not* on their existing shares in the property according to the principles of land law. It was said (at pp. 93–4) that:

> Parliament recognised that the wife who looks after the home and family contributes as much to the family assets as the wife who goes out to work. The one contributes in kind. The other in money or money's worth. If the court comes to the conclusion that the home has been acquired and maintained by the joint efforts of both, when the marriage breaks down, it should be regarded as the joint property of both of them, no matter in whose name it stands. Just as the wife who makes substantial money contributions usually gets a share, so should the wife who looks after the home and cares for the family for 20 years or more.

Thus, should the marriage of Mark and Sally Mould (11 Trant Way) end in divorce, Sally will be in a far better position than the unmarried Henry Mumps (see *Burns* v *Burns* [1984] Ch 317).

CONCLUSIONS

From the foregoing two main conclusions can be reached. The first is that it is likely that pressure will mount for the law to be changed so as to provide better protection for the increasing number of unmarried couples who live together as man and wife. (In *Hammond* v *Mitchell* [1992] 2 All ER 109, Waite J made express comment on the difficulties which can arise.) The second conclusion is that the number of unrelated remedies available to married persons is unwieldy and that a rationalisation of these rules is highly desirable.

7 Mortgages

Very few individuals or companies have sufficient liquid assets to pay for the purchase of property outright. The normal method of financing such a purchase is to obtain a loan from a building society, bank or finance house. Since large sums of money are involved, the lender will seek security for the money advanced and this will normally take the form of a mortgage of the property to be purchased. There can also be tax advantages to a purchase by means of a mortgage. Accordingly a large proportion of real property in this country is mortgaged. In addition to such mortgages for purchase, it is also common to offer a mortgage of land as security for any sizeable loan. Such a loan might be taken in order to improve the land (e.g., to install central heating) or for purposes unconnected with the land (e.g., to finance the owner's business ventures). In this chapter we examine the types of mortgages of land which may be created and consider the rules regarding their administration and their protection against later acquirers of interests in the land.

Factual background

When they purchased 1 Trant Way the Armstrongs were able to pay their own removal expenses and legal fees, and provided 10% of the purchase price of the property from their own resources. They obtained the remaining 90% of the house price by way of a loan from the Double Gloucester Building Society (DGBS). As security for the loan, the society took a charge by deed over 1 Trant Way. This charge was registered at the same time as the transfer to the Armstrongs and a Charge Certificate was issued to the DGBS.

Henry Harding, who is buying a 99-year lease of the maisonette at 2 Trant Way, also needs to raise money by way of a mortgage. He plans to borrow 95% of the price from his bank, the Wensleydale Bank plc.

Mildred Mumps wishes to borrow a large sum of money from her bank (the Royal Windsor Bank), in order to start her own business. The bank has insisted on security for the loan. 8 Trant Way is already mortgaged to the Red Leicester Building Society but Mildred has offered her bank a second mortgage on the property, as security for her business loan. Mildred has not told Henry of her plans.

Nigel Neep, the owner in fee simple of 14 Trant Way, has asked his bank manager for overdraft facilities for one month. The bank manager has said that this is possible but has suggested that the bank take Mr Neep's title deeds and hold them as security for the loan. Mr Neep bought the property in 1960, raising the bulk of the purchase price by a loan secured by a mortgage. He finished repaying that debt in 1980. He is happy to deposit the title deeds (which are normally stored for safe-keeping by his solicitor) with the bank as suggested.

WHAT IS A MORTGAGE?

A mortgage may be defined as 'a conveyance of land . . . as a security for the payment of a debt or the discharge of some other obligation' (*Santley v Wilde* [1899] 2 Ch 474). Throughout this chapter we will speak mainly of mortgages granted as security for the repayment of loans, and, although it is possible to charge any type of property in this way, will deal solely with the types of mortgage which relate to land.

The purpose of a mortgage is to enable the lender (the 'mortgagee') to take the property in whole or partial satisfaction of the debt if the borrower (called the 'mortgagor', since he creates the mortgage) fails to repay the loan (see p. 257). It is worth spending a moment in considering this terminology, because common usage these days speaks of the house buyer as 'getting a mortgage' and newspaper headlines announce 'more mortgages from building societies'. This implies that it is the *loan* which is the mortgage, and this terminology is sometimes adopted by law students, with resulting uncertainty about which party is the mortgagor and which the mortgagee. It is therefore emphasised that it is the borrower (mortgagor) who grants the mortgage of his property, as security for the loan made to him by the lender (mortgagee).

Types of mortgage

There are seven basic types of mortgage which relate to land: three are legal mortgages, four equitable. We will consider the legal mortgages first.

LEGAL MORTGAGES

Legal mortgage of a fee simple under LPA 1925, s. 85

One of the main concerns of the legal mortgagee is that he should obtain some interest in the mortgaged property. At one time, therefore, a mortgage of a fee simple was effected by the mortgagor transferring his whole estate to the mortgagee. In return, the mortgagee promised to reconvey the estate to the mortgagor when the loan was repaid. Today this method of creating a mortgage has been abolished, and, under the provisions of LPA 1925, s. 85, the mortgagor, instead of transferring the fee simple, will grant a long lease of the property to the mortgagee. This lease will be expressed to be terminable when the loan is repaid: it is said to be subject to 'cesser on redemption'. This method has the advantage that the mortgagor retains his estate in the land, but the mortgagee also has an estate (the lease) which gives him certain rights in relation to the land. In order to ensure that the lease will not end before the debt is repaid, it is normal to grant an extremely long term of years. Indeed the statute provides that, should one try to create a mortgage by the old method of transferring the fee simple, this will be converted into a grant of a lease for a term of 3,000 years from the date of the mortgage (s. 85(2)), and those drafting mortgages in accordance with s. 85 usually adopt a similar period of lease.

This method of creating a legal mortgage has an advantage over the older form of mortgage. Now it is possible to create a second legal mortgage over the same land, by giving the second mortgagee a lease which is longer than the lease of the first mortgagee. This creates a leasehold reversion in the second mortgagee, giving him the landlord's rights towards the first tenant. (As we have already explained, it is possible to grant several leases which take effect at the same time in the same piece of land — see p. 96). It would not, in fact, matter if the leases given to the various mortgagees were all the same length, but it is usual to give a slightly longer term to each successive mortgagee; and we will see that this is also done in mortgages of leasehold property.

Before 1926, the mortgagor, having transferred the legal estate to the first mortgagee, no longer had any legal estate which he could convey to the second mortgagee; and so, although second mortgages could be made, they took effect only in equity. Today, however, even if 8 Trant Way was mortgaged to the Red Leicester Building Society under s. 85, Mildred could still create a second legal mortgage in favour of her bank (and a third, and fourth, if anyone would lend on such security).

Legal mortgage of a term of years under LPA 1925, s. 86

Before 1926, mortgages of leases were also created by assigning the whole term of years to the mortgagee. This is no longer permitted. Under LPA 1925, s. 86, the correct method of creating such a mortgage is by granting a sublease to the mortgagee. Again, the mortgagee is thereby given an estate in the land, while the mortgagor retains his own estate. Should an attempt be made to use the old method of mortgaging, the disposition will be converted into a sublease. The period of the sublease will be the unexpired period of the mortgaged lease, less 10 days (s. 86(2)). The 10-day gap allows the creation of a second mortgage of the same lease, made by granting a sublease which is a day longer than the first sublease. Once again this allows for the creation of two or more legal mortgages of the same term of years. The mortgage of the maisonette at 2 Trant Way could be in this form though it is more likely to adopt the third possibility described below.

Charge by deed by way of legal mortgage under LPA 1925, s. 87

The third method of creating a legal mortgage is the method which is in normal use. Instead of granting a lease or sublease to the mortgagee, the mortgagor merely executes a deed which declares that he is charging his land by way of legal mortgage with the repayment of the sums specified. This form of mortgage may be used for both freehold and leasehold estates. LPA 1925, s. 87, provides that the effect of such a mortgage is to give the mortgagee 'the same protection, powers and remedies' as if the mortgage had been made by lease or sublease (whichever is relevant). Thus the mortgagee is treated as though he had a lease or sublease, although in fact no such estate is created. The effect of this provision is illustrated by *Grand Junction Co Ltd* v *Bates* [1954] 2 QB 160, in which leasehold property had been charged by way of legal mortgage under s. 87. Later, the landlord began forfeiture proceedings under s. 146 for breach of covenant by the tenant (see p. 144). Had he succeeded, the mortgagee's security for the loan would have been totally destroyed, for the lease ceases to exist on forfeiture. If the mortgage had been made by sublease, the mortgagee would have been able to apply for relief as a subtenant under s. 146(4) (see p. 144), but the question arose whether a chargee could do this when he had no legal estate in the property. However, the court held that the provisions of s. 87 gave him a right to apply for relief, just as though he held a mortgage by sublease.

The charge by way of legal mortgage does have several advantages compared with the other methods of creating a legal mortgage. It enables an owner to mortgage his freehold and leasehold property in one document, and in the case of leasehold property has the further advantage that since no actual sublease is created, the grant of such a charge will not amount to breach of a covenant against subletting (see *Grand Junction Co. Ltd* v *Bates* per Upjohn J at p. 168).

As a result of its simple form (a brief example is given in LPA 1925, Sch. 5, form No. 1), and the fact that it can be used to mortgage either of the legal estates, the legal charge has become in modern times the most usual method of mortgage. The mortgages of both 1 and 2 Trant Way are likely to take this form. The sample format of such a charge given in the LPA 1925 does not, however, give a true picture of the type of document which one would expect to see today. Most modern charges add to the statutory skeleton a long list of covenants between the mortgagor and mortgagee (e.g., preventing the mortgagor from granting leases or taking lodgers). There will also be detailed provisions concerning repayment of the sum advanced, together with interest, usually by instalments (and normally spread over a period of 20–25 years in the case of domestic mortgages). The modern mortgage is accordingly a longer document than the Act might suggest. The legal charge is also used when one is dealing with registered land, for LRA 1925, s. 25, provides that a legal mortgage of a registered estate should be created by charge (though any form may be adopted as long as the land is described by reference to the register). In line with the general policy applying to registered land, the completion of the deed does not, by itself, create a legal mortgage. It is the registration of the charge which perfects it and until registration the charge takes effect in equity only (LRA 1925, s. 26(1)).

EQUITABLE MORTGAGES

Contract to create a mortgage

Under the principle that 'Equity regards as done that which ought to be done', a contract to create a legal mortgage will be regarded as giving rise to an equitable mortgage from the date of the contract. This is dependent of course upon the contract being one which the courts would enforce by an order for specific performance (*Tebb* v *Hodge* (1869) LR 5 CP 73). A defective legal mortgage (e.g., one which has been signed but not witnessed) will be similarly treated, as long as specific performance is available. This is a similar rule to that which applies to defective leases (see *Walsh* v *Lonsdale* (1882) 21 ChD 9 and chapter 3). However, specific performance will not be available in any of these cases unless the mortgage money has actually been advanced, for traditionally equity has declined to force a man to make a loan. In such cases, providing a contract can be established which satisfies the Law of Property (Miscellaneous Provisions) Act 1989, s. 2, the mortgagor could fall back on his common law remedy of damages.

Informal mortgage by deposit of deeds

The protection and enforcement of a contract to make a mortgage (which we have just considered) is extended by equity's willingness to recognise as a contract any transaction which clearly shows that an estate owner intended to charge his property with the repayment of a loan. The classic example of this is found where the mortgagor deposits his title deeds or, in the case of registered land, his land certificate with the mortgagor in return for the loan. This was recognised as creating an equitable mortgage of the property in *Russel* v *Russel* (1783) 1 Bro CC 269, and continues in modern law under the saving provisions of LPA 1925, s. 13. For this type of mortgage until 1989 no written record of any kind was necessary, for the deposit of title deeds was regarded not only as constituting the contract to make the mortgage, but also as amounting to part performance for the purposes of LPA 1925, s. 40(2). Moreover the deposit and receipt of the deeds were regarded as part performance by both parties, so whichever side wished to rely on it might do so. Despite this, however, a written record was desirable in order to provide clear evidence of the nature of the transaction. Indeed, for reasons we shall consider later (p. 261), it was always best for such mortgages to be accompanied by a memorandum of deposit in the form of a deed. These mortgages were convenient and cheap when only a short-term loan was envisaged. The mortgage of 14 Trant Way which Nigel Neep intends to grant to his bank in order to secure the grant of overdraft facilities for one month would fall into this category.

The law relating to these informal mortgages has however been affected by the Law of Property (Miscellaneous Provisions) Act 1989, s. 2, because that provision relates to:

A contract for the sale or other disposition of an interest in land. . . .

Accordingly, for an equitable mortgage to be enforceable it will now be necessary to show that the agreement was *made* in writing. It will not do merely to have a later deed which states that the agreement exists (as was previously common practice) because that deed would merely purport to record an existing contract which would not satisfy s. 2, and accordingly would not amount to a contract at all. At present there are no cases which apply s. 2

to mortgages but the result of the reforms may be to prevent the creation of the most informal types of mortgage in which deposit of deeds was used without anything more being done. Nigel Neep's bank are likely to insist that his mortgage is made by a written agreement which satisfies s. 2. Of course, this may be a case in which estoppel will assist in the event of a dispute and courts of equity have long been careful to ensure that an agreement for a mortgage does not give rise to anything more than an interest by way of security for the money advanced. The danger now is that the mortgage may be ineffective due to s. 2 and that as a result the loan will become immediately repayable because the security has failed. The exact effect of s. 2 may however depend on the terms of the loan. Here 'only time will tell'.

Equitable charge

An equitable charge arises when a chargee appropriates specific property to the repayment of a sum of money in such circumstances that a legal charge does not arise. Now the charge should be made in writing. For an old example see *Matthews* v *Goodday* (1861) 31 LJ Ch 282. This type of arrangement is rare.

Equitable mortgage of an equitable interest

One obviously cannot make a legal mortgage of an interest which is recognised only in equity. This of course dates from the days of separate courts with separate jurisdictions. Common law did not recognise the equitable interests developed in the Chancellor's court, and accordingly would not enforce any legal dealings with them. Therefore any mortgage of an equitable interest in land, such as that of a life interest under a settlement, must be equitable in character. The creation of such mortgages was not changed in 1925, and thus they continue to be made by a transfer of the entire interest to the mortgagee, subject to an agreement that it will be returned to the mortgagor on repayment of the loan. The transfer must be made, at the least, by writing, in order to pass the equitable interest to the mortgagee under LPA 1925, s. 53(1)(c). (Note that this is a transfer and not an agreement to transfer.) Normally thereafter the mortgagee should give notice of the transfer to the trustees of the trust under which the interest exists (see p. 270).

RIGHTS OF THE MORTGAGOR

Having examined the methods of creating a mortgage we must turn our attention to the position of the parties after a mortgage has been made. We will look first at the rights of the mortgagor.

Right to redeem

The primary right enjoyed by the mortgagor is the right to *redeem* the mortgage on repayment of the loan and payment of any interest provided for by the charge. At law the right to redeem is a matter of contract: the mortgagor can redeem on the date or dates and in the manner provided for in the mortgage. Thus, should the agreement provide that the mortgage should be redeemed on a particular date, the mortgagee has, at law, a right to redeem on that date only. The legal rules do not allow him to insist on redeeming the mortgage either before or after the contractual date: see the discussion in *Kreglinger* v *New Patagonia Meat & Cold Storage Co. Ltd* [1914] AC 25 at p. 35. At common law, if the mortgagor did not pay on the contractual date, the mortgagor at one time forfeited the land to the mortgagee *and* could still be sued in contract for the repayment of the debt. Accordingly the legal right to redeem was, and is, very limited.

Fortunately equity took a very different view of the situation, particularly as there were examples of mortgagees absenting themselves so that it became impossible for the mortgagor to repay on the contractual date. As the purpose of the agreement was merely to provide the mortgagee with security for the loan, equity took the view that, as long as the advance and any interest was paid, the mortgagee should not be able to object to redemption. Originally equity intervened in cases of fraud by the mortgagee but soon came to recognise a general right to redeem in all cases (*Salt* v *Marquess of Northampton* [1892] AC 1). Thus equity allows the mortgagor to redeem even after the date fixed by the mortgage agreement for repayment has passed. Of course, since this right is enforceable in equity only, it is subject to the general principle that equitable remedies are discretionary in nature and that all the equitable maxims (particularly the 'clean hands' doctrine) will apply. Furthermore, in deciding whether redemption is possible, equity will look at the substance of the agreement, not its form. Accordingly a mortgage which is drafted to look like an outright transfer of the property, rather than the creation of an interest by way of security, will still be subject to the equitable right to redeem, if the facts are such as to indicate that only a grant by way of security was intended (*Darby* v *Read* (1675) Fin 226).

So far, we have spoken as though the full sum owed becomes payable on one date. The modern mortgage is more likely to provide for repayment by instalments, spread over a number of years. However, it usually will contain a provision that if the mortgagor defaults on the payment of an instalment the whole sum will become due. In law, the mortgagor will then have to redeem the mortgage or lose his property for ever, but equity will moderate the rigour of this in the way already described.

What does the mortgagor own?

Obviously a legal mortgagor retains his legal estate in the land but subject to the rights of the mortgagee (see below). In equity the mortgagor is described as owning the 'equity of redemption'. This must be distinguished from the equitable right to redeem which is mentioned above. The equity of redemption is the mortgagor's equitable interest in the property and it consists of *the sum total* of the mortgagor's rights in relation to the land (including, *inter alia*, the right to redeem). The equity of redemption is therefore an interest in land (*Pawlett* v *Attorney-General* (1667) Hard 465, at p. 469) and can be dealt with like any other equitable interest.

Before the changes brought about by the 1925 legislation, the equity of redemption was the only interest in the property retained by the mortgagor. If he wanted to create a second mortgage, he would transfer that interest to the mortgagee, but, as we have explained above, the mortgage of an equitable interest is itself necessarily equitable, so that all second and subsequent mortgages could take effect only in equity. Since 1925, it is now possible to create a series of legal mortgages.

No clogs on the equity of redemption

Equity is so protective of the mortgagor's equity of redemption that it will not tolerate any arrangement which either prevents or deters the mortgagor from exercising his right to redeem. Similarly any burdens imposed by the mortgage on the mortgaged property which may continue after the date of redemption are generally regarded with disfavour. They derogate from the principle that the mortgage should provide security only and that on redemption the mortgagor should recover the property without further fetter. In restricting the contents of mortgage agreements in this way, equity is recognising the fact that the mortgagor is often unable to dictate the terms of the mortgage, because of his need for the mortgage advance. It was therefore appropriate that he should be afforded some protection by the courts, but it may be thought that in some cases this approach has been taken to undesirable lengths.

Equity's approach is summed up in the rule that there must be no clogs (restrictions) on the equity of redemption, and this is applied to a number of situations, some of which we must now consider.

Prevention of redemption
Any provision in a mortgage which would operate to prevent the mortgagor from redeeming will be disregarded by equity and will be void. Thus a mortgagee cannot include in a mortgage a term that, should a specified event occur, the land would become his absolutely (*Toomes* v *Conset* (1745) 3 Atk 261). This rule has, however, been taken to extremes, so that it is not possible to give a mortgagee a valid option to purchase the estate as part of the mortgage transaction. The option, if exercised, would extinguish the mortgagor's right to redeem and is accordingly void. The original rationale for this rule was sound. As Lord Henley put it in *Vernon* v *Bethall* (1762) 2 Eden 110 at p. 113:

there is great reason and justice in this rule, for necessitous men are not, truly speaking, free men, but to answer a present exigency will submit to any terms that the crafty may impose upon them.

However, in *Samuel* v *Jarrah Timber & Wood Paving Co. Ltd* [1904] AC 323 the House of Lords applied (albeit reluctantly) the same rule to an 'arm's-length' commercial transaction. It was suggested that granting the option in a separate document might avoid the rule, but it seems that even this may not avail the mortgagee, unless the option is granted some time after the mortgage (this gives the mortgagor a chance to refuse an unfair agreement once he has received his loan) (*Lewis* v *Frank Love Ltd* [1961] 1 WLR 261; but see also *Reeve* v *Lisle* [1902] AC 461 in which an option was upheld).

Postponement of redemption
Any provision in a mortgage which attempts to postpone redemption to such an extent that the right to redeem becomes illusory may also be rendered void. The equitable right to redeem arises only once the contractual, legal date for redemption has passed. There is no general right in equity to redeem earlier (but see the Consumer Credit Act 1974, ss. 94 and 173, for rare cases of small mortgages which may be redeemed at any time). Accordingly, one way by which a mortgagee may try to obtain an irredeemable mortgage is to postpone the contractual date for redemption. In *Knightsbridge Estate's Trust Ltd* v *Byrne* [1939] Ch 441 a company had mortgaged its freehold property to an insurance company on terms that the mortgage would be repaid over 40 years. Later the mortgagor wished to redeem the mortgage before that period had expired, but the mortgagee objected. The court held that the term postponing redemption for 40 years was valid. The agreement was a commercial one made by businessmen and the mortgaged property was a fee simple. Due to the extended duration of the freehold estate (effectively it is perpetual) the company would recover an estate of equivalent worth when it did redeem the mortgage. The effect of this case is not, however, to make any postponement for a similar period valid. Were a domestic mortgage to be made irredeemable for such a long period, the court might still regard the bargain as oppressive and unconscionable. In fact most modern domestic mortgages expressly allow for early redemption, usually on payment of a small extra sum to compensate the mortgagee for the production of the necessary paperwork.
   Postponement of the date of redemption is rather more serious when one is concerned with a mortgage of leasehold property, for a lease is inherently of finite duration and therefore a wasting asset. In *Fairclough* v *Swan Brewery Co. Ltd* [1912] AC 565 the residue of a leasehold term of 20 years was mortgaged, the agreement being that the mortgage was not to be redeemed until a date six weeks before the lease was to end. Three years later the mortgagor sought to redeem early and the court upheld his right to do so. In this case, had the postponement been valid, the mortgagor would on redemption have recovered an estate which was nearly valueless and very different in character from that which had been mortgaged. In the case of leases, accordingly, postponement of the contractual date for redemption is likely to be rather more objectionable, even where the mortgage is a commercial bargain made between businessmen.

Collateral advantages for the mortgagee
The final type of clog on the equity of redemption which is commonly encountered is the creation of further advantages for the mortgagee, which are collateral to the mortgage. These are common in certain types of commercial mortgage. Thus breweries will often advance money on mortgage to the licensees of public houses, provided that the mortgagors agree that they will buy their beer from the mortgagee-brewery (subject to recent amendments of the law arising from concerns about competition policy), and similar

arrangements are made between petrol companies and garage owners. Such collateral advantages, if they are not unconscionable, are valid whilst the mortgage continues (*Biggs* v *Hoddinott* [1898] 2 Ch 307). They will not, however, normally endure once the mortgage is redeemed (even if the mortgagor has accepted a term that they shall continue beyond redemption), for otherwise the mortgagor would recover an estate encumbered in a manner that the estate he mortgaged was not (see also *Bradley* v *Carritt* [1903] AC 253). An advantage will not, however, invariably end once the mortgage is redeemed. In *Kreglinger* v *New Patagonia Meat & Cold Storage Co. Ltd* [1914] AC 25 a meat company mortgaged its property to a wool-broker (the mortgage was in the form of a floating charge, a special type of mortgage granted by companies). It was a term of the mortgage that the mortgagor would, for five years, offer its sheep's skins (a by-product of its meat business) to the mortgagees for purchase. The mortgage was redeemed after two years but the House of Lords held that the mortgagor was obliged to continue to offer the mortgagees first refusal on the skins for the full five-year period. The option was regarded as being reasonable in its terms (it was for a short period and at the best price) and was to be regarded as a separate agreement not really forming part of the mortgage. It was also, of course, a commercial transaction which had been agreed to by businessmen with 'open eyes'. It seems unlikely that such a collateral advantage could validly continue after redemption of a domestic mortgage.

Collateral advantages may also be held to be invalid, even during the continuance of the mortgage, if they are unconscionable or oppressive. Thus in *Cityland & Property (Holdings) Ltd* v *Dabrah* [1968] Ch 166 an agreement which imposed an extemely high premium, rather than requiring payment of interest, was rewritten by the court. In this case the mortgagor was allowed to redeem on repayment of the loan together with interest at a rate approved by the court. It is not, however, sufficient to show that the terms are unreasonable (certainly in a commercial bargain), even if they are extemely advantageous to the mortgagee. The agreement must be 'unfair and unconscionable' and imposed by the mortgagee 'in a morally reprehensible manner, that is to say, in a way which affects his conscience' (per Browne-Wilkinson J, infra).

The extension of the range of services provided by lenders has led to concerns that mortgagors may be forced into agreements which require them to use a prospective mortgagee to provide, for example, removal vans or estate agency services. The mortgagor might be told that unless he took such other items from the mortgagee the rate of interest on his mortgage would be higher. This problem has been addressed by the Courts and Legal Services Act 1990, ss. 104–107 ('tying-in provisions'). These sections have not yet been brought into force.

Right to grant leases

Having already granted a lease or sublease (or being in a similar position in the case of a charge by way of legal mortgage), the mortgagor would be unable, on general principles, to grant further leases of the same property which could bind himself and his mortgagee. Any further lease he did create would operate as a lease of the reversion (see pp. 97 and 246), and would not give the tenant any right to possession of the land which he could assert against the mortgagee. However, this caused difficulty, particularly in the case of large estates, where the mortgagor remained in possession of the land and continued to manage it, needing to grant new leases to, for example, tenant farmers and estate workers. The mortgagor is therefore given a statutory power by LPA 1925, s. 99: provided he is still in possession of the land he may create both leases and contracts for leases which will be binding on the mortgagee. Section 99 sets out a number of detailed requirements for the form and content of such leases, but we do not propose to consider them here, for in practice most mortgages will exclude the mortgagor's statutory power of leasing. This is because, in general, the mortgagee does not want the land to be burdened with a sitting tenant, for this will reduce its value if the mortgagee needs to realise his security (obviously different arrangements will still have to be made for the management of large estates and in commercial cases where the plan is to let the property).

The statutory power of leasing will almost certainly be excluded in any domestic mortgage, like that of the Armstrongs at 1 Trant Way, though mortgagees do sometimes agree to waive this exclusion in the case of approved tenants. Should the right to grant mortgages be excluded, any lease granted will nonetheless bind the mortgagor and tenant (a lease by estoppel, see p. 114), but will be void as regards the mortgagee and his successors (*Iron Trades Employers Insurance Association Ltd* v *Union Land & House Investors Ltd* [1937] Ch 313).

It should be noted that the mortgagor has power under LPA 1925, s. 100, to accept surrenders of leases as well. This may be done, however, only in order to replace the surrendered lease with a fresh lease and the new lease must be made within one month of the termination of the old.

Right to sue

In some cases the rights of the mortgagor to sue in relation to the land might be hampered by the fact that his estate is subject to the rights of the mortgagee. Any such problems are remedied by LPA 1925, s. 98, which allows a mortgagor in possession, who has not been notified that the mortgagee intends to take possession, to sue in a number of situations in which there might otherwise be difficulties. Generally therefore the mortgagor is free to bring any necessary action in relation to the land.

RIGHTS OF THE MORTGAGEE

Rights to title deeds or charge certificate

Under the pre-1926 type of mortgage the mortgagee necessarily had a right to hold the title deeds to the property, since the grant of the mortgage conveyed the legal estate to the mortgagee. Under the modern system, however, the mortgagee has only a lease or sublease and it is not normal for a tenant to hold his landlord's deeds. It is nonetheless desirable for the mortgagee to take the deeds, since this will prevent the creation by the mortgagor of later interests in the same property without the knowledge of the mortgagee (see p. 272). Accordingly ss. 85(1) and 86(1) specifically provide that a first mortgagee has the *right* to take the title deeds from the mortgagor. A mortgagee under a charge by way of legal mortgage is expressly given similar rights (s. 87(1)). In practice all banks and building societies, and any private mortgagee who takes proper advice, will insist on exercising this right. Of course, the mortgagor may well need upon occasion to see the deeds: he may, for example, need to check them to settle a dispute about the boundary line of the property. Accordingly LPA 1925, s. 96(1), gives the mortgagor the right to inspect the deeds and make copies, as long as this is done at a reasonable time and any costs incurred by the mortgagee are paid.

The equitable mortgagee has a similar equitable right to the deeds, but since the most common form of equitable mortgage is that which involves deposit of the deeds this is rarely a problem.

In the case of registered land a legal charge is created only when the charge is substantively registered. In order to effect this registration, the land certificate must be produced at the registry, and will be retained there until the mortgage is discharged (LRA 1925, s. 65). The owner of the charge, the chargee, will be issued with a charge certificate (LRA 1925, s. 63(1)). The charge certificate is similar in form to the land certificate but contains an entry of the charge on the charges register and includes a full copy of the deed creating the charge (Land Registration Rules 1925, r. 262).

Right to possession of the land

Since a legal mortgagee has a lease or sublease (or is treated as though he had) he has a right to possession of the land from the moment that the mortgage is created (see *Four-Maids Ltd* v *Dudley Marshall (Properties) Ltd* [1957] Ch 317 at p. 320 and *National Westminster Bank plc* v *Skelton* [1993] 1 All ER 242). This right may well be restricted by a term in the mortgage deed that possession will not be taken whilst the mortgagor makes regular payments (see, e.g., *Birmingham Citizens Permanent Building Society* v *Caunt* [1962] Ch 883).

Usually, the taking of possession is only normal as a preliminary to the remedy of sale and is not otherwise generally exercised. However, in recent years, due to the difficulties in selling properties and the drop in property values, it has become more common for lenders to seek possession of a property in order to let it. This may cause problems for a mortgagor because the interest under the mortgage will continue to mount. In *Palk* v *Mortgage Service Funding plc* [1993] 2 All ER 481, the Court of Appeal said that where sale was preferable in the mortgagor's interests a sale would be ordered instead (see further below on foreclosure for Court's power to order sale instead). The taking of possession must, in any event, be exercised peaceably (e.g., one may not break into premises) and this may necessitate an application to the court.

It might be thought that an equitable mortgagee would have an equitable right to possession of the property, since he is treated in equity in the manner in which a legal mortgagee is treated at law (compare with *Walsh* v *Lonsdale* (1882) 21 ChD 9 on equitable leases). However, there has been some disagreement in the courts about this, and we will return to the point when we consider the remedies available to an equitable mortgagee (p. 261).

Insuring at the mortgagor's expense

Normally the mortgagee will wish to ensure that the property is properly insured, since should it be damaged the value of the mortgagee's security will be diminished. Accordingly most mortgages include express terms concerning the maintenance of insurance. If there is no express agreement, LPA 1925, s. 101(1)(ii), implies into every mortgage made by deed a term allowing the mortgagee to insure the property against loss or damage by fire. The premiums paid become a charge on the property in addition to the mortgage advance. The amount of the insurance and the mode of application of any sums arising from the policy are further regulated by LPA 1925, s. 108.

Right to lease

A mortgagee who has taken possession has always had a right to grant leases. These, however, would be subject to the rule that there must be no clog on the equity of redemption, and so would not survive redemption by the mortgagor. There is, however, a statutory power to lease under LPA 1925, s. 99(1), which gives rights similar to those of the mortgagor described above. Any lease created under the statutory power will also bind the mortgagor. Since possession by the mortgagee is normally only a preliminary to sale, such leases used to be uncommon but may become more common due to the drop in property prices.

Right to tack further advances

This right is relevant only when there is a dispute about priorities, and so we will consider it in the section on priorities (p. 280).

Right to consolidate mortgages

This right applies when one mortgagee has vested in him two or more mortgages which were both made by the same mortgagor. This might occur if Henry Harding (2 Trant Way) had already granted a mortgage of, say, his business premises at 15 High Street, Mousehole to the Wensleydale Bank plc. The Bank would have the right to consolidate the two mortgages if, as is normal, this is expressly provided for in the mortgage (LPA 1925, s. 93).

The effect of the right is to allow the mortgagee to refuse to allow the mortgagor to redeem one of the mortgages without also redeeming the other. In the case of Mr Harding's mortgages, this right might prove important to the bank should the value of 15 High Street fall below the sums outstanding on the mortgage of that property. If Mr Harding chose to redeem the mortgage on 2 Trant Way, rather than the mortgage of his business premises, the mortgagee bank would be left with a mortgage for which the security is defective. By consolidating, the Bank can insist that Mr Harding redeems *both* mortgages. The right to consolidate is an equitable one, and is an unusual example of equity permitting a clog or fetter on the equity of redemption. It may be seen as the 'price' which equity exacts for allowing the mortgagor to redeem the mortgage when he could no longer do so at law. Accordingly the mortgagee has this right only *after* the contractual date for redemption has passed, when the mortgagor is relying on his equitable right to redeem. If the mortgagor should in fact repay the debt on the contractual date, the mortgagee would not be able to require him to pay off the other debt as well. The doctrine can affect subsequent purchasers if they buy land subject to the mortgage. Thus if someone bought 2 Trant Way from Mr Harding subject to the mortgage and then sought to redeem it, he or she would find that the bank's right to consolidate still applied, and that the mortgage on 15 High Street would also have to be redeemed. Fortunately it is extremely rare nowadays for estates to change hands without any mortgages first being discharged.

We have tried to give a relatively simple account of the doctrine of consolidation, illustrating it with a situation in which both mortgages are granted to the same mortgagee. This is not in fact an essential requirement: provided the mortgages are granted by the same person it does not matter that they are granted *to* different people. The rules governing the various different situations which may arise as a result of this are complicated, and beyond the scope of this book, but if you are interested you will find them fully discussed in Megarry and Wade, *The Law of Real Property*, 5th ed. (London: Stevens, 1984).

MORTGAGEE'S REMEDIES

The whole purpose of a mortgage is to provide security which the mortgagee can realise if the mortgagor fails to repay the loan. Obviously the mortgagee, like any lender, can always sue in contract for the repayment of the loan, but this may be a long process in which enforcing payment, even once judgment is obtained, can be difficult. The advantage of the mortgage is that it allows the mortgagee to use the charged land to repay the loan, often without the need for any court proceedings at all. The various remedies available to a mortgagee are therefore of crucial importance.

Remedies available to a legal mortgagee

Foreclosure
Any lover of Victorian melodrama will have heard the word 'foreclosure', and will know of it as a fearsome remedy by which a defaulting mortgagor is dispossessed. Indeed foreclosure was the traditional remedy by which a mortgage was enforced, though today it is extremely rarely used.

Although equity would allow a mortgagor to redeem after the contractual date, there would come a time in many cases when it was obvious that the mortgagor would never have the means to repay the debt. Foreclosure proceedings in equity were therefore the means whereby 'the court simply removed the stop it had itself put on' (*Carter* v *Wake* (1877) 4 ChD 605 at p. 606), and enabled the mortgagee to realise his security. For this reason foreclosure cannot be sought before the contractual obligation to repay has been broken (*Williams* v *Morgan* [1906] 1 Ch 804). A court order is required for foreclosure (*Re Farnol Eades Irvine & Co. Ltd* [1915] 1 Ch 22), and its effect is to vest the mortgagor's estate in the mortgagee in full settlement of the debt (LPA 1925, ss. 88(2) and 89(2)). Should the property be worth more than the debt, the mortgagee is not liable to pay the balance in value to the mortgagor. Since this is almost invariably the case, foreclosure is a remedy which is often unfair to the mortgagor (and to any subsequent mortgagees, who lose their security). Accordingly, on hearing an application for foreclosure the court will give the mortgagor a period in which he can redeem the mortgage (and will allow later mortgagees the chance to protect their security by redeeming the prior mortgage). Generally the mortgagor is in financial difficulties and is unable to repay the loan and redeem. Accordingly he is given the right to ask for an order for sale instead of foreclosure (LPA 1925, s. 91(2)). This is an advantage because on sale the mortgagee may keep only the portion of the proceeds which represents the debt, plus interest and costs. The balance must be returned to the mortgagor, or paid to anyone else entitled, such as later mortgagees. Sale may also be appropriate in any case in which it produces a better financial result for the mortgagor (see *Palk* v *Mortgage Services Funding plc* [1993] 2 All ER 481).

Another reason why foreclosure is an unpopular remedy (but this time from the mortgagee's point of view) is that even once a foreclosure order has been made the court may reopen the whole situation and allow the mortgagor to redeem the property after all. *Campbell* v *Holyland* (1877) 7 ChD 166 (in which an order for foreclosure was reopened three months after it had been made absolute) sets out the various matters which the court will take into account in considering such an application. These include: the speed of the mortgagor's application, his reasons for failing to redeem before foreclosure, and the nature of the property. The court would probably be more sympathetic in the case of 'an old family estate . . . which possesses a special value for the mortgagor and not the same value for other people' (at p. 173).

As might be expected, the court would be less willing to reopen foreclosure if the mortgagee had already sold the property to someone else, although even in that case this could still be done.

Possession and sale
We have already discussed the basic rules relating to possession (p. 255). Generally this right of the mortgagee is only used as a remedy and normally is a prelude to sale. The mortgagee might, however, take possession so that he can repay his debt from the income produced by the premises (e.g., if the premises are let to a tenant). However, in such cases it is more common to appoint a receiver instead so that, as we shall see (p. 261), the mortgagee is not personally liable for any mismanagement of the land. The chief purpose of taking possession is therefore to ensure that on a subsequent sale the mortgagee will be in a position to give vacant possession to the purchaser.

The power for the mortgagee to sell the land is implied into every mortgage made by deed by LPA 1925, s. 101(1)(i). This power *arises* when the mortgage money has become due (for instance, on the contractual date of redemption) but does not become *exercisable* until one of the conditions prescribed by LPA 1925, s. 103, has been met. These are that:

(a) a notice requiring payment has been served on the mortgagor and the default has continued for three months thereafter; or

(b) some of the interest payable is at least two months in arrear; or

(c) there has been breach of a covenant in the mortgage deed (other than that relating to the payment of money) or of some provision of the LPA 1925.

A purchaser must satisfy himself that there is power to sell under the mortgage (that is, that it was made by deed and that the power has arisen), but he does not have to check that one of the conditions for exercise of the power ((a) to (c) above) has been met (see *Bailey* v *Barnes* [1894] 1 Ch 25 at p. 35).

Sale has the advantage over foreclosure that it is generally not necessary to apply for a court order. The sale may be negotiated in any suitable manner (e.g., by auction or by private contract) and may be made subject to such conditions as the mortgagee sees fit (s. 101(1)(i)). As we shall see, the mortgagee may be liable to the mortgagor, and others, for any loss caused through his negligence in conducting the sale (see p. 265).

However, an order for possession (as a prelude to sale) may be delayed for a time if the Court believes that the mortgagor may obtain a higher price if he sells himself. (See *Target Home Loans* v *Clothier, The Times*, 7 August 1992.)

Effect of sale

On sale, the mortgagee will convey to the purchaser a good estate or interest (for example, the fee simple) free of the interests of the mortgagor and of any estates, interests or rights to which the mortgage has priority, but subject to any estates or interests having priority to the mortgage (LPA 1925, s. 104(1)). Thus if 1 Trant Way were subject to two mortgages:

(a) to the Double Gloucester Building Society, and

(b) to the Mousehole Bank plc

then on a sale by the DGBS the purchaser would take a title free of the second mortgage to the MB plc, but on a sale by the MB plc the purchaser would take an estate subject to the first mortgage to the DGBS.

It is perhaps worth emphasising that on sale the purchaser obtains the full estate belonging to the mortgagor, not just the long lease or sublease which was granted to the mortgagee (LPA 1925, ss. 88(1) and 89(1)).

Disposition of proceeds of sale
The selling mortgagee becomes a trustee of the proceeds of sale of the property (LPA 1925, s. 105), and should apply the proceeds in the following order:

(a) in payment of any sums needed to discharge any encumbrance prior to the mortgage and to which the sale was not made subject:
(b) in payment of the costs, charges and expenses properly incurred in arranging the sale;
(c) in discharge of the mortgage debt, including interest and other sums due;
(d) any balance should be paid to the mortgagor or the other person 'entitled to the mortgage property'.

Thus were, in the example given above, the DGBS to sell 1 Trant Way it would first pay the costs of sale (e.g., legal expenses), and then would pay its own mortgage debt, interest and costs. Thereafter the balance of the proceeds of sale should be paid to the MB plc which at the time of sale was next entitled to the property (*British General Insurance Co. Ltd* v *Attorney-General* (1945) 12 LJNCCR 113). The MB plc will in turn become trustee, and after repaying itself, should (if there is sufficient money) pass the balance of the proceeds of sale to the mortgagors.

Should the sale not realise sufficient funds to repay the mortgagee, he may still sue in contract for the balance of the debt (*Rudge* v *Richens* (1873) LR 8 CP 358). However, since the property itself may well have been the mortgagor's only valuable asset, it may prove difficult to obtain satisfaction of any judgment.

Protection for the mortgagor
There are circumstances in which it would be unfair for the mortgagee to be allowed to sell the property. Thus, if the mortgage interest is only a few months in arrears and the mortgagor can show that he will be in a position to pay his debts very shortly it would be undesirable to allow the mortgagee to insist on sale. Accordingly the following means of protection is provided for the mortgagor.

As we have seen, the first step towards sale is for the mortgagee to obtain possession. The mortgagee may not do this by means of any force (e.g., by breaking a window) since this would constitute a criminal offence (Criminal Law Act 1977, ss. 5 and 6). Normally therefore an application to the court for possession will have to be made. This in itself will give the mortgagor extra time to pay. If the land is or includes a dwelling-house, further protection is given to the mortgagee by Administration of Justice Act 1970, s. 36. Under this provision the court may, on hearing an application for possession, adjourn the proceedings, stay or suspend judgment or postpone the date for delivery of possession, if it appears that 'the mortgagor is likely to be able within a reasonable period to pay any sums due under the mortgage'. This permits the court to give the mortgagor a 'second chance' to pay but will not be exercised where the mortgagor cannot make payments which will clear the debt within a reasonable time (whilst continuing to pay current instalments:

see *First National Bank plc* v *Syed* [1991] 2 All ER 250). As originally drafted, these provisions proved unsatisfactory when dealing with instalment mortgages, in which it is normal to provide that should one instalment be unpaid the whole sum becomes due. If the mortgagor has to pay 'any sums due' in such a case this would include the *whole* advance and few mortgagors could comply with this requirement (see *Birmingham Citizens Permanent Building Society* v *Caunt* [1962] Ch 883). Accordingly, an amendment was introduced by Administration of Justice Act 1973, s. 8, and now in the case of instalment mortgages the 'sums due' are only those payments which are in arrear and a clause requiring repayment of the whole loan can be disregarded by the court when exercising its discretion under s. 36 of the 1970 Act. The 1973 Act also extends the powers of the court to foreclosure actions even where possession is not also sought: s. 8(3).

Power to appoint a receiver
A receiver is a person who is appointed to take charge of the mortgaged land and either manage it (in order to produce an income to repay the debt) or sell it. Receivers are not commonly appointed in respect of mortgages of domestic property but are very frequently used in commercial mortgages.

The power to appoint a receiver may be granted expressly by the mortgage, but in addition, provided the mortgage is created by deed, the right to appoint will be implied by LPA 1925, s. 101(1)(iii). The power arises and becomes exercisable in exactly the same way as the statutory power of sale (see p. 258).

The receiver is appointed by a written document executed by the mortgagee (LPA 1925, s. 109). (For special rules on the appointment of receivers of company property, see the Insolvency Act 1986, ss. 33 and 34.) The receiver appointed under the LPA 1925, s. 101, power becomes an agent of the mortgagor (and not of the mortgagee who appointed him) and thus the mortgagee will not be liable for any negligence of the receiver (but see p. 266). Where a receiver obtains income from the land he should apply it in the following order:

(a) in payment of any outgoings in respect of the land (e.g., rates, and instalments on mortgages which have priority to that under which he was appointed);
(b) in payment of insurance premiums in respect of the land and his own commission (fees);
(c) in payment of interest on the loan;
(d) in payment of capital if the mortgagee agrees;
(e) payment of any balance should be made to the mortgagor (or other person entitled to income).

Problems regarding remedies when the mortgage is equitable

In describing the remedies available to the mortgagee we have, so far, concentrated on the position of the legal mortgagee. It is, however, important to note that in a number of ways an equitable mortgagee may not be in such a strong position. In several instances he may, in the end, obtain the

K

same remedy as a legal mortgagee, but he will often do this only after the trouble and expense of obtaining a court order, whereas the legal mortgagee may make use of such remedies without applying to the court. It must also be remembered that in any event remedies given by the court in protection of an equitable mortgagee will always be discretionary in character, because of the basic nature of the equitable jurisdiction.

We will now consider each remedy in turn.

Foreclosure
This causes little difficulty since it requires a court order in any event, and being an equitable remedy applies to equitable mortgages just as it does to legal ones.

Possession
As we have indicated (see p. 255) there appears to be no reason why an equitable mortgagee should not be regarded as having a right to possession in equity. It has, however, been said that the equitable mortgagee has no such right (see *Barclays Bank Ltd* v *Bird* [1954] Ch 274 at p. 280). By contrast, other authorities suggest that he may be so entitled (see *Ex parte Bignold* (1834) 4 Deac & Ch 259 and the article by Wade (1955) 71 LQR 204 and the decisions discussed therein).

The weight of academic opinion certainly seems to be that an equitable mortgagee does have the right to possession (see Megarry and Wade, *The Law of Real Property*, 5th ed. (London: Stevens, 1984), p. 951).

It should be noted that the issue under discussion here is whether an equitable mortgagee has the right to take possession *without a court order*, for it is certainly possible for him to do so on an order from the court (*Barclays Bank Ltd* v *Bird*). These days, few mortgagees would risk taking possession without a court order, even when they are entitled to do so and so the whole question, although interesting, does seem largely a theoretical one.

Finally, it seems to be the case that a chargee under an equitable charge will have no right to possession, since he cannot be regarded as having a contract for a lease or sublease, as can other equitable mortgagees (*Garfitt* v *Allen* (1887) 37 ChD 48). However, even this might be questioned if the equitable charge is regarded as a contract to create a charge by deed by way of legal mortgage, under which the chargee certainly does have a claim to possession.

Sale
The statutory power of sale under LPA 1925, s. 101(1)(i), applies only to mortgages made by deed, and therefore an equitable mortgagee will have no automatic power of sale unless he can rely on such a deed. In consequence, an equitable mortgagee normally required execution by the mortgagor of a memorandum under seal evidencing the transaction, which would be sufficient to satisfy the statutory requirements. Today it is likely that such a mortgage will be made by deed (at which point one might as well opt for a legal charge).

Even if the mortgagee has obtained such a deed he may still experience problems, since it has been held that he is not able to convey the legal estate because he has only an equitable interest in the property (*Re Hodson and Howes's Contract* (1887) 35 ChD 668). Although this view may be supported by the principle that no one can give more than he has, the same argument might appear to apply to the legal mortgagee, who has only a lease but is enabled by statute to convey the full estate (LPA 1925, ss. 88(1) and 89(1). It is difficult to see why the equitable mortgagee, selling in exercise of the statutory power, cannot rely on these provisions in the same way, and in *Re White Rose Cottage* [1965] Ch 940 Lord Denning MR expressed the view that there was no reason why he should not be able to convey the legal estate (at p. 951).

Uncertainty on the point, however, persists, and mortgagees continue to avoid any possible trouble by relying on the device traditionally used of inserting in the deed a declaration of trust or a power of attorney. The 'trust' method provides that the mortgagor is to hold the legal estate upon trust for the mortgagee, and gives the mortgagee power to appoint himself, or another, as a trustee in the mortgagor's place or to require the mortgagor to convey the property according to the mortgagee's direction. By exercise of this power the mortgagee can vest the legal estate in himself or a purchaser and can then transfer the equitable interest under his statutory power. By obtaining a power of attorney, the mortgagee will be empowered to convey the legal estate on behalf of the mortgagor. However, this second method suffers from the defect that, as the mortgagee sells on behalf of the mortgagor, the sale will be subject to any charges binding on the mortgagor and the mortgagee cannot thereby overreach any rights which rank after the mortgage to him (*Re White Rose Cottage*).

In the case of an equitable mortgage created without the formality of a deed the mortgagee may still apply to the court for an order for sale under LPA 1925, s. 91(2).

Appointing a receiver
The statutory power to appoint a receiver under LPA 1925, s. 101(1)(iii), applies only to equitable mortgages which are made by deed. However any equitable mortgagee may apply to the court for the appointment of a receiver (Supreme Court Act 1981, s. 37).

Disadvantages of equitable mortgages

From what we have said above, it can be seen that a mortgagee who accepts an equitable mortgage not made by deed may find the remedies available to him less satisfactory than those of a legal mortgagee. To some extent, although not entirely, these disadvantages may be overcome by the use of a deed, but as we shall see in the section on priorities (p. 276) this does nothing to meet the difficulties which an equitable mortgagee may occasionally encounter in enforcing his rights against later legal mortgagees or other purchasers of the legal estate.

Given the need for a deed to enable the equitable mortgagee to take advantage of the statutory remedies, a lender may regard it as being altogether easier to create a charge by way of legal mortgage (using a deed), and thereby avoid all the problems. In the case of the planned mortgage by deposit of deeds by Mr Neep of 12 Trant Way, his bank manager may well feel, on consideration, that a legal charge is to be preferred, but in any case will certainly insist on a deed. The Law of Property (Miscellaneous Provisions) Act 1989 also tends to discourage the creation of informal arrangements.

RIGHT OF CERTAIN THIRD PARTIES TO REDEEM

The mortgagor and the mortgagee are not the only people who may have rights in respect of a mortgage, for others may be entitled to exercise the right to redeem. This arises because *any* person who has a right in the equity of redemption is also allowed to redeem (of course by repaying the sums secured by the mortgage) (*Peace* v *Morris* (1869) LR 5 Ch App 227). Thus if Henry Mumps manages to establish that he has an interest in 6 Trant Way, he will be entitled to redeem any mortgage of the property should he choose to do so. A spouse who has a right to occupy the matrimonial home under the Matrimonial Homes Act 1983 has also been held to have a sufficient interest in the equity to allow him to redeem under this rule (*Hastings & Thanet Building Society* v *Goddard* [1970] 1 WLR 1544).

A second or later mortgagee is also a person who has an interest in the equity of redemption and he may also claim to redeem a superior mortgage. This reference to 'later' and 'superior' mortgages brings us to the notion of priorities, which we must briefly explain. Where there are several mortgages of the same property, those mortgages are ranked in order, with the mortgagees being entitled to receive the money owed to them according to their place in that ranking. Thus if the property is not worth the full amount of the debts secured on it, those ranking first take their money in full and those coming later may receive nothing. The rules which determine the order of priorities will be explained later (p. 266), but for the moment it is enough to know that mortgages are ranked in this way.

Where a later mortgagee wishes to redeem an earlier mortgage and this can be arranged by agreement, there is no difficulty. It may be, however, that the earlier mortgagee refuses to accept payment, either because there is a dispute about what is owed or because he is relying on his right to consolidate. In this case, the person wishing to redeem will have to seek a court order, and in doing this will find that he is subject to the rule that he should 'Redeem up and foreclose down'. This is best explained by reference to the following illustration.

Assume that land is subject to mortgages in favour of different creditors, A, B, C, D and E, the mortgages ranking for priority in that order. If D wishes to redeem the mortgage to B by court action, he is obliged to redeem also the intervening mortgage to C (redeem up). He does not have to redeem A's mortgage which simply keeps its priority. He is also required to bring foreclosure proceedings, which will extinguish the rights of E and the mortgagor. This apparently harsh provision comes about because B will be required to account for any payments he has already received and show what is still owed to him. The later mortgagees and the mortgagor are all interested in this, because if D redeems B's mortgage he will take over B's position, and be entitled to recover that amount of money from the value of the property in priority to all those who rank after B. They therefore have to be made parties to the action between D and B, so that they can watch the proceedings in their own interests and be bound by the court's decision about the amount owed to B. However, it was felt to be unreasonable to put all these people to the expense of coming to court simply to watch the proceedings, and therefore the rule developed that, while they were there, their claims on the property must be dealt with as well. Therefore, as well as redeeming B's mortgage, D must take the opportunity to quantify and pay off the debts due to any intervening mortgagees (here, C), and must also take foreclosure proceedings to vest the property in himself, free from the rights of later mortgagees (here E) and the mortgagor. Of course, if E or the mortgagor can pay off the debt owed to D, one or other of them can prevent his foreclosing. If neither of them has the resources to do that, it may be worth their while asking the court to order sale instead of foreclosure (see p. 258) in the hope that sale will produce enough money to pay off all the earlier mortgages and still leave enough for E and the mortgagor.

LIABILITY OF MORTGAGEES AND RECEIVERS FOR FRAUD OR NEGLIGENCE IN EXERCISE OF POWERS

Possession

When a mortgagee takes possession of land he is obliged to take a certain amount of care in relation to his management of the property. Thus he might be held liable to the mortgagor for letting the property at an undervalue (*White* v *City of London Brewery Co.* (1889) 42 ChD 237). The test applied is that the mortgagor is liable for any loss due to lack of due diligence in management, that is, that he is liable for wilful default (*Hughes* v *Williams* (1806) 12 Ves Jr 493).

Sale

A mortgagee or receiver who sells the property was once said to be liable only for fraud in relation to the sale (*Kennedy* v *De Trafford* [1897] AC 180). He was not to be regarded as being a trustee of his power of sale and was therefore entitled to exercise it in his own interest (*Warner* v *Jacob* (1882) 20 ChD 220). This is particularly important when choosing a time for sale, since the mortgagee may wish for swift repayment whilst the mortgagor requests a delay until a better time for sale (e.g., dwellings generally fetch a higher price in the spring than they do in winter). Many old cases indicate that the mortgagee or receiver may sell when he chooses, that his motives for selling are immaterial (see, e.g., *Nash* v *Eads* (1880) 25 SJ 95) and that the mortgagor cannot complain (in the absence of fraud) of a sale at an undervalue (*Davey* v *Durrant* (1857) 1 DeG & J 535). Later cases, however, indicate that now both mortgagees and receivers will be generally liable for negligence as well as fraud. In *Cuckmere Brick Co. Ltd* v *Mutual Finance Ltd* [1971] Ch 949 a mortgagee who sold land without informing prospective purchasers that planning permission had been obtained to build flats, as well as houses, was held to be liable to the mortgagor for the resulting shortfall in the sale price. Salmon LJ indicated that the mortgagee was obliged to obtain the proper or 'the market' value of the premises, but reasserted the principle that the mortgagee might choose his own time for the sale. In *Standard Chartered Bank Ltd* v *Walker* [1982] 1 WLR 1410, however, the Court of Appeal indicated that in future receivers and mortgagees would be generally liable for any negligence on sale, and Lord Denning MR indicated (*obiter*) that this should include liability for negligence in choosing the time of sale. (See also *Predeth* v *Castle Phillips Finance Co Ltd* [1986] 2 EGLR 144.)

Generally a mortgagee cannot be held liable for the carelessness of his receiver since the receiver is deemed to be the agent of the mortgagor. If therefore a mortgagee wishes to collect income from the property in order to satisfy his debt, he is usually better advised to appoint a receiver than to take possession of the land himself. However, if the mortgagee intermeddles in any way (e.g., by urging a swift sale) he may thereby render himself liable for any negligence which results (*Standard Chartered Bank Ltd* v *Walker*).

Since liability does now appear to exist in negligence this appears to extend to all who fall within the 'neighbour principle'. Accordingly the selling mortgagee or receiver will presumably be liable to anyone who has an interest in the equity of redemption.

Where a building society is concerned the duty to take care is governed by statute (see Sch. 4 to the Building Societies Act 1986).

TERMINATING A MORTGAGE

Obviously, apart from a termination by use of one of the remedies set out above, a mortgage normally ends when the mortgagor repays his debt. At that point any estate granted to the mortgagee will terminate automatically (cesser on redemption). However, the mortgagor will require evidence that he has repaid the mortgage sums, so that future purchasers can be assured that the land is free of any encumbrance. In the case of unregistered land, this is usually done by asking the mortgagee to execute a memorandum of discharge, which is usually endorsed on the back of the mortgage deed itself. In the case of mortgages of registered land, it will be necessary to clear the registered charge off the register. This is usually done by obtaining a completed form of discharge and the charge certificate from the mortgagee, and forwarding these to the registry (though any clear proof of discharge will suffice). The registrar will thereupon cancel the charge and reissue the Land Certificate to the registered proprietor (LRA 1925, s. 35, and Land Registration Rules 1925, r. 151).

PRIORITIES

Often, when a person is asked to lend money on the security of a mortgage, or when he later comes to enforce that mortgage, he will discover that there are a number of people who have interests in the property. When Mildred's bank is considering her request for a loan secured by a mortgage of 8 Trant Way, it will have to take into account the claims of: (a) the first mortgagee, the Red Leicester Building Society; (b) Laura Lymeswold's lease/licence; and (c) Henry's possible rights arising from contribution. The bank will be concerned with these other rights, beause it wants to be sure that if Mildred fails to repay the loan it will be able to sell the property (or exercise its other remedies) without any difficulty, and that the proceeds of sale will be sufficient to repay the debt. The bank therefore will need to consider:

(a) The amount of the loan secured by the first mortgage. If the property was sold, and the debt to RLBS discharged first, would there be enough left to repay the bank?

(b) The nature of Laura's interest. If she has a lease, this would decrease the value of the property, because a purchaser is unlikely to pay as much for a house with a sitting tenant as he would for one with vacant possession.

If Laura has a licence enforceable against third parties, this would, of course, decrease the value of the property in the same way.

(c) Whether Henry has any rights arising from contribution, such as an irrevocable licence or an interest under a resulting trust. Either of these might give him a right to remain in the property, which would effectively prevent sale; and if he had an interest under a trust, the bank might find that the mortgage attached only to Mildred's share of the beneficial interest.

The existence of other interests in the property is therefore of considerable importance to mortgagees. The mortgagee needs to know which interests he can ignore because they are *postponed* to his rights, and which interests he must take into account because they have *priority* to his mortgage.

The rules on priorities are in the main merely a practical application of the rules on the enforceability of legal and equitable interests against third parties, which we discussed in chapter 2. However, these rules often appear rather confusing when applied to mortgages, because there are so many of them, and there seem to be so many different situations to consider. In fact, if you can work out which situation is presented by the facts before you, you should find that applying the relevant rule is not too difficult.

We suggest that when dealing with a question of priorities, you begin by arranging the competing mortgages in chronological order, that is, according to their date of creation. The final order of priorities may be very different from this, but it at least provides a starting-point and a basis from which to apply the rules. Having done that, we think you will find it helpful to ask yourself a series of questions, in a prescribed order, which we work through in the following pages, and have tried to summarise in Figure 7.1.

In what follows, we usually refer to competing *mortgages*, but in general the same principles will apply where questions of priority arise between a mortgage and any other interest (such as that of a purchaser of the fee simple). Begin by asking yourself:

What is the nature of the property which is subject to the mortgage: is this a mortgage of the legal estate or of an equitable interest (such as a beneficiary's interest under a trust)?

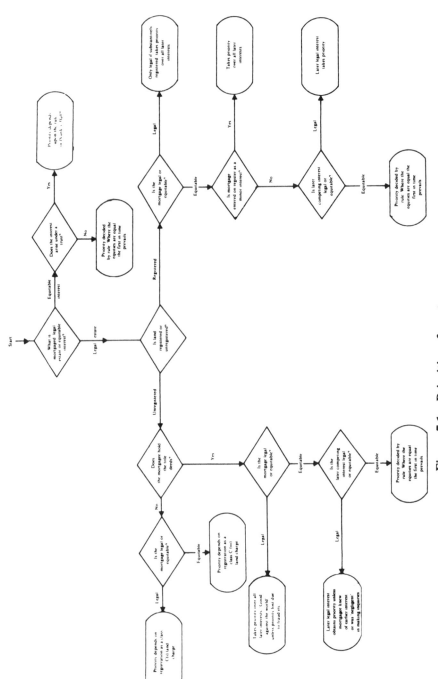

Figure 7.1   Priorities of mortgages

We will deal with mortgages of the equitable interest straight away, because the rules can be stated relatively shortly, and we can then concentrate for the rest of the chapter on mortgages of the legal estate.

PRIORITIES OF MORTGAGES OF AN EQUITABLE INTEREST

We have already seen that any dealing with an equitable interest must itself be equitable (p. 249), so we are concerned here only with successive equitable mortgages. Where there is a competition between equitable interests, the general rule is expressed in the maxim: Where the equities are equal, the first in time prevails. Therefore the interests will rank chronologically, according to the date of creation, provided each mortgagee has, in equity's view, acted fairly in regard to those who come after him.

However, where the property which is mortgaged consists of a beneficial interest under a trust, questions of priorities are regulated by special rules. We will consider registered and unregistered land separately.

Unregistered title

Where the subject-matter of the trust is unregistered land, competing assignments of the beneficial interest are regulated by the rule in *Dearle* v *Hall* (1823) 3 Russ 1, as applied to trusts of land by LPA 1925, s. 137. This rule applies to all successive assignments of the beneficial interest, and provides that priority of competing assignments (which include mortgages) depends on the order in which notice of the assignments is received by the trustees. Therefore in the following situation:

(a) mortgage to A,
(b) mortgage to B,
(c) B gives notice,
(d) A gives notice,

B would normally gain priority over A. However, since one is dealing with the equitable jurisdiction, B is not allowed to gain priority by giving notice first if he knew of the existence of A's mortgage when the second mortgage was created, for to allow this would be patently unfair. Thus only a second mortgagee without notice can improve his priority under the rule (*Re Holmes* (1885) 29 ChD 786). If B had no notice at the date when his mortgage was created, but learned of A's mortgage before giving notice, B may still obtain priority by giving notice first (*Mutual Life Assurance Society* v *Langley* (1886) 32 ChD 460). It is important to note that the crucial time for the operation of the rule is the date at which the trustee *receives* the notice, rather than the time at which notice is given. Accordingly, a mortgagee who posted a notice through the trustee's letter-box one evening, was held not to have given notice until the following day when the notice was opened and read (*Calisher* v *Forbes* (1871) LR 7 Ch App 109).

When giving notice under *Dearle* v *Hall* the assignee of the equitable interest should take care to give notice to the correct persons. Usually the trustees to be served will be the persons, or person, in whom the legal estate is vested. However, in the case of land which is settled under the SLA 1925, notice should be given to the trustees of the settlement and not to the tenant for life, in whom the estate is vested. Great care should be taken to give notice to *all* the trustees, whatever the type of trust. If this is done, the notice is effective for priority purposes even if later those trustees who received the notice retire, or die in office, and leave their successors without any knowledge of the notice which was given (*Re Wasdale* [1899] 1 Ch 163). However, if, where there are several trustees, notice is given to one only, that notice becomes invalid when that trustee retires or dies, unless that trustee had told the others that he had received notice (*Timson* v *Ramsbottom* (1836) 2 Keen 35, but see also *Ward* v *Duncombe* [1893] AC 369). If giving notice proves unduly difficult or expensive a 'purchaser' (this includes a mortgagee) can require that a memorandum be endorsed on the document which created the trust and under LPA 1925, s. 137(4), this is effective in place of giving notice to the trustees.

LPA 1925, s. 137(3) provides that 'A notice, otherwise than in writing, . . . shall not affect the priority of competing claims of purchasers in that equitable interest'. The meaning of this provision is not entirely clear: it may mean that all notices for the purpose of *Dearle* v *Hall* must since 1925 be in writing, or it may be that an oral notice is sufficient to maintain an assignee's existing chronological priority, although inadequate to give him priority over an earlier assignee.

Registered title

Where the subject-matter of the trust is registered land, the priority of assignments of the beneficial interest used to depend upon the order in which the assignments were entered in a special index called the Index of Minor Interests (LRA 1925, s. 102(2)). Relatively little use was made of the index and therefore it was abolished by LRA 1986, s. 5: now the rule in *Dearle* v *Hall* applies to both registered and unregistered interests.

PRIORITIES OF MORTGAGES OF THE LEGAL ESTATE

Where it is the legal estate which is subject to the mortgage, one begins by asking:

Is title to the estate registered or unregistered?

Registered title

In the case of registered title, the next question is:

Is the mortgage legal or equitable?

Legal mortgages

We have already seen that the only way of making a legal mortgage of registered land is by way of registered charge (p. 247). It is possible to create several registered charges of the same estate. LRA 1925, s. 29, provides that, subject to any entry to the contrary, the priority between such charges depends on the order in which they are entered on the register, and not on the order in which they are created.

The registered charge will also take priority over all equitable mortgages created after its date of registration. In addition, it will take priority over *earlier* equitable mortgages, unless they have been protected by entries on the register or take effect as overriding interests under LRA 1925, s. 70(1)(g) (see below).

Equitable mortgages

Equitable mortgages of registered land arise in a number of ways, including all those by which such a mortgage may be created in unregistered land (i.e., defective deed; contract to make a mortgage; deposit of documents of title, in this case the land certificate). In addition, an equitable mortgage may arise as a stage on the way to the creation of a registered charge, for you will remember that even if the charge is created by deed it does not become a *legal* charge until completed by registration. Where the parties have gone to the trouble of using a deed, the mortgage will presumably be completed by registration and its priority will then depend upon the rules which we have just described. If for any reason this does not happen, however, the mortgagee has only an equitable interest, and his position will be governed by the same rules as that of any other equitable mortgagee.

All equitable mortgages should be protected as minor interests by an entry on the register of a notice or caution (depending on whether the land certificate is, or is not, available). Once this is done, any later disposition by the registered proprietor will be subject to the mortgage, which accordingly will take priority over every later mortgage, whether legal or equitable.

What happens, however, if such an entry is not made? The answer depends on the nature of the later interest, which is seeking to gain priority over the earlier, unprotected equitable mortgage. Thus the next question to ask is:

What is the nature of the competing interest — legal or equitable?

If the later interest is *legal*, having itself been completed by registration, the legal purchaser or mortgagee will take free of the earlier equitable mortgage, unless, by any chance, the equitable mortgagee was in actual occupation of the land, and could claim an overriding interest under LRA 1925, s. 70(1)(g). This, of course, is not very likely to be the case.

If the later interest is *equitable*, for example, a later equitable mortgage, one might expect that the same rule would apply, and the unprotected earlier mortgagee would be postponed to the later one. However, in *Barclays Bank Ltd* v *Taylor* [1974] Ch 137, the Court of Appeal held that, since LRA 1925 contained no express provision for priority between competing minor interests, the general equitable rule that 'Where the equities are equal, the first in time prevails' should apply. Accordingly, in that case an unprotected equitable mortgage was still held to take priority over a later equitable interest under a contract to sell the registered estate. This rule applies even if the second charge has correctly been protected by entry on the register as a minor interest (*The Mortgagee Corporation Ltd* v *Nationwide Credit Corporation Ltd, The Times*, 27 July 1992).

One should not, however, overlook the opening words of the rule: it applies 'where the equities are equal'. In *Barclays Bank Ltd* v *Taylor*, the mortgagee bank held the land certificate, a fact which would have given warning of its position if any enquiries had been made, and the Court of Appeal took the view that there was 'nothing in the conduct of the bank . . . to justify postponement of its equity' (at p. 147). This is very different from the position where an earlier mortgagee does nothing, on or off the register, to protect his position and thus allows the mortgagor to represent that the property is unencumbered. In such a case, the earlier equitable mortgagee might well find that in the court's view the equities were not equal, and that he was postponed to a later equitable interest.

One final point should be mentioned before we leave mortgages of registered land. Later on, in connection with unregistered land, we shall see that an earlier mortgagee may lose his priority to a later one if he has been guilty of fraud, misrepresentation or gross negligence. These rules are of wider application than the equitable principle we have just considered, and apply to legal mortgages as well as to equitable ones. It is not easy to see how these rules could apply to registered land, nor how the holder of a registered charge (or of a mortgage protected by notice or caution) could lose his priority in this way, for evidence of his interest is on the register for any prospective mortgagee or purchaser to see. However, as the matter has never arisen in respect of registered title, it cannot be said with certainty that the same principles would never be applied, and thus it is worth bearing in mind that they might be found to do so, if the earlier mortgagee had in some way misled or deceived the later purchaser.

Unregistered title

The first question to ask in the case of unregistered title is:

Does the mortgagee hold the title deeds to the property?

You will remember that taking the title deeds is a standard precaution to prevent the mortgagor from making further dispositions of the property, and has the effect of ensuring that anyone dealing with the mortgagor is alerted to the fact that the land is already encumbered (see p. 255). Although cases could be imagined where a fraudulent mortgagor could divide his title deeds in such a way as to be able to give a convincing set of deeds to more than one mortgagee, the general position will be that only one mortgagee can take the deeds, and that any other mortgagee will not have that protection. A mortgagee without title deeds is, however, able to protect his position by registering his mortgage as a land charge.

Position where the mortgagee does not hold the title deeds

If the mortgagee does not take the title deeds when the mortgage is created, his mortgage is a registrable land charge. Such a mortgage, if legal, is known as a 'puisne mortgage' and should be registered as a class C(i) land charge, while if it is equitable, it is a general equitable charge and registrable in class C(iii) (LCA 1972, s. 2(4)(i) and (iii)). Registration constitutes actual notice (LPA 1925, s. 198) and so all later mortgagees, whether legal or equitable, will take subject to a mortgage which is protected in this way.

What happens if a registrable land charge is not registered? You will remember that some classes of land charge, if unregistered, are void only against the purchaser of the legal estate, while others are void against the purchaser of any interest (legal or equitable) in the land. Class C(i) and (iii) land charges, with which we are concerned here, fall into the second category, and thus any later mortgagee, whether legal or equitable, will take free of an earlier unregistered mortgage, or, in other words, will gain priority over it.

The basic position we have just described is quite straightforward, but there are two possible problems associated with it of which you should be aware.

(a) Writers have asked what would happen if a mortgagee took the title deeds at the creation of the mortgage, which was therefore not a registrable land charge, but later returned them to the mortgagor. Does the mortgage then become registrable? The general view seems to be that it does not become registrable. This is based partly on considerations of convenience (for otherwise the mortgage would fluctuate between being registrable or non-registrable as the title deeds moved backwards and forwards between the parties), but also derives support from the wording of the relevant sections. These refer to a '*deposit*' of deeds, rather than to a 'retention', and so it is thought that an initial deposit of deeds is sufficient to make the mortgage unregistrable for the rest of its life (see further, Megarry (1940) 7 CLJ 243). Of course, if the mortgagee does return the deeds to the mortgagor, he is placing himself at risk, and could in extreme cases lose his priority to later mortgages (see p. 275).

(b) The second problem could arise only where there is more than one mortgage which is not protected by a deposit of deeds, and consequently there are two or more registrable land charges. In such a case, a conflict could arise between two statutory provisions: LCA 1972, s. 4(5) (replacing the earlier LCA 1925, s. 13, which was in exactly the same terms) and LPA 1925, s. 97.

We have already mentioned the provisions of LCA 1972, s. 4(5), but now need to look at the exact words of the section:

[A] land charge of class C . . . shall be void as against a purchaser of the land charged with it, or of any interest in such land, unless the land charge is registered in the appropriate register before the completion of the purchase.

LPA 1925, s. 97, provides:

Every mortgage affecting a legal estate in land . . . (not being a mortgage protected by the deposit of documents relating to the legal estate affected) shall rank according to its date of registration as a land charge pursuant to the Land Charges Act.

In general, there will probably be no difficulty about the operation of these two provisions. If the first mortgage is not registered, the second mortgagee will take free of it, and if he then registers his own mortgage as a land charge no complications can arise. There may however, be a conflict between the two provisions if transactions occur in the following order:

  (i)   registrable mortgage A created;
  (ii) registrable mortgage B created;
  (iii) mortgage A registered;
  (iv) mortgage B registered.

According to LCA 1972, s. 4(5), B should take priority, because A was not registered when B was created. However, if you apply LPA 1925, s. 97, then A should take priority, because it was registered as a land charge before B was registered.

There are a number of suggested solutions to this problem (see, for example, Megarry (1940) 7 CLJ 243 at p. 255; Hargreaves (1950) 13 MLR 533 at p. 534; Sir Robert Megarry and H.W.R. Wade, *The Law of Real Property*, 5th ed. (London: Stevens, 1984), pp. 999–1001; and note that the earlier articles refer to LCA 1925, s. 13, which was in exactly the same terms as the present provision in the 1972 Act). Some writers favour the provisions of the Land Charges Act, saying that it is a later enactment (even LCA 1925 was technically later than LPA 1925), and that an interest which is void can scarcely be revived by subsequent registration. Others support LPA 1925, s. 97, pointing out that it specifically relates to mortgages, while the LCA provisions apply to mortgages only because the interpretation section provides that 'purchasers' shall include 'mortgagees'. (On the other hand, in the technical sense that 'purchaser' means 'one who takes by act of parties' (p. 69) a mortgagee has always been a purchaser, quite independently of any statutory provision.) A third approach suggests that there is really no conflict between the two sections: s. 97 is seen as a signpost, pointing on to the Land Charges Act and saying, in general terms, that the priority of these mortgages shall depend upon the detailed provisions of that Act.

The point is a fascinating academic conundrum, on which each reader may form his own views. It is, however, perhaps worthy of note that there has been no reported decision on the point in the 68 years since the two conflicting provisions were first enacted, which suggests that the problem does not give rise to any real difficulty in practice. This view is perhaps further supported by the fact that Parliament had an opportunity to resolve the conflict in 1972, when repealing and replacing LCA 1925, but in fact merely re-enacted the old s. 13 in the same terms.

Position where the mortgagee does hold the title deeds
In this case, one needs to begin by asking:

Is the mortgage legal or equitable?

Legal mortgages In general, the legal mortgagee with the title deeds can rely on the basic principle that legal rights bind all the world. This means that anyone who later acquires an estate or interest in the land will take it subject to an earlier legal right. This is so even if the later purchaser did not know of, or could not discover, the existence of that right, although in the case of a mortgage he will usually be forewarned by the fact that the mortgagor cannot produce his title deeds. Thus a legal mortgage will take priority over all mortgages, legal or equitable, which are created after it, *unless the first legal mortgagee acts in such a way as to lose his natural priority.*

Loss of legal mortgage's natural priority due to mortgagee's fraud, misrepresentation or gross negligence

(a) *Fraud.* If a mortgagee colludes with the mortgagor in some kind of fraud on a later acquirer, it would be manifestly unjust to allow him later to depend upon the natural priority of his own mortgage. Neither law nor equity will assist a cheat, and in such a case the fraudulent mortgagee will lost his priority to the person whom he has deceived. In this way even a legal mortgage can be postponed to a later equitable interest (*Peter* v *Russel* (1716) 1 Eq Ab 321).

(b) *Misrepresentation.* Similarly a mortgagee who enables the mortgagor to make some false representation to a later purchaser will be prevented from claiming a priority which conflicts with the representation made. Thus allowing the mortgagor to recover the deeds (or, before 1926, to retain them) in order to create a later mortgage is regarded as holding the mortgagor out as being able to mortgage the property. In such a case, the second mortgagee will get priority if he did not know of the first mortgage, and thus even an equitable mortgagee may take priority over an earlier legal mortgage. In *Perry Herrick* v *Attwood* (1857) 2 DeG & J 21, the legal mortgagees left the title deeds in the hands of the mortgagor, so that he could raise a further loan of a prescribed amount, secured by a mortgage which, it was agreed, should take priority over the earlier mortgage. In fact, the mortgagor then created two further mortgages, for a greater amount than was intended, and it was held that in these circumstances the first legal mortgagees lost their priority to both later mortgagees.

(c) *Gross negligence.* The suggestion that it is possible to lose one's priority due to gross negligence in the protection of one's own interests causes rather more difficulties.

In *Northern Counties of England Fire Insurance Co.* v *Whipp* (1884) 26 ChD 482 a mortgagee company, which allowed the mortgagor access to a safe in which his deeds were stored, was held not to have lost its priority when the mortgagor recovered the deeds and created a second mortgage. Oddly, the court held the first mortgagee's action to be merely careless, and said that priority could only be lost in a case of gross negligence. In *Walker* v *Linom* [1907] 2 Ch 104, a purchaser of the legal estate, who asked for the title deeds but failed to check that all had been delivered to him, was held to take the land subject to a later equitable mortgage. It may be that the purchaser in this case was regarded as having been grossly negligent because he was a solicitor and accordingly should have been aware of the need to check the deeds carefully. A contrary decision was reached in *Cottey* v *National Provincial Bank of England Ltd* (1904) 20 TLR 607. One may contrast this decision with that in *Hunt* v *Elmes* (1860) 2 DeGF & J 578, where a solicitor mortgaged two properties, A and B, to a client. The client-mortgagee received a parcel bearing a label which stated that the deeds of both properties were enclosed. In fact the deeds of property B were missing, and the solicitor later sold that property to a third party. In this case the mortgagee was held not to have lost his natural priority because he was entitled to rely on the solicitor-mortgagor. It was accepted that the mortgagee had been imprudent, but not so imprudent as to lose his priority.

Equitable mortgages
In the case of an equitable mortgage with deposit of title deeds, the first question to ask is:

What is the nature of the later competing mortgage — legal or equitable?

Position where the competing mortgage is legal This situation, of an earlier equitable mortgage and a later legal one, would seem likely to turn on a straightforward application of the doctrine of notice. If the purchaser for value of a legal estate has actual or constructive notice of an earlier equitable interest (that is, knows or ought to know of it) he will be bound by it, whereas if he does not have that notice he will take free of the interest. Here, the later mortgagee is a 'purchaser for value of the legal estate' (*Brace* v *Duchess of Marlborough* (1728) 2 P Wms 491), and one would expect that the mortgagor's inability to produce the title deeds would give the later mortgagee actual or constructive notice of the earlier equitable mortgage which is protected by deposit of those deeds.
    There are, however, a number of decisions which do not deal with the matter in these terms, but are instead concerned with whether the legal mortgagee has been so *negligent* in investigating title that he should be postponed to the earlier equitable mortgagee. Thus, in *Hudston* v *Viney* [1921] 1 Ch 98, in which a legal mortgagee did not investigate the mortgagor's title for the full statutory period and therefore failed to discover an earlier equitable mortgage, Eve J said that something more than mere carelessness was necessary to make the legal purchaser subject to the equitable interest:

[I]t must at least be carelessness of so aggravated a nature as to amount to the neglect of precautions which the ordinarily reasonable man would have observed and to indicate an attitude of mental indifference to obvious risks.

Several cases in which the decision is based on negligence rather than notice are concerned with the situation in which the legal purchaser has enquired for the title deeds and has been given some excuse by the owner for their non-production. In *Oliver* v *Hinton* [1899] 2 Ch 264, a purchaser who accepted the excuse that the deeds related also to other property was held to be guilty of gross negligence, and postponed to an earlier mortgagee, Lindley MR specifically saying: 'I do not base my judgment upon constructive notice of the charge' (at p. 273). In *Hewitt* v *Loosemore* (1851) 9 Hare 449, however, a mortgagee who accepted the rather weak excuse that the mortgagor was busy and would produce the deeds at a more convenient time, was allowed to take free of an earlier equitable mortgage, the court saying that a legal mortgagee was not to be postponed to an earlier equitable one 'unless there be fraud or gross or wilful negligence on his part' (at p. 590). This decision may, however, have been affected by the fact that the mortgagor was a solicitor, whilst the mortgagee was a farmer and the mortgagor's cousin. A later acquirer was also protected in *Agra Bank Ltd* v *Barry* (1874) LR 7 HL 135, when he accepted the excuse that the deeds were in Ireland, which, since the land was in Ireland, may well have appeared reasonable, at least in the context of gross negligence. One cannot help but feel, though, that these excuses should have put the legal mortgagees on their guard, and they might well have been deemed to have had constructive notice if the courts had been employing the doctrine of notice rather than the concept of negligence.

It was for this reason that we mentioned earlier, when comparing the position of legal and equitable mortgagees (p. 263), that the equitable mortgagee might also find himself at a disadvantage on questions of priority. In the days before 1926, when these cases were decided, there was nothing more that equitable mortgagees could do to protect themselves. Today, however, they might perhaps be better advised not to take the title deeds, for without them they have a registrable land charge, registration of which gives actual notice to all later purchasers.

Position where the competing mortgage is equitable Here there will be two competing equitable mortgages, and accordingly the principle which we have already mentioned several times will apply: where the equities are equal, the first in time prevails.

Thus equitable mortgages rank for priority in chronological order, unless the earlier mortgagee loses his priority through fraud, misrepresentation or negligence in failing to retain the title deeds. The general principles involved are very similar to those discussed in connection with the postponement of a legal mortgage (p. 275), although there have been suggestions that an equitable mortgagee will be postponed by a lesser degree of negligence than is needed in the case of a legal mortgagee. There is, however, no known decision in which an equitable mortgagee has been postponed for anything less than gross negligence, and in *Taylor* v *Russell* [1891] 1 Ch 8 the court expressed the view that the same standard should apply to both.

PRIORITIES OF THREE OR MORE MORTGAGES

So far, we have described the rules about priorities as though we were concerned only with a competition between two mortgages. It is, however, possible to have three or more mortgages of the same estate, and you may therefore have to deal with questions of priorities in such a situation. We suggest that you should continue to apply the approach adopted so far: begin by listing the mortgages according to their date of creation, and then consider the earliest one in relation to each successive mortgage. When you have done this, take the next one to be created, and consider it in relation to each one that follows it. If you proceed in this way, considering each pair separately, you will often find that at the end you can list all the mortgages in order of priority.

Take, for example, three mortgages of a legal estate, title to which is not registered, which have been created in the following order:

(a)   legal mortgage to A, who takes the title deeds;
(b)   legal charge to B, who registers a class C (i) land charge; and
(c)   equitable mortgage to C.

Now compare the mortgages in pairs:

(a)   *A and B.* A has a mortgage protected by deposit of title deeds, which is therefore not a registrable land charge. He has a legal mortgage, so his right is good against the world, and there is no suggestion of any conduct on his part which would deprive him of his priority.
Result: A before B.
(b)   *A and C.* The position is exactly the same as in the case of A and B.
Result: A before C.
(c)   *B and C.* B has a legal mortgage not protected by deposit of title deeds. It is therefore a registrable class C(i) land charge, and having been registered as such will bind all those who take a later interest in the property including C.
Result: B before C.

On this occasion, then, this method of approaching the problem produces a clear and simple set of answers:

A before B
A before C
B before C

and the mortgages can be sorted into a neat straight line of priority:

A   first
B   second
C   third

It is possible, however, to think of situations in which the order of priorities is not so easy to determine, as the following example will show. Again, there are three mortgages of the legal estate, in unregistered land, created in the following order:

(a) legal mortgage to D, who takes the title deeds;
(b) legal charge to E, who registers a class C(i) land charge.

D then foolishly returns the deeds to the mortgagor, who creates:

(c) an equitable mortgage by depositing the deeds with F (and making a written agreement).

Again, one compares the mortgages in pairs:

(a) *D and E.* The position is exactly the same as between A and B in the previous example, for D retained the deeds at the time of the mortgage to E, and has done nothing to lose his priority.
Result: D before E.
(b) *D and F.* Here, despite the fact that D has a legal mortgage and F only an equitable one, it seems likely that D will be postponed to F, for D's returning the title deeds to the mortgagor enabled him to represent to F that the property was unincumbered.
Probable result: F before D.
(c) *E and F.* The position is the same as between B and C in the previous example.
Result: E before F.

When you consider the answers you have obtained here, you will find that the results cannot be arranged in a neat list, but instead go round in a circle:

D before E
F before D
E before F

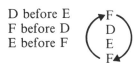

How you break into this circle is unclear, because the point has never come before the courts. Two possible solutions would be either that all the mortgagees should bear an equal loss (for there is only a problem if the value of the property is less than the sums outstanding on all three mortgages), or that the mortgages should rank in the order in which they were created. (Some authorities have suggested applying the rules of subrogation, but this produces a manifestly unfair result. (See Megarry and Wade, *The Law of Real Property*, 5th ed. (London: Stevens, 1984), p. 1001, and Gilmore (1961) 71 Yale LJ 53.) Happily , the circular priority problem is rarely likely to arise in practice, and in general you should be able to arrange competing mortgages in order of priority without too much difficulty.

MORTGAGEE'S RIGHT TO TACK FURTHER ADVANCES

As we have seen, 8 Trant Way is already subject to a first mortgage to the Red Leicester Building Society (RLBS), and a second mortgage may soon be created in favour of the Royal Windsor Bank (RWB). At some later date, after the creation of the second mortgage, Mildred, the owner of No. 8, might return to the RLBS and ask whether it would extend her mortgage to cover an additional advance. If the building society considers doing this, it will wish to know whether the fresh advance is effectively a third mortgage, ranking for priority after the RWB's mortgage, or whether it can 'tack' (add on) this further advance to the first mortgage, so as to gain priority for the later advance.

Again, the need to tack further advances will often arise where a mortgage has been given to a bank to secure the mortgagor's overdraft. As each cheque is presented for payment, the bank makes a further loan to the mortgagor, but it is obviously desirable, from the bank's point of view, that all these loans should rank for priority with the original mortgage.

The circumstances in which further advances may be tacked are governed by different statutory provisions in the case of registered and unregistered title.

Unregistered title

The rule is that under LPA 1925, s. 84, a mortgagee has the right to tack further advances in three situations:

(a)   Where all the subsequent mortgagees agree. This is relatively unlikely to happen.

(b)   Where the mortgagee seeking to tack did not have notice of the existence of the subsequent mortgage at the date at which the further advance was made.

It may be thought that this second category would be of little use to the earlier mortgagee if the later mortgage was registered as a land charge, since registration constitutes notice. However, under s. 94(2), the first mortgagee is not deemed to have notice of the second mortgage merely because it has been registered as a land charge, provided that:

(i)   the first mortgage was expressly made for the purpose of securing further advances; and

(ii)   the second mortgage was not registered at the date when the first mortgage was created or when the first mortgagee last searched the register, whichever is the later.

Therefore, if a later mortgagee wants to prevent tacking in these circumstances, he must give express notice of his position to the earlier mortgagee.

(c)   Where the first mortgage obliges the mortgagee to make further advances. Here he may tack even if he has notice of the later mortgage. Thus, should a mortgagee agree to finance the building of a new estate, it might be agreed that the advance should be paid in stages as each house is finished. In such a case the mortgagee can tack the separate loans together, even if he has knowledge of a later mortgage.

Registered title

LRA 1925, s. 30, covers two of the situations which are dealt with in the case of unregistered land by LPA 1925, s. 94:

(a) Where a registered charge is made for securing further advances, such advances may be tacked until such time as the registrar notifies the chargee of any later mortgage which he intends to register as a charge (s. 30(1) and (2)).

(b) Where there is an obligation to make further advances, any subsequent registered charge takes effect subject to those advances — in other words, the first mortgagee may tack the advance.

INTERESTS PRIOR TO THE MORTGAGE: A CAUSE FOR CONCERN TO THE MORTGAGEE

Finally, before we leave mortgages, we need to look again at the position at 8 Trant Way. Mildred is seeking a loan from the Royal Windsor Bank (RWB) on the security of a second mortgage of No. 8, and the bank will need to consider the extent to which it will be bound by the existing interests in the property. The title is unregistered.

The RWB must first consider the earlier legal mortgage to the Red Leicester Building Society (RLBS). If the RLBS has the deeds (as is normal) and has not done anything to forfeit its natural priority, it will take priority over any second mortgage to the RWB. Should the RLBS not have the deeds, its mortgage still takes priority if it is registered as a class C(i) land charge. If it does not have the deeds, and its mortgage is not registered when the second mortgage is created, the second mortgagee will gain priority, even if the RWB knew of the earlier mortgage (*Midland Bank Trust Co. Ltd* v *Green* [1981] AC 513). Accordingly, before making any advance, the RWB should check the situation with regard to the RLBS mortgage. Thereafter, it will need to have 8 Trant Way valued, and should ensure that it does not lend more than the balance of the value after deduction of the sums due to the RLBS.

The RWB needs also to consider the situation of Laura Lymeswold, who has a licence or lease of 8A Trant Way. If she has a lease (as is very possible after *Street* v *Mountford* [1985] AC 809), the RWB will take a mortgage *subject to* the pre-existing legal estate vested in her. It should ensure that its valuation takes account of the existence of a sitting tenant. Should Laura have only a licence, it appears that it will not bind the bank (and a later purchaser on sale by the mortgagee) for the licence would be contractual: see *Ashburn Anstalt* v *Arnold* [1989] Ch 1.

The greatest problem for the RWB would be the uncertain position of Henry

Mumps. If Henry has an equitable interest in the property due to his contribution, this will bind the RWB, unless the bank can claim to be a bona fide purchaser for value of a legal estate without notice. Since Henry is in occupation of the premises the bank is likely to have notice under the rule in *Hunt v Luck* (see p. 71). (For the position if the title to No. 8 were registered, see *Williams & Glyn's Bank Ltd v Boland* [1981] AC 487, and note the overriding interest which Henry might claim under LRA 1925, s. 70(1)(g).) The existence of such a binding interest would mean that the bank's mortgage would attach only to Mildred's interest in the property and not to Henry's share. Thereafter, since as an equitable co-owner Henry would have a right to reside in the property until sale (*Bull v Bull* [1955] 1 QB 234) and as the mortgage would not affect his interest, Henry could prevent the second mortgagee selling the property (see *Williams & Glyn's Bank Ltd v Boland*). This would prevent realisation even of the partial security with which the bank would be left. The possibility of such interests arising has accordingly created a minefield for the building societies and banks. One solution to the problem would be for Mildred to appoint another trustee to join with her in receiving the mortgage money, so that Henry's interest would be overreached and attach only to the mortgage advance: *City of London Building Society v Flegg* [1988] AC 54.

Of recent years, the professional mortgagees (e.g., building societies and banks) have been increasingly concerned about the position of people such as the mortgagor's family and friends, who occupy the property with him at the date of the mortgage and may have rights to the property which can be enforced against the mortgagee. The *Boland* decision caused much debate in the financial institutions, and in 1985 a Bill was introduced into Parliament which was intended to amend the rule in *Hunt v Luck* and the effects of LRA 1925, s. 70(1)(g), as interpreted in *Williams & Glyn's Bank Ltd v Boland*. By virtue of the proposed amendment, a mortgagee or purchaser would not be bound by the beneficial interests of a person living in the property *with the legal owner* (i.e., reversing *Hodgson v Marks* [1971] Ch 892 and affecting someone in Henry's position). The position of a spouse would, however, have still been protected. The Bill was withdrawn at second reading and indeed it appears that it may be extremely difficult to produce a rule which fairly protects both mortgagees and parties with beneficial interests in the property.

8 Easements and Profits à Prendre

The title 'easements and profits à prendre' may make you imagine that this chapter is concerned with strange rights known only to land lawyers and having archaic names. In fact both easements and profits are commonly encountered and most of us use such rights every day of our lives: for example, when we walk across the courtyard in the block of flats in which we live, or enjoy the continuing support of our houses which is provided by walls belonging to our neighbours. Once you have read this chapter you can, on your next train journey, play a variant on a childrens' game, and spot from the train windows the situations in which easements and profits are likely to arise. Is the woman driving up a shared driveway exercising an easement (a right of way)? Is the little boy leading his pony into that field exercising a profit (grazing)? Does the path across the back gardens of those terraced houses indicate an easement (right of way on foot)? From this you can see that the interests discussed in this chapter are often quite straightforward and essential to our daily life. The common strand to all these arrangements is that they are all rights exercised over land which belongs to another person, and so come into the category of third party interests in land.

Factual background

The plan of 14, 15, 16 and 16A Trant Way in figure 8.1 (overleaf) may assist you when reading this chapter.

In 1935 the then owner of 15 Trant Way decided to install modern drains in the property. The nearest main drain was in Gouda Grove. After discussion the then owner of 16 Trant Way agreed that the drains could be laid across his front garden into Gouda Grove. A deed was drawn up which contained the following words:

> The grantor [the owner of 16] as beneficial owner hereby grants unto the grantee [the owner of 15] full right and liberty to use the sewer or drain marked [with a dotted line] on the plan attached hereto for the passage or conveyance of sewage water and soil from the said 15 Trant Way to the public sewer.

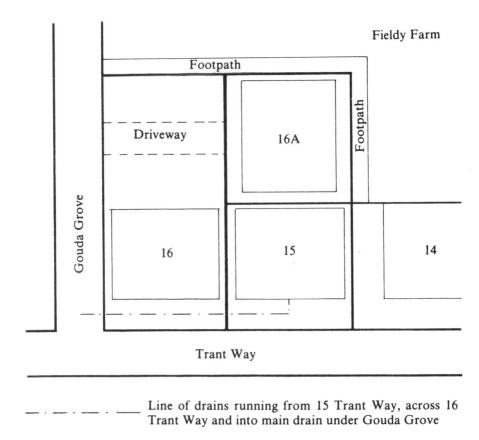

_._ _._ _._ _._ _._ _._ Line of drains running from 15 Trant Way, across 16 Trant Way and into main drain under Gouda Grove

Figure 8.1   Nos. 14, 15, 16 and 16A Trant Way

The current owner of 15 Trant Way is Charles Chive.

The current owner of 14 Trant Way (Nigel Neep) keeps a goat which he grazes on Fieldy Farm (to the rear of 14). Fieldy Farm is owned in fee simple by Farmer George.

There is a footpath leading from the back of 14 Trant Way to Gouda Grove. This path runs across Farmer George's land. The path has been in regular use by the owners of 14 Trant Way for many years.

For the last 50 years the fence separating 14 Trant Way from Fieldy Farm has been maintained by Farmer George or his father (who was his predecessor in title).

At one time 16 and 16A formed one plot of land. In 1975 the then owner of 16 Trant Way (Marjorie Marjoram) sold the freehold of the property now known as 16A Trant Way to Basil Borage. The only access to 16A is across the driveway on 16 Trant Way (see figure 8.1) but this fact was not mentioned in the conveyance to Basil Borage. In 1985 Miss Marjoram sold 16 to Dan Dill (who has made a first registration of title). Mr Dill dislikes Mr Borage and wants to prevent his use of the driveway.

At present 16 Trant Way enjoys an uninterrupted view of fields to the rear of the property over Fieldy Farm. Farmer George has just obtained planning permission to erect a corn silo on the farm and Dan Dill believes that this will spoil his view.

You will recall from chapter 3 that Fingall Forest, the fee simple owner of 2 Trant Way, has granted a tenancy of the basement flat at No. 2 to his friend Gerald Gruyère. When Mr Gruyère first moved in he had only an oral lease. At that time he asked Mr Forest if he could keep his dustbin in the back garden of 2 Trant Way (which Mr Forest retained for his own use) and Mr Forest agreed. About two months ago the two friends decide to formalise their arrangement, and Mr Gruyère was given a written lease of the flat for a period of 2 years. The agreement was recorded in a written document, not under seal, which did not mention the right to keep the dustbin in the garden.

WHAT IS AN EASEMENT?

Easements are rather like elephants: easy to recognise but very difficult to define. We are easily able to identify rights which are commonly accepted as being easements, for example, rights of way and rights of light. However, the label 'easement' covers such a wide range of interests that it may be difficult to discern any similarity between them. One might as a result be inclined to ignore the difficulties of definition and merely construct a list of rights which have been recognised as easements. However, although this may be helpful, it is not sufficient, for the courts have recognised that the list of easements is not closed and that the need for new easements will be met as the circumstances of life change (*Dyce* v *Lady James Hay* (1852) 1 Macq 305). Thus an easement allowing the erection of a television aerial is obviously a modern addition to the list. We must accordingly return to the question of a standard against which a claim to a new right can be tested. This standard is provided in the judgment of the Court of Appeal in *Re Ellenborough Park*

[1956] Ch 131 which, although it does not define an easement, provides rules for its recognition.

The rules in *Re Ellenborough Park*

The original owners of Ellenborough Park also owned the surrounding land, which they sold off in plots for building purposes. Each conveyance granted to the purchasers the right to use the park, subject to an obligation to make a contribution towards the cost of maintaining it. The plaintiffs in the case acquired the park itself from the original owners, and intended to build upon it. The owners of the surrounding plots claimed the right to use the park and the Court of Appeal upheld these claims, saying that the rights to use the park were legal easements. Since these rights were legal interests in land, they bound the purchasers of the park, and thus prevented them from building upon it. The court approved four rules of recognition for an easement:

(a)   There must be a dominant tenement and a servient tenement.
(b)   Dominant and servient owners must be different persons.
(c)   The easement must accommodate the dominant tenement.
(d)   The right claimed must 'lie in grant'.

We will now look at these rules and their application in greater detail.

Need for a dominant and servient tenement
An easement is a right enjoyed over one piece of land (the 'servient tenement') for the benefit of another piece of land (the 'dominant tenement'). In the case of the easement of drainage given in our practical examples, 16 Trant Way is burdened and is the servient tenement, whilst 15 Trant Way is benefited and is the dominant tenement.

It is essential that there is a dominant tenement, for an easement cannot exist 'in gross', that is, without being attached to a particular piece of land which derives benefit from it. It is this which distinguishes, for example, an easement of way from a public right of way: in the latter, anyone may use the way, whereas the easement is available only to those connected in some way with the dominant tenement.

Accordingly, when a claim is made to an easement, the two pieces of land must be readily identifiable, and therefore, when an easement is being created, care must be taken to ensure that the two tenements are clearly identified. This is particularly important in the case of the servient tenement and, in our example of the right to drainage, the burdened land is clearly identified by the dotted line showing the line of the drain as it passes under 16 Trant Way. In a properly drafted document, the dominant tenement should also be clearly defined, thus the use of words such as 'for the benefit of the land known as 15 Trant Way' is desirable. However, it is not fatal if such an express mention is omitted as long as it is clear from the deed which land is to be benefited (see *Thorpe v Brumfitt* (1873) LR 8 Ch App 650).

Dominant and servient owners must be different persons
This is how the rule is stated in *Re Ellenborough Park*, but it is perhaps easier to understand if one says that the two tenements must not be both owned and occupied by the same person. An easement is essentially a right over another's land for the benefit of one's own, and one cannot exercise a right against oneself. Thus if a person owns two pieces of land and walks across one piece in order to reach another, he cannot be exercising an easement (*Roe* v *Siddons* (1888) 22 QBD 224 at p. 236). Sometimes, however, such a situation is said to give rise to a 'quasi-easement': this is, as it were, a potential easement which could develop into an easement if the plots came into separate hands.

We have emphasised the requirement that the same person must not own *and* occupy the two tenements, because it is possible for a tenant to have an easement over other land belonging to his landlord, and equally for the landlord, during the period of the lease, to have an easement over land occupied by the tenant. Thus in the case of Fingall Forest and Gerald Gruyère at 2 Trant Way it is perfectly possible for Mr Gruyère to have an easement in respect of the land owned and occupied by Mr Forest, although Mr Forest owns the fee simple of both dominant and servient tenements.

Should one person acquire both the servient and the dominant tenement this will extinguish a pre-existing easement, if at the same time the two properties come into common occupation. If, at some future date, the same person were to buy both 15 and 16 Trant Way, this would bring the easement over 16 Trant Way to an end.

The easement must accommodate the dominant tenement
This rule requires that the right must confer an advantage on the dominant land. It is not sufficient for the right to confer a merely personal advantage on the current owner. Such a personal right is said to be an interest 'in gross' and, as we have seen, it is not possible to have an easement in gross. All easements must be 'appurtenant', that is, they must benefit identifiable land. In *Re Ellenborough Park* the right to use the park was held to benefit the surrounding plots of land because a domestic property is always improved in character by the availability of a garden. Unfortunately it is sometimes difficult to distinguish between personal benefits and benefits conferred on land, though, if it can be shown that the right increased the value of the land or its saleability, this would be sufficient. It may help to consider whether *any* possible owner of the property would regard the right as advantageous. Obviously any owner would regard the availability of drainage into the main drains as an advantage.

A problem may arise where the right claimed tends to confer an advantage, not on the land itself, but rather on some trade or business which is being carried on upon the land. In *Hill* v *Tupper* (1863) 2 H & C 121 the right claimed as an easement was the right to put pleasure-boats on the canal which bordered the 'dominant' land. It was held that this right did not amount to an easement, because it did not benefit the land. Rather it benefited the business which Mr Hill happened to be running upon his land. The fact that the right benefits a business is not necessarily fatal, however, to a claim that the right is an easement. In *Moody* v *Steggles* (1879) 12 ChD 261, a right to hang on neighbouring land a sign pointing towards a public house was held to be capable of being an easement. This may well be because it is common for land used as a public house to remain in such use for prolonged periods, sometimes for centuries, so that the business run on the land and the land itself become inextricably linked.

The requirement that benefit be conferred on the land does, however, mean that the servient tenement and the dominant tenement must be reasonably close together. Normally the two properties will adjoin one another (as is the case in all our practical examples) but this is not absolutely necessary (*Pugh* v *Savage* [1970] 2 QB 373). The two pieces of land must, however, be close enough to support a claim that the dominant land receives an actual benefit from the right, and thus one could not have an easement exercisable over land at the other end of the country (*Bailey* v *Stephens* (1862) 12 CB (NS) 91 at p. 115).

The easement must be capable of forming the subject-matter of a grant
Easements are interests in land which can be legal interests, and as such they must 'lie in grant'. This means that a right must be capable of being granted by deed if it is to be recognised as an easement. A number of rules result from this requirement, the first of which is that the right claimed must be specific and definable, for it would have to be carefully defined if included in a deed. This can be a problem if the right claimed involves issues of taste, since such matters cannot be defined. Thus one cannot claim a right to a prospect (a fair view) as an easement, for one cannot define such a right (*William Aldred's Case* (1610) 9 Co Rep 57b). Thus Dan Dill at 16 Trant Way cannot complain about Farmer George's silo on the basis of an easement to a view. He should have made his complaints at the stage at which the farmer applied for planning permission (though he might not have been able to prevent the grant of permission). The vague nature of the right claimed may also result in its failing this test. Thus in *Mounsey* v *Ismay* (1865) 3 H & Co 486, a claim to use land for general recreational purposes was held to be too vague to amount to an easement, although a right to use a garden for similar purposes was upheld in *Re Ellenborough Park* itself.

The second important consequence of the rule that easements lie in grant is that, at the date at which the right arose, there must have been two persons who were capable respectively of granting and receiving the easement. This is of importance where easements are acquired otherwise than by express grant and will accordingly be discussed later when we consider methods of acquisition.

Some examples of easements

It is not possible for us to list all the rights which have been recognised as amounting to easements, but we will mention some of the most common.

(a) *Rights of way.*
(b) *Right to light.* This must be a specific right, so that light is claimed

for particular windows or skylights, and there cannot be a general claim for light over the whole piece of land (*Colls* v *Home & Colonial Stores Ltd* [1904] AC 179). The amount of light which one can claim is that which is necessary according to the ordinary notions of mankind. Thus this right would be infringed were the light so obstructed that in a dwelling the electric light had to be lit all day. A mere diminution in the light is not sufficient, nor can one claim extra light because of the activities carried on on the land unless the special use contemplated was known to the owner of the servient land at the time at which the easement was acquired.

(c) *Rights to water*. One has no general right to water which percolates through the soil, but an easement may exist in respect of water in a defined channel, e.g., a pipe or stream (see, for example, *Race* v *Ward* (1855) 4 E & B 702).

(d) *Rights to air*. Once again there is no general right to the passage of air but a claim to air flowing in a defined channel can amount to an easement. This might include, for example, rights in respect of ventilation ducts (*Wong* v *Beaumont Property Trust Ltd* [1965] 1 QB 173).

(e) *Rights to storage*. This is now a well-accepted easement, provided that the right is sufficiently definite (*Wright* v *Macadam* [1949] 2 KB 744). A vague right or one which excludes the servient owner from the use of his own land is not, however, acceptable (*Copeland* v *Greenhalf* [1952] Ch 488 and *Grigsby* v *Melville* [1974] 1 WLR 80). Mr Gruyère's right to keep his dustbin in the garden of 2 Trant Way seems to qualify as an easement in this category.

(f) *Right to support*. This right is very important where one is dealing with a semi-detached or terraced house. In such a case the boundary frequently runs down the centre of the connecting wall. Were one owner to remove his half, the remaining portion would probably soon collapse. Accordingly an easement of support is recognised in this, and other similar cases (*Dalton* v *Angus & Co.* (1881) 6 App Cas 740); this right is limited, however, so that whilst the servient owner may not pull his wall down he may let it fall down for lack of repair (*Jones* v *Pritchard* [1908] 1 Ch 630 at p. 637).

(g) *Fencing*. This easement obliges the owner of the servient tenement to maintain a fence between the servient and dominant tenements. This is unusual, because easements do not usually impose expense on the servient tenement. There is no requirement, for example, to make up or maintain a road or track across one's land, and similarly we have just seen that there is no duty to repair a wall which is supporting one's neighbour's house. For this reason, the easement of fencing has been described as a spurious easement, but its existence was recognised by the Court of Appeal in *Crow* v *Wood* [1971] 1 QB 77.

Farmer George's habit of fencing off 14 Trant Way may possibly fall into this category (see also *Egerton* v *Harding* [1975] QB 62).

(h) *Use of facilities*. Common examples include the use of a lavatory (*Miller* v *Emcer Products Ltd* [1956] Ch 304), of a letter-box (*Goldberg* v *Edwards* [1950] Ch 247) or a kitchen (*Haywood* v *Mallalieu* (1883) 25 ChD 357).

The types of easements described above merely provide some examples, and reference should be made to C.J. Gale, *Gale on Easements*, 15th ed. (London: Sweet & Maxwell, 1986), for a fuller list.

Establishing a new easement

If one wishes to establish a claim to a hitherto unknown easement one must first show that the right claimed satisfies the four rules of recognition adopted in *Re Ellenborough Park*. Thereafter it is necessary to satisfy the court that the claim to a new type of easement is justified. This is considerably easier if one can show that the nature of the right claimed in analogous to that of some existing easement. Thus Mr Gruyère might wish to show that his claim to store a dustbin is similar in character to the right to store coal which was accepted in *Wright* v *Macadam* [1949] 2 KB 744. In addition there are certain other rules which should be considered:

(a) The courts will never accept as an easement a right which has the effect of excluding the servient owner from his own use of the land. An easement is by nature a limited right, and if the dominant owner seeks to oust the servient owner he is claiming a right which is considerably greater than that conferred by an easement (see *Grigsby* v *Melville* [1974] 1 WLR 80).

(b) Any interest claimed must be in the nature of a *right*, rather than a permission (in which case it will amount to a licence). Thus in *Burrows* v *Lang* [1901] 2 Ch 502 a claim to an easement to take water from an artificially filled pond was rejected, because exercise of such a right depended on the owner filling the pond and could not be enjoyed without his cooperation. The 'right' was, therefore, too precarious and could not qualify as an easement. In *Green* v *Ashco Horticultural Ltd* [1966] 1 WLR 889 a claim to a right to park a van failed because the claimant had always moved his van when asked to do so by the servient owner and accordingly exercised his right only as far as the servient owner permitted.

(c) Easements may broadly be divided into two categories: positive and negative. In the case of a positive easement the dominant owner must *do* something in order to exercise his right. A right of way is thus positive because the dominant owner must walk, drive or ride on to the servient land in order to exercise his right. A negative easement is a right which is enjoyed without any action by the dominant owner (e.g., a right to light). In *Phipps* v *Pears* [1965] 1 QB 76 it was said that the courts would not readily accept the creation of new *negative* easements, because they have a tendency to restrict the servient tenement owner and hamper development of his property. The court rejected a claim to an easement of protection from the weather, which was argued by analogy with the easement of support, and which, like that easement, would have the effect of preventing one from demolishing one's own property.

(d) Normally the courts will not accept an easement which requires expenditure by the servient owner. Thus in *Regis Property Co. Ltd* v *Redman* [1956] 2 QB 612 it was held that a claim to the supply of hot water was not an easement. The easement of fencing is an exception to this rule. Another exception arose in the case of *Liverpool City Council* v *Irwin* [1977] AC 239. Here, the House of Lords, in construing a very incomplete contract between the tenants of a multi-storey block of flats and their landlords, found, first, implied easements giving the tenants the use of stairs, lifts and rubbish chutes, and then identified a further implied term requiring the landlord to take reasonable care to keep in reasonable repair the common parts over which those easements were exercised. This decision was undoubtedly influenced by considerations of general public policy, but it is important to remember that their lordships were concerned with interpreting the terms of a particular contract and were not laying down rules of general application.

Subject to these general principles the list of easements will continue to expand as circumstances change, and the courts seem happy to see new rights arise as and when they prove to be useful or necessary.

WHAT IS A PROFIT À PRENDRE?

A 'profit à prendre' is a right to take something from land which belongs to another person. The 'something' which is removed may either be part of the land itself (e.g., sand), or something growing on the land (e.g., grass) or wild creatures found naturally on the land (e.g., fish, deer or pheasants). There are a number of traditional forms of profit, although others can still arise.

(a) *The profit of pasture* is an ancient right. It is a profit because the grazing animals take grass and other plants from the land. This cannot exist as a right to graze an unlimited number of animals as this would exhaust the land, and the traditional limit is the maximum number of animals which can be supported through the winter (*Mellor* v *Spateman* (1669) 1 Wms Saund 339). Mr Neep's right to graze his goat would probably be a profit of pasture.
(b) *The profit of piscary* is the right to take fish.
(c) *The profit of turbary* is the right to cut turf or peat, usually in order to burn it.
(d) *The profit of estovers* is the right to take wood for use as fuel or for domestic or agricultural purposes (e.g., to build fences).

Unlike an easement, it is not necessary for a profit to be appurtenant to land. It may exist in gross, in which case it may be exercised for the personal benefit of its owner. Thus a profit of piscary in gross would allow the fisherman to take fish in order to sell them, whilst a profit of piscary appurtenant allows fishing only to the extent of the needs of the land to which the right is attached (e.g., to feed those who reside there). Furthermore, profits may exist to the exclusion of the servient owner, as well as in common with the servient owners or other persons. Thus Mr Gruyère's right to graze his goat may be for the benefit of 14 Trant Way (appurtenant), or for his own benefit (in gross), and may be to the exclusion of Farmer George (sole) or, more probably, a right shared with Farmer George (in common).

EASEMENTS AND PROFITS MAY BE LEGAL OR EQUITABLE

Easements or profits, like other interests in land, may be legal or equitable. In order to constitute legal interests, they must satisfy certain rules concerning the period for which they last and the method by which they are created. The first requirement is derived from LPA 1925, s. 1(2), which defines legal easements and profits as being granted for a period 'equivalent to a fee simple absolute in possession or a term of years absolute'. This means that the easement or profit must last either, in effect, for ever, or for a fixed period. Thus an easement granted 'for 10 years' would be legal, whilst an easement 'for life' cannot be legal because it is not for a period equivalent to a legal estate. Easements which do not satisfy the requirements of s. 1(2) take effect as equitable interests.

The second requirement, concerning the method of creation, is found in the general rule that all legal estates and interests must be created by deed (LPA 1925, s. 52(1)). If no deed is used, the purported grant is ineffective in law but equity may construe the arrangement as a specifically enforceable contract to grant an easement or profit, and treat that right as being in existence from the date of the contract. There is one apparent exception to the requirement for a deed for the creation of legal easements and profits. As we shall see, these rights can be acquired, without any formal grant, by 'prescription'; that is, by use over a long period of time (see p. 299). No deed is in fact used in such a case, but, with only one exception, the various methods of prescription are all based on the fiction that a grant has been made in proper form, so that in this method, too, legal interests are created by deed—even if only by a fictitious one!

Whether an easement or profit is legal or equitable is of great importance when one comes to enforce it against someone who has bought the servient tenement. We have already dealt in some detail with the enforcement of third-party rights against purchasers and so we will do no more than remind you of the relevant rules. In the case of registered land a legal easement or profit is an overriding interest under LRA 1925, s. 70(1)(a), and accordingly will be automatically binding upon a purchaser. Generally an equitable easement or profit will be a minor interest and should be protected by entry on the register by way of notice or caution. You should, however, note that in the case of *Celsteel Ltd* v *Alton Holdings Ltd* [1985] 1 WLR 204 the Court of Appeal accepted that an openly enjoyed equitable easement could be an overriding interest due to the operation of r. 258 of the Land Registration Rules 1925. In the unregistered system, a legal easement is enforceable against any purchaser, under the principle that legal rights bind the whole world. Equitable easements in unregistered land are registrable as land charges if created on or after 1 January 1926 (LCA 1972, s. 2), though some passages in *E.R. Ives Investment Ltd* v *High* [1967] 2 QB 379 suggest that some equitable easements may be binding without registration but this point has not been further developed. Equitable easements and profits in relation to unregistered land and which were created before 1926 are subject to the old equitable rules of notice.

METHOD OF ACQUISITION

Express grant or reservation

The story of the installation of the drains of 15 Trant Way (see p. 283) shows that an easement or profit can arise by agreement between two owners who already hold separate properties. In such a case, the owner of the land which is to become the servient tenement executes a deed granting the easement to his neighbour.

Very often, however, easements or profits are created when land is divided on sale. The vendor may sell only part of his land, keeping the rest for himself (as happened with 16 and 16A Trant Way), and he and the purchaser may each want to enjoy rights over the other's property. Where the purchaser is to be given easements or profits, they are granted by deed, usually by the same deed which conveys the legal estate to him. Where the vendor wishes to retain certain rights over the land he is selling, he must 'reserve' those rights in the conveyance. The purchaser takes his rights by express grant, while the vendor obtains his by express reservation.

The reservation of an easement requires care because the document will be construed strictly against the vendor/grantor (*Cordell* v *Second Clanfield Properties Ltd* [1969] 2 Ch 9).

Implied grant or reservation

In certain cases in which a conveyance of land makes no mention of the grant or reservation of an easement or profit, it may be possible to say that one arises by implication. As we shall see, it is easier to establish an implied grant, in favour of the purchaser, than it is to set up an implied reservation on behalf of the vendor.

Implied grant

Traditionally, it has been said that easements, and in some cases profits, arise by implied grant as follows:

(a) easements of necessity;
(b) intended easements and profits;
(c) easements under the rule in *Wheeldon* v *Burrows*.

However, recent case law (*Nickerson* v *Barraclough* [1981] Ch 426) suggests that the first two of these are not really separate categories, and that easements of necessity are really a form of intended easement.

Easements of necessity An easement of necessity is an easement which is so essential to the enjoyment of the land that the land cannot be used without the easement. It used to be said that such easements would be implied into a transaction because to hold otherwise would be to allow the grantor to derogate from his grant. The classic example of such an easement arises in the case of 'the land-locked close'. This is land which, like 16A Trant Way, is totally inaccessible, unless an easement to permit access is implied into the conveyance or transfer. On this basis an easement of way would have been implied in the conveyance of 16A Trant Way by Marjorie Marjoram to Basil Borage, as otherwise Mr Borage would have acquired a useless estate. In *Nickerson* v *Barraclough* [1981] Ch 426, however, which did involve land-locked land, it was held that this method of acquisition also depended upon the intentions of the parties. Thus an easement of necessity could not be implied where the original vendor had expressly stated that no right of access was being granted. (For a useful plan which assists the understanding of this case see (1980) 130 NLJ 204.)

The overlap between necessity and intention can be illustrated by the older case of *Wong* v *Beaumont Property Trust Ltd* [1965] 1 QB 173, in which basement premises had been let upon the express understanding that the property was to be used as a restaurant. Later, after assignment by the original tenant, the assignee was required to improve ventilation if the restaurant business were to continue. The assignee claimed an implied easement for passage of air through a duct to be constructed on the landlord's property, and was successful on the ground that this was necessary if the contemplated use of the premises were to continue. On the facts, one can see that the case might have been similarly decided by implying that the parties *intended* all rights which permitted the use of the premises as a restaurant. Another important case in this area of the law is *Liverpool City Council* v *Irwin* [1977] AC 239 in which easements were implied giving the right to use rubbish chutes, stairs and lifts in a multi-storey block of flats. In addition the grant of a flat was held to include an implied right to have the facilities maintained in a reasonable state of repair. Again, is this a matter of intention or is it that a lessee cannot make any real use of a flat at the top of a tall block unless there is a lift, kept in working order?

Intended easement and profits   As we have seen above, it may be that rights which are necessary for the use of the land are to be presumed to be within the intention of the parties unless expressly excluded. This second category, however, includes more than easements of necessity, for under this heading a grantee may claim a profit or any easement, even though *not* necessary to the enjoyment of the property, provided he can show that both parties intended to grant it. An example of this is found in *Cory* v *Davies* [1923] 2 Ch 95, where a row of terraced houses had been built with a drive in front and an exit to the road at each end. One of the owners barred the exit at his end of the terrace, requiring all traffic to go the other way. There was no express grant of an easement in favour of all the house owners over all parts of the drive, but the court found that the original parties had a common intention that the drive should be used in this way, and thus an intended easement was implied.

Stafford v *Lee, The Times*, 10 November 1992, is a recent case which shows how the question of the intention of the parties was addressed in a case of 'land-locked' land and which therefore might properly appear to fall into the area of easements of necessity. Here the defendant's predecessor in title had conveyed an area of woodland and a pond to the plaintiff's predecessors.

The land fronted a drive but no right of way over the drive to the nearby highway was conferred. The plaintiffs wished to build a house on part of the land but the defendants said that there could be no right of way over the drive for residential purposes (including construction work). The Court accepted that it was appropriate to infer an easement to give effect to the intentions of the original parties but indicated that this could only be done in cases in which the parties intended that the dominant land should be used in some definite and particular manner. In this case because the plan on the relevant conveyance showed other neighbouring buildings the Court was ready to infer that the woodland would be used for similar purposes. Accordingly the claim to an easement for domestic purposes succeeded.

The rule in Wheeldon v Burrows   In order to understand this rule, it is necessary to remind ourselves about quasi-easements (see p. 287). Although a landowner may derive benefit from one piece of his own land in favour of another, he cannot be said to have an easement, because there are no separate tenements. For example, if he enjoys the uninterrupted passage of light over his garden to his windows, he cannot say he has an easement of light, although, if the garden were in separate ownership he might very well have such a right. This situation is sometimes described as giving rise to a quasi-easement.

The rule in *Wheeldon v Burrows* (1879) 12 ChD 31 provides that if, in such a situation, the owner sells that part of his land which is benefited (e.g., the house) and retains the land which is burdened (e.g., the garden), the purchaser may acquire an easement over the land retained by the vendor. Thus, in the example given above, the quasi-easement would become a true easement of light.

In *Wheeldon v Burrows*, Thesiger LJ stated the principle as follows (at p.49):

[O]n the grant by the owner of a tenement of part of that tenement as it is then used and enjoyed, there will pass to the grantee all those continuous and apparent easements (by which, of course, I mean *quasi* easements), or, in other words, all those easements which are necessary to the reasonable enjoyment of the property granted, and which have been and are at the time of the grant used by the owners of the entirety for the benefit of the part granted.

There seem to be three elements of this rule, for the quasi-easement must be:

(a)   'continuous and apparent';
(b)   'necessary to the reasonable enjoyment' of the land sold; and
(c)   in use at the time of the sale.

If all three requirements are satisfied then a grant of a legal easement is implied into the conveyance or transfer of the portion of the land which is sold. In *Wheeldon v Burrows* itself, requirements (a) and (b) appear to have been regarded as alternatives. It was suggested in *Ward v Kirkland* [1967] Ch 194 at p. 224, by Ungoed-Thomas J, that requirement (a) applied to positive easements (e.g., a right of way) and requirement (b) applied to negative easements (e.g., a right to light). The best view appears to be that (a) and (b) are alternatives, though in a number of cases the court appears to have discovered both.

The words 'continuous and apparent' have sometimes been construed widely, so that a right of way which can be in regular but hardly 'continuous' use, has been held to satisfy the test (*Borman v Griffith* [1930] 1 Ch 493 at p. 499). The requirement that the right be 'apparent' arises because this rule is based on the principle of non-derogation from grant. On inspecting the land a purchaser may see visible signs of a quasi-easement and assume that he will obtain the benefit of the right. In the case of 16A Trant Way, if there was a house on the property when Mr Borage bought it and a driveway across 16 leading to it, the driveway would render apparent the quasi-easement being used by the vendor. The requirement that an easement should be 'necessary for the reasonable enjoyment of the land' does *not* produce a test as strict as that for easements of necessity. All that is needed for *Wheeldon v Burrows* is that the right claimed should facilitate the reasonable enjoyment of the property.

Implied reservation
In general the courts will not readily accept a claim to the acquisition of an easement or profit by implied reservation because of the rule that documents are to be construed strictly against the grantor. This is because it is presumed that the grantor is in a position of strength and is able to reserve any rights which he chooses to retain. Should he fail to reserve these rights he has only himself (or his conveyancer) to blame. Moreover, it can be said that an implied reservation derogates from the grant, for the grantor has apparently given the grantee an unencumbered estate and is then trying to burden it with an easement or profit.

However, there are a few cases in which easements or profits may be claimed by implied reservation, and the rules relating to easements of necessity and intended easements or profits can apply to reservations as well as to grants. Thus an easement giving a right of access to landlocked land may be acquired by implied reservation (*Pinnington v Galland* (1853) 9 Exch 1) as may an easement of support (*Richards v Rose* (1853) 9 Exch 218).

There is, however, no possibility of an implied reservation under the rule in *Wheeldon v Burrows*, for the court in that case rejected the vendor's claim to an easement over the land he had sold. (It is interesting to note that the rule which takes its name from this case is in fact derived from *obiter dicta*, for the court was not dealing with any question about implied grant.)

Express grant by virtue of LPA 1925, s. 62

LPA 1925, s. 62(1), provides that:

A conveyance of land shall be deemed to include and shall . . . operate to convey, with the land, all buildings, erections, fixtures, commons, hedges, ditches, . . . liberties, privileges, easements, rights, and advantages whatsoever, appertaining . . . to the land, . . . or, at the time of conveyance, . . . enjoyed with . . . the land.

At first reading the subsection appears to be nothing more than a word-saving provision, designed to make it clear that on the conveyance of an estate in land the grantee obtains the benefit of houses, fences and other things upon the land and any rights, interests and privileges existing for the benefit of the estate, without any express mention of them being made in the conveyance. However, the section has been interpreted in such a way that it is capable of creating new legal easements and profits in favour of a purchaser, as well as transferring those which already exist.

An examination of the case of *Wright* v *Macadam* [1949] 2 KB 744 illustrates how this may occur. While in possession as a protected tenant under the Rent Acts, Mrs Wright was given permission by her landlord, Mr Macadam, to store coal in a garden shed, which was retained by the landlord. Later a fresh lease of one year was made (by an unsealed document in accordance with LPA 1925, s. 54(2)) which did not refer to the shed. After some time, Mr Macadam tried to charge for the use of the shed and Mrs Wright refused to pay, claiming that she had an easement of storage. It was held, by the Court of Appeal, that the creation of the fresh lease was a 'conveyance' within the meaning of LPA 1925 and that it operated to grant Mrs Wright a legal easement of storage. Thus, by virtue of s. 62, a conveyance can convert a pre-existing licence into a legal easement. A further example is found in *Goldberg* v *Edwards* [1950] Ch 247, where a permissive use (licence) of an alternative route of access was regarded as becoming a legal easement on the grant of a lease. It is not easy to see why s. 62 should have this effect, for the words of the section would suggest that the licence should pass as a licence, rather than changing into a legal right. However, this interpretation was first adopted in 19th-century decisions on similar provisions in earlier statutes, and it is now well accepted.

If we now consider the situation of Mr Forest and Mr Gruyère at 2 Trant Way, it appears that Mr Gruyère has acquired the legal easement of storing his dustbin in the garden by virtue of s. 62. The right to store is capable of being an easement and the creation of a legal lease (even in the absence of a deed) provides the necessary 'conveyance' for the operation of s. 62. In order to prevent such a development, a landlord who is granting a fresh lease should either revoke any licences he has previously given, or include a term in the lease which will exclude the operation of s. 62.

In both the cases we have mentioned so far the two properties were in separate occupation before the date of the relevant conveyance, and the owner had given a permissive right to the occupier of the dominant land. What if the land had been previously owned and occupied by the same person (as was the case, for example, with 16 and 16A Trant Way)? In *Long* v *Gowlett* [1923] 2 Ch 177 it was said that in such a case there was no 'privilege, easement or advantage' being exercised at the date of such a conveyance, for the owner-occupier of both plots could not be exercising rights against himself. In such a case there are no rights which can mature into easements on the conveyance. This view is confirmed by *obiter dicta* of Lord Wilberforce in *Sovmots*

Investments Ltd v *Secretary of State for the Environment* [1979] AC 144, in which his Lordship said (at p. 169):

The reason is that when land is under one ownership one cannot speak in any intelligible sense of rights, or privileges, or easements being exercised over one part for the benefit of another. Whatever the owner does, he does as owner and, until a separation occurs, of ownership or at least of occupation, the condition for the existence of rights, etc., does not exist.

(But see the articles by Jackson (1966) 30 Conv (NS) 342, and Smith [1978] Conv 499.)

Profits, as well as easements, may be acquired by the s. 62 method, where a right capable of amounting to a profit has been given and thereafter a conveyance satisfying s. 62 has been made (*White* v *Williams* [1922] 1 KB 727 (grazing sheep)).

Since s. 62 operates by importing certain words into the conveyance, it has the effect of making an *express*, not implied, grant of the easement or profit (*Gregg* v *Richards* [1926] Ch 521). The fact that the section works through a conveyance in this way means that it is subject to a number of limitations. For example, it will not operate on a contract to convey or create a legal estate, for this does not constitute a conveyance (*Re Peck's Contract* [1893] 2 Ch 315) (we have already mentioned (see p. 104) that this is one way in which a contract for a lease is not as good as a lease). Nor can it convert into an easement or profit a right which does not satisfy the tests for such rights (*Phipps* v *Pears* [1965] 1 QB 76 (claim to easement of protection from weather)). It is also probable that a short lease granted informally under LPA 1925, s. 54(2) will only amount to a conveyance for these purposes if there is a document making the grant. Although an oral lease will be legal under s. 54(2) if it is for not more than 3 years, in *Rye* v *Rye* [1962] AC 496 it was held that the definition of conveyance in LPA 1925, s. 205 requires there to be an instrument. This case was in fact a decision in relation to LPA 1925, s. 71 but there is no reason why the same reasoning should not apply to cases under s. 62, so that the wording of this section would be taken to cover only those grants made by some form of document. A claim under s. 62 will also fail where the express words of the conveyance manifest a contrary intention.

Comparison of the rule in *Wheeldon* v *Burrows* and LPA 1925, s. 62

Space does not permit us to make a detailed comparison, and indeed it will be more useful to you to make this for yourself, but we will indicate briefly the main differences:

(a) *Wheeldon* v *Burrows* relates only to easements, whilst s. 62 applies to both easements and profits.

(b) *Wheeldon* v *Burrows* operates where, before the conveyance, the two pieces of land have been occupied by the same person, whereas diversity of occupation is required for s. 62. This distinction is not one which, however, can be given without the warning that not all writers upon land law are agreed that s. 62 can only apply when before the date of the relevant conveyance the two plots of land were at least in separate occupation. Indeed the leading texts on this area of the law dispute this view (see Jackson, *The Law of Easements and Profits* (1978), p. 100 and Gale, *Easements*, 15th ed. p. 140). Accordingly the matter should not be regarded as settled. However, support for the view that s. 62 only applies where there has been diversity of occupation can be found in *Long* v *Gowlett* [1923] 2 Ch 177; *Ward* v *Kirkland* [1967] Ch 194, 228, and in the decision of the House of Lords in *Sovmots Investments Ltd* v *Secretary of State for the Environment* [1979] AC 144, in which this view was expressly stated (by Lord Wilberforce at p. 169 and by Lord Edmund-Davies at p. 176). Obviously an express statement of this type cannot be ignored but Jackson points out that the remarks in *Sovmots* are no more than *obiter dicta* and were made without full consideration of the authorities. A number of cases do suggest that diversity of occupation is not essential (*James* v *Plant* (1836) 4 A & E 749; *Barkshire* v *Grubb* (1881) 18 ChD 616; *Broomfield* v *Williams* [1897] 1 Ch 602 and *Wright* v *Macadam* [1949] 2 KB 744, 748. For the moment it is, however, likely that lower courts will follow the *dicta* in *Sovmots*, though until there is further authority the matter remains subject to some doubt.

(c) The types of easements which can pass under *Wheeldon* v *Burrows* are restricted by the three requirements of the rule, whereas there are no such restrictions in the case of s. 62.

(d) *Wheeldon* v *Burrows*, unlike s. 62, is apparently not limited to conveyances. Thus it seems that a contract to grant a lease may be sufficient to create an easement in favour of the tenant under *Wheeldon* v *Burrows* (*Borman* v *Griffith* [1930] 1 Ch 493).

Acquisition by prescription

Both easements and profits may be acquired as the result of long use, as well as by the means of grant and reservation described above. This method of acquisition is called 'prescription', of which there are three forms:

(a) common law prescription;
(b) the fiction of lost modern grant; and
(c) under the Prescription Act 1832.

All these types of prescription will give the acquirer a legal easement or legal profit, even though there has in fact been no grant by deed. With the exception of one of the forms of prescription under the Act, all these methods are based on the fiction that such a grant has been made at some time in the past, and long use is regarded merely as evidence of that grant. Some of the rules about prescription which may seem strange will be more easily understood if you remember that they are designed to maintain this pretence.

There are three basic rules which apply to all the methods of prescription and we will discuss these first and then consider each of the three forms of prescription in turn.

Use must be as of right
It is essential for the claimant to establish that, throughout the period of use, he has enjoyed the right he claims 'as of right'. His use (and that of his predecessors in title, if relevant) must be consistent with the fiction that the right was granted at some time in the past, and that he has been acting in reliance on this. Any inconsistent behaviour will be taken to show that he does not have such a right. It appears that it is irrelevant that the claimant of the easement has been exercising the right in the mistaken belief that it has in fact been granted to him (*Bridle* v *Ruby* [1988] 3 WLR 191). It is said that the use must be *nec vi, nec clam, nec precario.*

Nec vi   This means that the right claimed must not have been exercised by force. Thus if Farmer George were to have erected a gate blocking access to the footpath on his land, Mr Neep would be using the path by force if he broke down the gate, or even if he simply climbed over it. Even a protest by the servient owner can prevent user as of right, for ignoring a protest is regarded as use by force (*Eaton* v *Swansea Waterworks Co.* (1851) 17 QB 267). This rule prevents people obtaining interests in land by use of 'strong-arm' tactics.

Nec clam   The right must not be exercised secretly, for such use prevents the servient owner from objecting to the acquisition of the right and appears inconsistent with a claim of right. In *Liverpool Corporation* v *Coghill & Sons Ltd* [1918] 1 Ch 307 a claim to an easement of drainage was unsuccessful because the claimant's drain had entered the general sewer below ground and it was impossible for the corporation to ascertain that one more load of effluent had been added to its general burden. Thus if Mr Neep had used the farmer's path only at dead of night and in a manner designed to conceal his use, he would be regarded as not having exercised an easement of way as of right.

Nec precario   This means that the right must not be enjoyed precariously, i.e., by permission. If the servient owner has given the claimant permission, the right is a licence and not an easement or profit and (unless contractual, or binding due to an estoppel) is revocable at the will of the licensor. Thus if Farmer George has given Mr Neep permission to use the path, the use is not made 'as of right'. Of course, if permission was given very far in the past it may be deemed to have lapsed in time, so that the more recent use may be regarded as not being by permission (*Arkwright* v *Gell* (1839) 5 M & W 203).

The right must be acquired by a fee simple owner against a fee simple owner
Again, this rule originates in the pretence that the right has been properly granted at some time in the past, for the only way to explain its continuance is that it was granted in fee simple, rather than for a limited period of years. This implies a grant by a fee simple owner to a fee simple owner. Thus, even if the use in question is by a tenant, any easement or profit acquired as a result will attach to the fee simple in the dominant land, rather than

to the tenant's lease (though of course the tenant will still have an interest in claiming). As a result, it is never possible for a tenant of dominant land to acquire rights by prescription against his own landlord (*Gayford* v *Moffat* (1868) LR 4 Ch App 133), for such a tenant can only claim to acquire an easement on behalf of the landlord, and the landlord cannot have rights against himself (*Ivimey* v *Stocker* (1866) LR 1 Ch App 396). It is emphasised that what we are saying is only that a tenant cannot acquire easements against his landlord by *prescription*, for we have already seen that he may acquire such rights by express or implied grant. Similarly it was held in *Simmons* v *Dobson* [1991] 4 All ER 25 that a tenant could not obtain by prescription against another tenant of the same landlord (see also on this point *Wheaton* v *Maple* [1893] 3 Ch 48 and *Kilgour* v *Gaddes* [1904] 1 KB 457).

Where an easement is acquired by prescription it binds the fee simple estate in the servient land. If that land is let to a tenant during the prescription period it seems unfair to allow the dominant owner to claim the acquisition of an easement or profit by prescription. The tenant on the servient land may well not be concerned about the exercise of the right, whilst the fee simple owner may not be aware of the user since he has given exclusive possession of the land to his tenant. It is therefore the rule that there should be no tenancy of the servient land at the start of the prescription period. If, however, the fee simple owner is in possession when the use begins, he has the opportunity to discover what has happened and can make enquiries of his tenant in order to ascertain whether the use is continuing. Thus in *Pugh* v *Savage* [1970] 2 QB 373 an easement was acquired by prescription even though the servient land had been let for 10 years in the middle of the prescription period. If, however, the land is let when the use began, the prescription period will only start when the fee simple owner re-enters (*Daniel* v *North* (1809) 11 East 372).

The use must be continuous

The infrequent use of a right is not sufficient if one is claiming an easement or profit by prescription. Thus if Mr Neep had used Farmer George's path on only three occasions in the last 12 years this would not support a claim to an easement by prescription (see *Hollins* v *Verney* (1884) 13 QBD 304). As we have mentioned previously, the exercise of a right of way can never be continuous in a literal sense, but in such cases regular usage will suffice. Also the right exercised should not generally be varied during the period for prescription, although in the case of *Davis* v *Whitby* [1974] Ch 186 it was regarded as acceptable if a minor variation was made for the sake of convenience (here the alteration was to the exact path used in the case of a right of way).

Prescription at common law

In order to establish a claim to an easement or profit by prescription at common law, it is necessary to establish that the interest has been enjoyed, as of right, since *time immemorial* or, to use the traditional phrase, 'from time whereof the memory of man runneth not to the contrary'. Under the Statute of Westminster, the First (1275), c. 39, the date of legal memory is 1189, and so this method of prescription requires that the right in question was in existence before that date.

The reader will appreciate that it is practically impossible to establish positively such a long period of use. Accordingly the rule has developed that proof of use during living memory will raise a presumption that the right has been enjoyed since 1189. Originally user during living memory was established by asking the oldest inhabitants of the area whether the right had been exercised as long as they recalled. Today all that is needed is evidence that the right has been used for at least 20 years (*Darling* v *Clue* (1864) 4 F & F 329).

However, the presumption raised by the 20-year use is a rebuttable presumption, and the claim to prescription at common law can be destroyed by evidence which shows that the right claimed must have begun later than 1189. Thus if the claim were to an easement of light, proof that the building on the dominant tenement had been built after 1189 would destroy the claim at common law (*Bury* v *Pope* (1588) Cro Eliz 118). Similarly, if the dominant and servient tenements have been in common ownership at any time since 1189 this claim at common law will fail. Even if the right had been granted before 1189, it would have come to an end when the two pieces of land came into the same hands (see p. 310), and any grant when they separated again would be after the date of legal memory (*Keymer* v *Summers* (1769) Bull NP 74). Thus, were Nigel Neep to claim his right to use the footpath on Farmer George's land by common law prescription, he would be able to raise the presumption of use since 1189 if he and his predecessors in title had used the path for 20 years, but his claim would easily be defeated if Farmer George could prove that 14 Trant Way and Fieldy Farm were once owned by one person (which is very likely to be the case). As a result claims by prescription under the pure common law rule are rarely successful today, although, as we shall see, some assistance is provided by the Prescription Act 1832.

Lost modern grant

Because it was so difficult to obtain an easement or profit under the general common law rules, the courts eventually developed a second method of prescription at common law known as the fiction of the lost modern grant. This requires that the claimant should first establish user during living memory (for at least 20 years). Once this has been established the court is prepared to presume that the right is being exercised as the result of a modern grant by deed, *but that the grant has been lost*. This is recognised as a complete fiction (see *Dalton* v *Angus & Co.* (1881) 6 App Cas 740). It appears that the presumption cannot be rebutted by proving that no grant *has* been made but it will destroy the claim if the servient owner can show that, at the date at which it is alleged the grant occurred, there was no person capable of making the grant (for example, because the land was subject to a strict settlement, under which no grant could be made). Similarly the claim may be opposed by showing that at the relevant time the dominant and servient tenements were in common ownership (see *Neaverson v Peterborough Rural District Council* [1902] 1 Ch 557).

This method of prescription, based on a blatant fiction, was disliked in the 19th century, and it was hoped that the changes introduced by the Prescription Act 1832 would make it unnecessary to use it. However, as we shall see, this Act has proved to be most unsatisfactory, and so the method of the lost modern grant is still in use today (see p. 308).

The extent of the fiction is well illustrated by *Bridle v Ruby* [1988] 3 WLR 191. There a developer built and sold a number of houses. Originally it was intended that the purchaser of plot 12 was to be granted an express right of way over a drive. In fact the relevant clause was deleted from the conveyance so that the grant of the right was never made. The purchaser and his successors, in the mistaken belief that they had the right to do so, used the driveway for 22 years. Here the Court of Appeal held that the right could be claimed on the basis of lost modern grant. The fact that the relevant clause had been deleted from the original conveyance did not prevent the operation of the theory that at a later date a grant had been made. It was even irrelevant that the owners of plot 12 had used the right believing that the right to do so arose from the original conveyance. This case clearly demonstrates that the legal fiction is alive and well today. For a further illustration see *Mills v Silver* [1991] Ch 271, in which the Court of Appeal considered at length the issue of permission in relation to the doctrine of lost modern grant. The usual common law rules apply to lost modern grant, thus for example it applies only by a fee simple owner against a fee simple owner (see *Simmons v Dobson* [1991] 4 All ER 25).

Prescription Act 1832

The Prescription Act 1832 may very well have the dubious honour of being the worst drafted Act of Parliament on the statute book. Indeed it is even generally presumed that there is a misprint in s. 8 of the Act and lawyers have accordingly adopted the habit of reading the section as though the misprint did not exist (thereby substituting the word 'easement' for the word 'convenient' where it appears in s. 8). The Act was intended to remove the difficulties which arose with the common law forms of prescription; however, it did not abolish them, so that the three forms now exist alongside one another, and the Act has introduced fresh complexities of its own.

The Act divides the easement of light from all other easements and profits and deals with it separately. Furthermore it creates two different prescription periods (a 'short period' and a 'long period'), with different effects, for profits and easements other than light. The provisions relating to the short period merely assist a person claiming under the common law rules, but those relating to the long period do introduce a form of statutory prescription which does not depend on any fiction.

Profits and easements other than light under the Prescription Act 1832

Short period
The short period for easements is 20 years (Prescription Act 1832, s. 2), and for profits is 30 years (s. 1). The Act provides that, where use can be shown for the appropriate period, no claim to prescription at common law shall be defeated by showing that the right 'was first enjoyed at any time prior to such period'. The effect of this provision is quite simple, but understanding why the statutory words have this effect is not so easy. The explanation is as follows. Legal memory does not go back before 1189, so, if the right was first enjoyed before that date, it would not be possible to show when it started. Thus the fact that one *can* show when it started means that that beginning must be *after* 1189, which would be fatal to a claim at common law. Therefore the Act is saying, in a roundabout way, that once the period had been completed, common law prescription cannot be defeated merely by showing that the use began after 1189. The claim can still be defeated in any other way that would defeat common law prescription, such as showing that the use is not as of right, or that the right claimed lacks the characteristics of an easement or profit. Accordingly, if permission has been given, orally or in writing, at any time, this will prevent a claim under the short period because the right would have been exercised precariously. (If the permission were of considerable antiquity it may be disregarded as lapsed, particularly if it is oral: see p. 300.) In much the same way in *Diment* v *Foot Ltd* [1974] 1 WLR 1427 a claim to an easement of way based on 36 years use failed because the use was not known to the servient owners (*'clam'*). A similar result was caused by secret use in *Union Lighterage Co.* v *London Graving Dock Co.* [1902] 2 Ch 557, in which the claimed easement of support was being exercised secretly, below water level.

Deductions
In order to provide some protection for a servient owner who is subject to a legal disability, s. 7 of the Act provides that certain periods should be deducted when one computes the 20 or 30-year short period. The effect of these provisions, as modified by later reforms of the law, is that one should deduct any period during which the servient owner was:

(a)   an infant;
(b)   a patient under the Mental Health Act 1983 (or the Acts which preceded it); or
(c)   a tenant for life.

Thus if Nigel Neep had exercised his right of way for 35 years but for 20 of those years the owner of Fieldy Farm had been insane (e.g., Farmer George's father had become senile for 20 years before his death) Mr Neep can only claim 15 years of user for the purposes of the short period. He can, however, add together the use before the old man's senility overcame him and the use after Farmer George inherited on his father's death. He does *not* have to restart the period once the disability is removed (*Pugh* v *Savage* [1970] 2 QB 373).

Long period
The long period is 40 years for easements (s. 2) and 60 years for profits (s. 1). The benefit of proving use for the longer period is that the right claimed 'shall be deemed absolute and indefeasible, unless it shall appear that the same was enjoyed by some consent or agreement expressly given or made for the purpose by deed or writing'. This is the statutory form of prescription, and does not depend on the common law rules, nor on any fiction.

Consents
It is clear from the statutory provisions we have quoted that written consent can destroy a claim under the long period, whether it was given before the period started or during the period. At first reading this may seem to imply that purely oral permission cannot destroy the claim. However, this is not the case for it is still necessary for the dominant owner to show that his use of the easement or profit during the 40 or 60-year period has amounted to use as of right. As we have seen already (p. 300), if the servient owner has given oral permission the use is precarious and *not* as of right. Accordingly oral permission given *during* the long period will destroy the claim but oral permission given *before* the period can be ignored.

Does the use have to start against a fee simple owner?
As we have said (p. 300), at common law the prescription period could not start at a time when the servient land was let to a tenant. In *Davies* v *Du Paver* [1953] 1 QB 184 the Court of Appeal appeared to apply the same rule to a case brought under the Prescription Act 1832. However, in the earlier case of *Wright* v *Williams* (1836) 1 M & W 77 (which was not cited in *Davies* v *Du Paver*) it was held that the common law rule did not apply because of the positive wording of the Act. It would appear that the better view is that the rule *does not* apply, particularly as in s. 8 special provision is made for deduction of periods during which the servient land is subject to a lease (see Megarry (1956) 72 LQR 32).

Deductions
Deductions from the long period are governed by s. 8. It should be noted that these rules bear no real relation to the deduction from the short period prescribed by s. 7. Assuming that the word 'convenient' in s. 8 is a misprint for 'easement', s. 8 provides for the deductions from the long period of any term during which the servient land was:

(a)   held by a tenant for life;
(b)   held by a tenant under a lease for more than three years.

However, the s. 8 deductions may only be made if the servient owner resists the claim to acquisition by prescription within the three years following the end of the life interest or lease. The following example may make this clearer:

1 January 1954	The then owner of 14 Trant Way started to use the footpath on Fieldy Farm.
1 January 1982	Lease of Fieldy farm for 10 years granted.
31 December 1991	Lease ends.
31 December 1993	49 years' use of right of way.

In this example if Mr Neep claims under the longer period on 1 January 1994, Farmer George would be able to claim a deduction from the period of use, under s. 8. For in these circumstances the servient tenement, Fieldy Farm, would have been subject to a lease for more than three years (10 years) and that lease would have ended less than three years before the date of the action. (Action started on 1 January 1994 and lease ended two years earlier on 31 December 1991). If, however, the use continues, but no case is brought to court until 1995, more than three years will have elapsed since the end of the lease, and Farmer George will accordingly not be entitled to make any deduction. Thus if a matter comes to court in 1994 Nigel Neep will only have a claim based on 30 years' user (40 years' actual use, less 10 years during which the servient land was let), whilst if the case is started in 1995 Nigel Neep can claim 41 years' use (no deduction is permitted). This result may seem odd at first sight but one should remember that the purpose of s. 8 is to provide limited protection for the reversioner who takes action swiftly on recovering the land. This may be particularly important to the freehold reversioner or a remainderman, following on after a tenant for life, who should accordingly make immediate enquiries about such matters as soon as his interest vests in possession.

Rules common to both short and long periods
Certain rules are common to both the long and the short periods.

User as of right   We have already seen that the Prescription Act 1832 does not exclude the common law requirement that the user relied upon must be as of right during the period claimed, and this has been held to mean not only that the use should be *nec vi, nec clam* and *nec precario*, but also that use must be by and against fee simple owners (*Kilgour* v *Gaddes* [1904] 1 KB 457).

Period must be 'next before some suit or action'   Under s. 4 the period relied upon must be 'next before some suit or action wherein the claim or matter to which such period may relate shall have been or shall be brought into question'. Thus a period of use which ceased some time before the commencement of an action cannot be relied upon for the purpose of statutory prescription, although it may be effective to support a claim to prescription at common law. Thus in *Tehidy Minerals Ltd* v *Norman* [1971] 2 QB 528 claims based upon user which had ceased in 1941 (when the land was requisitioned by the army) were ineffective under the Act, although some claimants succeeded in establishing their rights under the principle of lost modern grant (see also *Mills* v *Silver* Ch 271). Another effect of s. 4 is that no right to the easement or profit can exist under the statutory rules until some action is started, regardless of the length of use involved (*Hyman* v *Van den Bergh* [1908] 1 Ch 167). Of course, in order to secure his interest in the land, the dominant owner has only to apply to the court for a declaration that an easement or profit has been secured under the Act.

There must have been no interruption   A claim based on either period may be destroyed by proof that there has been some 'interruption' to the claimed interest and that the dominant owner has acquiesced in that interruption for the period of one year. An 'interruption' is any action which interferes with the right claimed. In the case of the footpath on Fieldy Farm, Farmer George could create an interruption by erecting a gate, or other barrier, preventing access to the path. Thus in *Davies* v *Du Paver* [1953] 1 QB 184, the servient owner erected a fence in order to exclude the dominant owner's sheep and thereby to prevent the acquisition of a profit. This case illustrates, however, that there must not only be an obstruction but that the obstruction must be *acquiesced in* for one year by the claimant. In *Davies* v *Du Paver* the dominant owner immediately protested at the erection of the fence, but did not issue proceedings to establish his claim to a profit until 13 months later. The Court of Appeal found that he had not acquiesced in the interruption for one year because his initial protest must have been effective for some period (at least a month) in which case at the start of the action there had been less than one year's acquiescence. However, mere discontent which is not sufficiently communicated cannot amount to sufficient action to indicate a lack of acquiescence (*Dance* v *Triplow* [1992] 17 EGLR 103).

As a result of this provision about acquiescence, it is not possible to rely on an interruption to prevent the claimant succeeding under the Act once 19 years and 1 day have passed with respect to the short period (29 years and 1 day for profits) and 39 years and 1 day (59 years and 1 day for profits) for the long period. For, if an interruption were made, for example, to an easement after it had been used for 39 years and 1 day, the dominant owner could still issue proceedings 364 days later, as soon as the 40-year term is up, and claim that he had not acquiesced in the interruption for a year. By protesting at the interruption, he can extend the time still further. Thus, once usage has entered the last year of one of the periods, the only safe way for the servient tenement owner to act is to commence proceedings immediately for trespass, for until the period is completed his opponent will not be able to rely on the existence of an easement or profit by prescription by way of defence.

Right to light under the Prescription Act 1832

The right to light is dealt with by the Prescription Act 1832 in a way different from its treatment of all other easements. There is only one period (not a 'short' and a 'long' period) and that requires user for a period of 20 years. Section 3 of the Act provides that if the 'use of light' to 'any dwelling-house', workshop, or other building' has been 'actually enjoyed . . . for the full period of 20 years without interruption, the right thereto shall be deemed absolute and indefeasible'. There are a number of differences between this provision and those relating to other easements and profits. In particular s. 3 does not require the satisfaction of the common law requirements for prescription. Accordingly the use need not be as of right, nor is it necessary for the use to be by a fee simple owner against a fee simple owner. Accordingly, a tenant can acquire an easement of light by prescription against his landlord, or against a fellow tenant holding from the same landlord.

The rules on interruption, however, *do* apply to easements of light in the same way as they apply to other rights claimed under the Act, and it has also been held that the 20-year period relied on must be next before suit or action, even though s. 3 does not specifically mention this (*Hyman* v *Van den Bergh* [1908] 1 Ch 167).

It can be seen that it is far easier to acquire an easement of light than any other easement or profit. Accordingly a 'servient' owner may well wish to take action to prevent his neighbour acquiring such a right. Unfortunately, in order to do this he would need to interrupt the use of the right and the erection of some structure (e.g., a hoarding) in order to do this will probably be contrary to the planning regulations applicable to the property. As a result, the Rights of Light Act 1959 was passed in order to provide a simple means by which a claim to light can be interrupted. Under this Act, instead of building a hoarding, a servient owner may register a notice in the Local Land Charges Register specifying the size and position of the obstruction which he would otherwise have erected. Notice of this entry should be given to the dominant owner unless the case is one of exceptional urgency (s. 2). The entry upon the register operates as though a real obstruction had been built and therefore if the dominant owner takes no action for a year he will be deemed to have acquiesced in the interruption.

How to apply the three forms of prescription

We have now looked at a bewildering variety of rules, and you must wonder how they fit together and which method to use. At one time it was thought that the courts would generally be unwilling to accept a claim based on a lost modern grant, but the decision in *Tehidy Minerals Ltd* v *Norman* [1971] 2 QB 528 appears to have produced a rehabilitation of the doctrine (see also *Bridle* v *Ruby* [1988] 3 WLR 191 and *Mills* v *Silver* [1991] Ch 271).

There are thus still three main methods to consider, and it appears that they should be applied in the following order. Begin with the long period under the Prescription Act 1832. If there is not a sufficient period of use, or it is not 'next before the action', or for some other reasons that method does not succeed, apply the common law rules, assisted if possible by the short-period provisions of the Act. If that is not successful, as a last resort you should apply the doctrine of the lost modern grant. This is in effect the order in which the various forms of prescription were considered in *Tehidy Minerals Ltd* v *Norman*. This judgment of the Court of Appeal does provide a very good example for anyone who has to deal with a problem of this kind, and so we will end this section with an account of that case.

The plaintiffs owned an area of downland on which local farmers had grazed their animals since the 19th century. For some time during and after the Second World War the down was requisitioned, and when grazing was resumed it appeared to be by permission. The plaintiffs fenced the down and excluded the farmers, who broke down the fences. The plaintiffs alleged trespass and the defendants claimed that they had a profit of grazing.

It was not possible to support the claim under the long period of the Act, for the period of requisitioning and permissive use broke into this. The long use, dating back to the 19th century did, however, enable some farmers to raise a presumption that the right had existed from time immemorial, and they succeeded at common law. The other defendants, however, could not rely on the common law, because their farms and the down had been in common ownership at some time after 1189; they were not assisted by the shorter period under the Act because it was interrupted by the requisitioning. They were, however, able to show over 20 years use before the war, and the Court of Appeal held that this was sufficient to raise a presumption of a lost modern grant and found that they had acquired a profit by this means.

REMEDIES

We will now consider briefly the remedies which may be used to protect an easement or profit.

Abatement

Theoretically if any obstruction to the lawful exercise of a profit or easement is erected, the dominant owner may exercise a 'self-help' remedy and may simply 'abate' (remove) the obstruction. This may be done without informing the servient owner (*Perry* v *Fitzhowe* (1846) 8 QB 757) but the right should be used with care. The dominant owner must not use unreasonable force, nor may he injure any person in attempting to enforce his rights. It would, however, be permissible to break down a fence or gate. In general, however, it is inadvisable for the dominant owner to rely upon self-help, and indeed in *Lagan Navigation Co.* v *Lambeg Bleaching, Dyeing & Finishing Co. Ltd* [1927] AC 226 at p. 245 Lord Atkinson indicated that the law preferred that a remedy be sought through the courts, and that abatement should only be used in cases of extreme urgency.

Action

Normally a person claiming that his easement or profit has been infringed will apply to the courts for a suitable remedy. Obviously it is possible to seek a declaration to clarify the rights of the parties (useful where a right is claimed by prescription). The plaintiff may, however, go further and seek damages to compensate for any loss caused by the infringement but if he does so he must establish some serious interference with his rights, rather than some trivial incident (*Weston* v *Lawrence Weaver Ltd* [1961] 1 QB 402). Generally, the remedy which will be sought is that of an injunction restraining the interference of which the dominant owner complains. Once again, the courts will not intervene where the act complained of is only a trivial interference with the dominant owner's rights (*Cowper* v *Laidler* [1903] 2 Ch 337).

EXTINGUISHMENT OF EASEMENTS AND PROFITS

Once easements and profits have arisen they will, as interests in land, endure through successive ownerships of the land. Indeed they may well endure for very long periods. We must therefore consider the means by which such rights are brought to an end.

Dominant and servient tenements coming into the same hands

Because a man cannot have rights against himself, an easement, or a profit appurtenant to land, will be extinguished if the dominant and the servient tenements come into common ownership and possession. It is essential that *both* ownership and possession become common, and that both tenements are acquired for an estate in fee simple (*R* v *Inhabitants of Hermitage* (1692) Carth 239). Thus if the fee simple owner of one tenement takes a lease of the other this does *not* extinguish the easement or profit. All that happens is that the exercise of the easement or profit as a *right* is suspended for a period of the lease and will revive when it ends (*Simper* v *Foley* (1862) 2 John & H 555). If, however, the two tenements do come into common ownership the easement or profit will be completely extinguished and will not revive if the plots are separated again at a later date.

Release

An easement or profit may be 'released' (given up) by the dominant owner at any time. Obviously at law such a release should be effected by deed, but equity will recognise an informal release if it would be inequitable to allow the releasing owner to go back on his word (e.g., *Waterlow* v *Bacon* (1866) LR 2 Eq 514). The effect of a release is to return the easement or profit to the servient owner, at which point it merges with his estate and is thereby extinguished.

Implied release — abandonment

In general the mere lack of use of an easement or profit, once it has been acquired, will not lead to the extinguishment of the right (*Seaman* v *Vawdrey* (1810) 16 Ves Jr 390), for a man is never obliged to exercise the rights which he may have. However, a prolonged non-use may be adduced as evidence that the dominant owner has impliedly abandoned his right. It should, however, be noted that if the dominant owner explains the non-use he may still be regarded as not having abandoned the right. Thus in *James* v *Stevenson* [1893] AC 162 a right was not lost due to a long period of non-use because the dominant owner explained that he had simply had no occasion to exercise the right (but presumably might wish to in the future). In *Benn* v *Hardinge, The Times*, 13 October 1992, the Court of Appeal said that non-use, even for 175 years, was not enough on its own to indicate an intention to abandon. The Court said the abandonment of such a right would not be lightly inferred.

If, however, the dominant tenement has been altered in such a way that the right claimed becomes unnecessary or impossible to exercise, then the alteration may be regarded as evidence of an intention to abandon the right. This presumption may be rebutted by evidence that the original character of the land may be restored in the future and that the need for the easement or profit would revive. Thus, in the case of a right to light, the easement will not be extinguished merely because the house on the dominant land is destroyed, as long as it is intended to erect another building in its place (*Ecclesiastical Commissioners for England* v *Kino* (1880) 14 ChD 213).

LAW REFORM

By this point the reader may well have concluded that the law relating to easements and profits is sadly in need of reform. It may be of some comfort that the authors agree with this conclusion. The existence of three methods of prescription is in itself an unnecessary complication and the nightmarish quality of the Prescription Act 1832 has been a cause of complaint for generations. Indeed in 1966 the Law Reform Committee recommended that all the existing rules on prescription should be abolished and replaced by one simpler method of prescription providing for a single period of 12 years (14th Report, Cmnd 3100). In addition it has been recommended that a more far-reaching reform be contemplated in order to bring the law relating to easements and freehold covenants in line with one another (Law Commission Working Party, Working Paper 1971, No. 36). We will consider possible reforms at greater length once we have explained the rules relating to freehold covenants (see p. 331) but will mention at this point one small reform which has already taken effect.

Access to Neighbouring Land Act 1992

In the absence of an easement giving access, in the past there has been no right for a neighbour to gain access to his neighbour's premises in order to enable the carrying out of maintenance work to his own premises. Thus, if one bought an estate in premises which were build right up to the boundary of the land concerned, it was essential to check that express rights had been provided in order to allow access to neighbouring property for the purpose of pointing brickwork, repairing windows or doing any other work which could only be carried out from the neighbour's premises. This was no problem where due care had been taken by those building premises which extended right to the boundaries of their land but in some cases caused undesirable problems. It was, of course, always possible to enter the neighbour's property with his permission (by licence). However, should such permission be refused, even if such refusal were unreasonable, nothing could be done. Following recommendations by the Law Commission that the law in this regard should be reformed to allow a limited right of access in cases where this was essential, a limited change in the law has been made by the Access to Neighbouring Land Act 1992, which came into force on 31 January 1993 (SI 1992 No. 3349).

Although this Act does allow access in certain cases in order to carry out works which are 'reasonably necessary for the preservation of the whole or any part of the dominant land', it does *not* create a form of statutory easement. It does not give rise to a new interest in land but merely gives a right to access, which right can be enforced against certain persons concerned with the 'servient' land. Nor is the right one to which the person seeking access has an immediate claim: the right only arises where a court makes an access order in favour of an applicant. An order can only be made where the works are reasonably necessary to preserve land and where they cannot be carried out, or would be substantially more difficult to carry out, without the access (s. 1(2)). Even where these requirements can be established, an order will not be made where the court concludes that it would be unreasonable to make an order due to the degree of interference caused to the neighbour's use or enjoyment of the land or due to any hardship which would be caused to the neighbour or anyone in occupation of the 'servient' land. Nonetheless this new rule will allow access for a wide number of works to be carried out: for example, clearing drains and sewers, repairing buildings or any part of a building, replacing windows, felling trees and so on. The Act does not restrict the type of works for which an access order may be sought; all that matters is that the works should be reasonably necessary for the preservation of the land, though certain types of work ('basic preservation works') are taken to be reasonably necessary (s. 1(4)).

Where an order under the Act is granted it may include conditions as to the days on and times at which work may be done and may include a wide range of other provisions (for example, specifying who must carry out the work and providing for payment to be made for any damage caused to the 'servient' land) (s. 2(4)). Where the premises to which the work is to be carried out do not comprise residential land, the court may require a 'fair and reasonable' payment to be made for the right of access (s. 2(5)).

One problem with the access order is that it only has effect to require the respondent(s) to the application to allow the applicant the necessary access in order to carry out work. As you are already aware, it is perfectly possible for a number of different persons to have co-terminous rights to one piece of land and this means that the applicant must try to ensure that he joins as respondents to his action all persons who might have a right to prevent him gaining access to the neighbouring land. This might give rise to difficulties if, for example, the current occupant of the neighbouring land is a licensee (without exclusive possession) or if the portion of the land to which access is sought is subject to third party rights (for example, a right of way in favour of another neighbour which would be interrupted by the access conferred by the order). However, once an order is made, it will be binding on anyone acquiring an estate or interest from or under the respondent after the making of the order. Accordingly, whilst the order does not confer an interest in land it does create a right which, to an extent, runs to bind later acquirers and thus has some of the characteristics of an interest in land. Accordingly the 1992 Act provides for the registration of orders made under it and any such right may, and should, be protected by entry of a notice in the case of registered land (s. 5(2)) and, in the case of unregistered land, by registration of the order as a 'writ or order affecting land' (s. 5(1)).

9 Covenants Relating to Freehold Land

We saw in chapter 3 that it is usual for covenants to be included in leases. Similarly, covenants are quite commonly made in respect of freehold property, particularly if land is divided and the vendor wishes to ensure that his new neighbour does not behave in an inconvenient or disturbing manner. In the case of a new estate, the developer may well wish to impose covenants upon all the purchasers, in order to ensure that the estate is maintained in good order. Thus covenants are frequently imposed upon freehold estates. However, once the land burdened with the covenant is sold, the question will arise whether the covenant is binding upon the purchaser of the property. Over the years, special rules have developed in order to settle the question of which covenants can run with freehold land. These rules have some links with the rules governing covenants in leases, but the two systems are not the same and should not be confused with one another. In many cases a covenant by a freehold owner will not bind a purchaser from him, although a similar covenant, if contained in a lease, would bind the tenant's assignee.

Factual background

In 1970, Nos. 17 and 18 Trant Way were both owned in fee simple by Olive Orange. Miss Orange occupied 17 Trant Way, whilst No. 18 was let to a tenant. When the tenant left the property at the end of the lease, Miss Orange decided to sell 18 Trant Way. She sold the fee simple estate in the property to Robert Raspberry and, because she was concerned that her new neighbour should not inconvenience her, or, as she expressed it, 'allow the tone of the neighbourhood to fall', she insisted that Mr Raspberry should enter into a number of covenants in the conveyance. The covenants were:

(a) not to use No. 18 'for business purposes';
(b) to keep the exterior of No. 18 in good repair;
(c) to contribute one-half of the cost of maintaining the driveway shared with No. 17;
(d) not to sell No. 18 to a family with children (Miss Orange was elderly and found the noise of children at play disturbing).

In 1975, Miss Orange died, and her executors sold 17 Trant Way to Paul Peach.

In 1976, Mr Raspberry sold 18 Trant Way to Silvia Strawberry. Mrs

Strawberry has proved to be rather a difficult neighbour to Mr Peach and causes him considerable trouble. As a piano teacher, she gives lessons at home and the noise of children playing their scales throughout the day and early evening disturbs Mr Peach greatly. Furthermore, Mrs Strawberry has failed to repair the outside of No. 18, which has become something of an eyesore, and when Mr Peach had repairs made to the joint driveway she refused to contribute to the cost.

19 Trant Way was the old rectory, which had a very large garden and an orchard. In 1985, a development company, Big Builders plc, bought the old rectory, demolished it and built a new crescent of six bungalows. The gardens of the properties were landscaped and are 'open plan' in style. The six bungalows have now been sold, and the new owners of the fee simple estates have been registered as proprietors at HM Land Registry. The crescent is called Rectory Crescent, and the bungalows have been numbered 1 to 6, and were sold in that order. 1 Rectory Crescent was bought by Alfred Alpha, and 6 Rectory Crescent was bought by Oscar Omega. On each sale, the purchaser covenanted with Big Builders plc not to fence the garden of the plot being purchased.

We now need to consider the extent to which the covenants we have just described are enforceable, not only between the original parties but also between their successors in title.

ENFORCEABILITY OF COVENANTS: ORIGINAL PARTIES

When Olive Orange sold 18 Trant Way to Robert Raspberry in 1970, the covenants contained in the conveyance to Mr Raspberry constituted a contract between the parties. We have already explained that a covenant is a promise by deed (p. 118). Here, Mr Raspberry is the 'covenantor', and assumes the 'burden' under the covenant, and Miss Orange is the 'covenantee', and takes the 'benefit'. If Mr Raspberry had broken a covenant, Miss Orange could have sued for damages for breach of contract or sought an injunction restraining the breach. In this situation the basic rules of the law of contract apply.

It is easy enough to see that Miss Orange and Mr Raspberry have a contractual relationship with one another, for both signed, sealed and delivered a document which contained their agreement. However, it is possible for someone to take the benefit of such a covenant, even though he was not a party to the deed or perhaps did not even know that the contract had been concluded. In the case of 6 Rectory Crescent, Mr Omega clearly has entered into a contract with Big Builders plc, for both parties have signed, sealed and delivered the transfer (sealing was needed to execute a deed at the relevant date). If, however, Big Builders plc had put a clause in the transfer saying that the covenant not to fence the garden of No. 6 was made with Big Builders plc and with 'the owners for the time being of land forming part of Rectory Crescent', then Mr Alpha (and the owners of plots 2–5) would also be able to enforce the covenant made by Mr Omega. This effect is produced by LPA 1925, s. 56(1), which provides that, 'A person may take . . . the benefit of any condition, . . . covenant or agreement over or respecting land, . . . although he may not be named as a party to the conveyance or other instrument'. In *Re Ecclesiastical Commissioners for England's Conveyance* [1936] Ch 430, it was held that the effect of s. 56 was that a person, expressed in the conveyance to be one for whose benefit the covenant was made, was to be regarded as an original covenantee, even though he was not a party to the deed. As a result, the covenant may confer enforceable benefits on other persons, even though they may have been unaware that such a covenant had been made! Accordingly, if Mr Omega broke the covenant not to fence, Mr Alpha could sue him for breach of contract, provided that he could satisfy the court that the covenant did purport to be with him as covenantee, although he was not a party to the agreement (*Re Foster* [1938] 3 All ER 357 at p. 365).

ENFORCEABILITY OF COVENANTS: SUCCESSORS OF THE ORIGINAL PARTIES

In time, as we have seen from our examples, the benefited and burdened pieces of land will change hands, and pass to new owners. We must now consider whether the new owner of the benefited land obtains the right to enforce the covenants, and whether the duties under these covenants bind the new owner of the burdened land. In other words, do the benefits and burdens of the covenants run with the respective pieces of land?

Position after sale by the covenantee: does the benefit pass to the new owner?

In 1975 Olive Orange, the original covenantee in relation to the covenants burdening 18 Trant Way, sold her fee simple estate in No 17 to Paul Peach. At this time, the original covenantor, Robert Raspberry, was still the owner of 18 Trant Way. If Mr Raspberry had broken one of the covenants contained in the 1970 conveyance to himself, could Mr Peach have enforced the covenant against him? Obviously there is no privity of contract between Mr Peach and Mr Raspberry, but common law does allow the benefit of such a covenant to pass to a successor in title of the original covenantee, provided four conditions are met:

(a)   The covenant must 'touch and concern' the land of the covenantee.

(b)   At the time when the covenant was made, it must have been the intention of the parties that the benefit of the covenant should run with the land to the covenantee's successors in title.

(c)   At the time when the covenant was made, the covenantee must have held the legal estate in the land to be benefited.

(d)   The claimant must derive his title from or under the original covenantee (this is the common law rule as amended by LPA 1925, s. 78).

We will look at each of these requirements in greater detail.

'Touching and concerning' the land of the covenantee
Common law rules do not allow the successor of the original covenantee
to claim the benefit of a covenant unless, at the date when the covenant
was made, the covenantee had land which was benefited by the covenant.
This emphasises the fact that only the benefit of covenants which are
appurtenant to land can be claimed under these rules.

In addition, the covenant must 'touch and concern' the covenantee's land.
The purpose of the rule is to distinguish between covenants which confer
a benefit upon land and those which confer a purely personal benefit upon
the covenantee. In the case of 17 Trant Way we may well feel that the covenant
not to sell No. 18 to anyone with children was purely for the personal benefit
of Miss Orange. Such a covenant does not seem to confer any benefit upon
17 Trant Way itself. The test here is the same as that used in relation to
leases (see p. 135): the test in *Spencer's Case* (1583) 5 Co Rep 16a. The other
covenants made by Mr Raspberry do, however, appear to confer a benefit
upon No. 17.

The parties must have intended the benefit to run
This condition requires proof that, when the covenant was made, the parties
intended that it should run to benefit successors of the covenantee. Evidence
of such an intention can be provided by the covenantor covenanting with
'the covenantee, his successors in title, and those deriving title under him'.
These words are, however, now deemed to be contained in the covenant,
by virtue of LPA 1925, s. 78(1):

> A covenant relating to any land of the covenantee shall be deemed to be
> made with the covenantee and his successors in title and the persons deriving
> title under him or them, and shall have effect as if such successors and
> other persons were expressed.

*At the time when the covenant was made, the covenantee must have held the
legal estate in the land*
At common law, covenants attach to the legal estate and pass with it, and
so it is essential that, at the time the covenant was made, the covenantee
was the owner of the legal estate in the land on which the benefit is to be
conferred (*Webb* v *Russell* (1789) 3 D & E 393).

*The successor claiming to enforce the covenant must derive title from or under
the original covenantee*
At one time, a successor claiming the benefit of a covenant at common law
had to show that he had acquired the same estate as had been held by the
original covenantee, for common law regarded the covenants as attaching
to the estate, so that only a person who took the estate could obtain the
benefit of the covenants. Thus a purchaser of the fee simple from the covenantee
could enforce a covenant, whilst a tenant acquiring a term of years (even
if it were for 999 years) could not do so. Today, however, a tenant may
claim the benefit of a covenant which is attached to the freehold estate in
the land of which he is a tenant, for in *Smith and Snipes Hall Farm Ltd*

v *River Douglas Catchment Board* [1949] 2 KB 500 it was held that LPA 1925, s. 78, has the effect of extending the right to enforce a covenant to such a person. Section 78 appears to have been intended to be merely a word-saving provision, but over the years has been held to create important substantive changes in the law. In this instance it was said that, because the section refers to persons 'deriving title under' the covenantee, it extends the benefit of such covenants to tenants, who derive their title *under* the covenantee (or his successors). Were such persons incapable of obtaining a benefit under the legal rules, the inclusion of the reference to them in s. 78 would be meaningless and thus the section has been interpreted as creating an amendment to the law.

The benefit of a covenant amounts to a chose in action, and thus it is possible for the holder of the benefit to assign it to any third party in accordance with the ordinary rules of law. Under LPA 1925, s. 136, any such express assignment should be made in writing and notice of it should be given to the covenantor.

Application of the rules

One can see from these rules that when Miss Orange sold 17 Trant Way to Paul Peach, he would have obtained the benefit of all Mr Raspberry's covenants, except perhaps that of the covenant not to sell No. 18 to a family with children, which appears to be purely personal in nature. Apart from this, the benefit of all the covenants, both positive and negative, would pass with the estate to the new owner, for at common law the benefit of both types of covenant can run to a successor of the covenantee.

Position after sale by covenantor: does the burden pass to the new owner?

In 1976, Mr Raspberry sold the fee simple in 18 Trant Way (the burdened land) to Silvia Strawberry, and it appears that Mrs Strawberry is in breach of a number of the covenants originally made between Mr Raspberry and Miss Orange. The current owner of the benefited land, Mr Peach, needs to know whether Mrs Strawberry is in fact bound by these covenants.

Burdens do not run at common law

Unfortunately for Mr Peach, the basic rule is that the burden of covenants does not run at common law. Common law dislikes restraints being placed on a man's use of his own estate, and accordingly applies the strict rule of privity of contract in such cases. The leading decision on this issue is *Austerberry v Corporation of Oldham* (1885) 29 ChD 750, in which it was held that at common law the obligation to make up a road and keep it in good repair could not pass to the successor in title of the original covenantor. Thus Mrs Strawberry will not be liable *at law* for breach of any of the covenants made in respect of 18 Trant Way. This rule is in line with the general principles of the law of contract, which allow the benefit of a contract to be transferred to a third party, but not the burden.

The burden of certain covenants can run in equity
The common law rule caused considerable inconvenience, because the owner of benefited land could find that covenants became unenforceable merely because the burdened land changed hands. Equity took note of this difficulty and, through applying general equitable principles, arrived at the conclusion that where a purchaser acquired the burdened land with knowledge of the covenants it was quite fair that he should be bound to observe them. The enforceability of the burden of certain covenants against a successor in title to the covenantor was settled finally in the famous case of *Tulk* v *Moxhay* (1848) 2 Ph 774. In this case, the burdened land formed the centre of Leicester Square in London, and the original covenantor had covenanted with the owner of adjacent property that he would maintain the square as a garden. Later the square was sold, and the purchaser, relying on the common law rule that burdens do not pass on sale, intended to build on the property. It was held that the owners of the neighbouring benefited land had a right *in equity* to enforce the covenant against the purchaser of the burdened land, because he had known of the restriction when he acquired his estate. (The Leicester Square covenants were again the subject of litigation in *R* v *Westminster City Council, ex parte Leicester Square Coventry Street Association* (1989) 87 LGR 675.)

Since 1848 the courts have, in later cases, identified the rules which must be satisfied before equity will regard the burden of a covenant as passing under the *Tulk* v *Moxhay* doctrine. These rules are derived from *Tulk* v *Moxhay* but are not (apart from the last) expressly mentioned in the case. In their modern form, the rules may be stated as follows:

(a) The covenant must be negative.

(b) At the date of the covenant, the covenantee must have owned land which was benefited by the covenant.

(c) The original parties must have intended that the burden should run to bind successors.

(d) As the rule is equitable, general equitable principles (and the need for notice or its modern equivalent) apply.

The covenant must be negative This rule may seem odd when one remembers that the covenant in *Tulk* v *Moxhay* was to maintain Leicester Square as a garden. However, it is the substance of the covenant which matters, and not the form in which it is expressed. Thus the effect of the covenant in *Tulk* v *Moxhay* was that the owner should keep the square in an open state and *not* erect buildings. In the case of the covenants relating to 18 Trant Way, the covenants to keep the exterior in good repair and to contribute to the cost of maintaining the driveway are both positive, and thus cannot run to bind Mrs Strawberry under the rule in *Tulk* v *Moxhay*. This can produce rather inconvenient results, and reform of the law has been recommended (see p. 331). Indeed, some writers have argued that *Tulk* v *Moxhay* makes no mention of such a requirement, and that in the past positive covenants had been enforced against the covenantor's successors (see Bell [1981] Conv 55). However, this limitation on the rule has been accepted since the case of *Haywood* v *Brunswick Permanent Benefit Building Society* (1881) 8 QBD 403, in which Lindley LJ said that 'only such a covenant as can be complied with without expenditure of money will be enforced' against a successor in title. Thus a covenant 'not to allow the premises to fall into disrepair' would be regarded as a positive covenant, even though it is worded in a negative form, because compliance with the covenant will require action, and expenditure, on the part of the owner of the burdened land.

At the date of the covenant the covenantee must have owned benefited land Equity will not enforce a covenant unless it confers a benefit upon land. This involves two requirements: (a) that the covenant touches and concerns land; and (b) that at the date of the covenant the covenantee must have retained land which was benefited by the covenant. In *London County Council* v *Allen* [1914] 3 KB 642 a builder covenanted that he would not build on a particular piece of land. The covenantee was the council, which did not own land in the neighbourhood. Mrs Allen bought the plot with knowledge of the covenant, but was held not to be bound by it, because it was not made for the benefit of land owned by the Council. This decision emphasises the fact that equity will protect only covenants which are appurtenant to land.

There are, however, a number of exceptions to the rule that the covenantee must retain land which is benefited by the covenant:

(a) If you think of the situation in Rectory Crescent, you will realise that Big Builders plc, after selling plot 6 to Mr Omega, did not retain any land in the Crescent, and so, on the basic rule, the burden of the covenant would not run with that plot to any new owner. However, if it can be established that the development of Rectory Crescent constituted what is known as a 'building scheme', the burden will run with the last plot, despite the fact that the developer did not retain any land in the area. We will explain how building schemes work later in this chapter (see p. 324).

(b) There are also a number of statutory exceptions to the rule, for example in favour of local authorities or the National Trust. These exceptions allow such bodies to enforce covenants on behalf of the whole community (for example, to ensure that an area of natural beauty is not disturbed: National Trust Act 1937, s. 8).

(c) The rules relating to restrictive covenants in leases require a special mention in this context. Such covenants are capable of amounting to restrictive covenants binding under the rules of *Tulk* v *Moxhay*. This is of little importance where assignees of the tenant are concerned, for most of the covenants in the lease may be enforced against them under the rule in *Spencer's Case* (see p. 135), However, covenants which fall within the *Tulk* v *Moxhay* principle are binding on anyone who derives title from or under the covenantor, or one of his successors, and thus such covenants *can* be enforced against a subtenant, with whom the enforcing landlord has no privity of estate. You may remember that we mentioned this in the chapter on leases, while saying that in general the head landlord cannot enforce covenants in the lease against the subtenant (p. 136). Where this is the case, it is not necessary to show that the landlord has retained other neighbouring land which is benefited. It is enough to show that a benefit is conferred on the landlord's reversion (which is normally the case) (*Hall* v *Ewin* (1887) 37 ChD 74; *Regent Oil Co. Ltd* v *J.A. Gregory (Hatch End) Ltd* [1966] Ch 402).

The parties must have intended the burden to run   It is essential that the parties should have intended the burden to pass to later owners of the affected property. Normally this intention will be expressly evidenced by the covenantor covenanting on behalf of himself and his successors in title, and those deriving title under him or them. In the absence of an express provision, the covenantor is deemed to have covenanted in these terms by virtue of LPA 1925, s. 79. However, this provision, unlike s. 78, may be excluded from the agreement by an express term to the contrary. If the document creating the covenant is silent on the matter, the parties will be presumed to intend that it will bind later owners.

The application of equitable principles, and the need for notice or its modern equivalent   If Mr Peach is to enforce the covenants relating to 18 Trant Way against Mrs Strawberry, he will be obliged to rely on the assistance of the equitable jurisdiction of the court. As a result, the general principles and maxims will apply to any action which he brings. The most important of these is that 'He who comes to equity must come with clean hands'. This may be of importance where there are reciprocal covenants between neighbouring owners (as we shall see, this is the case in Rectory Crescent), and the owner seeking to enforce is himself in breach of covenant. In such a case, it would be inequitable for the court to assist the person who is himself in breach of his agreement.

More importantly, the fact that the burden of the covenants runs only in equity means that one must bear in mind the need to protect the right to the covenant by registration as a land charge or entry on the register in the case of registered land. As we have seen, *Tulk* v *Moxhay* was decided primarily on the basis that the purchaser of Leicester Square bought with notice of the covenant restricting the use of the land. Where one is dealing with unregistered land and with restrictive covenants created *before* 1 January 1926 the old equitable doctrine of notice (see p. 69) will still apply. The reader should not assume that such old covenants can be ignored, for they are still frequently encountered and can still be enforced where the rules in *Tulk* v *Moxhay* are satisfied. Where the title to the land is unregistered, and the covenant was created on or after 1 January 1926 then it requires registration as a class D(ii) land charge (LCA 1972, s. 2(5)). If such a covenant is not registered, it will be void against a purchaser of a legal estate for money or money's worth, regardless of notice (LCA 1972, s. 4(6)). The date by which the covenant must have been registered is the date on which the burdened land was conveyed to the purchaser. In the case of 18 Trant Way, Mrs Strawberry will *not* be bound by the restrictive covenants relating to the property unless they were registered as land charges before she bought the fee simple in 1976.

If 18 Trant Way were to change hands today, the new owner of the fee simple would be obliged to register his title to the land with HM Land Registry (see chapter 2), because Mousehole is now in an area of compulsory registration. On any such registration, the purchaser must tell the Registrar of any pre-1926 covenants of which he has notice and present to him a land charges search, which will reveal any registered covenants made after 1925.When the estate is registered, the Registrar will also enter on the register notice of any such encumbrances (Land Registration Rules 1925, r. 40; LRA 1925, s. 50(1)). These burdens on the land are minor interests, and will affect a purchaser only if entered on the register relating to the burdened land. Usually the Registrar will insert a full copy of the terms of the covenant in the charges section of the register and this information will be repeated in the land certificate.

Any covenants created after the title becomes registered must also be entered against the burdened estate. Most new covenants are created on transfer of the estate, and in the transfer deed. These covenants will be entered automatically on the register by way of notice. In the case of a covenant created at another time, the person with the benefit of the covenant should apply to have his interest noted on the register of the burdened land. This entry will be by way of notice if the land certificate or charge certificate can be produced, but otherwise will be by way of caution.

Where the burden runs in equity, the benefit must be made to run in equity
Having established that Mrs Strawberry may be bound by certain covenants burdening 18 Trant Way, it must still be established that Mr Peach has a right to enforce the covenants. Where he has to argue that Mrs Strawberry is bound *in equity* by the covenants, he must also establish that he has obtained the benefit of the covenants according to *equitable* rules: it is not enough to show that the benefit passes at common law. However, in general the equitable rules are more generous to the person claiming the benefit.

In equity, there are three ways in which a purchaser of the benefited land can acquire the right to enforce the covenant:

(a)   By annexation (which may be express, implied or statutory).
(b)   By express assignment of the benefit of the covenant.
(c)   Under the special rules relating to building schemes.

Express annexation   Where 'words of annexation' are used, the benefit of the covenant is annexed or attached to the land, so that for ever after it passes automatically with the land to the new owner. In order to achieve express annexation, it is necessary that the words of the covenant should show that the original parties intended the benefit to run, and one way of doing this is to state expressly that the covenant is made 'for the benefit of' named land (*Rogers* v *Hosegood* [1900] 2 Ch 388). Another method which will have the same effect is for the covenant to be made with the covenantee as 'estate owner', that is, describing him as the owner of the land to be benefited. For example, Mr Raspberry may have covenanted with Miss Orange as 'the owner for the time being of 17 Trant Way', and these words would have the effect of attaching the benefit of the covenants to No. 17. It is not enough, however, for the covenant to be made with the covenantee and his 'heirs, executors administrators and assigns' (or any similar set of words), for such a phrase does not link these people with the benefited land (*Renals* v *Cowlishaw* (1878) 9 ChD 125).

Where a claimant seeks to establish express annexation, a problem will arise if the wording of the deed creating the covenant purports to annex it to an area of land which is so large that it cannot reasonably be said that the covenant confers actual benefit on the whole property. In *Re Ballard's Conveyance* [1937] Ch 473, a covenant was said to be for the benefit of the whole of a large estate (approximately 690 hectares). In fact, the covenant could confer a benefit on only a small portion of that estate. Here the court said that, since the covenant did not confer a benefit on the whole estate, it could not run on a sale of the estate. Nor would it run when a part of the estate which *was* benefited was sold, because the court would not sever the covenant and attach it to parts of the land where the express wording of the deed did not allow for this (but see also *Earl of Leicester* v *Wells-next-the-Sea Urban District Council* [1973] Ch 110). As a result, when one drafts a covenant and wishes to attach it to a large area of land, it is wise to say that the covenant is for the benefit of 'the whole or any part of' the named land; this will allow the covenant to run with any part of the large estate which is actually benefited, and will also allow the benefit to be divided between several plots if the estate is ever sold off in that way (*Marquess of Zetland* v *Driver* [1939] Ch 1).

Implied annexation   In recent years, it has been suggested that, where words of express annexation are lacking, it may still be possible for the court to identify the benefited land by looking at the circumstances of the case. Where the facts are held to indicate with reasonable certainty the land which is to be benefited, the benefit will thereafter run with that land. This way of proceeding has been called 'implied annexation'.

The notion of implied annexation is usually said to be derived from two decisions: *Newton Abbot Co-operative Society Ltd* v *Williamson & Treadgold Ltd* [1952] Ch 286 (the 'Devonia' case) and *Marten* v *Flight Refuelling Ltd* [1962] Ch 115. The first of these cases was in fact concerned with assignment of the benefit, rather than with annexation, but it was welcomed as 'a useful guide' in *Marten* v *Flight Refuelling Ltd* (at p. 133). Here there had been no assignment of the benefit, and the court looked at the burdened land and the surrounding area, and came to the conclusion that the covenant had been taken for the benefit of land retained by the vendor. Wilberforce J mentioned with approval (at p. 132) that there seemed to be support for the view 'that an intention to benefit may be found from surrounding or attending circumstances'.

It has to be said that this decision stands very much on its own, and, further, that it has been suggested that the issue of annexation does not arise here (Ryder (1972) 36 Conv (NS) 26). The covenant was made with the executors of the previous owner, who were holding in trust for an infant beneficiary, and it was these executors and the former beneficiary, now absolutely entitled to the property, who sought to enforce the covenant. The decision has also been criticised as tending to increase the general uncertainty about the enforceability of covenants, for while questions of express annexation can in general be decided from a study of the documents, a claim of implied annexation cannot be decided without an application to the court (Report of the Committee on Positive Covenants Affecting Land (Chairman: Lord Wilberforce) (Cmnd 2719, 1968), para. 15).

Statutory annexation These rather complicated rules about express annexation, and the uncertainty about implied annexation, may be of less importance since the decision of the Court of Appeal in *Federated Homes Ltd v Mill Lodge Properties Ltd* [1980] 1 WLR 594, which suggests that in certain cases statutory annexation may be effective. The case before the court concerned a covenant by the defendant not to build more than a certain number of dwellings on the burdened land. It was clear from the wording of the document that the land to be benefited was neighbouring land retained by the covenantee, but there were no express words annexing the benefit of the covenant to that land. Later the covenantee sold this land and eventually it became the property of Mill Lodge Properties Ltd. In the case of part of the benefited land no problem about annexation arose, because the benefit of the covenant had been expressly assigned (see below). In respect of the other portion of the land, however, there had been no assignment, but the court held that this did not matter because it was clear which land was intended to benefit, and accordingly the covenant was annexed to that land by LPA 1925, s. 78. In the words of Brightman LJ (at p. 605):

If, as the language of section 78 implies, a covenant relating to land which is restrictive of the user thereof is enforceable at the suit of (1) a successor in title to the covenantee, (2) a person deriving title under the covenantee or under his successors in title, and (3) the owner or occupier of the land intended to be benefited by the covenant, it must, in my view, follow that the covenant runs with the land, because *ex hypothesi* . . . every other owner and occupier has a right by statute to the covenant. In other words, if the condition precedent of section 78 is satisfied—that is to say, there exists a covenant which touches and concerns the land of the covenantee—that covenant runs with the land for the benefit of his successors in title, persons deriving title under him or them and other owners and occupiers.

One strange feature of this case, which should be noted, is that the defendant was the original covenantor. There was no need, therefore, to show that the burden had run with the land in equity, and accordingly one would have thought that the court would have been concerned only with whether the benefit ran at common law. Consideration of the equitable requirement of annexation was, strictly, unnecessary for the decision of the case, and it would therefore be open to a later court to treat the statements about statutory annexation as *obiter dicta* (but see the discussion in *Roake v Chadha* [1984] 1 WLR 40). For the moment, however, the decision does suggest that the Court of Appeal will accept a claim to the benefit of a covenant by virtue of statutory annexation in any case in which it is clear which land was intended to benefit. Also it appears that the statutory annexation will be to every *part* of the benefited land since the court assumed that every successor or derivative proprietor could claim under s. 78. If this is the effect of s. 78 it renders obsolete many of the traditional difficulties associated with express annexation, including the need to annex to the 'whole or any part' of the benefited land.

Assignment   Even where the benefit of a covenant has not been expressly annexed to land, it has always been the case that the covenantee could transfer that benefit by express assignment. The benefit of a covenant, like the benefit of any other contract, is a chose in action and can be assigned at will. If one relies on this method it is, however, necessary to show that there is an unbroken chain of assignments, so that on each sale of the benefited land the benefit has been passed to the new owner and has finally come to the person who now seeks to enforce the covenant (*Re Pinewood Estate* [1958] Ch 280). It is also essential that the right should be assigned to the purchaser of the estate at the time of the conveyance to him, and an assignment made after the estate has been transferred is not acceptable (*Re Union of London & Smith's Bank Ltd's Conveyance* [1933] Ch 611 at p. 632).

Building schemes   Some of the rules discussed above would cause difficulty when applied to the development of a new estate, such as Rectory Crescent. As we have seen, each purchaser entered into covenants with the developer, but now the estate is completed Big Builders plc will move on to work elsewhere, and will not be concerned with enforcing these covenants. What the purchasers want is to be able to rely on a sort of 'local law' for the area (*Re Dolphin's Conveyance* [1970] Ch 654 at p. 662), which each householder can enforce directly against his neighbours if he needs to do so. To a large extent, this could be achieved by the existing rules, but it would be complicated and would depend on knowing the exact order in which the plots had been sold.

In our example, plots 1 to 6 Rectory Crescent were sold in that order. If some time in the future, the successor of the original purchaser of No. 3 should fence his garden in breach of the covenant, those holding plots sold after No. 3 (i.e. 4 to 6) could claim that they held land retained by the developer at the time of the sale of No. 3. The benefit of that purchaser's covenant would therefore be annexed to the retained land (assuming of course that the covenant had been drafted correctly), and it would have passed to them, or their predecessors in title, when the later plots were sold. Those who bought before the sale of No. 3 (i.e. 1 and 2) might be able to rely on LPA 1925, s. 56, provided that the covenant purported to be with the owners of those plots and that, if they are not the original purchasers, they can show that the benefit has passed to them under the usual rules.

Proceeding in this way may not seem too difficult, but that is because we have simplified matters by saying that plots 1 to 6 were sold in that order. In real life, the houses on a new estate will be sold in no particular order, as purchasers present themselves and make their choices, and after 50 years or so it could be quite difficult to know, in respect of a particular breach, who could proceed under s. 56 and who could rely on annexation.

There is further the problem we mentioned earlier: because Big Builders plc retained no land when the last plot was sold, an essential rule for the running of the burden is not satisfied, and so the successor to the original purchaser of No. 6 would take free of the covenant.

However, all these difficulties are avoided if it can be established that the development satisfies the legal requirements of a 'building scheme'.

The traditional requirements for a building scheme were established in the Edwardian case of *Elliston* v *Reacher* [1908] 2 Ch 374, in which a building society had laid out an area for development in separate plots and had sold these using identical conveyances and imposing identical covenants upon each purchaser. The court held that the covenants were enforceable against a successor to the original covenantor, and set out four rules to be satisfied in order to establish a building scheme (sometimes called a 'scheme of development'):

(a)   The purchasers must derive their titles from a common vendor.

(b)   Before selling, the vendor must have laid out his land in lots (or plots).

(c)   On sale, the same restrictions must be imposed on all the plots, and it must be clear that those restrictions are intended to be for the benefit of all the plots sold.

(d)   Each purchaser must have acquired his plot on the understanding that the covenants were intended to benefit all the other plots in the scheme.

In later cases, however, it has been established that these four rules provide only guidance, and that what is crucial is the intention of the parties to create a building scheme. Accordingly, a scheme was found in *Baxter* v *Four Oaks Properties Ltd* [1965] Ch 816, even though the whole area had not been divided into lots in advance of the first sale, because it was desired to allow purchasers to choose lots of varying sizes. Again, in *Re Dolphin's Conveyance* [1970] Ch 654, a single scheme was established, even though the purchasers had not acquired from a common vendor. The first sales were made by two co-owners, but later the land came into the hands of their nephew, who continued the sale of plots and imposed covenants identical to those imposed by his aunts. The court considered that this satisfied the essential requirement, since it was quite clear the the various vendors did intend to create a local law for the area. If however a common intention cannot be established, for example because the covenants vary between the plots of land, a building scheme will not exist (see *Emile Elias & Co Ltd* v *Pine Groves Ltd* [1993] 1 WLR 305).

Once a scheme has been established, and Rectory Crescent would appear to be a clear example of such a scheme, it is necessary to consider what benefits will accrue. The first is that, although it is still necessary to establish that the rules in *Tulk* v *Moxhay* have been satisfied, these rules are modified slightly in one respect, so that the burden will run with the last plot sold (here, No. 6) despite the fact that the developer does not retain any land capable of being benefited. With this exception, though, all the basic rules have to be observed: so there is no question of the burden of positive covenants being enabled to run under a building scheme, and the usual registration or protection by entry on the register is needed if successors of the covenantors are to be bound.

M

The second advantage of a building scheme is that all purchasers of plots in the scheme are enabled to enforce the covenants between themselves, irrespective of the date on which they, or their predecessors in title, bought their plots. There is thus no need to distinguish between the earlier purchasers, proceeding under s. 56, and the later purchasers, who rely on express annexation. Earlier purchasers will be able to obtain the benefit of later covenants, and that benefit will run with their plots automatically, provided that they can establish that a building scheme has been created.

The third use of a building scheme is that in equity it will ensure that the benefit of the covenants imposed on other plots will automatically run to all sucessors of the original purchasers, without the need for express annexation or for assignment (although this may be less important since *Federated Homes Ltd* v *Mill Lodge Properties Ltd* [1980] 1 WLR 594).

Besides the three advantages of the building scheme described above, such a scheme appears not to be subject to some of the other general principles relating to covenants. In *Brunner* v *Greenslade* [1971] Ch 993, it was established that both the benefit and the burden of covenants in a building scheme will run to affect someone who acquires only part of the original plot. Thus where a plot is subdivided, the purchaser of one part may enforce the covenants against the purchaser of the other part and against all the other owners of plots forming part of the scheme. This rule was accepted because the aim of the scheme is to create a type of local legal system, and this aim would not be fulfilled if 'islands of immunity' developed in which covenants could not be enforced (as would happen if the owners of subplots could not enforce the covenants between themselves).

Similarly, it appears that should two plots come into common ownership and then later be divided again, the original covenants will revive automatically between the subsequent owners (*Texaco Antilles Ltd* v *Kernochan* [1973] AC 609). In general law this would not occur, for the common ownership would extinguish the covenants as between the two plots and the rights and duties created by the covenants would not revive when the plots were once more separated. The only way in which the covenants could be revived would be for the common vendor to require fresh covenants from the purchasers from him. However, when a building scheme can be established, the rights and duties under the original covenants will spring up again automatically when the plots are separated. Thus the building scheme provides a useful exception to the ordinary rules on this issue.

THE PROBLEM OF POSITIVE COVENANTS

The fact that the burden of a covenant will not normally run at law, and that equity declines to enforce a positive obligation against the successor of the original covenantor, can prove decidedly inconvenient. You will recall that when 18 Trant Way was sold originally to Mr Raspberry he undertook to contribute towards the cost of the maintenance of the driveway which is shared with No. 17. Undoubtedly the same conveyance gave him an easement of way over the same drive. When Mrs Strawberry bought No. 18, she will have acquired the benefit of the legal easement, but may claim that she is not obliged to contribute to the maintenance of the drive, as the burden of positive covenants does not run to the covenantor's successors. This would produce an unfair result, and over the years conveyancers have developed a number of ways in which positive obligations can be made to bind successors. In addition, the common law has recognised one exception to the basic rule that it will not enforce burdens on later owners of the covenantor's land. These methods of avoiding the disadvantages of the basic rules can accordingly be of considerable importance, and we will now consider them individually.

The exception to the rule—*Halsall* v *Brizell*

In the case of *Halsall* v *Brizell* [1957] Ch 169, the purchaser of a plot of land on an estate had been given various easements including an easement of way over the estate roads, and in return had covenanted to contribute to the cost of maintaining the roads, walls and other facilities from which he derived a benefit. A successor of the original purchaser claimed the benefit of the easements affecting the property, but denied that he was obliged to make any payment, on the basis that the burden of a positive covenant would not run at law or equity. The court refused to accept this argument, holding that the successor in title could not take the benefit of an agreement unless he was also prepared to accept the related burdens (see also *E.R. Ives Investment Ltd* v *High* [1967] 2 QB 379, and *Tito* v *Waddell (No. 2)* [1977] Ch 106 at p. 290). For the rule to apply, the burden and benefit probably do have to be related to one another in some way (but see *Tito* v *Waddell (No. 2)* on this point, in which a different view seems to have been taken). The principle in *Halsall* v *Brizell* may therefore assist the current owner of 17 Trant Way, in compelling Mrs Strawberry to contribute to the cost of the repairs recently made to the shared driveway. The rule is frequently of considerable importance when one is dealing with a building scheme in which positive covenants for the maintenance of shared facilities may be necessary.

Evasion of the rules by techniques of drafting

There are a number of ways in which the burden of a positive covenant can be imposed on a later acquirer of burdened land.

Granting leases
Where a lease is granted, covenants in the lease which fall within the rule in *Spencer's Case* (see p. 135) will bind the tenant's assignees. In such cases, the law makes no distinction between positive and negative obligations, and covenants to contribute to the cost of maintenance or to an insurance premium are common. As a result, a vendor may well choose to grant a long lease of property, rather than selling the fee simple estate. In the case of blocks of flats, where the enforcement of positive obligations may be crucial, it is exceptionally rare for the flat owners to hold estates in fee simple, and leases are the norm. In such cases, the purchaser may well pay as much as he would have paid to acquire a freehold estate, but will obtain only a wasting asset. In addition his ownership will be subject to the landlord's rights of re-entry

and to a continuing obligation to pay ground rent. He may also encounter the difficulty that mortgagees are often less willing to lend money on the security of a leasehold property. All this is quite a high price to pay to enable the vendor to ensure that the burden of positive covenants passes to the successors in title of the covenantee.

Indemnity covenants
Another method of circumvention is to impose upon the covenantor an obligation to require an indemnity covenant from his successor. Should the covenant be broken, the covenantee can then sue the original covenantor, who remains liable on the covenant; *he* will sue his successor, and so on down the line. This method is not, however, very effective, because it is dependent on the maintenance of an unbroken chain of indemnity covenants. In addition, after some years it may prove impossible to find the original covenantor in order to enforce against him.

Creating estate rentcharges
Another possible method is for a vendor to require the purchaser to grant him an estate rentcharge over the land. You will remember that a rentcharge imposes a duty on the current estate owner to make regular payments of money to the person entitled to the charge (see p. 6), and so a rentcharge can be useful where it is wished to impose an obligation to contribute to the cost of maintenance; it might, for example, have been used in relation to the shared driveway at 17 and 18 Trant Way. However, in addition to this, the rentcharge can be used to enforce other positive obligations beyond the mere payment of money, for the owner of the charge has a legitimate interest in maintaining the value of the land, and so can require the estate owner, when he grants the rentcharge, to enter into covenants for repair and maintenance. The rentcharge, and its associated obligations, run with the land to bind successive owners. The right of re-entry which supports the rentcharge enables the owner of the charge to enter on the land and do the work himself, if the estate owner fails to do so.

The estate rentcharge was exempted from the general bar on the creation of rentcharges imposed by the Rentcharges Act 1977 (see s. 2), and so may still be created. It takes effect as a legal interest in land, and is good against the world in respect of unregistered land (LPA 1925, s. 1(2)). In the case of registered land, the rentcharge must be substantively registered in order to be legal (LRA 1925, s. 19(2)), and see p. 50), and on registration will automatically be noted upon the charges portion of the register of the burdened land (Land Registration Rules 1925, r. 107(2)).

Creating long leases which are then converted to freehold estates
A long lease with more than 200 years to run, which satisfies the other requirements of LPA 1925, s. 153 (see p. 111), may be converted by the tenant into a freehold estate. On such conversion, any obligations on the tenant, including positive covenants, will become burdens enforceable against the freehold estate. This method is rarely used as it is very cumbersome, and,

in the main, untested, but it is usual to include it in the list of devices enabling positive covenants to run with the land.

Covenants restraining sale of registered land without consent of the original vendor

Under LRA 1925, s. 58, a vendor of registered land may place on the register a restriction preventing the transfer of the registered estate to any person without the vendor's consent. The use of this provision would enable the vendor to require an intending purchaser from the covenantee to enter into fresh positive covenants with the original vendor before he will consent to the sale.

Fencing

It should be remembered that an obligation to maintain a fence may be drafted as an easement of fencing, rather than as a positive covenant, and the obligation will then run with the servient tenement (*Crow* v *Wood* [1971] 1 QB 77).

Statutory powers of local authorities

Local authorities are able to impose positive obligations and to enforce them against successive owners, under the provisions of a number of statutes. For example, under s. 30 of the Town and Country Planning Act 1971, a local authority, on granting planning permission, may impose a condition that works be carried out within a specified period, and this will be enforceable against future owners of the land.

Need for reform

These methods of avoiding the restrictions imposed by the present law are clumsy, and may not prove suitable in all cases. As a result, there is considerable pressure for reform of the law on this matter (see further below).

REMEDIES

Should a covenant be broken, the normal contractual remedies of damages for breach, or an injunction restraining breach may be sought. In cases in which a positive covenant has been broken, an order for specific performance or a mandatory injunction may be the most suitable remedy. Frequently, the real problem with a covenant is not in enforcing it, but in establishing whether it is binding on a particular person, or whether the person seeking to enforce it is entitled to do so. Suitable relief in the case of such a dispute is provided by LPA 1925, s. 84(2) as amended by LPA 1969, s. 28(4), which allows an applicant to ask the court to declare whether or not land is affected by 'a restriction imposed by an instrument' and 'the nature and extent' of the restriction. In addition, a declaration may be sought 'whether the same is or would in any given event be enforceable and if so by whom'.

N

DISCHARGE OF COVENANTS

A covenant will be extinguished automatically should the burdened and benefited land come into common ownership and occupation (*Re Tiltwood, Sussex* [1978] Ch 269) but remember the special rule relating to plots within a building scheme (*Texaco Antilles Ltd* v *Kernochan* [1973] AC 609). Otherwise it is open to the parties affected to agree to discharge the obligation (the discharge itself being made by deed). Apart from these methods, a covenant would continue to affect land in perpetuity, under the rules of common law and equity. This causes considerable inconvenience, where after the passage of many years the covenant has become redundant or unreasonable. As a result, a statutory method has been provided whereby certain covenants may be discharged or varied.

Under LPA 1925, s. 84, an application to discharge or modify, 'any restriction arising under covenant or otherwise as to the user [of land] or the building thereon' may be made to the Lands Tribunal. The party who is applying must establish one of four grounds on which he seeks discharge or modification of the covenant.

First, he may show that the restriction has become obsolete due to 'changes in the character of the property or the neighbourhood' or to other relevant circumstances. This would apply, for example, to a covenant to use premises only as a dwelling, if the surrounding area had come into business or mixed use. Secondly, it may be established that the covenant impedes a reasonable user *and* either does not provide any practical benefit of substantial value to any person or is contrary to the public interest. Thirdly, it may be established that those entitled to the benefit have agreed, expressly or impliedly 'by their acts or omissions' to the discharge or modification. Finally, the claimant may succeed if he can establish 'that the proposed discharge or modification will not injure the persons entitled to the benefit of the restriction'. In considering applications for discharge, the Lands Tribunal must take into account the development plan for the area and any declared or ascertainable pattern for the grant or refusal of planning permission (s. 84(1B)).

If the Tribunal agrees to discharge or modify a covenant on any grounds, it may require the payment of compensation to the owners of the benefited land. It should be noted that the wording of s. 84 is such that the powers of the Lands Tribunal do not apply to positive covenants.

A further statutory power to discharge a covenant requiring property to be kept as a *single* dwelling exists under Housing Act 1985, s. 610. This permits a county court to authorise an alteration of the property in breach of a covenant (for example, into several flats) if the property cannot be disposed of readily as one unit due to a change in character of the neighbourhood. The aim of this provision is to prevent land falling into disuse because of a limitation imposed by a covenant, and thereby to prevent a diminution in the number of dwellings available for occupation.

REFORM OF THE LAW RELATING TO BURDENS RUNNING WITH THE LAND

After reading the last two chapters, the reader may well be left with the impression that the rules relating to burdens running with the land are in considerable need of reform. Indeed it must be said that all are agreed on the need for reform, although how this is to be accomplished may be more debateable.

The rules relating to the running of covenants have been particularly heavily criticised and have been the subject of three major reports in recent years: (a) the Law Commission report on restrictive covenants (Law Com. No. 11, 1967); (b) the Wilberforce Committee report on positive covenants affecting land (Cmnd 2719, 1968); and (c) the Law Commission report on the law of positive and restrictive covenants (Law Com. No. 127, 1984). The last of these reports was a detailed attempt to make some sense of the confusion of the rules relating to easements and covenants. The position regarding positive covenants was particularly criticised, since such covenants do not run to bind a subsequent owner, and accordingly the original covenantor, who remains liable on his contract, can find himself being held responsible for the acts of some later owner long after his own interest in the land has ceased (para. 4.3).

The horrors of the rules regarding restrictive covenants are cogently summarised in para. 4.9 of the report:

The burden of a restrictive covenant does not run at all at law, but it does run in equity if certain complicated criteria are met. The benefit, by contrast, runs both at law and in equity, but according to rules which are different. These rules are, if anything, more complicated than the rules about the burden, and some of them are particularly technical and hard to grasp: as examples one may cite the rules about 'annexation' and those about 'building schemes'.

Recently, there has been further pressure to reform the rules about covenants, as part of a wider campaign for changes in the law to facilitate the sale of flats as freehold rather than as leasehold properties. At present, as more and more flats are built or converted, the number of leases on the market is increasing. Such leases may be all very well at the start, provided that there are no undue problems with the landlord about the management of the block, but as the lease wastes it becomes an increasingly unsellable commodity, for lenders are unwilling to advance money on the security of a diminishing estate. The wish to reform this area of the law once again gives rise to difficulties with covenants, for, as we have seen, one of the main reasons for granting leases rather than selling the freehold is that in this way positive covenants can be enforced against the purchaser's successors. If the sale of freehold flats is to become more common, the problem of positive covenants must be tackled.

What reforms are possible?

The 1984 Law Commission report took the view that the existing rules on covenants should be abolished and a new class of rights, 'land obligations', should be created to replace them. Such rights would be subject to rules similar to those applying to easements (which the Commission regarded as more satisfactory), and should subsist as legal interests in land, binding on successive owners under normal rules. After sale, the original parties would lose their contractual rights and obligations, thus destroying the present continuing contractual liability of the original covenantor (see para. 4.22). Under such a scheme, no distinction would be made between positive and negative covenants.

Easements

The 1984 report accepted that in general the law relating to easements is preferable to the rules on covenants. Whilst this may be true with respect to expressly created easements, the law on implied grant, the provisions of LPA 1925, s. 62, and the law on prescription are also sorely in need of reform. In 1971, the Law Commission Working Paper, *Transfer of Land: Appurtenant Rights* (Working Paper No. 36), recognised the difficulties in this area, and made a number of recommendations. In particular it was suggested that certain important easements (for example, the right to support) should become automatic statutory rights (para. 50). Further recommendations were made in relation to acquisition of easements by other methods. In particular, it was suggested that the prescription period should be reduced to 12 years in order to bring it into line with the limitation period for actions in respect of land (para. 101). In 1966 the Law Reform Committee, when considering easements and profits (Cmnd 3100), had been divided on whether prescription should be abolished in its entirety, but was unanimous in agreeing that, if retained, the law required drastic reform.

The various suggested reforms were, to some extent, drawn together in the consultation paper on 'Commonhold' presented to Parliament in November 1990 (Cmnd 1345 (1990)). This proposed a new system of ownership to be available where several 'units' of property share services and facilities and thus require some form of communal management and ownership of common parts (para. 3.1). At present, as we have seen this situation is usually dealt with by the grant of long leases. The suggestion made is that in future the owners of the various units should participate in a 'commonhold association' which would own and manage the common parts of the property. The owner in respect of a unit would however own the fee simple estate in his unit. The expenses in relation to the common parts would be apportioned between the unit owners. The proposals are intended to be suitable for both blocks of flats and ordinary development schemes. It is suggested that as part of this exercise the Law Commission proposals in relation to 'land obligations' (easements and covenants, including positive covenants) should form part of any Bill intended to implement the commonhold system.

Although the period for consulation on commonhold ended on 28 February

1991, as yet no Bill has been introduced in order to amend the law. However, a commitment to reform has been given by the Government and some small steps have been taken towards a new system by a limited extension of the rights of tenants to purchase the freehold in their properties (in the Housing and Urban Development Act 1993). More general reforms await future developments.

10   What is Land?

Thus far we have said very little about the definition of land. At first it may seem odd that there should be any question about the matter at all: surely everybody knows what land is? However, as we will see, the word 'land' to a lawyer means far more than it does when the word is used in normal speech. As well as defining 'land', we will also consider some of the other terminology which is applied to estates and interests in land, as this is relevant to the rather complex statutory definition of land.

'Land' is defined in LPA 1925, s. 205(1)(ix), as follows:

'Land' includes land of any tenure, and mines and minerals, whether or not held apart from the surface, buildings or parts of buildings (whether the division is horizontal, vertical or made in any other way) and other corporeal hereditaments; also . . . a rent and other incorporeal hereditaments, and an easement, right, privilege, or benefit in, over or derived from land; but not an undivided share in land.

This definition requires some thought and so we will now consider its individual parts.

EARTH, MINERALS, BUILDINGS AND FIXTURES

It is easy to accept that 'land' includes the earth beneath our feet and any minerals contained therein. However, the legal definition of land goes further and includes in the definition plants growing on the land *and* any other thing which is actually fixed to the land. 'Buildings' and 'parts of buildings' are actually mentioned in s. 205(1)(ix) and, after a moment's thought, it is not altogether surprising that they are included in the term 'land'. It is perhaps more surprising, at first thought, when one discovers that any item affixed to the land becomes land itself. Thus in *Buckland* v *Butterfield* (1820) 2 Brod & Bing 54, it was held that a conservatory which was attached to a house by eight cantilevers, each 9 inches long, formed part of the land. This is important, because should one wish to retain and remove such a fixture when selling the freehold estate in the land, one must specifically contract to exclude the fixture from the sale. Thus, should a vendor intend to remove the rose bushes from the garden of a house which he is selling, he should provide for this when the contract is made. *Buckland* v *Butterfield* also illustrates the point that since the house is land, because it is fixed to the earth, anything fixed to the house also becomes land. However, something which is merely placed upon the land, and not fixed to it, will not be regarded as forming part of the land, however heavy it is and even if it would be very difficult to move it. In *Berkley* v *Poulett* (1976) 242 EG 39, a large statue, made of marble and weighing nearly half a ton, was not regarded as part of the land, because it was not fixed down in any way.

The basic rule is therefore that anything annexed to land *is* land. However, the courts have long accepted that something which is affixed merely to facilitate its display, or in order to steady it, is *not* to be regarded as becoming part of the land. Thus in *Leigh* v *Taylor* [1902] AC 157, a tapestry tacked to strips of wood, which were then affixed to the wall, was not regarded as being part of the land. The degree of annexation in this case was merely that which was necessary for the display of the tapestry. In *Hulme* v *Brigham* [1943] KB 152, printing machines weighing between 9 and 12 tons were not regarded as fixtures, even though they were attached to motors which were fixed to the floor. In this case the degree of annexation was slight and was necessary merely to render the motors stable.

In rare circumstances something which is not actually fixed to the land but which appears to form an integral part of it, may be regarded as forming part of the land for legal purposes. The best example of this is *D'Eyncourt* v *Gregory* (1866) LR 3 Eq 382, in which stone statues, seats and garden vases were held to be part of the land, even though they were free-standing as were certain tapestries and pictures hanging upon the walls. The basis of the decision is that the ornaments formed an integral part of the architectural design of the house on the property. Thus it appears that the existence of a 'master plan' concerning the property may render items part of the land, even though there is no real annexation. Another illustration was supplied by Blackburn J in *Holland* v *Hodgson* (1872) LR 7 CP 328 at p. 335, when he explained that a pile of stones lying in a builder's yard would obviously not form part of the land upon which it lay. However, were the same stones to be constructed into a drystone wall (which uses no mortar and no method of fixing the wall to the ground) on a farm, the wall obviously would form part of the land of the farm.

HEREDITAMENTS

Before 1926, 'hereditaments' were those rights which were capable of passing to heirs by way of inheritance. The term is defined in LPA 1925, s. 205(1)(ix), as 'any real property which on an intestacy occurring before the commencement of this Act might have devolved upon an heir'. This includes the estates and interests in land which we have discussed in this book, and which are not purely personal rights. Thus a licence is not a hereditament because it was a personal permission and not an interest which would have passed to an heir.

Corporeal and incorporeal hereditaments

Having defined 'hereditaments' as 'inheritable interests', the common law went on to distinguish between 'corporeal' and 'incorporeal' hereditaments. Corporeal hereditaments are physical objects: the physical land and its attachments. Incorporeal hereditaments are rights, not things, and there is a fixed list of such hereditaments, which includes rentcharges, easements and profits.

This traditional classification may cause you some surprise, for the two groups, corporeal and incorporeal, seem strangely unrelated, though they are supposed to be subdivisions of one category. To paraphrase Austin (*Jurisprudence*, 5th ed. (London: Murray, 1885), vol. 1, p. 362): one class consists of intangible rights over objects (incorporeal), and the other of physical objects over which rights may be exercised (corporeal). Further, the notion of corporeal hereditaments seems to conflict with the basic principle of English land law, which we emphasised in chapter 1, that one cannot own the land itself, but only an estate in it. No provision for estates in land seems to be made in this classification; they are certainly not within the accepted list of incorporeal hereditaments, but one cannot describe them as corporeal because they are intangible rights rather than tangible objects.

This is a classification which has always caused difficulty and debate and we would not trouble you with it if it were not for the fact that you will see references to 'hereditaments' in the statutory definition of land. It is also important that you should realise that easements, profits and rentcharges are not merely interests in land but are themselves 'land' within the statutory definition. We suggest, though, that it is enough to note the meaning of the terms and that you should not spend too much time on this rather difficult point until your studies of land law are very advanced.

The statutory definition of 'hereditaments' includes the term 'real property' and this leads us to the next set of technical terms.

REAL AND PERSONAL PROPERTY (OR, REALTY AND PERSONALTY)

Often you may see references to 'real property' which suggest that this term is synonymous with 'land' (e.g., in the book title, *Cheshire and Burn's Modern Law of Real Property*). This is not, however, entirely true, for, as we shall see, some interests in land do not amount to real property.

The distinction between real and personal property is an ancient one and is still of importance today. The term 'real' property refers to that property which the early courts would protect by a 'real' action (an action *in rem*). In this context the adjective 'real' does not have its usual meaning of 'genuine' but is used in a technical sense. The word 'real' derives from the Latin word '*res*' (thing). A 'real action' was one in which the court would order that the property itself (the '*res*') be restored to an owner who had been dispossessed, rather than giving the defendant the choice of returning the property *or* paying damages to compensate for the loss. If someone takes your table, a remedy in damages will usually suffice, for you may take the money and buy another table. However, land is unique in its character and, at a time when status in society depended upon one's relation to land, it was felt that where land was lost it was essential that it should be recovered. Thus there was a distinction between 'real' property (where the property could be recovered by an action *in rem*) and 'personal' property, so called because it could be protected only by an action '*in personam*' (an action against the person of the wrongdoer). Where an action *in personam* was concerned the wrongdoer would in general pay damages rather than return the property. Thus the history of English forms of action has led to a labelling of property which is still used today.

Most of the rights considered in this book amount to real property because they are rights in land which would have been subject to an action *in rem*. There are, however, two main exceptions. The first of these is the right of a beneficiary under a trust for sale. Since the doctrine of conversion notionally transforms the trust property into money (a form of personal property) the beneficiaries' interests under the trust are seen to be interests in personalty.

The other exception is not so obvious and results once again from the manner in which the law has developed. When leases first came into common use, they were regarded as commercial contracts creating rights *in personam* between the parties. Unlike freehold estates they did not affect the tenant's position on the feudal ladder, and were not subject to one of the real actions. If the tenant were dispossessed by his landlord, he could not recover the land but would only be awarded damages for breach of contract. Since it was protected only by an action *in personam* the lease came to be regarded as personal property. After a time, the tenant was enabled to recover the land by action, whether he was dispossessed of the land by his landlord or by some third party, but by this time it was too late to alter the classification of the lease. A lease was therefore a 'chattel' (another name for personal property, derived from a French word from which 'cattle' is also derived— livestock being an important form of personal property). However, recognition of the rather special nature of the lease led to the rather paradoxical nomenclature of 'chattel real', which emphasises its hybrid nature.

Leases remain personal property to this day and the distinction can sometimes prove to be of importance. Thus if a testator were to make the following disposition in his will: 'All my real property to my son Alfred and all my personal property to my son Bernard', Albert would receive any freehold property owned by his father, but Bernard would be able to claim any leasehold property, together with any equitable interests his father might have had in a trust for sale and all his father's chattels. In this case the freehold property is obviously an estate *in land*. It should be recalled, however, that the lease, whilst being personal property, is also an estate in land (LPA 1925, s. 1(1)). The equitable interest behind a trust for however, not only *is* personal property but also *is not* an interest in land, although in *Williams & Glyn's Bank Ltd v Boland* [1981] AC 487 the House of Lords did accept that it was an interest in relation to land.

We said at the start of this book that it was our intention to avoid a discussion of purely historical matters. However, you will have found that historical issues have intruded rather often into this last chapter. The reason for this is that modern land law is still, to a certain extent, tied to its past. The 1925 property legislation was not a complete break with the past but rather reformed and built upon the existing law, which had developed over the centuries. The relationship between land law ancient and modern is particularly noticeable when dealing with the technical definition of 'land' because in this area the 1925 statutes attempted no radical reforms. Accordingly we feel that, although a knowledge of the historical development of land law is not essential to the modern student, it may be of interest and assistance to those who wish to deepen their understanding of the subject. We hope that this book has shown you that land law is a fascinating and lively subject and that we have encouraged you to extend your reading into such areas.

Glossary

abatement. A 'self-help' remedy by which the owner of the dominant tenement may remove an obstruction to the exercise of an easement.

absolute interest. An interest which is not determinable or conditional (see p. 86–88), i.e., it is not granted on such terms that it is liable to end prematurely on the occurrence of some specified event.

administrators. See 'personal representatives'.

adverse possession (acquisition of title by). The process of acquiring title to land by dispossessing the previous holder and occupying the land until his right to recover it is time-barred under the Limitation Act.

alienation. The act of disposing of one's property, i.e., passing it from one owner to another.

annexation. The procedure of attaching the benefit of a restrictive covenant to the land of the covenantee, so that it will run automatically with that land, without any need for the benefit to be assigned (transferred) to the new owner when the land changes hands.

appurtenant. See 'profit à prendre'.

assent. A disposition by personal representatives, by which property is vested in the person entitled under the deceased's will or on his intestacy.

assignment. A transfer of property (used particularly in respect of the transfer of a lease or a reversion).

barring the entail. See 'disentailing'.

base fee. The interest created when the holder of an entailed interest tries to transfer it to another person, without satisfying the requirements for 'disentailing' (converting the interest into a fee simple). The recipient takes only a base fee, which lasts as long as the entailed interest would have lasted, and ends when the original grantor becomes entitled to enforce his reversion.

caution, inhibition, notice, restriction. Methods of protecting minor interests in registered land by entry on the register.

cesser on redemption. The process by which a mortgage automatically comes to an end when the obligation which it secures is performed.

charge. An encumbrance securing the payment of money.

charge by way of legal mortgage. See p. 246.

chattels real. Leases — see p. 337.

choses in action. See p. 13.

choses in possession. See p. 13.

clog (on the equity of redemption). Any restriction imposed by the mortgage on the mortgagor's right to redeem the mortgaged property.

conditional interest. See p. 86.

consolidate (right to). The right of the mortgagee to refuse to allow the mortgagor to redeem one mortgage unless some other mortgage is redeemed at the same time.

co-ownership. A form of ownership in which two or more people are entitled to possession of the property at the same time. See 'joint tenancy' and 'tenancy in common'.

concurrent lease. See 'lease of the reversion'.

conversion. A change in the nature of property, from realty to personalty, or vice versa. Actual conversion of this kind occurs when land is sold, so that the purchaser's property changes from money into land, and that of the vendor changes from land into money. Under the equitable doctrine of conversion, this change notionally takes place at an earlier stage, as soon as the contract to sell is concluded (see p. 203).

conveyance. An instrument (other than a will) which transfers property from one owner to another.

corporeal hereditament. See p. 335.

covenant. A promise made by deed.

covenantee. The person with whom a covenant is made, who takes the benefit of the covenant and has a right to enforce the promise.

covenantor. The person who makes a covenant, and has the burden or duty of performing the promise.

deed. A document which is signed in the presence of a witness as a deed and is then delivered (see p. 10).

deed of discharge. See p. 200.

determinable interest. See p. 87.

disentailing. The procedure by which an entailed interest is converted into a fee simple (see p. 179).

distress (to levy distress to distrain). The legal seizure of chattels in order to satisfy some debt or claim; in particular, may be used by the landlord against the tenant in respect of unpaid rent.

dominant tenement. A piece of land which is benefited by some right (see 'easement').

easement. A right enjoyed over one piece of land (the 'servient tenement') for the benefit of another piece of land (the 'dominant tenement'), e.g., rights of way, rights of drainage, rights of light. See also 'quasi-easement'.

encumbrance. A liability burdening property.

entail. See 'entailed interest'.

entailed interest. An interest in land inheritable only by the issue (child, grandchild etc.) of the original grantee; since 1925, exists only as an equitable interest.

en ventre sa mère. Literally, 'in one's mother's womb', i.e., conceived but not yet born.

equity of redemption. The mortgagor's interest in the property during the continuance of the mortgage.

estate. An interest in land which entitles its owner to exercise proprietary rights over that land for a prescribed period.

estate contract. A contract to sell or grant an estate in land. Both parties are bound by the contract, so that either can enforce against the other. The statutory definition of estate contracts which are registrable as class C (iv) land charges (LCA 1972, s. 2(4)(iv)) includes two further rights, the option to purchase and the right of pre-emption, but these do not create the reciprocal rights and duties of the full estate contract.

An **option** (to purchase an estate or to renew a lease) gives the person entitled the right to compel the owner to sell or grant the estate, but does not impose on him any duty to buy. He is free to exercise the option or not, as he chooses.

A **right of pre-emption** (or right of first refusal) gives the person entitled a right to be offered the property if the owner decides to sell, but does not impose any duty to sell on the owner, nor any duty to buy on the person entitled.

estate rentcharge. A rentcharge (q.v.) created to ensure that the owner of the land, subject to the charge, contributes to maintenance costs or performs some other positive obligation (see p. 328).

excecutors. See 'personal representatives'.

fee simple absolute in possession. The larger of the two legal estates in land (the other being the term of years absolute: LPA 1925, s. 1) which will last indefinitely, as long as there are persons entitled to take the property under the will of the previous owner or on his intestacy.

fee tail. See 'entailed interest'.

fine. A premium, sometimes payable on the grant or assignment of a lease.

fixed-term tenancy. See p. 98.

foreclosure. The procedure by which a mortgagee asks the court to extinguish the mortgagor's equitable right to redeem, and his other rights to the property, and to permit the mortgagee to take the property in satisfaction of the debt or other obligation for which it is security.

freehold estate. Fee simple absolute in possession.

hereditament. See p. 335.

incorporeal hereditament. See p. 335.

infant. A minor; a person who has not attained the age of majority, being under the age of 18.

in gross. See 'profit à prendre'.

inhibition. See 'caution'.

in possession. Denotes that an interest so described gives a right to present enjoyment of the property, rather than to enjoyment that will not commence until some time in the future.

instrument. A legal document whereby a right is created or confirmed or a fact recorded.

intestacy. The condition of dying without having made a will.

inter vivos. Literally, 'among the living'; the phrase denotes that a disposition so described takes effect during the lifetime of the grantor, rather than under his will (which takes effect at death).

joint tenancy. The form of co-ownership in which each owner is entitled to the whole property, rather than to an undivided share in it. The right of survivorship *(jus accrescendi)* applies here, so that the last surviving tenant becomes solely entitled to the whole property, while those joint tenants who predecease him have no share in the property to pass with their estates. (Compare 'tenancy in common'.)

lease. The second legal estate in land ('term of years absolute', LPA 1925, s. 1(1); an interest which gives the person entitled exclusive possession of the land for a fixed period of time, usually but not essentially in consideration of the payment of rent. The term 'lease' is used to describe both the estate and the document creating it.

leasehold estate. The term of years absolute.

lease of the reversion (or concurrent lease). A lease which is created where a landlord grants a second lease in respect of property which is already subject to a lease granted by him (distinguish 'reversionary lease').

lessee. Tenant under a lease.

lessor. Landlord under a lease.

licence. Permission (in this context, usually permission to use land).

limitation of actions. The procedure whereby the right to bring an action is barred after the lapse of a prescribed period of time.

minor interest. An interest in registered land which requires protection by an entry on the register.

mortgage. The grant of an interest in property as security for the payment of a debt or the discharge of an obligation.

mortgagee. The person to whom a mortgage is granted and the interest in the mortgaged property conveyed (see 'mortgage').

mortgagor. The person who creates the mortgage and conveys an interest in his property as security for the payment of a debt etc. (see 'mortgage').

nec vi nec clam nec precario. Literally, 'not by force, nor by stealth, nor by permission'. The phrase describes the way in which one who claims an easement or profit by prescription must have acted during the prescription period.

notice. 1. See 'caution'. 2. Knowledge. (a) **actual notice**—real knowledge; (b) **constructive notice**—knowledge which a person is deemed to have, usually because he failed to make the necessary inquiries and is taken to know what they would have revealed; (c) **imputed notice**—notice belonging to an agent which is ascribed to his principal.

notice to quit. The method whereby landlord or tenant may end a periodic tenancy.

option. See 'estate contract'.

overreaching. The statutory procedure which enables a purchaser to take the legal estate free from certain equitable interests (arising, for example, under a Settled Land Act settlement, a trust for sale or a mortgage), provided the purchase money is paid to two trustees or a trust corporation.

overriding interest. An interest in registered land, which does not require protection by entry on the register and binds the registered proprietor and all who acquire later interests in the land.

partition. The physical division of land between several co-owners, so that each becomes the sole owner of a separate plot.

periodic tenancy. See p. 99.

perpetually renewable lease. See p. 95.

personal property (personalty). See p. 336.

personal representatives. Persons authorised to administer the estate of a dead person. There are two types: **executors**, who are appointed by will; and **administrators**, who are appointed by the court in cases of intestacy (i.e., where the deceased leaves no will), or where there is no executor willing or able to act.

possibility of reverter. The right of a grantor to recover the land if a determinable interest comes to an end (see p. 87).

pre-emption (right of). See 'estate contract'.

prescription. A method of acquiring easements or profits by long use.

profit à prendre. The right to take something (such as sand, wood, pasture) from land belonging to another. A profit may be **appurtenant** to a piece of land, that is, it may benefit that land and run with it; or it may be **in gross**, that is, it may belong to an individual without being attached to a specific piece of land which is benefited by it.

puisne mortgage. A legal mortgage of unregistered land which is not protected by the deposit of the title deeds with the mortgagee, and so is registrable as a class C (i) land charge (LCA 1972, s. 2(4)).

purchaser. A person who takes an estate or interest by act of parties rather than by operation of law (p. 69). When used as a technical term, the word does not have its colloquial meaning of 'buyer', and so one who buys has to be described as 'a purchaser for value'.

quasi-easement. A potential easement. The term is used to describe the situation in which land, which is owned and occupied by one person, is used in a way which would constitute an easement if the land was divided into two tenements which were separately owned or occupied (see p. 287).

real property (realty). See p. 336.

registered proprietor. The person registered as the owner of a legal estate in registered land.

remainder. An interest in land granted under a settlement to take effect after some previous interest (e.g., to A for life, **remainder** to B in fee simple). A remainder gives a right to possession of the land in the future and so, since 1925, exists only in equity.

rentcharge. A right entitling the holder to receive a periodic sum of money from the owner of land charged with that payment. Provision may be made, for example, for the payment of annuities in this way. See also 'estate rentcharge.' A rentcharge should be distinguished from **rent service**—the rent due from a tenant to a landlord under a lease.

rent service. Payments (generally in money, although sometimes in goods or services) made to a landlord by a tenant holding under a lease.

reservation. A method of creating an easement or profit, whereby a grantor retains these rights over the land which he conveys to the grantee.

restriction. See 'caution'.

reversion. The right remaining in a grantor after he has granted some interest shorter in duration than his own. The term is used in respect of both settlements and leases. 1. Settlements: the owner of a fee simple, for example, who grants a life interest or an entailed interest, has not disposed of his full estate, and therefore retains a right to the land when the interests he has granted come to an end (the property will 'revert' to the grantor). A reversion gives a right to possession of the land in the future and so, since 1925, exists only in equity. 2. Leases: an estate owner who grants a lease retains his own legal estate in the land (fee simple or superior lease) throughout the duration of the lease. This interest in the land, which includes the right to receive rents and profits, if any, during the lease, and to recover the physical possession of the land at the end of the term, is called the 'landlord's reversion'.

reversionary lease. A lease creating a term which will begin at a future date (distinguish a 'lease of the reversion', which arises where a landlord grants concurrent leases of the same property).

rights *in personam*. Rights enforceable against only certain categories of persons, e.g., the right of a beneficiary under a trust.

rights *in rem*. Rights in respect of a piece of land which are enforceable against any person who acquires an estate or interest in that land, e.g., in the case of unregistered land, a legal easement or a legal lease.

seisin. Possession (historically, the type of possession enjoyed by the holder of a freehold estate).

servient tenement. A piece of land which is burdened by some right (see 'easement').

settlement. A disposition of property, made *inter vivos* or by will, whereby the settlor (the estate owner making the settlement) creates a series of successive interests in the property, e.g., a grant to A for life, remainder to B in fee simple.

severance. The procedure by which a joint tenant converts his relation with the other co-owners into that of a tenant in common, so that he has a notional undivided share in the property and is no longer affected by the right of survivorship. Distinguish 'words of severance'.

socage. The surviving form of tenure, by which land in England and Wales is held of the Crown.

statutory owners. A person who acts where there is no tenant for life of a Settled Land Act settlement (p. 185).

sublease. A lease granted by a landlord who is himself a tenant of a superior estate owner.

tack (right to). The right to add a further advance (i.e., a later loan) to an earlier debt secured by a mortgage, so that the additional loan shares the priority of the earlier debt and thus takes priority over any intervening mortgages.

tenancy. A lease; the two terms, 'tenancy' and 'lease', are used interchangeably throughout the book.

tenancy at sufferance. See p. 113.

tenancy at will. See p. 114.

tenancy by estoppel. See p. 114.

tenancy in common. The form of co-ownership in which each owner has a notional, although undivided, share in the property, which passes with his estate at his death; the right of survivorship does not apply to this form of co-ownership. Compare 'joint tenancy'.

tenant for life. The beneficiary under a Settled Land Act settlement who has the right to present (current) enjoyment of the property. Under the Act, the tenant for life holds the legal estate and has statutory powers of management over the settled land.

tenure. The set of conditions on which a tenant held land from his feudal lord; today all land is held in 'socage' tenure.

terms of years absolute. A lease.

title. A person's right to property, or the evidence of that right.

transfer. The deed used to pass the legal estate in registered land from one owner to another.

trust corporation. The Public Trustee or a corporation either appointed by the court in any particular case to be a trustee or entitled by rules made under Public Trustee Act 1906, s. 4(3), to act as a custodian trustee (LPA 1925, s. 205(1)(xxviii)).

trust for sale. A trust which imposes a duty to sell the property.

trust instrument. See p. 186.

undivided shares in land. The interests of tenants in common; sometimes used as another name for tenancy in common.

usual covenants. A term of art, denoting a fixed list of covenants to be included to a lease (see p. 129).

vesting deed. See p. 187.

volunteer. A person who takes property without giving value for it.

waste (liability for). The liability of a limited owner, such as a tenant under a lease or a tenant for life of settled land, for any act or omission which alters the state of the land whether for better or worse. (See ameliorating, permissive and voluntary waste, p. 124.)

words of severance. Words in a grant of property to co-owners, which indicate an intention that the grantees should hold as tenants in common and not as joint tenants.

Subject Index